Crossing Frontiers

Travels in India and Pakistan
(1977-1981)

Judy ·
with very
best wishes

Jo

Crossing Frontiers

Travels in India and Pakistan
(1977-1981)

JOSEPHINE E. BLANEY

© Josephine Blaney, 2013

Published by Woodsome Publishing

A CIP catalogue record for this book is available from the British Library.

ISBN 978-0-9575645-0-3

Book cover design and layout by Clare Brayshaw

Prepared and printed by:

York Publishing Services Ltd
64 Hallfield Road
Layerthorpe
York YO31 7ZQ

Tel: 01904 431213

Website: www.yps-publishing.co.uk

Foreword

This book is based upon a four year stay on the Indian subcontinent. I resided mainly in India and Pakistan with a month in Sri Lanka.

The period covers 1977 to 1981. Regarding the countries mentioned, the rupee to pound exchange rate varied between three states. For example the exchange rate for India was about 17-18 rupees to the pound in 1977.

Several of the descriptions apply to a land that has changed considerably. I have retained former place names such as Bombay for Mumbai, Madras for Chennai and Calcutta for Kolkata.

I have changed some names of people to avoid any upset. Many rural people I stayed with in India lived in villages only found on detailed maps. The enclosed map refers mainly to the major towns.

I owe a mighty thanks to all the people who gave me hospitality.

Josephine E Blaney
Hebden Bridge

About the Author

Josephine Blaney née Scholes was born in Huddersfield, Yorkshire. After various work experiences ranging from social work jobs to fish factories she embarked upon adult education. Graduating at the University of Birmingham in Archaeology and African Studies and later at the University of Manchester in Social Anthropology.

Contents

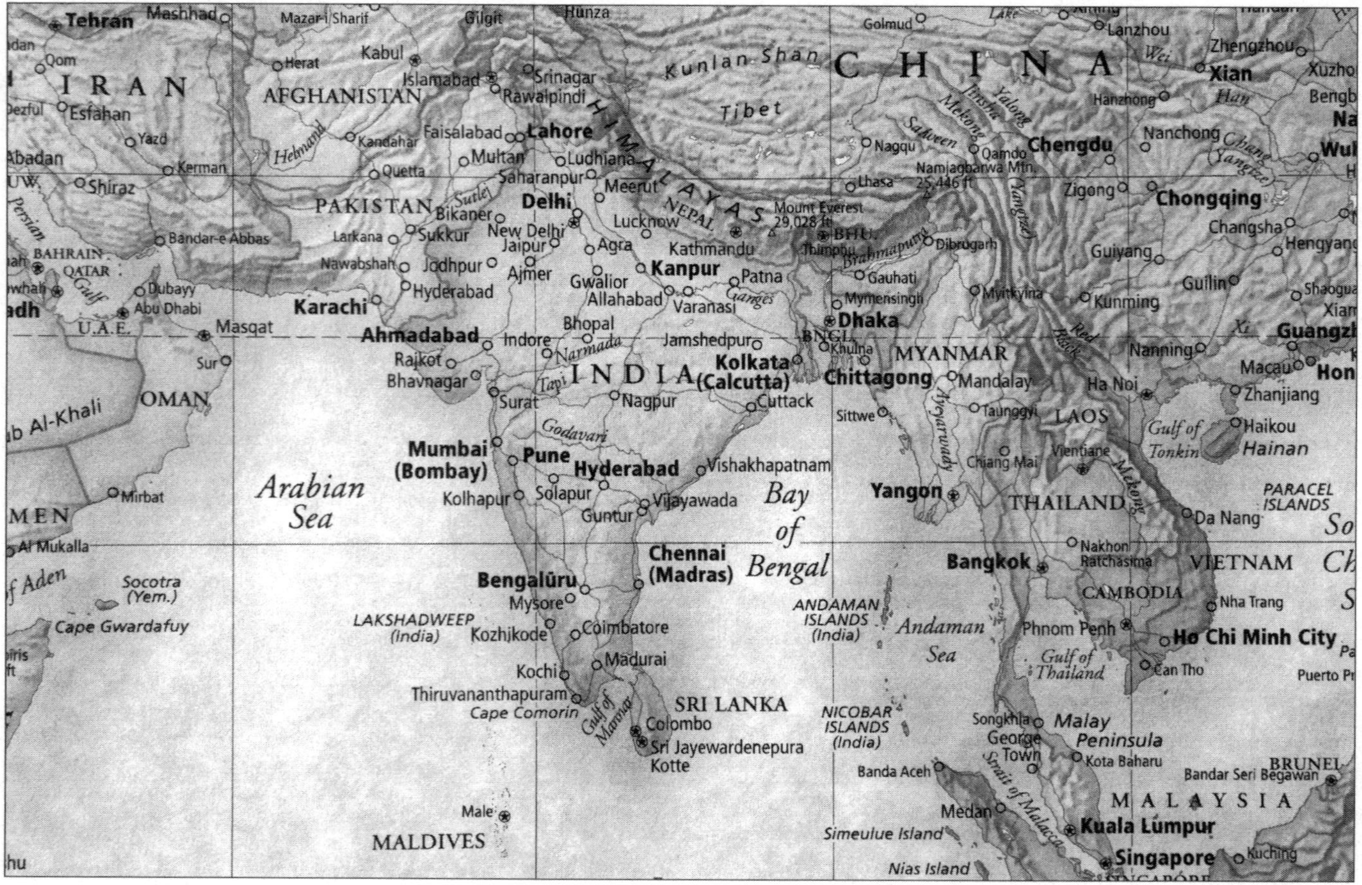
IRAN
AFGHANISTAN
PAKISTAN
INDIA
CHINA
NEPAL
BHU.
BNGL.
MYANMAR
LAOS
THAILAND
VIETNAM
CAMBODIA
MALAYSIA
BRUNEI
SRI LANKA
MALDIVES
OMAN
U.A.E.
QATAR
BAHRAIN
Tehran
Mashhad
Qom
Esfahan
Yazd
Kerman
Shiraz
Bandar-e Abbas
Dubayy
Abu Dhabi
Masqat
Sur
Mirbat
Al Mukalla
Socotra (Yem.)
Cape Gwardafuy
Mazar-i Sharif
Herat
Kabul
Kandahar
Quetta
Helmand
Islamabad
Rawalpindi
Gilgit
Hunza
Srinagar
Faisalabad
Lahore
Multan
Ludhiana
Saharanpur
Meerut
Delhi
New Delhi
Bikaner
Sutlej
Sukkur
Larkana
Nawabshah
Jodhpur
Hyderabad
Karachi
Ahmadabad
Rajkot
Bhavnagar
Surat
Indore
Bhopal
Narmada
Tapi
Jaipur
Ajmer
Agra
Gwalior
Allahabad
Lucknow
Kanpur
Varanasi
Ganges
Patna
Kathmandu
Jamshedpur
Kolkata (Calcutta)
Cuttack
Nagpur
Godavari
Mumbai (Bombay)
Pune
Hyderabad
Solapur
Kolhapur
Guntur
Vijayawada
Vishakhapatnam
Chennai (Madras)
Bengalūru
Mysore
Kozhikode
Coimbatore
Madurai
Kochi
Thiruvananthapuram
Cape Comorin
Gulf of Mannar
Colombo
Sri Jayewardenepura Kotte
Male
LAKSHADWEEP (India)
ANDAMAN ISLANDS (India)
NICOBAR ISLANDS (India)
Arabian Sea
Bay of Bengal
Andaman Sea
Persian Gulf
HIMALAYAS
Mount Everest 29,028 ft
Tibet
Kunlan Shan
Golmud
Lhasa
Nagqu
Qamdo
Namjagbarwa Mtn. 25,446 ft
Salween
Mekong
Jinsha
Yalong
Yangtze
Thimphu
Brahmaputra
Dibrugarh
Gauhati
Mymensingh
Dhaka
Khulna
Chittagong
Sittwe
Myitkyina
Mandalay
Taunggyi
Ayeyarwady
Yangon
Chiang Mai
Vientiane
Bangkok
Nakhon Ratchasima
Phnom Penh
Gulf of Thailand
Ho Chi Minh City
Can Tho
Nha Trang
Da Nang
Ha Noi
Gulf of Tonkin
Hainan
Haikou
Zhanjiang
Macau
Nanning
Kunming
Guiyang
Guilin
Red
Black
Chongqing
Zigong
Chengdu
Nanchong
Hanzhong
Lanzhou
Wei
Xian
Zhengzhou
Han
Changsha
Hengyang
PARACEL ISLANDS
Songkhla
George Town
Kota Baharu
Malay Peninsula
Strait of Malacca
Kuala Lumpur
Singapore
Kuching
Bandar Seri Begawan
Banda Aceh
Medan
Simeulue Island
Nias Island
Puerto Pr

Chapter One

The Musk Filled Mosque

Amritsar, that most hallowed city of the Sikhs, greeted me one late afternoon after I had crossed the border from Pakistan to India.

Kashmir was to be my first destination. Owing to an electric power cut while I was sitting in the waiting room at Amritsar railway station, I struck up conversation with a Pakistani from Britain named Syed and his daughter Lubna who were also heading for Kashmir.

We were informed that no sleeper was available in the second class carriages. After a small payment to one of the ubiquitous scarlet clad coolies, Syed obtained a luggage rack for use as a bunk. On the train, the three of us took turns in the horizontal position. The lower seats were crammed to capacity with passengers who willingly co-operated, squeezing two of us in at a time alongside themselves. They did not hesitate in telling us how the coolie had overcharged us by two rupees. We had only paid the coolie four rupees.

The overnight train journey to Jammu was followed by an exhausting twelve hour bus journey north from Jammu to Srinagar, the capital of the state of Jammu and Kashmir. As we climbed northward we passed acres of chenar (plane), spruce and deodar (Indian cedar) trees.

On arrival at Srinagar, the exhausted and defenceless traveller faced an onslaught of touts, perhaps locusts would be a better word. Many Indian cheap hotel owners employed touts in fervent competition with each other. Later on in my travels while in hotter regions, their patter would always be 'room ten rupees with fan' or 'five rupees mosquito' or 'good room no bed bugs'.

The three of us were eventually commandeered towards the Jhelum River, which traverses Srinagar and waters the Vale of Kashmir. The Jhelum is also one of the major rivers of the Punjab (Land of the Five Rivers). The cheaper houseboats are moored all along parts of the river. Our tout called into the darkness and the muffled tones of one of the boatmen could be heard. Mahmud, our boatman, rowed across to collect us and take us to his houseboat situated centrally in Srinagar.

There were four classes of houseboat in Kashmir consisting of A, B, C. and D, the last offering dormitory accommodation only. Our boat was C class. The most costly boats had a special kitchen vessel attached, in which a family, who were not the owners, served the guests. On C class boats, the owners' families lived on the same boat as the guests.

The boatmen or 'Havjis' claimed a proud tradition of boat building from Noah. Our boat had a steep sloping tiled roof and sliding wooden doors. All water for washing and drinking was brought by bucket from the river.

For Kashmiris, the tourist season is short as their home is snowed up for months. Kashmiris are well known in all India for being thrifty. Old travellers' tales continually remark upon the untrustworthiness and cunning character of Kashmiris. The early 19th century traveller William Moorcroft's comments were typical, 'Selfish, dishonest, ignorant, supple, intriguing, clever ...'

Cargo boats daily paraded their wares up and down the river carrying anything from driftwood and flowers to shawls and carpets. As good salesmen, they would climb into your boat and inundate the traveller with fabulous Kashmiri shawls plus any local trinket, invariably making a sale.

Mahmud and his family spent much of their time squatting in front of their tiny kitchen clay fire, the women wearing a colourful tent-like garment called a phiran, and the men wearing a plainer woollen version of this dress. Both sexes wore the baggy shalwar trousers. Kashmiri women also sported a handsome head cloth tied at the back.

When a Kashmiri is squatting, the phiran is voluminous enough to allow space for the kangri heater only found in Kashmir. It is a small earthen bowl with hot embers on the inside and supported on the outside by a wicker frame. For all the kangri's utility, unpleasant accidents have occurred.

Each morning Mahmud's daughter would hand out some thick sweetened Indian tea presuming that this delicacy was preferred to the Kashmiri kawah tea, which is sometimes salted and often has almond added. Indian tea is always heavily sweetened and milky and all contents are boiled together until it is stewed. Unlike English tea, it is never weak. In richer households, spices such as cinnamon and cloves might be added to the milky brew.

Many Kashmiris still have the lovely old samovars (heated metal containers) whose ancestors must have crossed over the mountains from central Asia. The last time I saw so many samovars was on an Israeli kibbutz in 1966 where many of the inhabitants were of Russian origin.

My houseboat bill had been paid in advance and Mahmud, in common with many other cheaper houseboat owners, had the unfortunate habit of diminishing the quality and quantity of food as the month went by. Increasingly, he began to moan about the bazaar prices. Unlike the richer houseboat owners on Dal Lake, he did not have a floating vegetable garden made of woven reeds. Perhaps he was lucky, as these gardens occasionally floated away during inter-houseboat quarrels! My daily lunch consisted of huge Kashmiri apples, walnuts and goats' cheese.

Early evening was one of the best times to take a shikara journey. These boats were the gondolas of Kashmir. In the declining light, one passed all the houseboats moored at the river bank waiting to go to Dal Lake. Each boat family was huddled over its tiny fire or hurricane lamp, each with their own life experiences, the occasional laughter or raised voice, lovemaking, birth and death. Glimpsing into the boats gave me the same exciting curiosity as examining a cross section of a coal mine or doll's house in a museum!

The vast majority of the Kashmir Valley folk are Muslims. Prior to Partition, Kashmiris were ruled by proud Hindu Rajput Dogras whose Dogra homeland was Jammu to the south. The Dogra rulers opted for India at independence.

Friday, the Islamic rest day, offered what sounded like a cacophony of muezzins emanating from the mosques. One Friday I counted four sermons all starting at about two o'clock in the afternoon. Most mosques do use loudspeakers and the imams (prayer leaders) always sounded as if they were shouting at the 'congregations'. Having not been brought up on a diet of strict Calvinism, I never understood why many of the imams, during a sermon, had to sound as if they were pouring torrents of anger at their congregations. A superficial onlooker might interpret Islam as purely an aggressive faith, rather like judging Christianity by Ian Paisley and the Free Presbyterian Church in Ulster.

Indian Kashmiri architecture had similarities across in north Pakistan. All along the riverside, timber framed houses filled in with ancient-looking bricks, appeared to prop each other up. Many of them had upper floor jetties projecting over the lower storeys. Most magnificent of all were the wooden cedar mosques with horizontal wooden strips and wooden pagoda style roofs instead of the Persian arch so loved by Islamic architects.

One such mosque named Shah Hamadan, which faced a busy quayside, was exquisitely decorated throughout the inside with papier mâché, the craft being a Kashmiri speciality. All the pillars of wood and moulded paper pulp were decorated with tiny red and green floral patterns. An absolute warmth, plus the smell of musk, came from the mosque and the inside of the building flickered with lively little oil lamps. As is usual in mosques, a number of men were inside, some prostrating in prayer, others reading or sleeping. There can be something so peaceful and relaxing about the simplicity of a mosque. I obtained a good view from the door but the mosque interior was banned to non-Muslims and Muslim women. There seemed to me something sad about some of the black-shrouded, burqa-clad women cringing around the entrance of the mosque, forbidden to seek sanctuary in one of the central edifices of their faith. Many Muslims, like some orthodox Jews, allow women a segregated presence in houses of prayer or say it is better for them to pray at home.

Outside the mosque, the area was dense with jumbles of old houses, which would have done justice to a Gustave Doré sketch. The boat repairers' yard was filled with heaps of straw, some of it being used for thatching the cargo boats. I went inside a tiny carpet weaving factory employing six to seven boys. The youngest worker was six years old. It was a dingily-lit place and on entrance, it was hard to spot the three horizontal looms. Patterns were being sung out by a senior boy. For weaving the intricate patterns, the minimum wage was 10 rupees paid on a piece rate basis. I wondered how many of the wealthy purchasers of these carpets would ever think of all the hard work that had gone into their prized possessions. Nearby was a turmeric grinding factory which was dark, being windowless and below stairs. Yellow turmeric, a powder used for colouring food, filled the atmosphere and I departed after only ten minutes as it was too claustrophobic.

At Srinagar's Kanyar district, I passed a handsome whitewashed mosque with wooden green shutters before arriving at what the minority sect, the Ahmadiyya community believes to be the tomb of Jesus Christ. According to A. Faber Kaiser's book 'Jesus Died in Kashmir', the descendants of Jesus are still living in Srinagar. There is a tradition that Jesus came to the East in search of some of the Lost Tribes of Israel and that his mother Mary died en route at a place now called Murree, in what is today Pakistan. The Ahmadis believe that Jesus was put on the cross but when he was taken down, he was still alive. It is a fact that even in Afghanistan, there is a tradition that some of the Pathan people are descendants of some of the Lost Tribes. The tomb of Jesus was situated amongst some Muslim graves which were orientated towards Mecca as is the custom of Muslims. The name of Jesus slightly varies in local terminology as he is known as Hazrat Isa Sahib. Isa is a common Arabic term for Jesus and this name is used by all Muslims.

If Jesus did die in Srinagar, he was not the only major holy man to die in Kashmir. Shah Hamadan, whose name is used for the mosque I have just described, fled from Samarkand because he was persecuted by its ruler. The story goes that he descended from the skies to the place where the present day mosque stands and ordered the original inhabitants of Hindu holy men to depart.

The majority of visitors to Kashmir tended to forsake old Srinagar for the beautiful countryside. In September, the Moghul gardens are glorious. The Persian gardens as a concept were first introduced into India by Emperor Babur in the early 16th century.

Moghul rulers of India enjoyed those gardens during the seasons when the dry, dusty plains of North India were unbearably hot.

The gardens are closed symmetrical plots, kept verdant with cascades and fountains. The present gardens do not date much before the 17th century. One feature which I found attractive was that the orchards are not separated from the flowers but form an intricate part of the whole garden. The names of some of the gardens are lovely. These are Nishat

Bagh (Garden of Gladness) and Shalimar (Abode of Love). The names are fine examples of literary Persian, the Moghul court language.

Naga (snake) worship is ancient in India as in many other cultures not influenced by the Judeo-Christian-Islamic religions. The serpent often symbolised Mother Earth and rebirth in one form or another. Names like Srinagar and Vernag in Kashmir are testimony to these origins. Vernag has a sacred spring at the source of the Jhelum in which resides a tutelary deity in the form of a snake. Mythology informs us that the ascetic aspect of God in the form of Lord Shiva's wife Parvati manifested herself here in the form of a river, also symbolised as a snake.

Yusmarg (Meadow of Jesus) was a place where I was pestered by 'ponywallahs' so I rode by mule to Dudh Ganga (Milk Ganges). While admiring the milky frothy waterfall and dense pine forest, I was nicely addressed by two army officers who befriended me and invited me to a quiet place where a party of officers and their wives were enjoying a sumptuous lunch during the Hindu festival of Durga Puja. Durga is another name for Goddess Kali, or the fearsome aspect of female energy in creation. In the Muslim dominated Kashmir Valley, this festival is ignored. The meal consisted of rice, onion, cauliflower, lentils, meat and beer. All the officers were new bloods from the military college established by the British at Dehradun. The meal ended with everyone enjoying a game of cards.

There were other festivities. A relative of my boatman was to be married. The nikah, or first part of the Muslim marriage ceremony, had already taken place wherein the contract was made before the qazi (judge). Mahmud rowed a German visitor and me along to a little cluster of boats and a marquee, which later collapsed into the river! The friend of the German visitor was indisposed with dysentery and so remained on our houseboat. True to Muslim tradition, the German visitor and I were separated. I was taken to the women's domain where all the women were sitting cross-legged or squatting in one big boat. All eyes were upon me instead of the gorgeously-bedecked bride in red, looking compulsorily miserable as an Indian or Pakistani bride is expected to appear, whether she is happy or not. Earlier, I had seen some women dancing and singing Kashmiri style in groups of eight or more with arms locked together.

During the meal, we sat and ate in groups of four from one platter called a trambi. A Hindu would rarely contemplate eating off the same dish as another, so in this sense Islam is a brotherly faith. Using right hands only, we plunged into the hot spicy food of saffron- coloured rice and saag, a form of spinach. This was accompanied by hot meat curry made with shish kebab. The food was cooked in enormous handleless metal pots by hired cooks.

I travelled by bus to Wular Lake, which was surrounded by orchard after orchard of apple trees and miles of poplar and willow trees that formed a delicate tracery. Wular Lake is the largest fresh water lake in India. En route, the bus stopped at Manasbal Lake, which had a rest house and gardens along the lakeside. The bus passed women carrying huge bundles of willows on their backs. Willows are used for canework. The rice harvesting season was in full swing and rows of workers thrashed out the husks in an up and down motion.

On the bus were a number of irritating middle class Bengali honeymoon couples. Their Kashmiri student guide looked despondently at me and asked 'did you enjoy your journey?' He told me that the Bengalis had been bored. I had already had a row on the bus with one of these visitors who had blasted everyone out with Hindi film music from his transistor. My crime was that I had requested him to turn the radio off, which he did. The end result being that his little group attempted mild intimidation of me whenever we encountered each other at a stopping place.

Kashmir is famed for its silk manufacturing. At the Government silk factory, two of the lower management kindly invited me to their homes. The rooms in their houses seemed bare to a western eye. In one house, I went to an upper room where the manager's family was assembled. There was no furniture, only rugs and carpets. After huge amounts of lumpy rice and meat, a jug of warm water was brought in for hand washing. Later, tea was served in handleless cups, together with sweetmeats. They were keen to know the difference between Catholics and Protestants and I questioned them about the passion for saint devotion in Kashmiri Islamic tradition. This was followed by the often to be repeated question 'Can you get me a job in England?'

Back in my houseboat, I continually had Mahmud's family going through my belongings and asking for gifts ranging from nail clippers to lipstick.

One day, by bus I joined groups of Hindu devotees taking the short cut up a hill one thousand feet above Srinagar to Shankaracharya's Temple. The stone temple was founded in the eighth century by Hindu sage Shankaracharya. The site offered a fabulous view of Dal Lake over to the fort taking in the white starkness of Hazratbal, where one of Prophet Muhammad's hairs is encased. The ancient temple of Shankaracharya stood high on an octagonal stone platform. The temple was reached by a flight of stone steps and then one tapped the temple bell to summon the form of God whom the temple is dedicated to, namely Lord Shiva. Inside the temple, a huge smooth black Shiva Ling (a phallic symbol of Shiva) dominated the centre. Images of the cobra and minor gods surround the Linga. Pilgrims bedecked the images with garlands and pour water over the Linga while chanting continuously.

After leaving the temple, I noticed that the Forestry Commission had planted various altruistic notices in praise of forest protection such as one proclaiming that the forest has more wealth than a rich prince, so it must be respected.

A community on the defensive in Kashmir was that of the Christians. Up a leafy lane in Srinagar behind the bund, one came across All Saints Church, which is denominationally part of the Anglican-derived Church of North India. The parish priest was of Tibetan origin, from eastern Kashmir state, namely Ladakh. His father was a Christian convert from Buddhism. The Rev Paljor invited me in for tea and told me that the previous church had been destroyed by Muslim mobs in 1967 because they believed that the Christians were giving moral support to Israel during the Arab-Israeli Six-Day War. The church was rebuilt. Misfortune hit the Christians again when that delightful church was destroyed during riots that followed the hanging of Bhutto in Pakistan because his hangman was a Pakistani Christian called Tara Masih! This is the tale I was told.

The second church was constructed with cedar wood and had a stone tower. Inside the church stood a huge lotus-shaped wooden font with mosaic inlay. The walls were whitewashed and above the altar was a lovely backcloth of cedarwood. On the whitewashed walls were murals depicting the raising of Lazarus and other Biblical stories displayed within a Kashmiri setting.

Soldiers from all over India were stationed in Kashmir as it forms part of the Indian border with China and Pakistan, but still it was a little surprising to find prayer books in the rounded Malayalam script of distant Kerala State in South India.

An excellent rural craft exhibition opened prior to my departure for Ladakh. The section dealing with sericulture or silk manufacturing was fascinating. The cocoons were boiled and the silk thread, which could be hardly seen by the naked eye, was then detached by rows of men latching the threads onto hooks. There were tanks of water full of cocoons. Village industries were well represented from handmade paper to shawl weaving.

Syed and Lubna had already departed from Kashmir after a ten day visit while I remained on the boat for the rest of the month before departing for Ladakh for two weeks. To delay the journey now in November would mean that I might be cut off by snow and unable to return to Srinagar by road. I bade a temporary farewell to my cosy abode on the houseboat and its accompanying bed bugs.

Chapter Two

Prayers and Rancid Tea

The bus to Ladakh, in the eastern part of Jammu and Kashmir State took an exhausting twenty four hours. The lushness of the Vale of Kashmir recedes at Sonamarg. Here the scenery rapidly changes on approaching the eleven thousand, three hundred foot Zojila Pass situated in the Zanskar Range of the Himalayas.

All along the increasingly precarious route through this central Asiatic landscape, the bus passed little groups of road workers handling barrels of tar. Positioned along the side of the road were sad monuments dedicated to the hundreds of men who had lost their lives constructing the pass. This was a scene that would be repeated on the Karakoram Highway in the far north of Pakistan.

These early morning road working scenes reminded me of similar surroundings on my descent in 1975 through the Drakensberg Sani Pass from Lesotho to the Republic of South Africa when I had hitched a lift on a lorry. We had passed huddled, blanketed Basotho women armed with pick axes mending the steep road in bitterly cold weather.

The Zanskar Range is desolate but the rock formations demonstrated a multitude of colour combinations on irregular surfaces without the aid of any foliage. Now and again, tiny oases of autumnal willows dotted the landscape.

We passengers, who were a varied group of Kashmiri merchants, Tibetan speaking Ladakhis and a few foreigners, halted at Kargil for a half-way stop for the night.

Kargil is a predominantly Shia Muslim town. Situated on the southern fringes of Baltistan, the locals had a slightly Mongoloid appearance though different from the Tibetan Ladakhi faces. Few women were on view and the men had staring eyes and grim public personas. The buildings in the town at dusk were an unprepossessing poverty-stricken mixture of mud and wooden structures with large verandahs. Normally I happen to like a vernacular style, perhaps it was the creepy atmosphere of the place that made me feel uneasy.

The Yak Tail Hotel was about as inspiring as its name. The entire bus disgorged itself beside this insalubrious place and once inside, we huddled up together to eat noodle soup and coarse Tibetan unleavened bread. Eventually, a number of eaters wisely departed and left about twelve of us sitting on benches. I was the only woman left but it did not make any difference. The rooms cost only three rupees. (In 1977, the rate of exchange was approximately eighteen rupees to one pound sterling). Three of us went into a tiny little room, which was dark and poky with three beds lurking together in the centre of the room as if in collaboration with each other. I doubt if the woollen bedding strewn over the charpoys had been washed in years. Soon I would get familiar with my old tireless bed bug pals.

The final stop before Leh, the small capital of Ladakh in eastern Lesser Tibet was a tiny village, which appeared to consist of nothing but tea shops and stalls. As in parts of Italy then, all the shops refused small change. On the bus afterwards, I noticed that all the passengers were devouring small orange sweets given instead of currency.

After the tiring twenty four hour bus journey from Srinagar, the vehicle descended into Leh by nightfall. I followed a more honest- looking fellow to a guest house where later on I would meet in bed the usual creeping companions. At least the kitchen was snug. It had a low horizontal iron stove, which occupied much of the kitchen, having a chimney at one end with bellows embedded into the clay floor below. One woman pumped the heavy bellows continually whilst the other female made the bread. I squatted with a couple of silent bearded foreigners munching the tasty local unleavened bread, which if not eaten immediately would turn into rubber. Dunked into local rancid buttered tea, it was palatable, this surely being one of the most ancient forms of bread known to man. The tea locally named boeja, is made in a long, narrow, waist-high churn. After boiling the tea Indian style, the strained liquid is poured into the churn and mixed up with salt and butter. My landlady would commence this ritual soon after dawn. Above the stove, bright gleaming pans were cheerfully displayed along soot-blackened shelves. Most Ladakhi ceilings were made of local poplar. These had a welcoming, cosy dinginess. The ventilation was none too good as smoke did not always make a clear exit. Maybe after a couple of weeks, my eyes would have stopped smarting.

Ladakhis are of Tibetan stock, of short stature with high cheekbones and other usual Mongoloid features. Regarding washing, they do it infrequently unlike the over fastidious Hindu plainsmen. Most traditional Ladakhis smelt forever of yak butter, which was smeared on the hair and skin to protect their bodies against sun and cold. Sun rays easily penetrate skin in the summer months because of the high altitude.

Both sexes wore maroon coloured cloaks called choga, which were tied at the waist by a kamarbund. Their boots and caps were made of sheep skin. The women also dressed in heavy skirts of the same material. One would occasionally bump into females wearing their inherited wealth in the form of a peyrak, which is an elongated leather head dress stretching from the crown down the shoulders, the leather base covered with studded turquoise. The precious stones for the dowry are collected from birth. However, most local women wore the ubiquitous high, heavy, black velvet-brimmed hats.

Tibetan diet is closer to Chinese rather than Indian cooking and is very simple. The whole of north India had wonderfully basic Tibetan cafes wherever the thousands of Tibetan refugees had settled. For the myriads of hippies with Delhi Belly, they offered a cool chilli-free meal. The popular dishes were noodle soups named thukpa stew and momo consisting of tasty mince meat and herb mixtures surrounded by a steamed pastry case.

Unlike many fellow Buddhists, the Tibetans in general are not fervent vegetarians partly because of the paucity of plants that can be cultivated in high places. Later on in my travels, I was to meet a few sanctimonious Hindus who would tell me that such people should up sticks and shift to more verdant pastures.

Barley is the staple cereal. Here it is called tsampa when roasted. Millet, beans and hardy wheat will also grow locally.

Local ploughs were still led by zhos (a cross between a yak and a cow). One of the most memorable sounds that I can remember was the solitary drone of ploughmen rhythmically cajoling their beasts of burden in the stone walled fields of Ladakh.

The chief places of worship for all Ladakhis as with other Tibetans are gompas. These monasteries are usually to be found in rather inaccessible fortress-like locations high up in the mountains. Scattered around in various remote places are mani stones, which have remnants of religious inscriptions carved into them. Tibetan Buddhism has another religious symbol namely chortens, which are domed structures with square bases, modelled on stupas (reliquaries) containing ashes of monks. Flying above the chortens are clusters of Tibetan prayer flags, fluttering in the breeze.

As in many other Buddhist lands, it is an honour for a young boy to spend a number of years in a monastery. They may enter as young as five years old. In most of the gompas I visited, one would see these seemingly irreligious little tearaways scurrying about the huge ungainly dwellings.

Many monasteries are extremely wealthy. For example, Hemis Gompa, which is twenty seven miles from Leh and dating from the seventeenth century, happens to own about two thousand acres of land, which is widely scattered in several districts. Inside Hemis, there was a pervasive smell of yak butter, especially in the prayer rooms and elsewhere for that matter. On many inside walls, there were a profusion of scrolled paintings called thankas. Some of them might as well have been faded for all one could see in the oppressive, dark shrine rooms. Thankas usually depict devils and demigods together with the Buddhist wheel of life and the most elevated lamas.

I spent four nights at the tiny guest house kept by the monks. The equally small room I shared was with two friendly German lads. One, named Wolfgang, was beardless and the other sported an enormous beard. Luckily for me, these two kind-hearted characters shared their food with me. Wolfgang had a little primus stove and we lived on rice and lentil stew. Because it was early November, it was freezing and each night I went to bed with my huge Ladakhi pullover; mittens of double knit wool, thick socks and a woolly hat. I still kept shivering the entire night.

During my visit, a minor winter festival was celebrated in the form of a masked dance by the monks. Some of the dancers wore masks of demented-looking animal heads or grotesque devils. In some ways, all this was hardly in keeping with peaceful Buddhism and an even stranger sight that puzzled me was to see dogs and horses being continually pushed around the inner courtyard of the gompa. Also, what looked like blood, was splashed upon the unwilling horses backs. Small boy novices were shoving around whilst chasing and roughly teasing one another, pulling each other's tatty robes when they were not tormenting dogs, a much maligned and taken for granted animal.

It must be said that in spite of the wealth of the monastery, the bulk of the monks wore very tattered maroon coloured robes. In my opinion, the clothes matched their equally rough behaviour. Perhaps the roughness was an aid to survival. What a refreshing change to the sanctimonious expressions so often found on the faces of western converts to oriental faiths! Some monks occasionally rushed up to the few poverty-stricken looking foreigners pressed amongst the crowd in the yard hoping for a few coins. Others were carrying large metal reliquaries studded with elaborate inlaid jewellery that glittered amongst the copper and gold work. Other monks performing as masked dancers teased the audience who stood around the periphery of the yard. A few visitors even had their hats and scarves pinched.

Later on several monks appeared bellowing enormous copper horns, which were either serpent-shaped and held aloft or just great big tubes held on the ground in front of the musician, being far too heavy to carry. The lucky ones held cymbals. The drama enacted allegorised the battle between good and evil. The climax of the drama was a series of masked dancers who in turns stabbed a mound of cooked barley tsampa, the very substance symbolic of their existence.

I travelled to Phyang monastery, to which I and a Canadian friend went after spending the night together at a delightful inn in Leh. We had difficulty in finding the lama with the key in order to get into the main prayer rooms. Later, we nearly stumbled over a lama who had squatted while he painted a large embossed golden dragon against a dark blue background. We asked him where to find the lama with the key and he pointed vaguely towards some huddled dwellings reclining on a hillside beneath the gompa proper.

On descending the hill, we followed the familiar deep rhythmic thud of Tibetan drums and groaning horns. We found ourselves amongst an assembly of six monks performing puja (prayer) as they sat cross-legged facing us. In front of each monk hung huge gongs suspended on poles. The monks also used small drums which had two tiny straps attached. These drums were played in a circular movement and when swung, they resounded. Next to the monks stood beautiful butter sculptures with intricate lace-like chevrons and diamond designs. One lad had the job of continually replenishing both worshippers and ourselves with cups of buttered and salted tea of thickish texture. This was supplemented by gigantic chunks of local bread with a very tough consistency. Thus after every few minutes, the monks would pause and sup as they chatted and joked in a very informal manner, as if it were part of the ceremony. Placed in front of them were Tibetan scriptures, which are written in the ancient script unique to Tibet – a form of wood block-printed writing. The old documents consisted of horizontal loose sheets about one foot long by three inches wide, all kept in loose leather binding.

By mid November, the Srinagar to Leh road would soon be snowed up. Before departing for Srinagar, I got myself invited by a couple of military police officers to go and visit Shiksey monastery in their jeep. To be posted in military service to these northern climes was probably the equivalent of being sent to Siberia, especially as a number were from south India. The previous day, I had shared a bottle of local rice beer called chang with one of the officers and he seemed alright.

On the day of the trip, they had taken alcohol and offered me some chang in the jeep, which I declined. After an hour on the road in the middle of nowhere, we stopped. A number of hands wandered in my direction. Of course, travelling alone, I was easy game. I told them quietly to remove their hands and the Madrasi driver yelled that if I did not let them have sex, they would leave me behind. Somehow, I kept calm and strangely enough, they drove onto the monastery. After our return, the following day the chief officer came and apologised and asked me if I wanted to go to Hemis with him. Needless to say, I declined!

The bus journey back to Srinagar got delayed at five o'clock in the morning and passengers had to wait three hours at nearby Drass for the army convoy to pass on the narrow road. In a tea shop, Sikh truck drivers explained how they drove in neutral thus saving petrol to then sell it. Also, they overloaded the trucks and sold parts of the vehicle!

After arrival back in Srinagar, I decided to leave the state of Jammu and Kashmir and head south. It was a cloudy day and the crowded bus passed fields of violet saffron in the Pampore district. I was amused by the caption in the bus, 'A gentleman will not smoke on the bus and disturb to all'. I stayed one night at an awful hotel in Jammu. Unfortunately, everyone seemed to wake up and rise at three o'clock in the morning. The mass movement would be swiftly followed by the never ending hawking of throats. I soon discovered that many Indians, especially Hindus, are obsessed with ablutions at the crack of dawn.

Next, I was off on another tiring twelve hour journey on a clapped-out old bus to the neighbouring state of Himachal Pradesh to the hill station Dalhousie.

Chapter Three

Nature Cure in the Himalayan Foothills

As the local bus climbed up to Dalhousie, we passed lush-growing deciduous trees. On arrival, one of my first sights was the Palace View Hotel, which reminded me of an English village church hall. It had wooden trellised arched windows outside, and inside a dance hall that must have witnessed many barn dances and tombola sessions during the Raj. This hotel commanded a fine view over the former British cantonment and the Indian bazaars called Tagore and Gandhi Chowk.

In typical hill station fashion, the bazaars had developed in a limpet-like way alongside the military quarter. Hill station architecture always displays a sea of corrugated iron roofs. It had become too costly for locals to cart slates up the steep lanes. On some of the road sides were painted lively pictures of Lord Buddha. It became second nature for me to adopt the Indian habit of calling Gods or great Beings by the title Lord. I still felt close to Tibetan culture because in Himachal state, there are thousands of Tibetan refugees whom India has offered freedom since China invaded their land. For years, I had corresponded with a Tibetan lama as a pen friend. Lama Lobsang Tseering had previously lived at Gyudto College monastery in Dalhousie after migrating from Tibet. I never met him and only heard of him through the UK based Tibet society. Now he had gone away again to distant Arunachal Pradesh on the borders of China, a forbidden area to foreigners in 1978.

The most striking form of animal life were monkeys with lovely red behinds who engaged together in glorious acrobatics, usually when they were not preening themselves. The heavy mists and low clouds looked as if they would never shift.

The dull weather aggravated an illness that I developed. I had found myself staying at a forlorn-looking guest house, which appeared to have only me in it. The rooms were plain with spartan bedding, the most memorable thing being the towering ceiling with a creaking fan. I had to spend several hours in bed each day as I got a sickly feeling and ate no food apart from bread and tea. The atmosphere was not helped by the pervasive smell coming from a local bush which penetrated my very being. I also gave work to the local police who kept asking me what my mission in India was. This was a question I was frequently to be asked while travelling there. I was never asked in Pakistan. Maybe there was still a belief in public service in India, being a legacy of Gandhi. Or perhaps not.

Why, I do not know but I was glad to leave Dalhousie and set off for the neighbouring hill station of Dharamsala, which at the time was surrounded by snow-capped peaks that descended into dense green shrubbery. Situated at over seven thousand feet, many of the houses, which were built in the most precarious positions, appeared to clamber parasitically up the hillsides.

Upper Dharamsala was mainly a Tibetan refugee settlement. The home of the Dalai Lama and Tibetan government in exile. The town was dominated by the Tibetan Children's Village. While walking towards the village, a boy on crutches insisted on accompanying me, and then went ahead of me as I panted exhaustively behind him. Eventually, I met Yangchen Dolken, an articulate woman. She lived in a pleasant hut, one of several designed by an English architect.

In 1978 the village held over one thousand children. They lived in units of twenty five people including their house parents. Their small hospital used both allopathic (western orthodox medicine) and Tibetan medicine. Yangchen thought that Tibetan treatment was better for preventative health care, which may have some truth as western medicine is often geared to curing symptoms rather than the cause of ailments. Many of the children were the orphans of Tibetan road workers who had died on the various mountain roads. Yangchen told me that relations with Indians were fine but intermarriage took place mainly with westerners, rarely with Indians. 'We Tibetans are on the same wavelength as westerners', I was told.

After having a Tibetan girlfriend pen pal who was a student of Tibetan medicine, I was dying to see the traditional training centre in Dharamsala. Luckily, the place exists as refugees carried the precious texts over the mountains from Tibet. The course took from five to seven years to complete in the 1970's. Students would study herbalism, gemology, acupuncture and astrology. In order to learn herbalism, students had to go into the local hills and pick the herbs thus seeing the plants in their native surroundings. One room in the medical centre held an automated collection of pestles rhythmically pounding into huge mortars crammed with herbal powders of different shades of green. At one end, there stood a machine for manufacturing tablets. One enthusiast pointed out that some tablets were for memory improvement!

The centre of Upper Dharamsala was McLeod Ganj and it offered the depressing sight of western hippies attempting to sell off all their possessions. What a desperate and unoriginal little group. However, many foreigners go to the town to study Buddhism and to see the Dalai Lama and the Tibetan government in exile.

I spent several nights at the dingy Goddess Kali temple, which had an orgy of the dirtiest and crudest statues of the goddess on display. The bearded priest informed me that it would cost me the magnificent sum of two rupees per night on 'backside of Kali'. He sat drinking cheap whisky while seated on terribly infested-looking bed clothes. At one point, a more sober man sat alongside him on a dilapidated arm chair. An assortment of broken cups, bottles and broken down charpoys were littered about the place. 'Do you smoke hash?' the priest enquired. A pretty sad place but then most faiths have occasional depth of degeneration and this was Hinduism's moment.

I climbed up to the Tibetan government in exile headquarters. The complex included a museum and library, the latter had a couple of western converts to Buddhism crouching over a number of ancient- looking Tibetan texts. Some stay one month or up to a year. I got hold of the autobiography of the Dalai Lama My Land and My People wherein he comes out as occasionally too accommodating to the Chinese. Somewhere else, I read that the Tibetan medical centre had invented a contraceptive that had to be taken seven days in succession at prescribed times, which would enable it to work for one year!

Since departing from Pakistan, I had joined an organisation called Servas International. It was really a set-up of hosts and travellers, except that I was not a host. Hosts may be families, individuals or communities from any background. In India, some members were linked to Mahatma Gandhi's work in the Sarvodaya movement which involves itself in working for the downtrodden all over India. Some folks lived in ashrams, which are welfare communities of varying sizes where people live together as a unit without payment. Of course, most ashrams are religious (Hindu) in inspiration and are fairly self- supporting or reliant upon donations.

Himachal Pradesh is a Himalayan state carved out of the former eastern Punjab and some small princely states. Its northern border joins troublesome Kashmir. It was here that I met my first Servas fellow Swami Poornachand. Living in a cave near the town of Jawalamukhi, a small town in the Himalayan foothills was this saintly looking white- bearded man aged eighty two years old. He spoke Hindi, the major language of northern India with a strong Pihari (hills) dialect. His later life had evolved around the Gita Bhawan Public Trust as a pilgrimage centre for the local Goddess Durga temple, Durga being one of the manifold aspects of the divine female energy Shakti. The trust also provided money to help poor students purchase food and medicines. Devotees could also worship at a small temple in the trust's own grounds.

I didn't sleep in the cave as Swamiji (ji is a term of respect in India) lived as a hermit high up in the surrounding hills. In common with so many pilgrimage centres found at many temples, this dharamsala (temple hostel) proclaimed itself loud and clearly at the dreaded hours of sunrise and sunset when recorded devotional music was blasted out from a fearsome, crackling loud speaker offering headaches rather than tranquillity.

At the nearby Devi (goddess) temple, a short walk away from my guest house, devotees sat cross legged whilst occupying the entire temple courtyard, singing hymns accompanied by the portable Indian harmonium, which looks like a tiny piano with a back that opens and shuts. The other instrument was a pair of tabla drums. This Devi temple was built up against a steep rock face and so had an impressive setting. It was famous for a perpetual sacred fire, which burnt from a source of inflammable gas issuing from a fissure in a nearby rock cleft behind the temple.

Visiting another temple in the vicinity, a local temple hand offered me sweet tea and roti bread. We smoked country leaf cigarettes called beedies. Like roll ups, they tended to go out if not continually smoked. This temple was for untouchables only. Untouchables in modern India are also called Scheduled Castes or by Gandhi's euphemistic name Harijan, literally Children of God.

My next Servas friend Maharshi Tirathram turned out to be a remarkable man over seventy years old. His tiny ashram in the hamlet of Oel, I considered to be one of my dearest homes in India. Maharshiji of Brahmin origin was a former freedom fighter against the British, the first of many such characters that I would meet on the subcontinent. He was once imprisoned by them as he had joined Gandhi's civil disobedience movement. The Swadeshi (own country first) movement initiated by Gandhi aimed at discouraging the use of imported materials, especially Lancashire cloth, thus encouraging home industries, even the humble spinning wheel and hand loom. One often finds that all those who claim to be followers of the Mahatma wear homespun and hand woven khadi (cloth). The purpose was to build up a pool of workers in labour-intensive industries. The khadi worn by most of these workers varies a little and Maharshi wore white cotton, fairly loose trousers, a long dull-coloured shirt under a sleeveless woollen waistcoat, different from the famous Nehru jacket. All this was topped by a white or brown boat-shaped Gandhi cap. The chief problem with khadi is that it is not long wearing, it is also more expensive than most of the locally produced factory cloth. The biggest joke is that this cloth was de rigueur for India's politicians who often mouthed Gandhi's slogans while developing fat bellies. Entering Gandhi Seva Ashram, the first thing to be seen within the compound was a bust of Gandhi with the caption 'Trust, Ahimsa (non violence) Love, Brahmacharya (chastity) Control of palate, Non stealing, Non possession, Poverty, Fearlessness, Removal of Untouchability, Swadeshi'. Quite a moral impact for the new visitor!

My hut, as I came to call it, was a rectangular mud building with a large overhanging thatched roof and a verandah the entire way round. Nightly, I would lie awake and listen to the everlasting sound of crickets and ubiquitous fireflies. The varieties of insects were enough to satisfy an entomologist.

Inside the hut were very dusty hanging photos of Nehru, Gandhi, Subhas Chandra Bhose (a revolutionary Bengali who, during the Second World War wanted India to join with Japan and Germany against Britain) and Sardar Patel, a conservative Hindu politician. The bulk of the room was occupied by a large table and a hard plain wooden base, which served as my bed. The two windows were composed of prison type bars with internal wood shutters. The double doors were of the common Indian type with a horizontal metal bar, which padlocked the two outward opening doors.

I always carried my own padlock around with me because at so many later hostelries, I never trusted the proprietors not to snoop around my belongings.

Maharshiji was a great believer in nature cure (the preferred term for naturopathy in India). This system is one amongst many practised in modern day Hindustan and Pakistan for that matter. Ayurveda is the oldest established medical system in India in that unlike folk healing, it has an ancient literary tradition. It is the Hindu method using herbs and minerals. Unani (Urdu for Greek) is the medicine favoured by Muslims. It is based on ancient Greek medicine and was introduced to the subcontinent by the Arabs. Ironically, today it is found no longer in Greece or any Arab land, only in Indo-Pak. Western medicine is labelled by the name of allopathy. Indians use these terms. Homeopathy is very big in the subcontinent and that is without the aid of the English Queen's patronage. At any school of homeopathy in Britain, a large number of the text books will have come from India and some students do their practicals in India. On a later visit to book-loving Calcutta, whilst wondering through the mile long second hand book Mecca named College Road, I came across a book shop that just specialised in homeopathic works, all well thumbed but now gathering dust.

All systems apart from allopathy are geared perhaps more to treating the causes of disease rather than the symptoms. I became chiefly interested in nature cure and eventually found out that Osmania University in Hyderabad, central India offered a four year degree course in naturopathy. This course was started by a dissatisfied student of western medicine. However, most nature curists are not formally trained though some of them dish out certificates like confetti.

In India as elsewhere, nature cure emphasises self sufficiency of the human organism that is based on natural forces operating within the body to help healing, with disease being viewed as a disturbance of natural equilibrium. Apart from natural disasters and accidents, naturopathy places the responsibility for illness on the patient who has become ill through choosing an abnormal lifestyle. Unlike all the aforementioned healing systems, nature cure is drugless, even herbs are out except perhaps in cooking. Its materia medica consists of elemental agents such as earth, water, air, light and even in some cases magnetism.

Yoga and diet play an obsessive role in India. All the nature curists were keen to tell me how they refused to accept the germ theory of disease as a primary cause of illness. Maharshiji ran a little hospital at the ashram for some older patients who plainly enjoyed the peace of the place. Remedial massage, yoga and fasting were the popular treatments. Other centres might have included chromotherapy (use of colour in treatment), hot and cold water therapy, special baths and mud packs.

A little way behind my hut was a similar one built by an English disciple of Gandhi called Mirabhen. Maharshiji said that she insisted on only using local materials for the hut. Gandhians are great believers in mud/dung for building. The efficacy of mud for walls and flooring is evident as it is warm in winter and cool in summer unlike concrete in modern dwellings, which has the opposite effect. Of course, a mud building needs far more upkeep.

Just before I ended my first visit to the ashram, the DDT man came and sprayed all the ashram premises. I entered my hut a few hours later and found the entire hut covered in white powder with masses of embalmed insects. That night, I slept in the hut. I must have been crazy, especially since the substance was banned in many western countries!

The panchayat is India's version of village democracy. Maharshiji was the local sarpanch (council leader) and held his meetings under one of the larger ashram trees. Most of the locals were illiterate so they got help with such basics as letter writing and court cases, something that can drag on for years in India.

Prior to my getting the slow bus to Delhi, a stranger came to the ashram. His name was Syed Razi. He was to become a type of mentor to me. He was a non-practising middle aged Muslim and a former advocate from Bihar state. In many ways, he seemed more of a Hindu than a Muslim if only because of his presence in an ashram, rather a Hindu institution in its origins. He even joined in ashram prayers and was very keen on meditation and nature cure. He was a handsome man with an engaging gap in his front teeth. Before growing his long beard, he sported a small British 1940's moustache. His hair was parted on one side and back off his forehead. In fact, he used to tell me that 'In my prime, I looked very dashing'.

His family situation was strange. As Muslims, his two brothers had migrated to Pakistan during Partition in 1947. During the 1970's, there were disturbances between Hindus and Muslims in the eastern state of Bihar. His wife Hamida and seven children all departed for Pakistan. After two years there, they found that they had had enough and left for the United States. Syed Razi was always an Indian first and never accepted the concept of Pakistan. He said that whenever there was a cricket match between the two countries and Indian Muslims could be heard supporting Pakistan, he would get mad.

He argued against the idea of the Muslim belief in Finality of Prophethood meaning that Muhammad was the final and the greatest prophet of all time. Mainly as the Arabic word in the Quran could be interpreted purely as latest.

One day at the ashram hospital whilst he was examining a patient with high blood pressure, all our voices were drowned out by a drone of bagpipe players gaily bedecked in colourful clothes. The pipers were accompanied by drummers performing on the infectious horizontal dholak drums. These drums are to north Indian folk music what the tablas are to classical music. This was followed by a colourful bridegroom being carried on a simple decorated wooden sedan chair with a domed canopy covered with a gay cloth. The groom wore a garland of flowers and rupee notes. The wedding group was entirely male as the groom was on his way to claim his bride. The festive party remained outside the ashram for an hour. Then a pathetically unrhythmic dance took place with one fellow within the circle who performed as if he was high on bhang (a drink from hemp.)

Chapter Four

From Punjab to Delhi and Misfortune on a Motorbike

The present day Punjab is only a microcosm of its former size. The former West Punjab went to Pakistan. Part of East Punjab went to the states of Himachal Pradesh and Haryana.

Chandigarh is the capital of Punjab and Haryana. It was designed by the French architect Le Corbusier on the grid pattern of streets. Each sector of the city was a self contained unit with many facilities including open spaces. No buildings were higher than a few storeys and there were plenty of trees and gardens. Considering its modernity, Chandigarh was a lovely city. Unfortunately, ugly building materials were used in the form of cheap bricks and cement.

My first Servas friends in Chandigarh were a wealthy Sikh family. The father was a lawyer and the mother, a close friend of Mrs Gandhi, had been a member of the state legislature and had received the Nehru award. The eldest daughter had been deserted by her husband. On her wedding, her family had paid a two lakh (200,000) rupee dowry. The family was a combination of good western education and pride in Sikh culture. She told me that it was wrong for either sex to cut their hair, her younger sister had cut a few inches off her own hair and was considered 'fast' even though she read the Sikh holy book the Guru Granth Sahib daily. The family kept the Holy Scriptures in a large wooden structure called a balki, which itself was held in their tiny prayer room that had on one of its walls a giant painting of the gentle face of the founder of the Sikhs, Guru Nanak. They denied that there were Islamic influences in Sikhism.

I was unconvinced. When reading from the Holy Granth, they recited a few words from a page newly opened each day.

My second Servas character in Chandigarh was to become one of my closest friends in India. Satinder Verma was a scholarly-looking man with a pleasantly intense face. His receding hairline gave him a distinguished appearance while his hair was quite long at the back. He and his wife were trained teachers. He lectured in English literature and like most Indian lecturers, he lived upon the university campus. Through an illness which badly affected his back, Satinder became interested in Christian Science. This group had a little section in Chandigarh, their membership including Sikhs. However, Satinder had retained his open-mindedness to all faiths and was still a Hindu. The entire family was vegetarian, including his daughter Shiela, though he hailed from a meat eating family. We discussed matters of religion and politics. Satinder had travelled to the USA giving talks on eastern philosophy. He found the Unitarians to be one of the most open-minded Christian groups.

To the south of Punjab lies the state of Haryana. This state was created from the former east Punjab during the craze in attempting to base the boundaries of individual states upon language. That part of Punjab which became Haryana was predominantly Hindu whereas the northern area of Punjab was just over fifty percent Sikh dominated. The presumption was that Punjabi Hindus spoke Hindi as a first language unlike the Sikhs who spoke Punjabi. This was nonsense as the Hindus in that area often spoke Punjabi as their first language whether or not they understood Hindi. In this area, the states were based upon religious differences. Of course, communities of both religions still lived together in many cases.

Haryana tends to be a state without any real identity. One traverses it en route to Delhi. It is best seen in early morning during the winter. The road to Delhi, although flat, offers its own feasts for the eye. During winter, myriads of lush green water weeds grow in hundreds of scattered ponds dispersed amongst verdant fields. Haryana is real buffalo country in spite of the presence of the large noble white Haryana humpbacked cattle. Many north Indians apart from rigid naturopaths and some Brahmins relish the much richer milk of the buffalo.

My first view of New Delhi was of one of the drab colourless concrete suburbs. I had arrived to visit my Servas 'friend' in the Janakpuri suburb.

I was in a bad mood being the last person to get off a small local bus and I had caught the bus conductor examining my luggage up at the front of the bus, which did not help my mood.

My host Mr K was a secondary school teacher and he invited me to talk to his class of blue uniformed school kids. Wearing shalwar and kamiz (baggy trousers and long shirt), I addressed the giggling multitude for fifteen minutes. They asked me if I was afraid to travel alone, why I was not married. Could I get them lodgings in the United Kingdom? I gave them frank replies.

Mr K took me back home and he kept apologising for the fact that he had no 'flush latrine'. That did not concern me. I mentioned that his house servant was continually staring at me. 'Oh, he is like one of your Negroes in your country', he said, pointing at his servant's dark skin.

The next day, Mr K and family took me to a lower middle class marriage party, which was the usual gaudy and glittering affair found at such assemblies. The women were conventionally attired in saris while the men wore western suits of all shapes and shades. Strange colour combinations such as brown suits and purple woolly hats! I thought that if they could not afford well-cut suits, then they would look far better in traditional clothes. Nobody spoke to me, they only stared.

Many Indian weddings are attended by awful western style bands, which play Hindi film music, usually out of tune with too many trombones and trumpets. At the same time that day the crudest Hindi film music was blasting out of loud speakers. For a short while the only saving grace was a traditional folk music group. The garlanded groom arrived on a white horse, his face covered by tinsel and tassels hanging down from his turban. The white horse gave the image of a man coming to claim his woman. A lot of these often overprotected and spoilt sons could not even manage three steps on a horse without someone holding the reins.

Guests mixed sweet and savoury foods together, not in the sweet and sour Chinese way but on the same thali (plate). There were placed very sugary sweetmeats called halawi, together with meat and vegetables. The meal was followed by a painfully long speech from the bridegroom's side of the family. Much of the speech involved praising the bride and telling amusing stories about her. The main presents transferred were from the boy's family who gave clothes and jewellery to the bride.

However the bride's family would have paid a costly dowry. Dowry giving is banned in India but this law is ignored by nearly everyone. Dowry giving often bankrupts middle class families and this is one of the reasons that baby girls are not so welcome in Hindu India. The bride's family as 'bride giver' is often inferior in status to the 'bride takers', the groom's family. Even within the same subcaste.

Mr K had the misfortune to have five daughters hence his life's wages went towards their dowries. Families continue to try for a boy and end up with girls. Mr K claimed 'Man is superior to woman in this country so the girl's family gives more'. No comment. Goddess worship does not automatically improve the lot of women.

The day before my departure from this household, a teaching colleague of Mr K came to the house. 'You like wine?' I hesitated with an answer. In India the term 'wine' can mean anything. Though there were no legal prohibitions in New Delhi, social conventions often forbade the consumption of alcohol in houses if women were present. This same practice could apply to meat eating. Some husbands and sons ate meat in restaurants but were vegetarians in front of their female relatives.

I was to regret accepting the invitation to drink alcohol. Naively, I believed that I was going to a family's house. Instead, the friend came to collect me by motorbike and we travelled in the pitch dark on a November evening about twenty miles out of Delhi.

The bike stopped at a small isolated brick house. I noted the presence of two other men. One of them was the school clerk who must have seen me the previous day at school. Not a woman in sight. I smelt trouble. Yet another group of frustrated Indian men with images of easy western females. A chicken was consumed with relish 'Our women are innocent, they see their men as gods' exclaimed one wag. The local red wine was repulsively thick and sweet. There was also an off white 'whisky' made from rose water, which tasted like perfume.

These men were unbelievably immature under the influence of alcohol. Perhaps they had never been alone with a woman before. The groping began. My 'host' tried to force a kiss. 'You will have to kill me before you get it', I asserted. I threatened to tell Mr K's wife. They relented. En route back to Delhi with three of us on the motorbike, (the groping still continued) we met a wealthy Sikh couple whose car had broken down. I attempted to waylay the woman and ask for a lift as they were going past Janak Puri suburb. Next thing I knew was that they had left. They must have thought me unbelievably cheap as my breath smelt of alcohol and I was alone with three drunken men. Mr K begged me not to tell his wife. Boy, was I glad to get home, I was really quite scared.

At four o'clock in the morning the following day, even grandmother's religious chanting was a welcome sound. I was surprised to see bottled milk delivered at the house. I had never seen this in Karachi where I had spent a year. In both Pakistan and India, one has to be wary of purchasing adulterated milk. Mr K's eldest daughter saw me with my radio and enquired if I was listening to a cricket 'commentary' as if that was the only happening on the BBC World Service.

Around some of the neighbouring muddy streets, feral swine scratch a living. These pigs are consumed by untouchable/scheduled caste 'sweeper' (latrine cleaner) colonies. Hindu India, like Muslim Pakistan considers the pig unclean. This is because they live on garbage and excrement. The poor things get little else to eat. On close inspection, even the sacred homeless cow eats most kinds of rubbish. In a few states like the Punjab, there are a few pig farms. On one alleyway, a group of children invited me to their homes 'will you write to us?' I said 'No'. Most of their countrymen or foreigners in the same situation would have replied in the affirmative even if they had no intention of writing. I was purely a curiosity, a novelty. 'Will you sing and dance?' Nearby, an elderly Sikh man asked in refined English 'Do you know Suffolk?' He was an ex-student of A.S. Neill's old progressive school Summerhill. I would again meet this man many months later in central India at a nature cure sanatorium near Pune.

Chapter Five

The Nationalist Saint and
the Shaven-Headed Swami

Remaining in New Delhi, I arrived in the early morning at Sri Aurobindo ashram.

I heard the sounds of devotional singing coming from a central building. Inside the hall were large photos of the Hindu sage Sri Aurobindo and his most famous disciple, a French lady called 'The Mother'. On the photo, Sri Aurobindo wore a white toga-like shawl draped across one shoulder. He had long white hair parted in the centre. He wore a long goatee beard and his eyes were penetratingly deep.

Sri Aurobindo lived much of his early life in England. His studies included Latin and Greek. On his return to India, he eventually became involved in the nationalist movement and studied Sanskrit and Hindu philosophy. Originally from Bengal, he went to live in French ruled Pondicherry to escape the clutches of the British authorities who wanted to arrest him for certain nationalist activities. Later, he founded an ashram in Pondicherry, now a part of free India.

On my second day, I assisted in making marigold garlands. These garlands are used for placing on statues and pictures on special occasions. That day was the anniversary of Sri Aurobindo's death and children of the ashram school recited various quotes from his writings. There were a few westerners living at the ashram and during the recitation, one western girl sat cross-legged in an intentionally ecstatic pose with palms turned upward on each knee. The Indians looked more relaxed. Why do converts have to go overboard in their zeal? At night, we all listened to recordings of Sri Aurobindo's voice. I found the voice uncanny and at once sacred. Sri Aurobindo died many years ago.

I next moved to Rajghat district where Mahatma Gandhi's samadhi (memorial place) stands. There an eternal fire burnt in an urn-shaped bowl. Nearby stood Gandhi Smarak Nidhi, a centre for organising Gandhian activities. This was my New Delhi home whenever I was passing through the area. Next to the centre was the Gandhi Museum, which had displays on Gandhi's life. His relics in the form of sandals, cloth, teeth and spectacles were shown in their simplicity. There was a good model of his birthplace in Gujarat and a beautiful picture of Gandhi made of ground-nut shells placed upon a peepul leaf.

One of the organizations with headquarters at Gandhi Nidhi was Himalaya Seva Sangh, which worked with the hill people of the Himalayas. The secretary was the kindly dignified Krishnamurti who was also an ex freedom fighter against the British. Some of the hills and plains people are classed as Adivasis or Adijatis (tribals) who are outside the Hindu caste system, which is divided into four major castes. At the top are the Brahmins or priestly caste followed by Kashatriya or warrior caste. Thirdly Vaishyas (traders) and finally Sudras (farmers). These are crude divisions and in reality there are thousands of subcastes within each group. These subcastes are themselves graded. Thus a little upward and downward subcaste mobility is sometimes possible on a group basis. Also outside the caste system are the untouchables or scheduled castes, which are often lumped together for government purposes as 'backward castes' in that their members may have reserved places in some government jobs and educational establishments. The tribals are supposed to be members of the original pre-Aryan or pre-Dravidian inhabitants of India. They can be of Animist, Hindu, Muslim, Christian religion or Buddhist. Tribals cannot always be clearly distinguished from their neighbouring low caste brethren.

Another organization at Gandhi Nidhi was a nature cure centre run by an austere Brahmin Sri Jawarbhai who gave up a wealthy lifestyle to follow Gandhi. Another member was the eccentric Dr Swaraj, a self-educated man from a gardening caste. He was a rough character who would always ask the most personal questions. He had boundless energy and constantly travelled all over India lecturing on nature cure. He claimed to eat only uncooked vegetarian food. Tea and coffee were banned from his room where we all would frequently gather for a good chat. Whilst squatting on the floor one day, my foot came near to a dish of cooked food, he yelled 'this is not our Hindu tradition', everybody laughed and I felt awful. I had nearly polluted the food. Cooked food is obviously more easily polluted than raw food, which may yet be cooked. We had purchased this food from a nearby restaurant.

'Hindustani Seva Sangh' was a curious organisation under the Gandhian umbrella. The term 'Hindustani' denotes a language, which is a combination of Urdu and Hindi. Both Hindi and Urdu have a similar grammatical structure. Their vocabulary is similar. Urdu uses more Persian, Arabic and Turkish words and the Persian script, while Hindi uses many Sanskrit words and Sanskrit Devnagari script. Urdu is spoken more by north Indian Muslims and Hindi by many North Indian Hindus. Gandhi wanted to prevent polarisation of the two communities so he suggested that the term Hindustani should be used for a language that used the much simpler Devnagari script rather than the complicated Persian cursive script, and retain many of the Persian and Arabic words. What has happened is the opposite of what Gandhi intended.

Since the creation of Pakistan at Partition from India, the languages have polarised because of nationalism. In India when one travelled in, for example, the Punjab, one could see a number of older Hindus reading Urdu/Hindi newspapers in Persian script and Devnagari script. This is because prior to Partition, many Muslims lived in that area. In modern times few, if any of the present Hindu children would be able to read the Persian script. In the schools of north India, they will learn only the Sanskrit derived script and a more 'Sanskritized' or 'purer' Hindi. They will learn in this 'purer' Hindi some words that they never use in conversation. I heard many people complain about 'Sanskritzation' on the radio, etc. Indirectly, this is an attack on Brahmin domination in certain quarters of the establishment as it is they who tend to form the bulk of the Sanskrit scholars. Sanskrit is a dead language and like Latin and ancient Greek insofar as it forms the source of many Indo-European languages. Pakistan has made Urdu its national language because this was the language spoken by the majority of Muslim migrants from India's old state of United Provinces who fled to Pakistan. It is not one of the original languages of geographical Pakistan such as Punjabi, Sindhi, Baluchi, Pushto and Kashmiri. Nationalism has polarised language. The concept of Hindustani is dead and buried.

In New Delhi I visited the National Small Industries Fair held in 1978. The best part of the exhibition related to Gandhi's ideas. A model of Gandhi's hut from Sevagram ashram was on display. This was surrounded by cottages exhibiting aspects of his teachings. One cottage was dedicated to his 'back to the village' ideal but with models of improved latrines and explanations about improving the diet.

In another cottage, there was discussion on untouchability and its eradication. It carried the legend 'If untouchability lives, Hinduism must die'.

A friend of Razi Sahib invited me to a 'sound and light' performance at the Red Fort in old Delhi. Perhaps it was advantageous for me to hear it in Hindi rather than English. It depicted vividly the Moghul rulers and concubines with the soldiers attacking, drinking and acting in a generally debauched manner. The wise rule of Akbar, who ruled at the same time as Elizabeth I of England, followed later by the zealous Aurangzeb who disliked music and drinking. The end showed the decline of the Moghuls and the coming of the British.

Razi Sahib joined me in Old Delhi and we wondered around the old bazaar of Chandni Chowk. One street was called informally 'Parathawali gali' (the lane of the paratha makers). Parathas are unleavened bread, which are deep fried and often stuffed with a variety of vegetables, the dough and vegetables are mixed together. A favourite shop of mine near the old Delhi Gate was the dudh (milk) shop. The shop was windowless and the cans, pots of milk and yoghurt stood on a raised platform. The dudh wallah sold lots of fresh milk, which was boiled on the spot in huge shallow pans and then scooped into glasses with its skin added. There was always lots of yogurt or curd as it was known there. We would treat ourselves to yogurt scooped into earthenware pots covered by a margosa or peepul leaf. A shop nearby the Jama Masjid or Friday Mosque served my favourite winter sweet made of carrots, nuts and raisins. The carrot was cooked in milk and then fried in ghee (clarified butter) and served from huge shallow pans. Old Delhi had a huge Muslim population. Many Muslims opted to remain in India rather than migrate to Pakistan.

I visited the government subsidised Institute of Research in Yoga. The fifty bed hospital was going to waste as they only had seventeen patients (in 1978) suffering from asthma, sinusitis or stomach disorders. The swami in charge looked bored with his job and too contented. A former administrator had been accused of sexual misconduct.

Razi Sahib and I went to the mock Gothic brick railway station of old Delhi to greet Swami Chidananda, a disciple of the Sivananda order. Accompanying him was a Lebanese who was dressed in simple white homespun cloth. The shaven-headed and beardless swami was attired in saffron robes. After Swamiji's group alighted from the train, each of our small welcoming group handed them garlands. This was followed by a solemn 'Om Hey Ram' ringing softly amongst the bustle around the train. Sweetmeats were distributed and Razi Sahib and I departed.

Indian railway stations always have many recumbent bodies lying about. All are homeless and they do not appear to get disturbed. They appear to be a bit luckier than the poor freezing 'dossers' in England who often get hounded from pillar to post.

Chapter Six

A Happy Life for Aged Cows and a Visit to Baba

Razi Sahib and I travelled north of Delhi into Haryana state to visit Pattikalyana Nature Cure Ashram situated within its own twenty five acre domain of well irrigated wheatfields, making it practically self-sufficient in food.

The leading characters at the ashram were Pittaji and Mataji (respected Father and Mother). Pittaji was of Pathan origin hailing from the North West Frontier Province (N.W.F.P.) of what is today Pakistan. Only seven per cent of the Pathans were Hindus. Pittaji had founded an ashram in Lahore but in 1948 it was destroyed by Muslim fanatics. He was an austere but serene character who kept the ashram working efficiently.

The ashram day commenced at four o'clock in the morning when we would all shuffle into the prayer room on hearing the ashram bell. The prayer room also housed a nature cure and yoga library. At four in the afternoon, a discussion hour was held in the same room. One day a few of us read aloud from Mirabhen's autobiography. The prayer room walls were covered with lovely paintings of Gandhi going about his daily tasks.

The ashram hospital had forty inpatients. The doctor had taken the four year degree course in naturopathy in Hyderabad. The treatments offered included massage, special diets, fasts and steam baths. Regarding the steam baths, Indian naturopaths prefer patients to keep the head cool while sitting in the bath. The steam bath I saw was a wooden cabinet with a hole cut out of the top. A small brazier was lit alongside it to provide the steam. They disapproved of sauna baths because of fear of overheating the head. Inscribed on the hospital wall was 'Three Causes of disease: Belief in Miracles, Love of Comfort, Human Indolence. A formula for living:

Be true to yourself. Not to be false to any man'. Underneath were pictures of various yogic postures and special baths.

I went to a nearby nature cure hospital at Semulka. Formerly, it was a farm, and then the hospital was established in opposition to Pattikalyana. It was run by a husband and wife doctor team who were expelled from Pattikalyana because they continually argued. The wife said 'They (patients) come home when all other pathies have failed.' Like Pattikalyana, they too maintained decrepit old cows but at Semulka, cattle were wondering all over the place.

As true Gandhians, they ensured that Pattikalyana's 'goushalla" (cow shelter) was well run. Many organisations connected with Gandhi's name are at the forefront of the cow protection movement. Cow slaughter was officially banned in all states except communist dominated West Bengal and Kerala. Slaughtering goes on illegally alongside a lot of interstate smuggling. Orthodox high caste Brahmins especially see the cow as sacred and highly intelligent. There is nothing inspiring about thousands of homeless cattle scrounging vegetables furtively off market stalls and getting kicked for their troubles. Gandhi intended that the banning of cow slaughter would lead to respect for all living creatures.

There was a small group of exclusive-looking western ashramites who were chelas (disciples) of their guru (teacher), a Dr Kershik. He was originally an allopathic practitioner who had turned to yoga. One foreigner, an Englishman addressed me in a dreamy, detached manner. Too much cliquishness for my liking. They were too full of their own cosy self-importance. Their daily lives were spent in study, meditation and discussion. Their guru was served by an especially close disciple, an American girl. In summertime, they would accompany Dr Kershik to Dalhousie where he had a retreat. The ancient Hindu scholars developed the concept of the ashramas or stages of life. A young man would pass at first through the Brahmacharya (self denial) stage spent studying and living with a guru. These studies might take years. One such student might learn ayurvedic medicine whilst he was serving his teacher and thus learn through example and humility. The next stage would be that of Grihast (householder stage) where he would dedicate his time to his family. Once his family had no real need of him, he would enter the Vanprast (social service stage) period and serve the community. Finally, he might become a Sannyasin (a seeker of truth) and take to the forest. The ashramas were there for all but obviously only a comparatively few people could have followed these four stages exactly. Thus Dr Kershik's disciples could claim to be Brahmacharyas because they looked after his every need as they were learning from him. The group took little interest in the nature cure treatments on the ashram. Like many converts, they appeared to be obsessively one-sided.

On return to Gandhi Nidhi in New Delhi, I was asked whether I would like to visit Vinoba Bhave's ashram at Wardha in the central Indian state of Maharashtra. Vinoba Bhave was the most famous living Gandhian (in 1978). The ascetic Vinoba or 'Baba' (father) as he was affectionately known joined Gandhi in 1916 not so much as a freedom fighter against British rule but more as constructive worker scholar. He started the Bhoodan or Land Gift movement. Publicity for this programme was carried out through padayatras, or walking from village to village all over India. At each village, he would hold public meetings as he hoped that sympathetic landowners would donate parcels of land to the landless. Often they offered only the worst land.

The train to Wardha was four hours late. I was accompanied on the journey by two ashramites from Pattikalyana. It was my second Christmas train journey and I was offered sweetmeats by a family of Hindu pilgrims travelling to one of Lord Krishna's shrines. (Krishna is the eighth incarnation of God Vishnu, the Preserver aspect of God).

The amount of luggage and bedding that Indian families carry on long journeys is staggering. There are pots and pans, mounds of cold chapattis/ rice and chutneys as well as enormous bedrolls. Many Hindus carry their own food partly to avoid pollution from bought food. The Krishna pilgrims also carried plastic bags stuffed with garlands for adorning the images.

One nearby Muslim disturbed passengers by prostrating himself hopefully towards Mecca at the five prescribed times. I cannot remember how he managed his ablutions as often there would be little water on the trains. On the bunk above the prostrating Muslim squatted a red-turbaned Sikh. All around us sat enormously fat sari- clad ladies who were part of the pilgrimage party.

The main purpose in visiting Vinoba's ashram was to participate in the Sarvodaya (welfare of all) conference. Small groups of us managed to get Darshan (vision and meeting) with Vinoba. He occupied a small green painted room with a woven bamboo ceiling. It had a clean and restful atmosphere. Vinoba was seated cross-legged upon a slightly raised wooden platform overlooking a group of squatting and cross-legged women. He wore his green coloured cape with ear flaps. This cape protected his eyes from too much light. Apart from the eccentric cape, his clothes were the usual hand-spun white dhoti (a loose cloth wound between the legs and around the waist) and shawl over a bare chest and a long, grey beard.

We visitors (mainly Indians) transmitted questions on bits of paper and he answered them. Vinoba told me to learn one hundred words of Hindi during my ten days at the ashram. We were lucky to see Vinoba as for some time just prior to my visit he had been fasting and remaining silent over a public issue, probably for a complete ban on cow slaughter.

During the conference, we all ate our meals in pandals or huge tents made of woven bamboo matting. There were no plates as all food was served on woven leaves placed on the ground in long rows. Each person had a separate leaf plate as Hindus rarely eat from the same plate to avoid pollution. Even the tea was drunk from non-used earthenware pots and then thrown away. Both leaf plates and earthenware pots were thrown away after use. India's sensible version of the 'throw away society'. Most of the conference delegates stayed at nearby Sevagram ashram where many workers had lived with Gandhi. I was told of a Sanskrit scholar called Shastvi who was a village worker but had contracted leprosy. In 1938 he came to Gandhi at Sevagram in search of asylum. Gandhi built a hut for him near his own hut and attended to the scholar personally, even massaging him.

A notice at the Ashram quoted Gandhi. 'To call a woman weaker is libel, it is man's injustice to woman. If by strength is meant moral power, then woman is immeasurably superior to man. Has she not great intuition? Is she not more sacrificing? Has she not greater power of endurance or courage? If non violence is the law of our being, the future is with women.'

Gandhi's little hut at Sevagram showed the bare essentials of earthly existence: lamp, spittoon, portable spinning wheel, first aid box of sandalwood, pen stand, ink stand, latrine, wooden sandals, walking stick, paper weight and the three monkeys, 'hear no evil, speak no evil and see no evil.' These were quotes from his magazine Young India where he mentioned the seven social sins as 'Politics without principles, wealth without work, commerce without morality, education without character, pleasure without conscience, science without humanity and worship without sacrifice'. The little hut was a summing up of Gandhi's ideals of simplicity in living. It was made of bamboo and palm leaf walls supporting bamboo beams and a red tiled roof.

At the Sevagram ashram school, children squatted in various corners armed with writing slates. They all chanted in unison by rote. Nearby, a written message in the hut said 'when you are in the right, you can afford to keep your temper and when you are in the wrong, you cannot afford to lose it'.

Gandhi believed that the untouchable category of scavenger 'sweeper of latrines' occupation should be eradicated. Sevagram had a permanent exhibition of model latrines that did away with the need for low or outcaste labour. Gandhi said that latrines should be as clean as a place of worship. He always cleaned his own and often others' latrines. Connected with these beliefs was his obsession against any useful thing being wasted. Through this philosophy, Indians have developed Gobar Gas plants, which convert cow dung to methane gas. The gas is without smell and the residue makes an excellent fertiliser. Usually gas plants are owned by families and occasionally communally.

In the village of Sevagram, there was a Martin Luther King colony of bungalows with little gardens surrounded by well-kept low hedges in English style. The local college had a Gandhian stress on rural development and all students had to serve local villages. Both allopathic and ayurvedic medicine were taught. In India, there are thousands of unemployed graduates, many of whom refuse to spend a few years serving the villages where the majority of the population lives. So it was good that a few colleges made students work with village people as part of their studies.

At six o'clock in the evening in Sevagram ashram, sandals were removed and all sat cross-legged in the prayer hall. Prayers were said from the major world religions though the atmosphere was distinctively Hindu.

After the bulk of the conference, delegates returned home. I settled down for ten days at Vinoba's ashram at Wardha. The day began at four thirty with morning prayers followed by a short rest. We cleaned and gardened before breakfast. Then, prayers again at ten thirty in the morning and five thirty in the afternoon. On Mondays, ashramites had a partial fast without an evening meal.

There were thirty five regular ashramites. Twenty two of them were celibate women who dressed in simple homespun saris. Vinoba had a strong belief in the potential spirituality of women and felt many had not been able to develop it because of hard work. One of the 'sisters' told me that some of them went months without speaking to Vinoba. Many of the women were well educated and came from high caste families. Often they had to learn to do manual work after years of seeing servants do such work. A sister told me that it had at first taken her one hour to light the kitchen fires while later it took her ten minutes. The food was good and their chapattis were very light and practically transparent in Maharashtrian style. As in all ashrams, the diet was strictly vegetarian, including no eggs. Each ashramite did two hours in the kitchen on a monthly basis. When Vinoba was younger, he dug trenches and latrines. In the footsteps of the Mahatma, he worked as a bhangi or scavenger caste labourer in cleaning out lavatories. The ashram held sixteen acres of land and they were mostly self-sufficient in food.

Many sisters faced great opposition from their families upon joining the ashram. Once, three sisters joined, however their father was a follower of Vinoba, so they faced little opposition. Even a Muslim lady who wished to join was afraid of her people's reaction. They didn't value celibacy.

Each day, after evening prayers, there followed what I called 'the ritual of Vinoba's going to bed ceremony'. A small group of devotees would stand and observe the ritual in the green room. First Vinoba would go to the bathroom, then return to his bed, clean his nose, neatly fold his handkerchief, look at his watch and then to sleep.

After days at the ashram, it still took time to appreciate the simplicity of Vinoba, even cleaning his nose in his domain, surely not a ritual for outsiders although there were always plenty of watchers. The 'performance' was a prayer in itself. The closest sisters to him would clasp their hands in prayer seconds before he retired.

His daily diet consisted of a ration of milk and a little honey. For one year, he stopped milk altogether. He was fanatic about cow protection and I was frequently told that he would sacrifice his life for the cow. As a Hindu, the cow was 'Gau Matha' (Cow Mother or Mother of Life). Even in death, she serves man in that leather is used and bone meal is fertiliser. In India, cows are often of greater use dead than alive once their milk has dried up. Vinoba once said 'Cow is our mother and we do not kill our mother'. This honouring of cattle is common to many societies based upon pastoralism. The Sudanese Dinka and Nuer are such an example. For example, the Nuer describes most form of beauty through their cattle.

My neighbouring ashramite had devised a couple of solar cookers and a solar clock. Another member was up half the night because he was an amateur astronomer. At three thirty in the morning one day, I looked through his telescope and got a good view of Jupiter and four of her moons.

'Saints are remembered in India, not politicians' said Vinoba. Few remember Emperor Akbar but the Tulsidas' translation of the Hindu epic the Ramayana can be found in many north Indian homes.

One day while gardening, I mistook the sacred holy basil plant tulsi for a weed and gleefully yanked it out of the soil. Luckily, it was undamaged and one of the sisters placed it back into the soil.

An Israeli girl was staying a short time on the ashram. Her name was Dahlia. One day, we went to Gopuri to see the village industries design centre. There they designed many looms and spinning wheels. Dahlia attempted to show me how to spin but I just did not have the patience. Two American Quakers who were founders of the United States Community Fund Trust visited Vinoba. Vinoba asked them if they were vegetarians. They replied a little self-righteously that they ate vegetables, fish and chicken. Vinoba asked them how the fish felt as it was being killed. He was often humorous at times. During early morning gardening, he would often appear with hands above his head, clapping merrily. All of us were expected to join in.

Archaeological remains were embedded in some of the ashram walls giving a shrine-like appearance along the temple courtyard surroundings. These antiques were found when the temple was being constructed.

One day, Dahlia and I saw Vinoba separately. He asked me if I was a vegetarian. I answered 'No'. He then gently pinched my arm and murmured in a deep plodding tone, 'You be vegetarian'. I tried to explain that it needs self discipline to give up a cultural habit. Vinoba had been a vegetarian since birth.

One of Vinobaji's closest women confidantes was the shaven-headed Kusum. She informed me that Baba (as Vinoba was usually addressed) was preparing for his death in spirit. He had told the ashramites 'I will go to God and come straight back'. Between his green room and the temple, Kusum showed me a white line on the wall where his presence would be. She lived separately from the other sisters. Unlike many of the other women, she was easy to communicate with. Some of these religious people lived in their own little closed worlds, which offered their own forms of selfishness.

Kusum said Vinobaji always believed that 'Mathematics is next to God', that there must be a balance of life even down to weighing food. The trouble was that although Vinoba was a balanced yet extreme man, some of his disciples were not. Disciples often lose themselves in their teachers. A French girl became so unbalanced that she was intoxicated with spiritual love for Baba. She ended up a mental wreck.

Vinoba in pre-Independence days had been imprisoned by the British. He got a duodenal ulcer while he was in prison. He became ulcerated because he refused first class category of prisoners' food and asked for food that the poorest got. This food was saturated with chillies. Eventually, through an improved diet, he conquered the ulcer.

During my stay at the ashram, one of the sisters was experimenting with a milk and banana diet. Another advocated raw vegetable and grape juice therapy for cancer of the nose. Four absent members of the ashram were about to complete their twelve year padayatra walk around India proclaiming Vinoba's philosophy on women's liberation.

I bade farewell to Baba and told him that some Indians were only vegetarian by name and that they would not be as truthful as Gandhi was in his autobiography My Experiments With Truth in admitting that he had actually eaten meat. Vinoba's last words to me were 'Baba eighty four years young'.

On the train journey north to Delhi, curious passengers wanted to know about Vinoba asking me what he ate and, what he was like as a man. One optimist enquired of me 'when are you going to become a saint?'

I arrived in Delhi in time for the minor Punjabi festival of Lohri, a winter feast in aid of giving thanks to God for the new growth of crops. A fire was lit in a courtyard and people walked around throwing peanuts and popcorn into the fire as offerings. All this was accompanied by singing, dancing and much clapping. After the festival, I visited some of old Delhi's monuments including the splendid tower Qutub Minar, a Muslim structure built upon the remnants of earlier Hindu temples. The central pillar is constructed of pink Rajasthani stone.

Chapter Seven

The Goddess Earns Good Money

Awaiting me at Gandhi Nidhi was an inland air letter from a Servas friend Mr Tej who lived in a village near Meerut in Uttar Pradesh state (UP) formerly United Provinces. Meerut was a squalid little town with a plethora of bicycle rickshaws scrabbling around in watery mud-filled lanes. Here I met Tej Bhai who had come to collect me in a hired horse and cart to take me to his home at Amarsinghpur village. On entering the village, we were greeted with the country salutation 'Ram Ram' ('God, God') and we replied with the Hindu greetings 'Nameste' or 'Namaskar'.

Amarsinghpur was a traditional Punjabi style village even though it was situated in UP. All houses and huts had flat roofs, the walls were constructed of kutcha, unbaked mud brick. Tej Bhai (brother) said that houses were plastered over twice yearly with mud mixed with cow dung. Many Hindus renew the appearance of their dwellings at the time of their major festivals. At Amarsinghpur apart from floods, they decorate at Diwali and Holi festivals or at marriages.

In this region of North India, it is usual for men and women in villages to live separately. Tej Bhai said that this was a good method of birth control! In many communities though, even when purdah is observed, men and women of the same household could sleep in fairly close proximity. Here, even husbands and wives were segregated. I ate in the women's compound along with Tej Bhai who broke convention in order to accompany me. Breakfast usually consisted of tasty brown sugar (usually white is reserved for guests!), parathas, which look like fried chapatis, plus fresh chutney made of grated radish and ginger. The yogurt curd was made overnight in earthenware pots. The buttermilk was made by boiling milk slowly and adding old buttermilk plus fresh milk and then removing the cream.

In this particular Hindu Jat (a farming subcaste) community, women observed purdah before older males. Purdah is a Persian word meaning curtain. As Jeffery notes in her book Frogs in a Well 'purdah is not confined only to Muslims'. For Muslim women, if complete veiling occurs, then it is after puberty and in reference to all men who are not closely related. Where purdah does apply to Hindus, it is after marriage and in relation to the husband's older male kin. Thus Tej Bhai had hardly looked upon his daughter-in-law's face. Whenever they were both present in the courtyard of the female quarter, his daughter-in-law kept her eyes lowered while covering her head with a shawl.

I slept in the men's compound in my own room. Tej never knocked on my door before entering nor did he give any warning of his presence. He was not being rude, it was only that some Indians often had an undeveloped concept of privacy than perhaps middle class English women. Nightly, he would bring me a huge pot of tea. He got upset when I told him that I did not want it simply because I could not find the latrine in the dark passing male bodies sleeping on charpoys (the string frame beds)!

The bulk of the owner cultivators of the Punjab and parts of Uttar Pradesh are Punjabi speaking Jats. The bulk of the Sikh community is also Jat. Tej Bhai's family were Jat and they were Hindus. The Jats had been a powerful caste in the areas for a long time. The bulk of the land around Amarsinghpur village was owned by his family or other Jats. The village had two thousand inhabitants. Most of them were Hindus. There were a minority of two hundred Muslims who worked as craftsmen in the area, in such work as carpentry and as blacksmiths. The rest were Brahmins and Untouchables. They appeared to live peaceably but did not have intimate relationships.

All the local children, including Tej Bhai's grandchildren had black kohl on their eyelids (an Arabic word for a fine powdery substance from antimony). The reasons given for them using kohl were health and keeping away bad spirits, although Tej Bhai denied that the latter purpose applied within his village! Another reason for the custom is that it is supposed to beautify a child's face, I thought it looked horrible.

Looking out of my bedroom window at sunrise, I had a panoramic view of the cows eating their breakfast. In India, cattle are rarely allowed to roam around freely when they are still of use. One never saw fields of grazing cattle. Usually they were tethered or well confined in a yard. Many villagers obtained little milk or milk products as the product went to the urban markets. Tej Bhai told me that previously, selling milk was held to be like selling your daughter in his locality. The situation was rather like poor fishing villages in the west of Scotland where the fishermen's families could not afford to buy the local fish.

We discussed vegetarianism. I explained that in the west because vegetarianism is a minority practice, then a conscious decision is usually made to become a vegetarian, which is quite different from inheriting vegetarianism as part of one's culture. Converts tend to examine such a matter more deeply than born vegetarians. Thus, I attempted to explain the western vegetarians antipathy to refined white flour, sugar etc., whereas many Indian vegetarians consider such foods good in themselves and proof of higher status. I offered to have a go at grinding the maize on a hand rotary stone grinder or quern. In Britain, these grinders are usually only found on archaeological sites or laying unused and forgotten in many a farmyard. Corn grinding must be an excellent way of developing the biceps because I found that turning the huge stone exhausted me after ten minutes.

Oxen were used for the rotary fodder cutter by Tej Bhai's family and in this locality, they still manufactured their own gur (brown sugar) because sugar cane grew abundantly. For making the sugar, the liquid passed by pipe to three circular basins embedded in a part of the ground, which formed a section of an underground oven. The juice was boiled and then it blackened.

Tej Bhai introduced me to the village committee. They were concerned to know whether we had capital punishment in England, whether the policemen were armed and if we had buffaloes. I thought that they might enquire about Asians in Britain. On a recent bus trip to Delhi, a man asked me about the 'raw deal' that Asians were getting in the United Kingdom. I agreed with his comments in many ways and then asked him what he would think of mass immigration in Delhi of those with very different cultures. He gave no answer.

I continued to enjoy the food at Amarsinghpur, eating mustard leaf that tasted better than spinach, which it looked like. The term 'curry' here consisted of ground chick pea flour called gram in India, mixed with yoghurt. We would drink a tasty yoghurt drink called raita mixed with mint, cucumber and cumin seeds.

The tall, slender serene faced Tej Bhai informed me that he had six months in prison under British rule for joining in Gandhi's Satyagraha (truth force movement) campaign plus detention during the Quit India movement. He was twice imprisoned under Mrs Indira Gandhi's emergency rule for distributing anti-government pamphlets against the emergency. I enquired as to why Vinoba Bhave, Gandhi's chief living apostle of non-violence, had implicitly supported Mrs Gandhi. Tej Bhai replied 'Because she's Nehru's daughter and they are both Brahmins'. Later he said that Vinoba had an emotionally-vested interest in supporting a woman as he had a strong belief in women's destiny.

Tej Bhai showed me a mustard seed crusher. First, the mustard seed was crushed in a grinding stone, and then the oil was removed by a rotary oil crusher driven by a cow. Later, he took me to the village silver goldsmith who made poor quality jewellery. The smith said that the objects he showed me were ninety per cent silver and ten per cent other metals but I think he was afraid to speak the truth in front of half of the village, which insisted on following me everywhere. As I looked behind me, I noticed a few timid women hiding their faces behind their shawls, probably amazed at the bold foreigner. The Hindu villagers did not wear saris or shalwar and shirt but a longish skirt, blouse and loose shawl. This form of dress was quite common with varying styles in much of North India from Sind in Pakistan to around Delhi and Uttar Pradesh.

In one house, the women were squatting silently just about out of sight whilst all the men of the house plus outsiders were standing about me as I was sitting on a charpoy. The head of the house informed me that they were honoured to have me in their houses. They even prepared tea for me when they went without. I told them that I was honoured to be amongst hard working people, especially the women who had less time to chatter than the menfolk! 'Do you have purdah in England?' one voice enquired.

I was shown a tiny temple, which was dirty inside. It had small marble statues of Siva and Parvati alongside the elephant god Ganesh. Many Hindus do believe in a supreme god called Brahma but he takes a variety of forms. The chief manifestation is the trinity of Brahma the Creator, Vishnu the Preserver and Siva the Destroyer and Reproducer. Parvati is the female aspect of Siva representing 'shakti' or female energy. Parvati is also goddess of beauty. The elephant god Ganesh is one of their sons. His statues shows an elephant head and a human pot bellied body. People pray to Ganesh before embarking on some activity.

Most Hindu households had little altars or niches in some of the inner walls where a little oil lamp might burn. Very popular were the dreadfully gaudy pictures of the Hindu pantheon, which were sold in many a street kiosk. The richer houses were distinguished in Armarsinghpur by old arched carved doorways, which formed the main entrance gates to the family compounds. Even these though had mud walls and inner courtyards where all the cattle lived.

During one group conversation, a Brahmin chipped in that Indians were not fit to rule themselves. Another man criticized the Brahmin for denouncing his country in front of me as so many people had had bad experiences under the Britishers.

I was taken to a sagai ceremony where I sat amongst a group of men. A marriage had been planned. The girl's father and the boy's father met for the first time. On the ground was a big metal thali or tray containing rice, chapattis, flour, brown sugar and saffron. Saffron donates hope for a colourful life, brown sugar for everlasting sweetness, water for fluidity, flour symbolises property and rice fertility. The Hindu Brahmin priest, following a hereditary occupation, performed the ceremony. He quoted the ancient Vedas written in Sanskrit. A rupee was handed to each guest, this money was then placed in the lap of the bride and groom to be. Handspun cotton thread was tied by the priest around the boy's wrist, and then the boy in turn tied the thread around the priest's wrist. The sagai ceremony was always held in the boy's home, but it was the bride's family who would have to pay for the future marriage and dowry. In the bulk of North Indian Hindu marriages, the families to be linked in wedlock must not be remotely related, only they must share the same subcaste. Thus, brides may have to travel hundreds of miles to live with their strange in-laws. Except when the wife has her confinement, she may rarely see her own natural family again. Her new in-laws as 'bride-takers' would often not demean themselves by accepting hospitality from her family. If she were to be unhappy in her marriage, she would not normally be welcome back home as this would shame and dishonour her family.

Tej Bhai had spent six months in Israel with a Gandhian group from India. There they studied the collective agricultural settlements or Kibbutzim and co-operative groups known as Moshavim. In Israel, they discussed Gandhi's concept of village industries. Gandhi gave great importance to the spinning wheel, which as Ved Mehta pointed out in his book Mahatma Gandhi and His Apostles he made into a by-word for economic independence and non-violent resolutions. I was told that sometimes prior to British rule, in many areas of India the spinning wheel and hand loom were non-existent and where they did exist, often their usage had been forgotten. Later, in Meerut district, many women learned to spin. At marriage, daughters were sent off with a charkha spinning wheel to 'set her up'.

My everlasting image of Amarsinghpur in winter was the sight of Tej Bhai wrapped up in a huge blanket over his shirt and dhoti making him look like a hooded monk.

I departed sadly from the village by horse and cart and was informed there was a good omen as a women passed us with a tray of cow dung cakes piled high above her head, so I was bound to have a good journey. En route to Meerut town, the cart passed a small hut on the roadside. Tej Bhai said that the girl who lived inside it was asked by her parents to watch over the picking of mustard from nearby wheat fields. During that time, she had a dream and in it she claimed that a man appeared riding on a blue horse and he told her to remain in the hut for a week until he returned. She informed her parents of the dream who believed that she must have seen Krishna. Eventually the news spread and now people come from far away to see the 'goddess' whose hut was on the roadside to prevent visitors from spoiling the crops. The visitors offered her money, which her family had taken possession of. The feeling was growing amongst some people that the family had done a 'put up job' and were cashing in on the whole affair. This was hardly a new idea in India or anywhere else. Thus the family might have been forcing the girl to remain alone in the hut. This episode reminded me of Satyajit Ray's non-commercial film Devi the Goddess where a father dreamt that his soon-to-be-married daughter was a goddess. She was then 'sentenced' to spend the rest of her life living in a temple.

Tej Bhai told me another story of a simple illiterate man who, while he slept, spoke in complicated Sanskrit mantras (magical verbal formulas used in worship or meditation). Some of the words were so ancient that they were rarely used today. When the audience was well educated, he adapted his performance to their requirements. He would lie down and after fifteen minutes, he gave a discourse. At least one could admire the man's enterprise in attempting one form of social mobility.

On arrival at Meerut, I was taken to visit the large Meerut ashram. Here, they had a well-stocked khadi goods shop of home-spun and hand-woven items. The ashram's carpentry section spent most of its time manufacturing a variety of improved spinning wheels. In the dyeing department, I was shown some manual screen printing. The ashram employed about five hundred people but only two hundred actually lived within the ashram compound. On a huge verandah, I saw heaps of raw and spun wool in various colours being sorted out by squatting workers. The actual spinning and weaving was done in the surrounding villages.

Before departing for Hyderabad in central India, I made a short visit to Shamley nature cure ashram and met Razi Bhai. He addressed a gathering on his favourite topic of psychic sleep whereas I spoke on Britain's welfare state. Afterwards, we were offered tasty wheat chapatis called shabby mixed with ginger and spinach!

Chapter Eight

The Human Body Servicing Station

Razi Sahib and I took a two night train journey south to Hyderabad. We must have looked like poor people because he insisted on carrying all our worldly goods in his huge 'motri' where the contents are wrapped up into an enormous knotted sheet. The purpose of our journey was to visit Dr Vankat Rao's hospital cum ashram in Secunderabad near Hyderabad – Deccan.

Hyderabad was a clean city by Indian standards with well maintained public buildings. Firstly, we visited Salarjung museum, which displayed the catholic taste of Nawab Mir Yousuf Ali Khan Salar Jung III. His family once ruled the former princely state of Hyderabad. Agents from overseas sent him catalogues and lists from antique dealers. He also patronised poets and artists and generally encouraged literary works. This was the strength of many of the former Muslim rulers, who, unlike many of the later British colonials, did their utmost to encourage local artists and musicians. Salar Jung's last purchase was a set of ivory chairs, which arrived after his death. One amazing exhibit was the entire text of the Holy Quran woven onto a man's waistcoat. There were also copies of ancient Hindu writings, that gave details of different types of sacred trees and plants, which could be used for carving the figures of gods and goddesses. Wood carving in southern India is well developed. This skill was used in monumental form on temple cars or chariots. 'Ralhakars' or builders of cars claim descent from the chariot maker tradition of Vedic times.

On arrival at Secunderabad station, I noticed that in central-southern India, there were large numbers of women sweepers employed on the railways and banks. In Pakistan only men worked in such public places, though in Karachi there were many Gujarati Hindu sweeper groups who worked in private homes, having been in that area since before Pakistan's creation.

Razi Sahib and I were housed in pleasant surroundings at the nature cure sanatorium. We had a discussion on Indian marriage and on the differences between Hindu and Muslim customs. Upon marriage, I was told for some castes, an orthodox, especially north Indian Hindu girl was considered to be a blank sheet whose personality was of little consequence as long as she showed no free spirit. The girl is prepared throughout her early life for a marriage where she must adapt completely to her new family. She is until she produces a male child, on the lowest rung of the joint family ladder and is the property of her husband. The ideal of womanhood is based on Sita, the virtuous wife of Rama, one of the incarnations of Vishnu. In the mythology of the Ramayana epic, Sita had been kidnapped by the evil Ravana, the demon king of Lanka (Ceylon). She was rescued but her husband Rama refused her love because she had lived under another man's roof, even though there had been no sexual relations. So she attempted to commit sati by throwing herself on a funeral pyre, a sacrifice refused by Agni, the God of fire.

Thus, she must serve her husband with no thought for self. Razi Sahib explained that in very orthodox arranged marriages, although the spouses to-be do not always know each other, it is believed that the parents will make a careful choice and that destiny plays a part, hence the important role of horoscopes in many such arrangements. Thus love will follow after marriage. Often social conventions are stronger than religious conventions. Under Islam, divorce is quite easy for a man, yet there are comparatively few divorces because such an action would bring social disgrace. Marriage is not a matter between individuals only but is a family affair. The problem of shame is present, thus if a divorced person has a sister, her marriage chances may be affected. The woman, upon marriage must be a virgin. This rule does not apply to the man. The woman's virginity is part of the trust between the two uniting families.

At the Hindu wedding I attended at Hyderabad, three priests officiated. When the bride came before the groom, a curtain was placed between them for several minutes, and then it was gradually lowered, the girl looking predictably submissive with eyes cast down while the boy was looking at her. They had never met before this ceremony. There was plenty of music from hired traditional players. Among the guests, there was little separation of the sexes.

At the wedding I attended in Pakistan, all the women had to wait for food until the men had eaten.

Razi Sahib introduced me to a kindly bearded Muslim called Muhammad Zainul Abedin. He presented us with a beautiful poem he had composed called The Rose.

Tell me oh rose the secret of your smile,
What tender touch you felt, what tickle awhile,
What passing warmth and embrace,
What silent whisper brightened your face.

Beauty drips from your lovely lips,
The opening whorl my wonder flips,
To know the treasure inside your hold,
As the soft silken veils slowly unfold.

Whose sacred skilful hand has gone,
Your blooming blushing hues to adorn,
Whose chirpy charming music was there,
That thrilled your holy heart lay bare.

Whose enchanting gleaming glance,
Made you dance in quick response,
Whose benign approaches from above,
Left on your cheeks soft signs of love.

When time seizes your petal sweet,
One by one you lay them at his feet,
Your brief life is, if closely viewed,
Indeed a smile of gratitude.

The nature cure hospital had about one hundred and twenty five beds. Running the place was a forbidding orthodox Hindu called Dr Vankatrao. He wore a south Indian white cotton lungi and a loose white shawl over a bare chest and shoulders. During the Quit India movement, he left Stanley Medical College for allopathic western orthodox medicine in Madras when he was in his fourth year of studies, because of harassment from the British authorities. In 1947-8, he studied naturopathy at Bhimavaram ashram, today in Andhra Pradesh state, because this was Gandhi's advice. Vankatrao's family was unusual in that his wife and two sons plus daughter-in-law were also involved in naturopathy. They were all graduates in naturopathy from Osmania University in Hyderabad. One son was also a qualified allopath. In many families I had found one enlightened member adopting a highly principled lifestyle whereas the rest of the family might be run of the mill materialists.

Vankatrao's 'Human Body Servicing Station' as he called the hospital was actually part of an ashram. Students of nature cure/naturopathy had to take a four year degree course from Osmania but these students lived as ashramites. The hospital/ashram had twelve acres of land making the centre self-sufficient in vegetables and fruit. Students lived a spartan existence attending prayers at four thirty in the morning and behaving in a disciplined manner. Some students were expelled because they had not stood up to Vankatrao's ideals. My complaint was that this rigid lifestyle might make the public believe that naturopathy was only for those leading an ascetic lifestyle. The hospital had twenty free beds for the poorest patients. These were classed as government research beds. As usual, the treatment offered was composed of yoga, massage, steam baths, spinal baths, sun baths, mud packs, enemas, etc. The library had over five thousand books. Vankatrao also ran summer health camps for young people.

The order of the day for all of us was to arise at four o'clock in the morning, take a glass of water and go to the lavatory before four thirty morning prayers. From five to six in the morning, the treatment commenced. Nearly all patients did yoga prior to the individual treatments. At ten thirty in the morning, fresh fruit was provided. I could never adapt to the Hindu habit of going to the lavatory at the crack of dawn before taking an early morning drink or 'bed tea' as it is called in

India. Many families do not take morning tea without having bathed or brushed their teeth. Most Indians would be horrified to hear of the oft-quoted Englishman's twice weekly bath in non-running water! Even in cooler areas, the orthodox bathe daily.

It was a well run place and we had excellent hospitality but I was glad to leave a place where I was unable to relax. I was beginning to find that the constant change of lifestyle was at the least very exhausting, especially when Indians constantly preached their particular pet theories!

Chapter Nine

Leave your Shoes and your Mind at the Gate

Whilst in Hyderabad, Razi Sahib and I decided for a change to go on an Indian tourist bus trip run by Janata Tourists Ltd. They turned out to be useless. The guide was dirty, uncouth and at the end of the trip to Mysore, arrogantly demanded money from passengers saying that guides were not paid. Only we two refused payment.

The bus took us to St. Philomena's Roman Catholic Church built in Disappointed Gothic. At nearby Chamundi Hills stood a magnificent giant stone statue of Nandi, the bull of Lord Siva. At Mysore Palace, a little section of it had stained glass roofing from Scotland, which gave the underlying room a cooling and contemplative atmosphere. Huge wall paintings depicted court life and the military of this former princely state of Mysore now in Karnataka state where the Kannadigas live who speak Kannada or Kannarese. At the end of the day, we visited a sandalwood soap factory and purchased a small bottle of sandalwood oil. It was no exaggeration to say that it smelt of disinfectant. One good thing about the trip was that the awful guide did not accompany us anywhere (I was the only European in the group) so it was not a guided tour at all!

I was most impressed by the Lalbagh gardens, less formal than Moghul gardens. Lalbagh contained lots of jackfruit, which is a large coarse type of bread fruit. Razi Sahib said that in his native Bihar, this was considered poor man's food though he ate it himself. It is sickly taken in large quantities but like all fruit, it is healthy. The glass house, now in a dilapidated state, was opened by Prince Albert. It had become neither a hot house nor a glass house.

On a later visit to the Mysore area of Karnataka state, I visited the magnificent temples of Halebid and Belur. These buildings date from twelve century A.D. The temples were built during the rule of the Hoysalas who ruled in Mysore district from the twelfth to fourteenth century. That part of Halebid Temple dedicated to Siva and his consort Parvati has huge bulls symbolic of Siva-Nandi. Many temple pillars were made of handsome black polished hornblende.

Onto Sravana Belgola, a pilgrimage centre for all Jains but especially the Digambara (naked or sky clad) Jains. One's fervour is tested by the fact that the object of pilgrimage, a free-standing fifty seven foot monolith of Gometeswara stands loftily at the top of a very steep (four hundred and seventy foot) flight of stairs cut into the rock. It took me over two hours to climb. The Jain saint stone colossus stands erect as a naked figure in what A.L. Basham's The Wonder That Was India calls the Kayotsarga posture of meditation. The standing figure's arms do not touch the body while he stands upright. The statue looks a little like an enigmatic Buddha with a slight smile on its lips. The naked man is depicted with creeper growing over his body showing his complete otherworldliness achieved through standing so long in meditation. Every twenty five years, the statue is anointed profusely with gallons of milk and ghee or clarified butter, which seemed a squalid waste of food in a country with so many poor people.

After seeing many of the magnificent South Indian temples, it is puzzling why the Taj Mahal is the most famous building in India. It is more Persian in style than Indian. Perhaps it is because the British found the simpler contours easier to comprehend than some of the complex baroque designs of the Hindu temples, together with their excessive statuary.

At Pune, Razi Sahib and I rested at the local Gandhian Sarvodoya Mandel and slept in the prohibition office by permission of a local Servas host. I met another host called Gokhale who taught transcendental meditation and was enthusiastic about eye bank donation. It took us a couple of days to recover from a ghastly bus journey from Bangalore to Pune after we had left the hospital at Hyderabad. It was an ordinary bus and there was no chance of sleeping because the bus stopped every twenty minutes during the twenty four hour journey for tea, causing a continual commotion of passengers climbing over the seats.

Pune was continually in the news because of the internationally famous Rajneesh ashram, which proclaimed itself as 'an experiment to provoke God'. We arrived just in time for the morning discourse by Rajneesh in the big circular tent. Direct entry into the tent was forbidden. We were all screened. Queuing up started well over an hour before the talk began. As we stood in crocodile formation, each of us was sniffed at by one of the disciples of Rajneesh. They not only checked for any perfumed soapy smell but also for any fluffy materials that we might be wearing. I carried in a thick Tibetan pullover to sit on and was instantly relegated on this, my first visit to the back of the tent. Rajneesh suffered from asthma and was allergic to any smelly soap, etc. One would think that he should have conquered these allergies as his followers did call him Bhagwan or God.

The audience sat cross-legged in orderly rows under the tent and waited patiently for Rajneesh. A few disciples were posted in different parts of the tent ready to pounce on anyone who dared to cough when the Master spoke. It is interesting how many 'free thinkers' can become so conformist themselves when it suits them and create their own new rituals.

Eventually, the great man arrived in a huge, orange car, all eyes turned towards him and we clasped our individual palms together and whispered the Hindu greeting 'Namaste'. He was a hugely bearded figure and wore a long plain shirt immaculately pressed by one of the privileged disciples. 'I want them to have tasted all those false gurus before they come here ... now work on them is possible, only one, who has seen the non-essential, can see the essential'. Near the tent, a notice proclaimed 'leave your shoes and your mind at the gate'. Rajneesh's beautiful soporific voice made me lose concentration.

The saffron clad ashramites were nearly all westerners as Rajneesh felt that only westerners were really ready for his philosophy though people of any nationality could join. Only a few of his followers actually lived on the ashram, the rest of the members including guests took over the surrounding hotels and generally monopolised that district of Pune. The conservative members of Pune city did not take too kindly to the 'corrupting' westerners. It is true that many westerners in search of gurus have serious personal unhappiness and to many uninvolved middle class Indians, they would appear a bit scruffy. In India, just to see people of the opposite sex holding hands is enough to obtain severe censure. If the same sex hold hands and put their arms around each other then that is acceptable. It is not seen as linked to homosexuality. It was amusing to see some of the middle class Indian visitors to the ashram who were not followers of Rajneesh. They were probably looking for exposed flesh.

At the ashram, my impression was of individuals seeking one close relationship for themselves. They did not want to experiment with all types of theories. Too much choice, itself, can be a mental strain. Apart from the cost, Sahib and I enjoyed the food served from the ashram kitchen. All food was vegetarian and consisted of brown bread, salads, open sandwiches and sweets and was prepared by the sanyassis (renouncers).

An entire Indian nuclear family once joined the ashram who formerly accompanied Rajneesh on his Indian tours. In 1978, at the time of my visit, Rajneesh refused to travel to the west unlike many teachers of less stature who took the first opportunity. 'In the name of religion, the west has turned into a market,' he claimed. Rajneesh said that the real seekers should go to Pune. At that time he hardly ever left his room. I found some truth in Rajneesh's ideas, even in such mundane matters as his belief regarding massage. He said that from birth many westerners had been starved of the 'nourishment of touch' hence the body became rigid and afraid.

At the ashram, I reflected that in India there often was total absence of national consciousness. Many people did not think beyond immediate boundaries of caste and religion. They may have become excited over the naming of a university or demarcation of a river boundary. If students were not permitted in some 'institutions of learning' to mass cheat then arson or an attack on the unlucky lecturer could be the result. The loud-mouthed, semi-literate students were indifferent to the major calamities of their country. Red tape and corruption sapped any initiative. The Indian masses had to be as stoic as water buffaloes. The overwhelming philosophy was 'it's not my business' over such public matters such as a conspicuous theft on a bus, which of course none of the other passengers saw or two conflicting types of music blasting out at a ceremony over discordant loudspeakers. No one complained. Perhaps it is because India was not a disciplined dictatorship that such matters went unanswered. I am not claiming that India is alone in having many such problems. Many similar problems exist in the west, especially in the United Kingdom.

Chapter Ten

A Woman of Substance and
Jaipur's Cure for Mental Stress

I travelled with Razi Sahib to Uruli Kanchen nature cure ashram (near Pune) founded by Mahatma Gandhi.

Gandhi wanted people to be independent in health matters. Uruli Kanchen's treatment programme put great stress upon fasting, and a forty days grape juice fast was offered as a popular treatment. All grapes were grown in the ashram's own vineyards. This was supplemented by the usual nature cure treatments I have described elsewhere. The scientific reason behind fasting is that it gives the individual a rest from digestion and it cleanses the body. Only plain water was allowed on the strictest fasts.

We were informed that Dr Vankatrao of Hyderabad had been offered four and a half acres of land through Vinoba's Bhoodan or Land Gift movement, in order to establish a 'Vanprasth' ashram. This would be an ashram for the actively retired who could participate in community service. Vinoba had requested Dr Vankatrao to spend thirty years at a Grihastha or family ashram. Then after his need for attachment was over, he should move to the next Ashrama or stage of life. The noble aim would be to prevent the retired from vegetating. Perhaps the west could learn something here.

It was a coincidence to find that one of the patients was the ex public school Sikh gentleman whom I had met in Janak Puri suburb in Delhi. He looked overweight so I presumed he was on a rigid diet

Before leaving Uruli Kanchen, I was shown how to make mud packs. Pure mud was sifted and all stones removed. Then it was soaked for twelve hours in small earthen pots, to be placed hot on parts of the body.

Dr Razi and I reached Bombay by electric train and stayed with an old friend of his from Bihar called Farida. She was widowed and living alone with three children in a small flat. By western standards there was nothing significant in that, but in India it showed some tenacity. Farida was widowed in her early twenties. In 'good' families, widows do not remarry even though she was a Muslim and her religion clearly sanctions it. In this custom, many Muslims have been influenced by Hindu tradition. One of the advantages of polygamy is that widows can be adopted into a new family as second wives. A man can remarry at any age, in fact, it is expected of him.

Farida hailed from a conservative middle class Muslim family. She disobeyed her family by leaving distant Bihar state for Bombay to fight her own battles. By that action, she severed all links with her family. She had no relations or friends in Bombay when she first arrived. Farida was in her mid forties and a woman of immense dignity. Her in-laws wanted her children in their clutches. She told me that she was self-educated. As she was sewing at the treadle machine in this tiny flat, she described how she educated herself by taking both a BA and MA plus a teacher's course. A PhD was being contemplated. She was able to educate herself by locking up her three small children and leaving them unsupervised while she went to college. Considering these difficulties, the children did not appear in the slightest bit maladjusted. They had few material goods in the dingy flat plus noisy neighbours but they never lacked their mother's love. Farida had refused many job offers, which would upset the education of her children, even when she was offered good money. At the time of our visit, she was teaching one class for poor children without pay. Her supplementary income came from sewing. Farida had shown double courage because not only had she brought shame upon herself, but alas her whole family, as she had chosen to operate a lifestyle which most Indian men would not have survived.

Bombay is noted for its Victorian Gothic buildings notably in the form of Victoria Terminus 'VT' railway station, the High Courts and Municipal Buildings. It is also a city of flat and tenement dwellers living in buildings, which range from the opulent to the squalid. Shanty towns litter the outskirts and are made of anything at hand including corrugated iron, cardboard and sacking. The real problems occur during the monsoons when the shanties become a quagmire. This is a situation replicated in most developing countries.

Near Bombay's Haji Ali Mosque situated on the waterfront, rows of people used to sit on the adjoining pier. Their business was to exchange rupee notes into small change, i.e. the ten paise (Rs 1-100 Paise) coins, which the Muslim pilgrims then distributed to beggars squatting in the vicinity of the Mosque. The paise acted as a symbolic offering to Allah. The money changers gave eighty paise for each rupee note. A lot of the money changers and beggars appeared to be physically handicapped and blind. Business varied from day to day on whether it was high or low tide, because access to the holy place became impossible at high tide. The main beneficiaries, the beggars, became themselves money changers and exchanged their coins for hopefully crisp one rupee notes from the pilgrims.

I said farewell to Dr Razi and departed alone for Rajasthan state. My first impressions of Rajasthan were ruined forts and bleak distant mountains amidst marshy land along the roadside en route to Jaipur. This town's pink plastered streets had an early afternoon oriental revelry about them. A cacophony of wedding groups including mounted bridegrooms paraded up and down the main thoroughfare amidst competing shouting loudspeakers and bands. A form of competitive gaudiness only found in Hindu marriages. Amongst the crowds, my bicycle rickshaw eventually manoeuvred itself towards my Servas host's house belonging to Trilokchand Jain, the current state health minister.

Inside his office-cum-sitting room, the minister's walls had the quotation 'Oh Lord, help me to keep my big mouth shut until I know what I am talking about'. This is a comment which has more relevance in India than elsewhere owing to the national obsession with ministerial speech-making. Sri Jain's house had the usual paintings of Gandhi but also murals of Buddha and Mahavir, Mahavir being one of the 'pathfinders' of the Jain religion to which my host belonged. Another picture was of a pensive looking Mr Nehru, India's first prime minister and Indira Gandhi's father. A huge calendar depicted the Hindu elephant headed god Lord Ganesh, son of Siva and Parvati. Ganesh represents God as a wise and prudent being. Before any big event, it is Ganesh who is propitiated.

Sri Jain told me a story about people feeding a monkey, which later got electrocuted. Somebody claimed that the monkey was an avatar (a reincarnated aspect of God), and then money poured in at the monkey's funeral and nearby beggars were ignored. Later on in my travels, I was to witness some passengers feeding a monkey at a station while the same bananas were refused to some beggars standing near the monkey. Usually I found individuals willing to drop a few coins to beggars rather than be abusive to them.

Sri Jain arranged for me to visit the Nature Cure and Yogic Research Centre at Jaipur. It was situated in a picturesque spot, being built in the 1950's on a traditional line with clean mud huts with straw roofs. I was told of one American girl who had broken her back in three places and was paralysed but through massage and other treatments, she had made a slow recovery. This was something of a miracle. During my visit there was a diabetic Finnish girl who was getting special diets and yoga treatment. Patients paid for lodging and a minimum of three rupees a day. The government gave aid for treatment in the form of research beds for the poor. The manager, Dr Sukramdas had trained at Benaras Hindu University in both Hindu ayurvedic and western orthodox allopathic systems of medicine. The Yogic Research Centre was run by Swami Anand and established in 1961 by the Rajasthan government, especially to treat diabetes, asthma and rheumatism. The therapies were evaluated by modern research methods. All yoga classes were free of charge. This part of the centre dedicated to yoga was called the Yoga Sadhna Ashram whose aim was to practice and propagate yoga as a freedom from bondage as outlined by the ancient rishis and munis (ancient seers who composed the early Vedic hymns) for the physical, mental and spiritual progress of mankind. The centre also hoped to establish a children's home and eradicate child crime through yoga. Swamiji felt that yoga was better for those suffering from heart troubles, blood pressures and some psychiatric problems.

I was taken to the white marble Padampura Jain Temple and pilgrimage centre. It had impressive architecture for a modern building. It was good to see that the skilled masons were still able to practice their art when there was wealthy patronage from communities like the Jains. Many Jains are rich merchants belonging to a faith, which encourages wealth creation combined with frugality. Lay Jains could not become farmers as this involved ploughing, which leads to destruction of many forms of life. Thus the Jain's obsession with non-violence influenced their predilection for business. None of Sri Jain's family ate any root vegetables such as carrots and potatoes because they are situated deep in the soil thus more creatures are killed in extracting them. So their vegetarian diet was more limited than many an orthodox Hindu's.

Nearby, the Padampura temple was the Galava Muni Tapasyn, a natural spring, which is the basis of a small complex of temples. What appeared to be an unlikely assortment of pilgrims stood slouching against walls smoking cigarettes, perhaps they were touts for the local monkeys who were believed to be connected with Hanuman, the monkey god who mythology depicts as the friend and servant of Rama, the incarnation of Vishnu and hero of the Ramayana epic. The temple monkeys were fed on grain. The spring is a sacred bathing place in its own right. In India, many water sources, river confluences and lakes are deemed sacred. Perhaps the nature cults are the oldest extant form of religious worship as they are found in many countries. Like much of Jaipur, the temples by the spring must have been handsome but time had led to decay into a uniform shabbiness only giving a glimpse of their former glory. The only unchanging objects were perhaps the wondering sacred cattle.

It was also arranged for me to visit Jaipur mental hospital, which housed three hundred patients. The atmosphere and the wards were drab but it was clean. All the beds had uniform red blankets. Having warned the hospital authorities of my visit, I was faced with all the patients sitting cross-legged to attention on their beds. The head psychiatrist's chief concern was 'Do you think it is clean?' The whole place was unnaturally calm. Unlike the old British mental hospitals, this new hospital had no grounds for the inmates to roam about in. If the true meaning of the word 'asylum' is refuge, then these patients would get little of that. The characteristic mental hospital atmosphere of patients rambling around was also absent. There were not any closed wards as the new hospital had changed from the old custodial concept of care. But an armed soldier kept guard over a ward of the more dangerous convicted criminals who were chained to their beds by foot manacles. Another ward was full of dejected mentally handicapped patients who had been left by their families to rot. All were villagers and for all patients, after-care was non-existent. Families did not participate at all in care partly because of the stigma of mental illness. I suggested that the hospital employ some social workers to educate the villagers. The average stay of a patient was about three weeks and about one third got readmitted. The only social worker around was a patient suffering with schizophrenia. Many paranoic experiences took the form of belief in demons and no doubt fearsome mothers-in-law.

After leaving the hospital, I visited the large handspun and hand-woven khadi centre. Two Servas members called Goyel and Agrawal who were well-off merchants, showed me the huge warehouses stacked high with wool and cotton khadi.

Jaipur is also famous for its Jantar Mantar, the early eighteenth century astronomical observatory erected during the reign of Sawai Jai Singh II, ruler of Jaipur. He issued a revised star catalogue, reformed the calendar and produced a set of tables of the sun, moon and planets. The instruments are built of huge masonry and are for measuring latitudes and longitudes besides reading altitudes. Other similar observatories were built at Delhi, Ujjain, Benares and Mathura.

Just outside Jaipur is the lovely Amber Palace. This place was part of the old capital of the Kachawaha Rajputs. It dates from the seventeenth century. There is a steep paved stoned path up to the palace entrance over which many people approach by elephant, the tourists looking extremely wobbly. The mirror work on the walls of the Shish Mahal or Palace of Mirrors is exquisite, alabaster inlaid with glass in the shape of flowers and cups.

I left Jaipur by bus to Ajmer. I wandered up the tiny narrow Mediterranean, rather than Indian, style of winding street to the shrine of the Muslim Sufi saint Shaikh Muin-ud-Din Chishti. He was a thirteenth century missionary who led a pious and simple life. All along the lane to his shrine squatted rows of shopkeepers with their gaudy displays of religious trinkets. The tomb looked garish, surrounded by Arabic inscriptions from the Quran embroidered onto a large velvet cloth. Everybody seemed to demand bakshees (or tipping)' at once. One corner near the tomb was crammed with beggars.

Pushkar is to the Hindus what Dargah Ajmer is to the Muslims. This camel fair centre has ghats beside its sacred lake. Unfortunately, Pushkar had become in the seventies the western hippie centre of Rajasthan. They clung together with their usual tired expressionless faces. I thought 'why pick on poor Pushkar?' Most of the temples constructed in the vicinity were paid for out of charitable donations. I was glad to leave the place for two reasons. Here any westerner was viewed as a drop-out, and as a non Hindu, I was refused admittance to a Vishnu Temple. I did not get further than the outer courtyard when an armed figure said 'This is a private temple'. I replied that I was sorry that their God was private and beat a hasty retreat.

Chapter Eleven

Spring Festival and a Prohibition Campaign

From Jaipur, I travelled by a wreck of a bus to Makrana town in order to visit a Servas friend and long time follower of Mahatma Gandhi called Swamiji. The bus broke down on four occasions during which time the driver was to be seen climbing right into the engine up front. The driving wheel, at one point, appeared to detach itself. The majority of these buses are built in India from scratch whereas in Pakistan, bus components are only assembled rather than locally manufactured. These buses, which soon become dilapidated, nevertheless take a lot of wear and tear and are constantly disembowelled and re-assembled rather like old bikes.

Prior to my arrival at Makrana, we stopped a fifth time as the bus coming in the opposite direction had come to a halt, and a fight was taking place between two passengers. All their bus passengers had got off to watch the fight so our bus stopped and its passengers got off to join in the fun from the other bus. Thus the four hour journey became seven hours.

Swamiji invited me to stay for the Holi festival. Holi is the celebration of the coming of spring and the departure of winter, and a time for planting crops. It is also a period to let one's hair down, the usual social prohibitions becoming a little lax. Rajasthan is the best state in which to celebrate Holi as here the festival has more gusto than elsewhere. Many Hindu festivals are joyous in that they are more like some of our pre-reformation medieval celebrations with big fairs and plenty of dancing. Rajasthanis smear each other with mauve-coloured water called rang. All the gutters in Makrana appeared overnight with the after-effects of the slaughtering of goats, which takes place during the Muslim festival of sacrifice commemorated in memory of Abraham's offering of his son, Ishmael.

The night before Holi, a huge bonfire was lit in order to burn old debris, signifying the end of the year. They asked me if in England we had a similar system. I told them that we had a secular version called Bonfire Night and many people would use their bonfires for burning old furniture. During the festival Swamiji told me to keep a low profile or wear my worst clothes if I wanted to be sprayed with purple rang. Nobody dared to spray him as he had given strict orders about the matter while dressed in his spotless white khadi dhoti and long shirt.

Swamiji was a tall, slender Brahmin with a calm, unflappable presence. His grey hair was closely cropped. As a youth, his family compelled him to wear the Brahmanical tuft of hair called chutia, which is allowed to grow from the crown of the head, believed to be a sensitive area. Once he had joined Gandhi's movement, he opposed his family and cut his hair in a casteless manner.

During Holi the unmarried girls collect ash and make it into balls, which they place near a temple wall. Days later these ashes are thrown into a well to signify a new life or day of birth of Parvati, goddess wife of Lord Siva. Ash is believed to purify water. Gaily-dressed girls balancing brass pitchers on their heads go into the temple for the ceremonial bathing of the deity, Parvati. The image is covered in flowers and the girls then ask for husbands 'such as the one you have been blessed with.'

At Makrana, during Holi, various caste group representatives came to visit Swamiji. He sat cross-legged in his furniture-less sitting room and awaited these visitors. Some folks came just to offer their greetings while others wanted help. Scheduled caste members who were marble quarry workers approached in an obeisant manner with hands clasped and heads slightly bowed. One quarry worker was an expert at reading foot prints and his services were frequently used in tracking criminals. Representatives of the Bowri Jats who were cultivators, plus a couple of goldsmiths arrived. Then the lowest local sub-caste of the scheduled caste or untouchables called Sansi arrived. They worked in leather goods and some of them produced liquor. Unlike many of his own Brahmin group, Swamiji would eat with Muslims and lower Hindu castes. By this action, he originally met great opposition in the small town and his own household because he had broken caste rules on commensalism. As a vegetarian who even rejects eating of eggs, this does not mean that he ate Muslim food, which included meat, nor meat of the lowest castes whose food often includes pig, but that they all shared his food, which was food acceptable to a good Brahmin. The point being that a Brahmin or another high caste member would traditionally be polluted just by being in such close proximity to a Sudra (member of the lowest major caste group of the Hindus) or outcaste untouchable. There are degrees of untouchability and the government has banned it officially with varying degrees of success. Forms of pollution have changed and today in many districts, it can be hard for an outsider to identify former untouchables and other low sub-castes.

Another festival followed Holi but it was a minor one celebrating the Goddess of Smallpox Shitala Mata, which literally means 'Cool Mother'. She is a local goddess vaguely linked with Durga or Parvati, the wife of Siva. As a minor goddess, she exists on the periphery of the major Hindu pantheon. As the local Gandhian leader and prohibition worker, Swamiji took me for two weeks around the local villages of Makrana district. It was at Gachhi Puri that we joined in the goddess of smallpox's celebrations where she is worshipped in aid of the prevention and cure of smallpox. We were served only cold dishes, which were cooked the previous night. Women take all the food to the statue of the goddess and offer it to her. They pray 'save our children from smallpox'. The cold food is offered as prasad (food that is blessed in the temples). Coldness is believed to prevent smallpox or chechak. No hot food or drink is offered on the day so fires remain unlit. Our meal consisted of millet kijri (a local kedgeree), churma (wheat pudding), chakr (brown sugar mixed with chickpea powder or gram), ker fruit, pod of ganwar, fruit of kejeni tree, cold curry and yoghurt. In Hindu ayurvedic medicinal theory, smallpox is understood as a 'hot' disease, which burns the body, hence the name 'Cool Mother'.

When Swamiji and I first set out in the jeep to go to the villages for the prohibition campaign, we had an auspicious start to our journey. A donkey passed us on the left side of the road and luckily there was not a snake on the right side.

Berwala had an active branch of the Servodaya (Welfare of All) movement. We met the village council or panchayat. One member leapt up and sprinkled vermillion on our foreheads. I noted thirteen male members of the council. During the meeting, Swamiji received a good response and a few women appeared at the door. As we left the austere little building, Swamiji pointed out 'that's cow excrement!' He was not even implicitly referring to the sanctity of Gau Mata (Mother Cow), so I replied dryly 'Yes, I know, we do have it in England'.

Barsu, a village with six thousand inhabitants, was more like a small town. A ruined palace in deep decay appeared to be haunted only by peacocks and it was all that remained of the erstwhile Rajput nobility. In Rajasthan state, there seemed to be a superabundance of many things such as men wearing turbans of all shades and handsome moustached men with earrings. There were also, monkeys, peacocks, camels, elephants, palaces and forts.

In most of the larger Rajasthani villages, the bulk of the landowning caste was and still is Rajput. They are a large subcaste of the Kshatriya or warrior caste of northern India. Present day Rajasthan was formerly the state of Rajputana, which was itself divided into princely states of various sizes ranging from the mighty states of Mewar, (Udaipur), Jaipur and Marwar (Jodhpur) to smaller states like Tonk and Pratapgarh. Past and present evidence of their dominance can be seen everywhere in Rajasthan. Most villagers live in mud huts of various designs whilst the Rajput dominant family mostly lived in the forts of differing sizes. Some Rajputs have deserted their forts for the towns and are absentee landlords. Rajputs were not only big landlords or zamindars but defenders of the village as a whole. Many of their canopied tombstones still dot the Rajasthani landscapes.

At Barsu village a noisy meeting was held for Swamiji's prohibition campaign, which was continually interrupted by a youth who considered himself to be like Rajput of old. He objected to having his name mentioned obliquely when Swamiji had proposed in a speech that panchayat members should not drink. 'We Rajputs always drink,' he yelled. It is true historically, that part of a Rajput's identity as a member of the warrior caste grouping has been linked to hearty living, which includes alcoholic consumption. Female Rajputs do not drink except perhaps in private. The lifestyle of some Brahmins like Swamiji is the opposite to that of a wealthy Rajput because the Brahminical ideal prefers intellectual refinement, non-violence and moderate consumption including no alcohol. While to repeat, the Rajput ideal stresses a readiness for violence, physical strength and pleasurable consumption, which for them includes meat and alcohol. Thus at once, between Swamiji and the quarrelsome Rajput, there was a clash of philosophies of life. The Rajput's exclamations were greeted with loud cheering when a large bullock twice disturbed the meeting with some aiding and abetting from the crowd.

After the Barsu meeting, Swamiji and I had tea at the council leader or Sur Panch's house. He belonged to a subcaste of the Vaishya or business caste community. Not surprisingly, he was a prohibition sympathiser. This might have been because Vaishyas, who are below the Kshatriya warrior group in the caste hierarchy, share many of the ideals of the Brahmins. Some extremely wealthy Vaishyas often lead what appear to be materially poor lives and adhere to a rigid form of vegetarianism.

Swamiji had formerly been verbally attacked by the Rajput landowners as he proved a threat to their dominance in the region. He had been a strong advocate of land redistribution. The bulk of the land was actually cultivated by Jats who represent in northern India the archetypal peasant, though unlike some in the Punjab to the north, these Jat peasants did not own the land but held it often in usufruct. Rajputs rarely demeaned themselves by doing manual work. Today many poorer Rajputs suffer economically as their women are kept in purdah within their compound walls and thus unlike many Jat women, they cannot work in the fields. The last big landowners of Barsu, prior to land reform, owned fifty two villages. The Government took control of the land thus the Rajput was reduced to being an ordinary tenant farmer. This feudal landowner then tried to snatch land back from the new tenants, causing many fights because the government was in the process of handing its newly acquired land over to the landless. The most vociferous of the former landless, the Jats opposed the Rajputs and made good use of the courts. It is a well-established fact that in many parts of India, the Land Ceiling Acts made precious little difference to the livelihoods of many. Former zamindars can pay henchmen including police to harass poor downtrodden tenants and landless labourers. Many Rajasthani Rajputs still employ scheduled castes on their new small amounts of land as they refuse to lower their dignity by cultivating, thus they impoverish themselves needlessly.

Vinoba Bhave's land gift Bhoodan movement got fifty three thousand bighas (one third to two thirds of an acre) of land donated in Nagour district around Makrana, and Swamiji supervised the land distribution. Vinoba was a strong believer in small-scale family farming rather than collectivisation, which as a concept he felt was not suited to India. In Hyderabad district in central India, the local communists had told the tenants to kill the landlords and grab the land for themselves. The government sent in the military. In 1951, Vinoba began his padayatra or footmarch calling 'who is the owner of the land?' When he got the reply 'we are', he answered 'Did you create it?' This approach touched the people, even the communists who had not thought of themselves as holding land in trust. So Vinoba attempted to distribute land by love rather than force. Usually, he was unsuccessful. Nehru, India's first prime minister wanted Bhoodan Acts to be passed in all states. Bhoodan boards were formed to regulate the transformation but failure ensued. In India laws are often made to be broken or manipulated.

After Barsu, the jeep took us onto Mangroth village, which was held in common under Vinoba's village gift or Gramdan movement. Here land was held in trust by all villages. Each of them surrendered ownership to the village society. Inheritance, mortgage, sale or transfer of holdings was forbidden without the sanction of the villagers. It proved to be a fairly peaceful socialisation of land at the village level. When villagers 'pledge for Gramdan' they had to form a village parliament of all adults and erect a village bank and a People's Court or Lok Adalat to settle disputes within the village. In short, gram swaraj, or village rule. At the next stage, what were called 'block dan' only operated if eighty percent of the villages in a regional block pledged for Gramdan. This had occurred in parts of states like Tamil Nadu and Bihar and failed because money was misplaced by corrupt officials and most important of all, the basic ideology of such socialisation was not understood. Both Vinoba and Gandhi hoped that eventually only defence, currency and foreign affairs would be discussed at national level. All other matters would be devolved. Many Hindus believe that India was once a land of self-governing village republics. It is true that village councils existed for centuries in India. The term panchayat referred to the five respected villagers in charge of administration. Much of the idealization of these village republics is partly mythology because in most cases only the dominant castes would have held power.

Our next village, Chandi, had two hundred families. It was here that Swamiji had first begun his Bhoodan movement. One villager had a licence for ayurvedic medicine and was presently involved in establishing a village industry by collecting the very bigger wild tustumba fruit, which is normally inedible. He soaked the pieces of fruit in lime water for a few days. He then washed the fruit with water and added sugar jelly so that it could be used for stomach troubles. Around Chandi the weaver caste also cultivated. Swamiji embarrassed me a little when he requested me to ask the assembled gathering to 'take their women out of purdah' and abolish the wearing of so many ornaments. In Rajasthan as in many other states, it is common to see women in villages carrying their entire wealth on their body in the form of heavy jewellery. Perhaps it is the only security they have. If a husband's family kicks his wife out of the homestead, she at least has some wealth on her body. Often the Rajasthani women's arms were completely covered in silver on ivory armlets. Heavy silver anklets were also worn as well as the usual nose ornaments and earrings. In much of Rajasthan, village women wore longish skirts and blouses rather than saris. Women did tell me that their jewellery was awkward to wear. I suggested a compromise in that the jewellery could be worn just for ceremonial occasions rather than as now, even when they did their daily chores. The main argument against this would be problems of storage and safety of the jewellery.

The next village was Rangaan where many of the pukka (kiln brick) houses had rose coloured stone arches and pillars with intricate lace-like filigree work around the doorways, entablature and outside columns on the verandahs. All the entrances to the buildings were raised up from the street by one or two steps. As in most of the villages, one was woken up at three o'clock in the morning by raucous peacocks and this performance was usually followed by village dogs. Villagers told us that at nearby Skaway village, the water situation was so bad that it had gone poisonous, even killing off the livestock. The village was dead, only existing in memory.

At Khardia our jeep passed the tombs of former landlords. All the tombs were built in pink stone with cupolas and pillars. Swamiji pointed out that many of the locals had signed the pledge against taking alcohol. He blurted out in a loud voice 'All who are signing are drunkards'.

Samawar village was famous for its numerous famines owing to years of draught. Later the situation altered, as the rains became too plentiful. Hence the ground was useless for millet, being the local staple food. The villagers had refused to change their crop because they were afraid to experiment with the unknown. In India, millet and sorghum are considered to be low grade cereals as well as poor man's food. Often villagers were shy on offering this lowly food to visitors and the wealthier Rajputs would offer their precious wheat chapattis. Swamiji tried to impress upon them that I wanted to taste the coarser millet or bajra chapattis. I heard about an Englishman who had been offered some meat on a millet chapatti. He took the meat and returned the coarse unleavened bread thinking it was an unbaked pot plate! It is true that some of the coarser breads in Rajasthan did closely resemble coarse unbaked pottery. This village also had poor water but recently they had been linked by pipe to the well of another village. I met one family who had formerly manufactured their own liquor and now they had smashed all their utensils. Swamiji requested that I photograph a dejected looking assembly of reformed brewers of illicit 'hooch'. The little group stood in front of their broken unhygienic utensils, looking distinctly uncomfortable.

At Biarkala village I gave a talk on village life in Britain while Swamiji translated it into Hindi. I had difficulty in standing having the previous day injured my toe on the back of a motorbike. A local family wrapped up the injured part with grape leaves using an ointment made with ghee and saffron.

The next village was Midian and I visited the potter's hut and was told that the Khadi and Village Industries Board were to provide him with an improved wheel. The manufactured pots were distributed to other villages in the neighbourhood. The potter's family offered us sugar-coated chapattis and rice pudding known all over north India as khir. On to Bhadjuli village, where I noticed that in common with the rest of the villages we had visited, at the public meetings, the bulk of the assembled gathering did not attempt to sit cross-legged on the large sheets provided. I enquired the reasons for this and a scheduled caste man answered 'the earth is our mother, we prefer to sit on the earth.' A few of the higher castes were also sitting or squatting off the mats. The custom is probably a hangover from the time when only top castes would even dare contemplate sitting on a floor cover.

The state government of Rajasthan had a scheme whereby certain villages were elected and their poorest seven families received a few sheep, land and a pension of forty rupees per month for their aged. The local Vishnoy community offered us a meal and informed me 'no wine drinker must touch our pots'. Luckily, they presumed that I was teetotal. Deer roamed in the Vishnoy area and I was told that these animals were unafraid of the Vishnoy's who are as non-violent as the Jains. The lower castes tried to eat deer when they could.

At Kamsheela Village, Swamiji and I sat in the dreary village school, which had rows of tiny desks where the children sat cross-legged behind them on the floor. The surrounding walls were covered in drab colourwash. Later we slept the night in the post office at Itawalaka Village run by the Sur Panch who had formerly been in the Indian navy and told me of his visits to Djarkarta and Liverpool. He was not optimistic about the prohibition campaign generally. 'Look what happened in the U.S.' The following morning, we watched boys pulling water from the well. It was always women who did this job in most villages, so perhaps this village was attempting a little social change. Later on, I met the panchayat and gave a talk on British social problems.

Next stop Rameshia, which was famed for its ornamental shoe making. I purchased a pair of multi-coloured embroidered leather shoes. For some reason this leather had a very strong smell. Only Muslims were involved in cobbling in this locality. Ramashia was once noted for its poisonous water, which had been eliminated by improved drainage. The village had a small ayurvedic dispensary plus a family planning centre called 'Family Welfare Centre' because of Mrs Gandhi's over-zealous officials who frightened villagers during the emergency of family planning. As soon as people saw a government jeep, all the males over a certain age would flee. During a talk on 'customs, I mentioned the obsession amongst many poorer Hindus of not drinking from the same cup as another and then drying up the utensil after washing it with the dirtiest towels imaginable. It seemed all right for men to share a cigarette with each other.

At Gedaklia village school, I addressed a group of children and told them that many English children kept pets. 'So do we' they all yelled in Hindi. 'Goats, dogs ...' I tried to explain the different concept in that in India the keeping of animals was often economic. At the same meeting I was told that those wishing to be village leader or Sur Panch often refused manual work. I did notice the lack of calluses on the hands of the current Sur Panch, plus his spotless white turban, dhoti and shirt. Most Indian officials understand manual work to be below their dignity.

Swamiji told me that the local hooch was made of a variety of concoctions consisting of molasses, bark of the twigs from the bobul tree plus root of jari. In the Udaipur area of Rajasthan they used maoowar tree, which had a sweet fruit and in South India, toddy is brewed from coconut palm trees and palmyra. The subject of alcohol plus much else, Indians tend to view in black and white terms. Swamiji, my prohibition-advocating host, had requested me early on our travels to speak against alcohol. I informed him that although we had heavy drinkers and alcoholism in Britain, most people drank moderately, even the Royal Family. In most of non-Christian India, no middle class women would drink even if it was well tolerated for their menfolk. For example, in Punjab, there were many 'beer halls' where Sikh males consumed alcohol but as a woman, I would never dream of going in such places. It was a different matter in the Buddhist area of Ladakh because in that area, women drank openly, even on the streets. Their favourite drink would be rice wine or chang (rice beer).

We arrived at Choundia. The jeep had broken down and needed fixing. Choundia was one of Vinoba's Gramdan (village gift) villages. We met the executive committee of the elected members who were all men. They were nominated by raised hands, not secret ballots. Policies were decided upon by the village parliament consisting of the entire adult population of the village. I commented upon the lack of women at the meeting. They rarely attended even the parliament except by sitting inconspicuously at the rear of any assembly. I muttered that the camels were less shy of attending the meeting and this comment caused a few giggles.

The sole village crop was millet but one former renegade youth had settled down and experimented with wheat successfully. There had been some years back, a decline in rainwater and the wells had dried up but the rains did come again. The only Muslim in Choundia was the school teacher who had come from Makrana Town. The thing that struck the visitor most of all was the absolute precariousness of life in a Rajasthani village or any other rural existence in India. Next year there may be no rains. In three years, there may be no village.

Ghakli Village was originally owned by the Maharaja of Jodhpur. It was a caste-entrenched village even though inter-caste relations were peaceful. Local Hindu lads had their heads shaved with only the tuft of hair at the back of their heads unshaved. They reminded me of the orthodox Hassidic Jews I had seen in Jerusalem with their shaven heads and long sidelocks. Swamiji and I ate the usual millet bread and porridge made of millet flour and yoghurt. Our hosts were amazed that I really enjoyed it as many city dwellers would have despised such food.

Our trip to the villages over a two and a half week period, was stimulating and exhausting. My only difficulty was always where to go to the lavatory because everybody around me would always know whenever I wanted to go and a private spot had to be found; so a woman would lead me amongst any available shrubbery.

Back in Makrana, Swamiji showed me a small Siva temple. Inside, it was an enormous white Siva Ling (representation of the penis, symbolic of Siva) hewn out of a block of marble. Opposite the temple there stood the beloved Gau Shala or cow shelter. One Brahmin friend of Swamiji's enquired 'any home for old cows in England?' Swamiji said 'cow is the mother of us all', that she was intelligent and that bulls were not lazy like buffaloes. He also stated that the cow's milk was healthier than buffalo's milk because it was less creamy.

The marble for the Taj Mahal came from Makrana quarries, which were formerly owned by the Maharaja of Jodhpur. Some families had a lease ownership of about five years. There were many mines and some huge quarries. The Moghul rulers were the first to quarry marble in the area. On my arrival at one of the quarries, I asked Swamiji's son how much the women who were hand-working the crane were paid. He replied, 'five rupees per day'. I suppose this was the average unskilled women's wage in 1980. The marble was then polished by hand and machine. Huge sawing machines cut the marble into thin slabs. At the small workshop, the Muslim carvers were creating Jain images of Mahavir in varying sizes.

One nearly-completed statue was ten foot tall but was useless as it had a big crack. The carvers had polished these uniform Buddha like faces with ember stone. Their job was hereditary and I found the situation ironic as the Muslim faith does not encourage image-making. For these carvers, there were thousands of worse ways to make a living.

Swamiji showed me the local scheduled caste/untouchable burial ground. They could not send their ashes to the Ganges so they buried the ashes in urns. Trouble arose when Muslims chose the same land for their Idgah, which is an open piece of land where Id prayers are held. The land was occupied by eight thousand Muslims armed with lathis (bamboo poles). The magistrate was in a hopeless position. Later, Swamiji as mediator, let the scheduled castes have a guarantee that the ground would be theirs if they burnt the corpses quickly. He negotiated with the Muslims. Then made the out caste Hindus prove to the Muslims that the land actually belonged to them (untouchables) so they dug up some old urns. Eventually, the matter was settled through a ceremony and a proper wall was built to separate the functions.

Chapter Twelve

Puppeteers and a Poisoned Foot

The bus to Udaipur was delayed by some temple-goers chanting the name of a Hindu deity when they were not singing folk songs and refusing to pay their fares.

On arrival at Udaipur in the southern part of Rajasthan, I visited Bharatiya Lok Kala Mandal Folk Museum. This institute conducted research into folk arts including puppetry, which is an ancient art form in Rajasthan. The hereditary puppeteers are Bharts. The puppets were used for educational purposes as well as purely as an art form and initially, institute workers had great difficulty in collecting puppets and performers for the centre, as villagers were panic-stricken. They were unaccustomed to townsfolk, apart from the fact that many items had sentimental value. Most of the villagers in question were tribals, supposedly the remnants of India's earliest known inhabitants. Museum workers had to gain the confidence of the tribals as protectors rather than destroyers. Later the Museum would train professional puppeteers from several countries. Traditional turban binders and puppet carvers were employed to teach non-hereditary puppeteers.

One local skill was the making of mobile wooden temples called Kavad. They had painted on them a narration of the religious stories of the deities painted by craftsmen. The little walls held many doors opened one by one until the last, displaying the main god or goddess such as Ram or Sita. Also a locally-popular custom was tattoo-like patterns 'mendahi' using henna on hands and feet. The effect was very cooling.

Udaipur Palace sits in the centre of a lake and was now a five star hotel so was well beyond my price range. The city has a good backcloth of hills covered with dry stone walls and crumbling stone huts, which cling to the hillsides. I climbed up to the seventeenth century Jagannath temple. At the temple entrance on either side of the steps are two handsomely-carved stone elephants. Within the temple compound by a shrine, is an image of Garuda the vehicle of Vishnu, the Preserver aspect of God. Garuda is half man and half bird. Many Hindu Gods have vehicles and two well known ones are the bull Nandi, carrier of Siva and Goddess Durga's tiger.

Inside Udaipur City Palace, constructed from 1600, the most memorable were the Manak Mahal or Ruby Palace, which has glass and porcelain ornamentation on its walls, and the Moti Mahal or Pearl Palace, which is famed for its mirrors alongside a neighbouring Shish Mahal, decorated with inlaid mirror work and Chinese tilework.

I spent a few days with a family called Dashotter who introduced me to an elderly local Gandhian called Mr Mehta, who was in bed recovering with a fractured arm from a lathi (bamboo stick) charge in an anti-government demonstration. This was also a house where I had to fight for barley chapattis, rather than the far commoner wheat ones, which can be obtained in any city. Once again, my hosts wished to serve me higher status foods such as wheat.

I had a painfully slow train journey to the huge fort at Chittorgarh, which is situated on an inaccessible looking precipice about five hundred feet above the surrounding countryside. The fort stretches over three square miles and it once housed its own town with market places and temples all of which were entered from one of the many imposing gateways, which are often named after the gods, Hanuman Gate, Ganesh Gate and Lakshman Gate. One gruesome reminder of the past is the 'mahasati', which is a wooden platform commemorating the cremation ground of the former rulers. Sati stones commemorate the self-immolation of widows. Mass immolation of Rajput women was common to prevent the enemy taking them.

I left the fort by the zig zag route I had come up in and haggled for a tonga (light two wheeled vehicle) to take me to the station.

On the border of neighbouring Gujarat state lies Mount Abu, the highest point of Rajasthan, set in the Aravalli Hills. It was here that I saw some wandering white clad Jain ascetics. They were all wearing white gauze puttika veils over their mouths and noses, which symbolsze the ultimate in non-violence. The veils are supposed to permit only the minimum of germs to be killed. The sadhus were clean shaven on both head and face. Jainism tends to be an atheistic and ascetic system of moral and spiritual discipline demanding a rigid form of non-violence. It was founded by Mahavir, one of the Tirthankaras or path-finders who lived in Bihar about the same period as Gautama Buddha in the fifth century B.C. While I stayed at my hosts in Udaipur, the Dashotters, some Jain nuns came begging. Their type of monasticism demands no form of social welfare work but many rich Jain business men do donate huge sums to temples and welfare organisations. In old Delhi, there is a Jain hospital for sick birds, most of whom are victims of the city's pollution and traffic accidents.

Mount Abu must have been lovely many years ago when it was just another sleepy hill station. Himalayan Dalhousie retains that gentle atmosphere. In Abu, walking in the English style church compound and old bungalow area, the sense of history was evident but was absent where modern Indian tourism screamed out. 'Rajasthani sarees' when most Rajasthani villagers who form the vast bulk of the population did not wear saris but skirts. It is a fact that foreigners equate Indian dress with the sari and that of all Indian costumes, the sari had the most chance of survival, followed by the Punjabi-derived baggy-trousered shalwar and long shirt. In much of North India, the villagers wear various forms of long skirts rather than saris, which if worn at all are only used for special occasions. In Bengal and much of South India, saris are worn by most sectors of the community but they are tied in numerous ways. Some saris reveal much of the female form, especially amongst lower castes. Many poor people do not wear a sari blouse under their sari while, others who work manually, tie up the sari between their legs so that by appearance, the dress looks a little like a man's dhoti.

Apart from some Christian women or very rich westernised females, it is usually only the males who wear westernised garb. The suit was nearly extinct in India and only worn within the country by more westernised business men. It is de rigueur for politicians to wear 'khaki' if only because of the Gandhian legacy. This dress usually takes the form of a long white collarless shirt with or without a waistcoat, plus either cotton trousers or Hindu dhoti, and a boat-shaped Gandhi cap. Thus unlike some African politicians who used to don Mao style jackets or three-piece suits, at least the Indian leaders did remain faithful to one mode of Indian dress. The form of dress adopted by many male youths in 1980 was pretty uninspiring. The models followed were the soft-faced male film stars. Many students wore frightful baggy terylene trousers and a loose shirt with a large collar.

Before leaving Abu, I visited a museum of the Brahma Kumari movement called the World Renewal Spiritual Museum. Here they displayed an illuminating array of pictures, all beautifully painted, depicting the life-cycles of man including his worldly life and heaven. Hindu mythology informs us that the present era is the Iron Age, which is characterized by feuds, crises of faith and character. This cosmology of the Hindus relates to a cyclical concept of time as opposed to the western evolutionary linear model of time. The cosmos is cyclical for all eternity and at its simplest level is divided into four ages or yugas. These ages represent a gradual decline in standards of morality, faith, longevity and happiness. It is the Hindu ideal of the golden age in that the First Age or Krta Yuga represents a state of human existence that is unified and classless, to the Kali Yuga, which is today when Kali, Goddess of Destruction ends the World in a cosmic holocaust. Then the world begins anew.

In a joint taxi from Udaipur, a fellow passenger told me that the Brahmakumari organisation was run by 'capitalists'. On a previous visit to Abu, he had met two women dressed in city clothes that he saw later at the Brahmakumari ashram dressed in white symbolizing poverty.

Brahmakumaris believe that Lord Siva promised five thousand years ago to reincarnate for the task of world transformation through spiritual awakening. Thus, he reincarnated in a human medium called Prajapita Brahma signifying his divine role of creating his progeny of viceless beings. Siva chose as his human vehicle a renowned diamond dealer from Hyderabad in Sind (now in Pakistan). After Partition, this Hindu diamond dealer migrated to Mound Abu. Today, the organisation he started teaches Raja Yoga in order to hopefully reduce vices such as lust, anger, greed and attachment. Two women dominated the centre and they were fondly called Dadi and Didi (older and younger sister) because of their motherly natures. In 1937, their founder Prajapata Brahma whom they called Baba (father) was given a vision of the twentieth century and he saw that man and beasts would be non-violent and that 'man and the cow would drink from the same stream'. Even the natural elements would be rendered harmless. This was hardly an original thought. The trouble is that each little group believes that it has the sole monopoly of the truth but at least, the Hindus acknowledge a diversity of culturally defined paths of reaching the truth or truths.

Mount Abu still had some fine mansions dating from British times, which were built in rather prominent positions apart from the humbler stone bungalows. They were all surrounded by overgrown foliage giving some of them a haunted appearance.

The five eleventh century Jain Dilwara temples are magnificently carved in white marble, much of it displayed as filigree work. Before entering the temple, devotees are requested to leave all leather goods outside. This is because the leather may have been taken from slaughtered animals rather than those that died naturally. Amongst the marble lace-like sculpturing stand rows of identical Jain statues of varying sizes. The odd sign stated 'Do not stretch your legs apart in front of the idols' or 'Sit with your back to the idols' or 'No betel chewing allowed, mouth must be washed before going into the temple'. At one point, I began to wish that they had the sign common in the inside of New Delhi's buses 'No Eve Teasing', which is a proclamation against teasing women. Even in the presence of their own women folk, some of the youths could not behave without teasing a westerner such as me.

Further out of Abu at Achalgarh are the remains of a fourteenth century fort and Hindu and Jain temples. At Achalgarh Siva temple, the priest pointed to the hole through which Siva thrusted his toe from his shrine at distant Varanasi (Benares)! Three carved buffaloes stand in isolation away from the temple. A little below is the artificial Nakki Lake, which was dug out by the nails of the Gods. It is quite attractive with many cattle islets dotted about it. Returning to Abu, I visited the totally uninspiring Raj Bhavan art gallery. It had more blank walls than art. More interesting was the expensive pink-stoned temple (new) prominently displaying the linga, symbol of Siva on the roof. It had another linga inside. Outside was a well- kept garden.

I stopped at a small café and noted the English menu had inscribed 'Catlats, Oreng, Oreng Pis Tost'. I opted for so-called tomato sandwiches, which had more pepper than tomato in them. Luckily there was lassi, a drink made of yoghurt, salt and ice. My last evening in Abu was ruined by hideous-sounding Hindi film music, which blasted out from every available loudspeaker. That suffering was to be as nothing as compared with what I had in store prior to a gruelling eight hour bus journey to Jodhpur. I did not know that I would wake up at three o'clock in the morning in the seedy Abu Road Hotel with a crippling pain in my leg, which was so bad that whenever my foot touched the ground, the sensation was about as bad as an electric shock.

My bus was to leave Abu Road at seven o'clock in the morning from the nearby bus stand, which was 'two furlongs' from my hotel. I paid a boy 1 rupee to carry my small shoulder bag to the bus stand while I hobbled behind him. Nobody offered any assistance during the journey simply because they did not know me. The journey was eight hours of misery. The whole of the central aisle of the bus was crammed with over thirty people thus blocking any cross ventilation at this hottest time of the year before the monsoon. If I had wanted water or to go to the lavatory, it would have been impossible. Usually there is a mass exodus at any tea shop en route, but not on this bus. At Jodhpur, I requested the last passenger to help me carry my bag down the steps of the bus to the rickshaw, which was only eight feet from the bus. For this middle class man to carry my bag down the steps of the bus to the rickshaw would have been too demeaning so he shouted to the rickshaw puller to carry it. He did not even help me off the bus. When travelling alone, one automatically goes through a toughening up process in both the physical and mental senses. When two travel together, it is easier to laugh at disasters. My rickshaw puller got lost, but eventually I arrived at the campus of the University of Jodhpur to visit a Servas member. He arranged for me to visit an allopathic doctor at the government hospital. Foreigners can get free treatment at such hospitals but they must pay for medicines. The doctor said that the poison from my injured foot had crept up my leg. It was a relief to know just what was wrong, but I felt guilty for being able to jump the queue as a foreigner.

Jodhpur at first sight, is a city encompassed by unrelenting flatness. Viewed from the solid five hundred year old fort, the mirage is of a distant sea. Pink stone is everywhere. The fort has a compact appearance with carved panels and pierced screens of sandstone plus a labyrinth of passages. Traditionally, each hereditary artisan group had its own street such as the potters, cobblers and tailors. The Chiton Palace was built of pink stone and had an enormous dome. On the lower storey, there was a lovely swimming pool and the walls surrounding it were painted in differing shades of Chinese style blue paintings.

The Ajit Palace was smaller and very English with plenty of old fireplaces, where there were stacked hunting trophies of African leopards, rhinos and tigers. There were endless photos and paintings of 'what I have killed'. Sometimes, one wonders what else some of the Maharajahs did with themselves. The palace was well kept. Occasionally, I anticipated the presence of a memsahib hovering about the English-style furniture and memorabilia.

My second host at Jodhpur, a nature cure doctor, placed a series of hot and cold compresses on my recovering leg. I gave him the money to purchase my ticket for the metre gauge train to Jaisalmar near the Pakistan border.

Chapter Thirteen

A Town Apart and a Hindu Saint

The train arrived at Jaisalmer early in the morning and the first thing that caught my eyes was the two day-old headlines in an English language daily 'Bhutto Hanged'.

This ancient sandstone town gives one a real feeling of apartness. The environs of Jaisalmer are semi desert scrubland and the town looms up on the horizon as if from nowhere. It was founded in 1156 A.D. by Jaisal, a member of the Bhati Rajputs and even if the bulk of the town is of a later date, a sense of history permeates every house. My host Sri Maheshwari was in charge of the 'khadi parishad', which operated the distribution of hand-woven cloth. His joint family lived in a large stone house, which was two hundred and fifty years old. Its entrance was raised up off a narrow street and on the opposite side of the street was an empty five-storied sandstone haveli (mansion), which was tall and narrow, having a large entrance with carved wooden doors. One part of the deserted house opened into a large square courtyard, which was exposed to the sky.

Maheshwari's house also had an exposed courtyard. The bare stone walls had carved stone alcoves and small wooden cupboards with equally small metal clasps upon the doors. Underneath these cupboards were lotus motifs, embossed to give a little ornamentation. All the ceilings were made of tightly-packed beams plus the permanent fixture, especially in the bathroom, of what seemed like hundreds of squeaking bats hanging upside down, which were as black as the wooden beams. The bathroom reminded me of a medieval castle, not only because of the bare stone walls but also because of the metal studded wooden door. Some of the inner walls were delightfully painted with colourfully-costumed Rajasthani ladies carrying a varied assortment of pots, while others played music such as the bearded and turbaned men holding woodwind instruments. These paintings stood about four foot high. On each side of one of Maheshwariji's main carved doorways were painted palms of two hands. This house alone was a national treasure. The place would last another millennium.

The Khadi centre employed three thousand wool spinners who were scattered around in various villages. There were three hundred weavers and dyers who were also commissioned. The goods on sale ranged from goat hair bags and camel hair carpets to woollen shawls and blankets.

Quite close to the house was the Mahavir Bhavan or Abode of Mahavir, the founder of the Jains. Here, any Jain pilgrim could stay for a pittance. Many temples own what are called in northern India dharamsala, or in south India choultries and are pilgrims rest houses. Inside Jaisalmer are eight Jain temples. On entrance, once again, all leather goods had to be left at the gate of the compound. In one temple, several priests with veiled faces were cheerfully performing their duties of cleaning the images of Mahavir. On the carved stone panels, dancing girls and musical instruments were abundantly depicted in marked contrast to the simple Buddha like Jain images. The Hindu deities of Vishnu, Kali, Krishna and Lakshmi were represented on other carvings. Another temple had a small library with books made of palm leaves with wooden covers. These books ranged from astrology to ayurvedic medicine. The Jains have always been big chroniclers. Most of the books are written in Sanskrit. Religious merit could be obtained by copying out an important religious manuscript. Thus, Jains have been able to preserve many ancient writings in their temples and monasteries, which might otherwise have been lost. The oldest temple dates from the fifteenth century and has one thousand and two hundred plus images. These images do not all represent Mahavir but also preceding 'pathfinders' or Jain saints and they are honoured by the number of images.

Jaisalmer grew wealthy as an entrepôt for the opium trade. Many of the local havelis were built by Seth Guman Mal Bapna, a wealthy banker and merchant who had thrived on the trade in opium. This form of business once stretched from China to Afghanistan. The result of this wealth can be witnessed in Jaisalmer's architectural heritage. All the important houses here have stone latticed windows and extravagantly carved walls with delicate floral tracery work. One group of havelis had sixty six balconies, all with individual carvings. Remains of wall paintings were crumbling day by day. Inside one haveli, there was an uncanny atmosphere of decayed opulence, the sole occupants being doves and hundreds of bats. The bats and their droppings clinging to many a gloomy staircase. On ascending the flat roof, all the storeys below could be seen by overlooking the central roofless courtyard. The haunted appearance was so penetrating that it is hard to imagine that once the place bustled with a thriving joint family household. From the roof, one got a fabulous view of the fort, which is second only to Chittorgarh in Rajasthan. It dates from the twelfth century and stands about two hundred and fifty feet above the town.

Former merchants had links with Gujarat to the south and Sind to the west. Both of these areas were famed for their Hindu business communities, though the bulk of the Hindu Sindis fled Sind province (now Pakistan) for India. Today, artists and scholars are no longer patronised as wealthy business families have deserted Jaisalmer. The town declined with the end of the Moghul empire and the rise of the British, partly because the opium trade was being increasingly geared towards China and the east, and also because Bombay and Calcutta became major centres of commerce and the major ports. The old land routes lost their strategic importance and later they were often deserted. To quote a brief acquaintance of mine, local historian N.K. Sharma's guidebook Jaisalmer the Golden City, 'the locked doors of the gigantic, havelis, the dirt laying therein, pigeons and bats voicing the tale of heartlessness of their masters who never returned.' Sharmaji was the son of a temple priest and follower of Vishnu hence a Vaishnavite. While showing me some of his beautiful slides of Jaisalmer, we were briefly interrupted by his wife who entered the small room to pray to Goddess Durga whose image was set upon a little makeshift altar above which was a symbolic, rather abstract-looking sketch of the eyes and nose of the goddess. Sharma's guidebook mentioned that species of bird 'the Great Indian Bustard' and he went on to say 'Even the Shah of Arab (sic) is very fond of these birds, yes so much so that if the government of Rajasthan had not crept in, they (the Arabs) would have exterminated them off the face of the earth.'

The streets of Jaisalmer were devoid of mechanised traffic. On the lane below Maheshwari's house, camels often sauntered. Formerly these beasts would have travelled down to Hyderabad in Sind. Now that frontier between India and Pakistan was closed. At night, while I slept on my charpoy on the verandah, just below in the lane a tethered calf rested next to its mother. In the early morning, the cow was milked in the same place. The stillness of the night was disturbed only by dogs barking.

Maheshwariji's household consisted of himself, his wife plus his three sons and their wives and children who all lived under the one roof. This was a real joint family in that there was often only one cooking hearth. Each evening, the wives served their husbands. A good conservative Hindu wife only eats after her husband. In many parts of orthodox Hindu India, it is rare to see whole families sitting and eating together even if all members are present in the house. There was only one bad thing to report on Jaisalmer and this was each child pestered foreigners, all called 'Angrez" (English) demanding 'give me pen'. Apparently, this is because some years back, Jaisalmer was 'discovered' by some French tourists who handed out ballpoints to all and sundry. The children only used the English word for pen, so there was still a bit of a mystery.

I departed from Jaisalmer by bus to Bikaner. What a dismal journey. The bus tyres punctured three times on the hot dusty road and it took exactly one and a half hours to mend each tyre! At times like this, Indians are stoical. I was worried because I knew that we would not get into Bikaner until ten o'clock that night. My only address was the local nature cure hospital. On arrival after a mind-shattering ten hour bus journey, the entire group of passengers yelled out in unison 'Jai Rama, Shri Ram, Jai Ram' ('Victory to God'). I hailed a tonga (horse and trap) to take me to the nature care centre, which stood behind enormous closed semicircular metal gates. This was certainly a forbidding sight at ten thirty at night. My letter giving notice of my arrival had not arrived and the 'chowkidar' (night watchman) informed me politely 'this is not dharamshalas. After speaking to him in broken Hindi, he admitted me with a friendly smile.

The bulk of the patients were sleeping in the open air at this exceedingly hot time of the year on simple charpoys. Most of them suffered with asthma. During the day, a hive of inactivity dominated the place. The hospital was neglected and facilities wasted. The excuse was 'no government help'. I received hot and cold fomentation for my foot and enjoyed a steam bath. To repeat, naturopaths in India dislike sauna baths because they believe in keeping the head cool. This bath was heated by a small fire and the steam went up a pipe into the small wooden cabinet in which the patient sat with only his head showing. This was followed by a cold bath. The hospital was owned by a local Jain Temple. Treatment was free and patients were charged for lodgings.

I left Bikaner by slow metre gauge train for the far north of Rajasthan, which borders on Punjab. Here, I visited Sri Ramachandra, another Gandhian who lived in the village Makassar near Hanumangarh Junction. He was a naturopath whom I had met previously at the Sarvodaya conference at Vinoba's ashram at Wardha. Ramachandraji was a pure soul and saintly in appearance and character. He was tall and slim with close cropped hair. He was a Hindu in an area where Sikhs were noticeable.

A lot of local men came to look at me as most of their wives were in purdah. Daily, my breakfast was roasted wheat grains, which were tasty, and milk. As a naturopath, Ramachandra was opposed to tea of the non-herbal variety. It was impossible to get a good night's sleep because April in the pre monsoon season is in Rajasthan noted for ghastly dust storms and sporadic rainfall. Each night was spent shifting beds around to avoid either dust or rain! Hanumangarh area in north Rajasthan has only flat and dreary scenery, which in a period before the completion of the new Rajasthan Canal, appeared only to consist of inferior-looking sand dunes.

The local school wall echoed Plato's wise words 'Great men discuss ideas, average discuss things and fools discuss persons.' At nearby Jundwali school, I spoke to the pupils about English rural life and answered their questions on politics in England. Afterwards, I had lunch with the 'doctor' who lived near the school who was more of an allopathic aid and compounder. At another school, I was introduced to the 'ladies' (Indians rarely use the word women'), or teachers, then I sat alone with the male staff. The female teachers were excluded because they could not sit alongside their male colleagues, though it was fine for the men to sit with me!

At nearby Sangaria village, I met Swami Keshwanen who had established many institutions including an agricultural college and some secondary schools. En route back to Makassar, I saw a veiled woman working in the fields collecting the harvest. She was veiled because her father-in-law and a male elder were chatting nearby. Usually women who worked in the fields were not in purdah as they were amongst their own sex and because veiling is impractical.

Ramachandra introduced me to a landlord's family, which still owned sixty acres of land after the Land Ceiling Act in his village of Leelavali. I ate with the men of the family and later on I met the women. At that time, Ramachandra made a speedy exit because of purdah. I commented that it seemed crazy that he, a deeply religious man, should have to leave the room as perhaps the women might benefit by meeting him. Under these circumstances, they would have been barred from meeting Mahatma Gandhi, the so called 'Father of the Nation'. One woman said that if they saw one man, then they should see them all, thus eventually leading to a breakdown of the arranged marriage system.

One afternoon, I met the Sur Panch's wife and her mother-in-law. The young wife spoke English well and told me that her son was at school in Simla up in the Himalayas. She explained that the local schools were poor 'we do not want him to be an animal.' She then added 'we honour our guests in India, we love you.' This ideal of duty from a western viewpoint is often an overdone formality, even when accompanied by a degree of warmth. At least unlike many women I had met, they did not reduce themselves to fits of giggles when confronted with a strange female such as myself. 'People laugh when they cannot understand you,' she added encouragingly. That probably explained why all the school kids had dissolved into laughter when I spoke in the schools, little horrors. The young wife went on to say 'we like our restrictions, we cannot go here and there, we love each other,' pointing to her elder female relations by marriage. I suppose it is the lack of choice for most Indian women that irk many westerners. Suddenly, the young wife added 'I will give you shoes, clothes or anything.' Was she being genuine? The family lived in a big compound but still the entire family lived and slept in only a few rooms as privacy was of little importance to them. Hospitality is one of the highest virtues and the family pressed food and drink onto me when it was clearly unwanted. They had a ghastly modern taste in furniture, which included a selection of cheap, plastic tables.

At Rajputra village I was taken to a small ashram where one ayurvedic doctor worked in a tiny room crammed with medicines of all descriptions. On the wall were various grubby-looking certificates and colourful gaudy pictures of the Hindu pantheon. Near Rajputra lived a Saddhu in grand seclusion. He did not speak by choice but he wrote with his fingers in the dust on the ground and also communicated by displaying certain mannerisms. Formerly, he had been a chela (disciple) of a guru (teacher) in a traditional ashram school or gurukul. The story goes that he was told rather abruptly that he spoke too much. He vowed silence for a year but he broke the vow so he extended it for five years and so on! We left the solitary loin cloth-clad figure to his chosen existence. I had hoped to see some traditional Rajasthani wrestling that was to be performed on my behalf in Makassar but it was cancelled.

Ramachandraji's sister kept asking me in Hindi 'do you want hair oil?' I explained that western women did not normally wear hair oil because of the different texture and style of hair. Indian women often wash their hair daily or at least pass water through it and then massage oil into it Ramachandra's sister used mustard oil.

Throughout my stay, my host had continually stressed the importance of cow protection. Like many of his ilk, he now dedicated his life to it. 'To protect the cow is to protect our agriculture and health. To worship the cow means to serve the cow and take care of her health.'

I was sad to leave Ramachandraji and departed for New Delhi and the Himalayan foothills.

Chapter Fourteen

A Conference of Naturopaths with Fire Healers

After the long journey, I arrived again at what was turning out to be my primary Indian home in the Sivalik foothills of the Himalayas, at the little Gandhi Seva ashram situated in Oel Hamlet in the Una district of Himachal Pradesh state. The place was still the same, especially my nature cure mud hut office where I slept with the old dusty naturopathic prints on its walls 'people spend their health to get their wealth and with might and main they labour hard to spend their wealth to get their health again.' The faded photos of the nationalists were still there covered in cobwebs.

Bed bugs were active and I managed to get head lice for the first and hopefully last time in my life. My head was thrust into a bucket containing vinegar to kill the lice. Hundreds of fire flies flitted around the hut by night like tiny torches. It was spring and the cuckoo was in full throat. Seasonal confusion was aided because many leaves were falling (April – May). The wild birds in India seemed to be quite tame and unafraid and they came in and out of my little hut constantly. They built their nests everywhere, usually around the open-raftered ceiling or behind the hanging photos of the eminent politicians.

I obtained the Tribune newspaper printed in Chandigarh and read an article about Rajasthan regarding arranged child marriages in Marwar district. Ten thousand babies and children were forced into marriage at an annual fair in 1979.

The night bus from Una to New Delhi was chaotic with arguments at the back, and continual shouting of "Indira Gandhi Zindabad" up front by zealous youngsters of the Youth Congress Indra.

I then went by train with Razi Sahib to Bombay and onto nearby Ulhasnagar for the sixteenth Akhil Bharat Nature Cure Conference. The venue was an ashram founded shortly after Partition by Hindu Sindi migrants from Sind, now in present day Pakistan. The competing ideologies and subgroups showed themselves up during the conference when in one of the larger meetings. Dr H, a major organiser of the conference grabbed the microphone out of another speaker's hand. This was followed by near pandemonium when one Swami spoke to the audience in a manner that was quite undignified. Apparently, he had been expelled from a hospital because of his liaisons with an unwed woman member of staff. It is doubtful whether he would have been kicked out for purely monetary corruption.

Before nightfall, we were all divided into sleeping areas allocated on the basis of the guests' home states. As I accompanied Dr Razi, I slept with the contingent from Bihar. My floor neighbours were from Tamil Nadu in south India.

The degree of nature cure fanaticism was most marked in the early morning. Even at three thirty in the morning, there were awakening shuffles of feet from the more enthusiastic practitioners of naturopathy. Most Indians do rise early unlike many westerners who may go through life without witnessing a sunrise. To be in one's bed roll at five o'clock in the morning was really lying in late. At five thirty in the morning, a few of us crept stealthily towards the ashram kitchen where non-herbal tea was being brewed. The second morning, a lady from Tamil Nadu and I were reprimanded by ultra orthodox Swaraji for drinking tea. I suggested that herbal tea should have been made available. Some Hindus are adverse to tea drinking for naturopathic reasons in that conventional non-herbal tea and coffee are banned from nature cure hospitals. While others object to tea because of nationalist reasons in that tea was mainly introduced into India in the 19th century during British rule. However, another tradition informs us that tea was introduced into China in 510 A.D. when a Buddhist missionary monk, Bodhidharma's disciple Ta-Mo, said that he would not sleep until his teacher's mission was successful. After some years, Ta-Mo succumbed to sleep. Because he broke his promise, he cut off his eyelids and threw them down but Buddha caused the eyelids to form a root and behold the tea plant symbol of wakefulness.

Swaraji, previously commented on in Delhi, was an interesting character who came from a gardening subcaste and epitomised the stereotype self-made man. He was about fifty years old with a rough looking face and a manner to equal it. He was extremely miserly with money and continually asking the price of everything, a common enough practice in India. He dressed in white cotton shirt and dhoti. Much of his money was earned by writing nature cure books in Hindi, which were partial translations from the writings of others. He ate only raw foods and had boundless energy being constantly on tour, speaking on nature cure in every corner of India, when he was not based in his room at Gandhi Nidhi in New Delhi.

During the conference at Ulhasnagar, I met a German disciple of Rajneesh who was conspicuously dressed in saffron. I suggested that his guru needed help for curing his asthma and the German replied that 'Bhagwan is hardly in his body for more than a few hours daily so why bother when he can still do his work?' People can make themselves believe anything.

Two enthusiastic Americans called Corolla and Barry introduced the conference members to an ancient Indian method of healing by using sacred ash called Agnihotra. To be efficacious, the ritual must be carried out exactly at sunrise and sunset. A special gold or copper pyramid-shaped container is used. The materials to be burnt are dried cow dung, rice, wood from any non-bitter fruit plus pure cow ghee. Corolla and Barry chanted a Sanskrit mantra adding a flavour of the ancient Vedas. Ash made from these burnt elements is believed to have healing properties. The container is pyramid shaped as it is thought that subtle energies collect at points in the pot. Barry informed us that in Europe, dysentery and TB were cured by cow dung ash mixture. Unfortunately, the pair did not go into further detail. The qualities of ghee are that it does not change weight before and after burning. Two minutes before sunrise or sunset, the fire is lit. Dead on sunrise, the fire should be blazing.

A cancer specialist in Germany had claimed that this ash was a 'miracle' weapon when used internally or externally. It can be used for fighting pollution according to the Vedas. In Baltimore USA, five year experiments were taking place by using this ash for curing some mental problems by attempting to alter and purify the atmosphere over a given period of time. It is believed that by situating these fires in particular places that the fire will affect the growth and health of both animals and plants. The ash may also be used as a fertiliser. I like to keep an open mind on such matters but when I questioned Corolla and her organisation about their claims that 'Sanskrit is the mother of all languages', she replied write to a university and find out.' So I wrote to the department of Sanskrit at Cambridge University and received a letter in reply from a professor of Sanskrit who was surprised to hear that such beliefs were extant in the twentieth century!

During the nature cure conference, Razi Sahib and I had the misfortune of becoming involved with one very fat bearded character who somehow latched onto us and offered to show us around Bombay. In the end, we used him as much as he used us. We left for Bombay and stayed at one of the Gandhian centres in a small room situated on their roof. At dawn we went by double deck bus to Colaba fish docks. Bombay takes its name from Mumbai, a Koli goddess and many Kolis are fisher folk. They are the oldest inhabitants of Bombay. That morning Colaba was thronged with fishing boats with their occupants involved in an assortment of tasks from mending fishing nets to cooking breakfast on deck in grimy looking vessels. There were no seagulls about, which seemed strange to me. Later, we returned to a shabby fish restaurant near the quayside and ate tasty fish curry.

Bombay's Elephanta caves situated on an island date from the seventh century and consist of rock cut cave temples dedicated to Lord Siva. There are massive sculptured panels chiselled out of rock walls. Each composition stands in a separate alcove. The lingam shrine has a three foot high cylindrical linga (symbolic of Siva) and at each entrance to that cave are sculptured dwarapals (door keepers) who rest against dwarfs. The Great Cave is famed for its central feature of Trimurti or three-headed figure of Siva in the guises of Brahma the Creator, Rudra (Siva) the Destroyer and Vishnu the Preserver. Much Hindu sculpture depicts the multiple appearance of a god simultaneously in various aspects, some lower, some higher and some approximately equal. Brahma is in essence the high god or the most unknowable aspect of god. Hindu trinitarianism, as Basham claims in The Wonder That Was India, tended to favour one god rather than all three. There are few temples dedicated to Brahma.

Near the three- headed figure within the Great Cave are two huge figures of husband and wife, Siva and Parvati. The Siva stands sixteen foot high and Parvati a little less. Part of Siva's head dress consists of the figure of Ganga, the river goddess of the Ganges, the river which is believed to have flowed from Siva's head. Another major statue is one depicting male and female aspects of the godhead in an androgynous sculpture of Siva uniting the two sexes, and including female energy or Sakti in one image. There are multitudes of other sculptures in Elephanta, which are far too numerous to elaborate upon here. I took the ferry back to Apollo Bunder feeling a little sad as so many of the impressive statues had been mutilated by Muslim image smashers.

I met up with Razi Sahib and we took the electric train to the low lying hill station of Lonavla. Swami Kawalyadhana had started a yoga centre cum hospital here back in the 1920's. Many foreigners came here and took a two or six month course in yoga therapy. The centre even had a laboratory for assessing the results of experiments on scientific lines. I saw some x-rays of a man's stomach showing what happened to his digestive system before and after he was insulted. A contraction of the organ was evident. I wondered how many of us constantly eat under pressure or without giving enough time to eating properly. Ideally, a meal should be eaten in silence, which in many Indian homes it is.

Later on in the day, I was invited by the foreigners to a small lake where they bathed in the nude away from prying Indian men. It was the first time I had participated in nude bathing since 1966 in Israel's Lake Tiberias. One man from Salford was very keen for me to join in!

Razi Sahib and I returned to Bombay and we spent the first night 'sleeping behind the door in the men's waiting room at Victoria Terminus Railway Station. The following night, we slept upstairs on the corridor in the same building. Unfortunately, a zealous railway official was combing the place for undesirable dossers. A neighbouring man crept up to Dr Razi's hitched up mosquito net and whispered 'give man ten rupees', so we handed over the money and he left us in peace. A couple of nearby foreign hippies refused to corrupt a public official and were ceremoniously kicked out. On the third day, Razi Sahib returned by train to New Delhi and I departed alone for a long visit to Gujarat state.

Chapter Fifteen

The Tribals and the Prudes

Gujarat state in western India is the birthplace of Gandhi and I planned to visit Swaraj (self rule) ashram at Vedchhi in southern Gujarat. The ashram was founded in 1924 by a worker whom Gandhi sent to labour with the local tribal population. In 1947, during the anti- British movement, the ashram and similar institutions were banned. They established schools specialising in Gandhi's ideal of Basic Education. This form of education aimed to fight the deleterious effects of the imported western system of schooling introduced by the British. Gandhi wished to make no clear cut separation between intellectual and physical work. Both the traditional caste system plus modern educational concepts of education have combined to downgrade manual labour. The end result being that once villagers learn to read and write or obtain a piece of paper, they believe that manual labour is below their dignity. The end product being that all over India, there are millions of graduates at all levels swelling the unemployment figures. In Punjab, for example, there were few unemployed illiterates but many so-called educated unemployed. The Vedchhi Swaraj ashram attempted to encourage youngsters to remain and work within the villages even after the students had had a literate schooling.

The Hindu caste system rests vaguely upon the concept of hereditary occupation whereby in many subcastes, individuals who transgressed the range of permitted occupation would be outcastes. Rigidity does vary considerably from district to district.

Unlike Pakistan, India is a secular state and there was no compulsory religious education in state schools. Even most of the fee- paying convent schools did not teach religion. The government had instituted civic studies to encourage national awareness, for the nation state is a modern idea. The ashram teachers told me that in many ordinary schools, teachers objected to classes on sewing, art, carpentry and cooking. Even the best schools in Britain tolerate one or all of these subjects. It would not be so bad if the academic tradition was transmitted efficiently in the bulk of Indian schools. Enter any village school in 1979 (when eighty four percent of India's population were villagers) and one saw rows of kids learning by rote. I had met more MA's in one week in India than in a year in Britain. I also met MA's in English Literature who had not opened a recommended original work of an author, they preferred to repeat the myriads of notes and commentaries churned out by underpaid academics.

In this southern area of Gujarat, Basic Education was continued up to university level at the Gujarat Vidyapith to the north near Surat on the coast. The Vidyapith offered a four year degree course in teaching and social services. All students were expected to return to the rural areas and assist these communities. The Vidyapith was mainly run by the tribals themselves. The vast majorities of the tribals no longer hunted but were landless labourers who had a history of ruthless exploitation by absentee proprietors of high caste Hindus. The most corrupt were the money lenders. One merchant could dominate and run the lives of thousands. Present day India still has millions of its population working as bonded labourers whereby labourers families are indebted over the generations.

My Servas friend Voraji joined Vinoba's Bhoodan movement and helped distribute eight thousand acres of land to the landless tribals. The two hundred Gramdan, village gift villages, he told me were 'only in name'. The industries encouraged were small scale ones in khadi, carpets and palm leaf products. Co-operatives had been started for diamond cutters who were formerly landless labourers. Other co-ops also arranged loans from the banks to help farmers obtain such basic necessities as buffaloes. Credit societies purchased and sold crops thus avoiding middlemen. Even the forest labourers had their own co-ops. Originally, all milk was dispatched to the cities and the peasants received none as they were constantly in debt over buffaloes.

Swaraj ashram had fifty acres of land and a population of about three hundred. I was impressed by the work of these Gandhians but I did have reservations. One day while sitting in Voraji's office, a tribal sari-clad woman entered. 'Look!' exclaimed Voraji, 'originally this lady went without any clothes.' This was seen as a great achievement, the fact that many tribals or Adisvasi's chose not to wear much clothing in their traditional habitats and even when they did so they did not traditionally view female breasts as sex objects. Many of the higher caste Hindu Gandhians were more prudish than some of the Christian missionaries. Gandhi had great admiration for the social work of the Christian missionaries but not for their efforts at religious conversion. On this subject, he reiterated the traditional Hindu view that people should follow their own faiths. Present day Gandhians quite happily condemn western missionaries for interfering with Hindu or Muslim religious sentiments while some of them will often, as higher caste Hindus, interfere with the lifestyles of India's tribals who after all are supposed to represent the remnants of India's oldest inhabitants. It was sometime later when I visited the Tribal Institute in Ahmedabad, when I would hear of severe cultural impositions upon tribals by so called Gandhians.

From Vedchhi, I travelled north to Servas member Mohan Parekh who lived in Bardoli district. He was an impressive looking man. He was tall and as pale as a northern European. My first glimpse of him was when he was seated on his verandah on a traditional Gujarati joli or swing, which was long and broad and nearly the size of a small bed. Noting my surprise at this furniture, he exclaimed 'but you have not seen them in Sind?'

Before conversing with Sri Parekh, I was offered mango juice mixed with ghee. He told me that Gujaratis had mastered the art of creating food that can be preserved for months. It is true that Gujaratis of certain castes are amongst the most widely dispersed groups in the world. They can be found in any corner of the globe from Trinidad to Fiji. Business communities who travelled previously by ship would carry supplies of, for example, bread that would last for months. This device was not only utilitarian but also it satisfied cultural necessities of maintaining caste rules as the majority of those travelling happened to belong to the business or Baniya group of subcastes collectively classified as part of the broad grouping Vaishya, the third major caste in the Hindu hierarchical system. In Gujarat, such common names as Patel and Parekh represent some of these Vaishyis. In India, they form one of the most diet conscious communities, adhering strictly to rites against polluting foodstuffs.

Sri Mohan Parekh ran a brilliant organisation which he had built up from scratch on Gandhian principles. Yantra Vidyalaya was an institute for rural technology with the lordly ambitions 'to enhance and enrich human efforts, not to replace human hands.' They offered a three year course in blacksmithing, welding machine repairing, electric wiring and a special section for training tribals in printing technology and book binding. Each student in 1980 received a monthly scholarship. In this part of Gujarat, the Adivasis or tribals constituted fifty two percent of the population. Interestingly enough, some tribal people were trained a century ago in typesetting by Parsi pioneers in the Bombay newspaper industry. The Parsis were the descendants of Pre-Islamic Persians who fled their country and came to India in the eighth century and later, in order to continue practicing their ancient Zoroastrian faith.

The fundamental aim of Sri Parekh's institute was not only directly practical including developing ideas about national unity but also had the major task of removing the idea of hereditary occupation based upon subcaste. This did not mean that a son should not have the choice to follow his father's work but that outside groups should also have the chance to join new occupational groups. Thus traditional Lohars or blacksmithing subcastes, taught tribals who were indebted landless labourers, a new skill.

Sri Parekh spent six months studying rural technology in Japan. On his return home, he elaborated his plan to up-grade village crafts, mainly by introducing 'science to the fields'. He showed me his improved designs for agricultural tools. I liked especially the tiny implements for rural kids who instead of playing Lego and Meccano would play with chakkhis (rotary grinding stones) buckets, wells, brick making tools, and little boards for rolling out chapattis. Sri Parekh was concerned with removing unnecessary strain from labouring so he redesigned traditional tools so that an altered posture was needed for working them. A further enthusiasm of this energetic man was solar energy. He had designed a number of solar cookers and had experimented with them. He showed me a couple near his house, which had huge reflecting mirrors.

Sri Parekh took me to Swaraj ashram in Bardoli, which was founded by conservative Hindu freedom fighter Sardar Vallabhbhai Patel. This leader also participated in the Dandi Salt March with Gandhi, which was linked to breaking a British law making it a punishable offence to possess salt not obtained from the government salt monopoly. This ashram ran a hostel for tribal girls and I was shown some of their work in the library. Above the bookshelves, they had displayed some projects on herbs and their medicinal use. Art projects included painting nests of weaver birds and girls spinning on charkhas or spinning wheels. The ashram offered a gentle environment, the buildings constructed in typical ashram style, with thatched or tiled roofs, mud brick and white washed walls, mud floors and a prison bar window without glass but with inner wooden shutters. This is what sets India apart from most other countries, especially in the so-called developing world. Only in India would one find idealistic educated people willing to praise the science of cow dung floors and the like, as many people believe that concrete is the best material because of its durability whereas mud is cool in summer and warm in winter and concrete is the opposite. There is nothing so restful on bare feet than a dried mud floor. Of course, mud would not be so attractive if one was living in a shanty during Bombay's monsoon. But the point I am making means that perhaps thanks to Gandhi, there are those in the population albeit a minority who do not wish to ape capitalist or Marxist models of development.

A man showed me around the lushly green ashram grounds and buildings. He had lived for twelve years in the United Kingdom. On this vegetarian ashram, he confessed that he had eaten meat 'If my father knew, he would jump off the roof.' To cap it all, he had even lived in a pub in the Yorkshire town of Haworth. It gave me a strange feeling just to hear somebody speak of a Yorkshire community situated near my own birthplace, as the ashram existence seemed culturally light years from the Bronte sisters' home village.

Chapter Sixteen

A Centre for Generating Peoples' Power

Leaving Sri Parekh, I had to travel through Broach district in central Gujarat for Bori village situated in the ancient cotton growing area of this state. After a long wait at the Ahmedabad bus station, I was informed that the eight forty five morning bus to Broach had broken down. In order to get to Bori, I was told to go by train via Nabipur. The train was one and a half hours late for Nabipur.

By luck, Banglawala Sahib, a friend of my future host at Bori, Sri Bikhubhai Patel was standing on the platform. He was an elderly Muslim gentleman attired in long white shirt, trousers and a skull cap. He wore the traditional Muslim beard without a moustache. After greeting me with a gentle smile, he told me he would contact Bikhubhai Patel.

The Banglawala's house in Nabipur was a hundred and fifty five years old. Externally, it looked shabby and neglected. On ascending the stairs to the female quarter of the house, my eyes feasted on a Gujarati spectacle of a huge kitchen, which displayed a magnificent collection of gleaming circular brass trays and patterned plates, jugs and cups all arranged about the walls on wooden shelves. Near some pictures of the Ka'aba at Mecca, gorgeous oil lamps with shapely glass bulbs hung near the walls and dangled from the heavily beamed ceiling. Without thinking, I gave the Hindu greeting of Namaste to the assembled female group who were seated on the floor and central swing. They appeared too shy to respond. Then they looked down and noted the baggy shalwar trousers that I was wearing, that in this area of Gujarat were only worn by Muslims. For my forgetfulness, they laughed when I muttered a hasty 'A Salaam Aleichum' with a quick touch of my forehead with my right hand. They replied 'Wa aleichum as Salaam'. This was an orthodox Muslim household and these women were in purdah.

Banglawala Sahib invited me to the male side of the house, which had its own separate outside entrance. His own room offered a late Victorian cum Edwardian scene dominated by a large heavy circular table. On the walls, old faded brown and white photos and equally ancient certificates hung. There were cupboards packed with long dusty articles and objects d'art including cups and saucers, glass cups, silverware, musical boxes and an old dip pen box ink bottle. Hanging from one wall was a circular Rajasthani water pot with floral designs and swords in ornately carved sheaths, including a silver shield from Mecca. Banglawala Sahib proceeded to show me a couple of old land registers. His family had formerly owned over six hundred acres of land. These registers were beautifully written by hand and bound in old leather covers. Some of the maps showed land divisions. He also brought forth a collection of old silk pyjamas and one beautifully embroidered saddle cloth for covering a horse's back.

Many traditional kitchens have separate alcoves to place the huge earthenware water pots. In India, the earthenware pot is a good refrigerator and keeps the water enclosed comfortably cool. The water has to be strained through a cloth into the pot. Before leaving the house, I managed to persuade the women to sit around the swing in the centre of the kitchen for a photograph. I have never sent them the photo (they did not request one) because I would have had to send it via the Patels and the Patels, although long friends of the Banglawalas had never seen their women.

Nabipur was entirely Muslim in 1980, apart from the tribals who had remained Hindu. These tribals tilled the land for such families as the Banglawalas for generations and later they were moving towards factory jobs, so the old landowners in spite of Land Ceiling Acts became short of labour.

I moved to Bori village and Bhikubhai Patel's house. The Patels formed part of the business community and also owned land. Bikhubhai's wife was a strikingly handsome middle-aged woman with a dark skin and delicate features. We took to each other instantly. Bharat, their son who lived with them during his holidays from college, was present. His mother wore a sari and father dressed in the usual Gandhian clothes including waistcoat while Bharat wore the awful baggy trousers with western cotton shirt hanging loose.

In this rich cotton area of Broach, it is the Patels who form part of the landowning hierarchy. Patels are thus an extremely powerful subcaste in Gujarat and they even dominate the farmers' co-ops. Bikhubhai took me to see a servicing co-op he established, which sold fertilisers, insect repellent oil, wheat and collected cotton from farmers. The capitalists were the sole shareholders. Workers got standard state wages and they worked seasonally. I noticed that one of the ginning machines in full production dated 1888 came from Oldham in Lancashire.

Back home, Bikhubhai's wife offered me a dish called dhokla, which consists of mixed pulses and sorghum with steamed rice. As it was now the pre monsoon season, I was offered much mango juice. Mango is truly the queen of fruits. Bikhubhai kept frightening me in his Gujarati pronunciation of English when he would ask, 'do you want snake?' Here the word snack sounds like snake! We ate our food on the kitchen floor where the food was placed on wooden boards. I never did learn to sit cross-legged so I devised my own weird methods of sitting on floors. The entire family slept on the roof verandah in order to benefit from the breeze. Electricity could not be relied upon and once the ceiling fans stopped, the mosquitoes began their vicious persecution.

It was a fabulous bus journey from Baroda to Rajpipla, a low lying hill station in the foothills of the Satpura Mountains. During British rule, Rajpipla was one of the numerous princely states which abounded in what is now Gujarat state. The bus on its gradual climb upwards passed lush green banana fields. I noticed that the former ruler's palace was now a training centre for forest rangers with one of India's few ayurvedic pharmacy training centres situated in the same building. The Maharajah had commissioned a German artist to paint murals on the walls of the former ballroom with delicate shades depicting nudes, lilies, swans and flowers. I doubted whether the average forest ranger reflected upon its quality or even noticed it. The palace only dated from 1939 and had a vaguely Art Deco appearance about it.

My new Servas friend Sri Pandya started to explain to me the intricacies of party loyalty in India. For example, my next host on my journey was to be the energetic Harrivallabhai Parekh, a leading Gandhian figure in Gujarat who unusually for such a man was a big supporter of Mrs Gandhi. (Mrs Gandhi was no relation of the Mahatma). Mrs Gandhi was also backed by such millionaires as the Parsi Tata family. Sri Pandya was correct in saying that the Gandhians of the Janata party such as Moraji Desai and Raj Narayan were in many ways more reactionary than Mrs Gandhi ever was. Sri Pandya worked as a freelance journalist and had a long history of concern with tribal welfare. Eating together, we ate the familiar papadum, which was homemade and eaten throughout the meal unlike in neighbouring Rajasthan where it is often consumed at the end of a meal. All the food was heavily fried though tasty but not ideal for hot weather. All my Gujarati hosts except the Banglawalas were vegetarians. Though one man claiming vegetarianism did eat meat in front of me and swore me not to tell his wife! Sri Pandya showed me his lovely little prayer room at the top of the house. His wife was so orthodox that she did not greet me when I first set eyes on her as she was clearing her domestic altar with her back turned to me. Her head was covered with part of her sari.

My last night in Rajpipla was spent in a house built in the great Victorian Rectory style, certainly more formidable than Disappointed Gothic. In the afternoon, I was taken to a local remand home run in connection with the Rajpipla probation and aftercare service. The boys were aged from six to eighteen years. But they were not strictly on 'remand' or 'under trial' as they are called in India but destitute tribals. That day, the food the lads were preparing was a local dish called dudhi made of gourd and gram flour. A few of the boys had families who had been entangled in murders. Many of these lads themselves were thieves. One of the teachers was of scheduled caste origin which had upset some caste Hindus because they felt that he should not have been appointed. Before I left, I was offered a nice jute bag, which was made by one of the boys when he was not attending the local schools.

Later, I was shown a maternity home where all the patients were able to bring an attendant from their own household. This was of course common practice in many non-western countries. The family attendant just slept on a mat by the patient's bed. Like many Indian hospitals, the wards had dingy unpainted walls. In another part of the hospital, I was shown the horrific side effects of sulphur tablets on one patient. The man had had a cut arm and had been prescribed sixty sulphur tablets. How many he had taken at a time I do not know but the end result was an upper part of the body with the appearance of third degree burns. His facial features were unharmed but his skin told another story.

Harivallabhai Parekh was a physically imposing man. He wore his homespun khadi clothes in an individualistic style. Head cloth tied at the back of his head, a long V necked Indian shirt and a lungi (a long cloth wrapped around the legs like a skirt). He was a stocky man and gave a welcome to anyone visiting the ashram 'Anand Niketan' (abode of Bliss), which he founded. The booklet he handed out called A centre for generating peoples' power for peaceful progress informed us that his father was a Diwan (chief minister) of a former princely state. Bhai (brother) as Harivallabhai was known was destined for a similar occupation. Eventually, he became involved in Gandhi's Quit India movement against British rule.

The area of Gujarat where the ashram was situated was a district of densely forested landscape. The majority of the locals were tribals. In common with many other tribals, they had a history of ruthless exploitation by money lenders and forest cum revenue officials. On the day of my arrival at the ashram, a whole crowd was assembled under a huge tree. This was one of the regular attendances at the Lok Adalat (People's Court), which was a remarkable social innovation. One endless form of exploitation was the costly sums involved in paying outside lawyers to deal with problems which already caused unbearable poverty. Understandably, the tribals felt that they were amongst the most oppressed and Bhai decided that a people's court would do away with ruthless professionals and that the court would be run by the tribals. It was Bhai who organised the court but the tribals watch the proceedings and were free to question any decisions.

When I attended the court, an ashramite explained some of the cases being discussed. One case featured the problem of wife beating by a third husband. The woman complainant sat on the ground with her legs outstretched. She wore a bead necklace and very heavy silver anklets and bracelets. These ornaments competed with a chunky object above the breast, which had coins dangling from it. The tribal wife was adamant for divorce while her husband opposed it. Her father chimed in that the husband was always beating his daughter. Her husband had previously admitted that he would pay a fine if he hit his wife again! But he had not paid up. She then exclaimed 'he always beats me at night when I cannot go for help.' The first thing that struck me was that among some high caste Hindus such frankness from a female would often be unthinkable. Even an eighteen year-old high caste Hindu widow of three days marriage had little chance of every remarrying, let alone a divorced woman. These tribal women did not sit with heads covered and faces downwards, they were bold by Indian standards. All tribals in this area were free to remarry many times. The jury at the trial consisted of two people from each side of the family and eventually only Rs 50 was paid by the husband instead of the usual Rs450 which was normally spent in that community after court cases. Any other money would be spent on fertilisers and seeds.

Another marital case involved a wife who did not want a divorce and her husband did. The court decided in favour of a divorce and the wife had to return some jewellery. A man appeared and prized off her heavy silver anklets with a hammer and anvil. The anklets were like manacles and they are fixed on a women for life and form part of her security so however heavy and uncomfortable, they cannot be removed. Money was exchanged and handed over to the wife's father, as her side of the family did not want the divorce.

Together with a group of visiting Indians, I was taken out to see some of the ashram projects. In some fields, I noticed tiny altars of plain headless clay horses with cylindrical bodies situated amongst some potsherds. From one of my books on tribal art, I noticed that the large Gujarati tribal group, the Dangs also designed them in a part naturalistic, part abstract character. I never understood why the horse was used as a cult figure here as there were very few horses or mules in the area. Of course, much of the so called tribal art depended upon non-tribal artisans as it was they who supplied metal tools to the tribals. The adjoining district of Chhota Udaipur, was noted for tribal cult objects including horses, dome shapes and human figurines. In one village, I heard how the males were expert in the use of bow and arrow. Holding up a bow, a man said that now it was only used for small kills such as birds and rabbits, as hunting was no longer a viable occupation and it declined when the tribals became agricultural serfs chained to absentee proprietors and money lenders.

The day before my departure from the ashram, I witnessed a tribal funeral. Some distance away from the ashram amongst an assembly of huge boulders was a bonfire surrounded by musicians heavily thumping their drums and blowing pipes. Many people squatted in the open rocky area in the scorching heat, some just laughing amongst themselves. I began to wonder if it was a funeral when suddenly a boy began crying loudly. Incense was sprinkled on the burning twigs and afterwards a small group circled the pyre. Then two of the mourners who carried burning torches ignited parts of the fire that were not already alight with the sweet smelling flames. Later, there were incantations within the small circling family groups. Then suddenly they all departed. I have always found the Hindu type of funeral with an exposed pyre far less depressing than the disappearing closed coffin witnessed in a western style crematorium.

I was glad to leave Bhai as I found him hard to talk to and once whilst seated at a table with Indian guests, he was asked, 'Who is she?' after introducing everyone else.

In Ahmedabad, I visited Gandhi's ashram situated by the dried up pre-monsoon Sabarmati river. This ashram was originally established by Gandhi in 1917. Intermittently, he stayed there until 1930 and departed for the Dandi Salt March with a vow not to return to Sabarmati until India got her freedom. The salt march was a symbolic gesture against British rule and more specifically against the imposed salt fare. (Sabarmati was dedicated to the untouchables or Harijans (Children of God) as Gandhi liked to call them. This was a label hated by many people as too patronising. I found the ashram had a commercialised atmosphere. The Mahatma's simple hut looked out of place amongst the modern concrete buildings. My impressions were not helped by the local ex- Servas man who after my polite 'Namaste', mumbled that he was no longer a member. Bhai had advised me to visit the character and that I just wanted to chat, perhaps he thought I was just another western drop-out.

It was an awful bus journey from Gandhigram to Kalol then onto Mansa to Gram Bharati. One had to kick and shove oneself onto these buses and aggressive natures emerge as a form of survival. The pre monsoon soporific air did not matter although the buses were windowless but were equipped with blinds that were only pulled down in a dust storm or if it was raining. If the entire aisle was crammed to capacity, then one forgot about circulating air. Apart from the most agile passengers on these rural buses, there was small opportunity of obtaining a seat because small boys would climb into the bus through the windows if they were unbarred or via the driver's seat. It was the survival of the fittest and God help the lame or old. Adding to the general confusion were the villagers who insisted on bringing all their possessions in huge bundles that did not always manage to reach the roof rack.

Gram Bharati was partly founded by my new friend P in 1958 as yet another experiment in Gandhi's concept of Basic Education for more than three hundred children. As usual, most of these children wanted white collar jobs. If many of these students took up agricultural work for life, it will only be because they could not get more favourable jobs.

Sri P was a member of the local proprietor Thakur subcaste who believed that they were originally Rajputs. They were no longer a ruler caste in the northern area of Gujarat but they still retained the mental superiority of the former rulers. Many Thakurs had no means of livelihood hence they still acted like feudals. As erstwhile landowners they refused to take up agriculture echoing the situation found in parts of rural Rajasthan. Unlike many of the Brahmins, Thakurs did not value intellectual work, consequently few of them entered educational establishments where they could have trained as administrators or teachers. Because of these factors, Sri P informed me that this former 'martial race' took to 'dacoity' or gangsterism. Under British rule many local Thakurs were labelled as 'Criminal Tribes' so the government attempted to regulate their activities. Part of the crime wave took the form of illicit hooch in a state like Gujarat, which was one of India's 'dry' prohibition areas.

Gram Bharati, like most ashram schools boarded its students in hostel with the aim of blending the castes together with the tribals. Industries such as rope making from jute had been taken up by widows and jobless women in Amrapar village. Another project was a potters' co-operative through which the co-op sold bricks and roof tiles. Another co-op made cement pipes needed for irrigation. They had established a model dairy to encourage famers to keep cattle rather than buffaloes. Looking at the children, Sri Patel said 'we know their parents and grandparents, how many fields they have got.'

I decided to head for north Gujarat including Kutch, which was close to the Pakistan border of Sind Province.

Chapter Seventeen

In Defence of the Cow and the Remittance Village

By bus to Vadnagar to meet old friend Dr Joshi, an allopathic doctor who established a hospital for one hundred patients. Formerly, he had practised in Bombay as a private practitioner and later trained as an eye specialist before joining Vinoba's Bhoodan campaign.

We walked to a Jain temple inhabited by several Jain monks. Some of these monks had never married and others had joined after they had raised a family during their Vanprast stage of life. One nun had been deposited by her parents in the temple at the age of six. Both monks and nuns dressed in white cloth and once or twice a year they all did penance by pulling out their hair and beard strand by strand. Somebody was an expert at this so unnecessary pain was avoided. One monk informed me that it could be done in a few hours only. Their pilgrim centre was situated on either side of the temple with one side for each sex as they were forbidden to mix. Jain monks and nuns had to travel around the countryside for about eight months every year. They could preach if they wanted but not all were academically inclined and unlike some Christian orders, they were not allowed to remain isolated from the larger community nor did they involve themselves in social work of any type.

Like the monks, Dr Joshi had dedicated his life to an ideal, namely to cow protection. Prior to my visit, he had travelled to Bombay to take part in cow protection campaigns. Western medical training had not displaced a deep respect for Gou Mata, (Mother Cow).

I travelled by train to Surendranagar, a typical dirty, small town with markets galore under a sea of red pantile roofs. My bicycle rickshaw puller peddled me to Wadhwan in the old part of Surendranagar in order to meet Sri Vyas, a former clerk from Kenya who had lost his job through Africanisation. His friend Sri Trivedi had a job advocating post office savings. Here, I met the elder brother of Bhai, the Servas secretary named Jayantibhai Parekh who was a retired language teacher. His character was unlike his extrovert brother, having a gentler disposition.

At one end of Surendranagar stood Bal ashram or Children's ashram, which was formerly known as Hindu Brahmacharya ashram, a conservative Hindu title symbolic of former attitudes to orphans because it literally meant Hindus who were chaste and kept lives of total self denial. The original centre was opened in about 1920. Until the present leaders took over, the orphans were expected to go out and beg for a living. No self respect or mutual co-operation was developed. In 1980 the husband and wife team who ran the place were a fantastic pair. The stocky white-bearded Nagjivaibhai Desai with his cheerful disposition belied a shrewd, hard working man. His bespectacled wife Shantibhen was slightly built but equally tough. She had faced incredible opposition from her father when she announced that she wanted to marry fellow primary school teacher Nagjivaibhai. Her community was Jain and he came from an impoverished community of shepherds. 'Love marriages' were still quite rare in India when, as in this case, none of the parents had played any part in the marriage arrangements. For twenty years, Shantiben's father had cut her off socially but as his death approached, he visited the ashram and witnessed the work being done and finally accepted his son-in-law. It is hard for a westerner to imagine what happens to an Indian who makes such a decision to marry against their parents' wishes. Such action disgraces the whole family and may even affect any other sibling's chances in marriage. Shame is the end result.

No physical punishment was used by staff and I have never been in such a place which resonated with such love and co-operation and at the same time had so much vibrancy. Shantibhen's own teenage boy Muni was severely mentally handicapped and her family and friends pressurised her into sending him into a home but she refused and as a result he was cared for by everyone.

The ashram had its own primary school attached to the main complex of buildings and they held a folk dancing session one day a month. One local dance performed was a kite dance and one in imitation of the peacock. Later on was an extraordinary dance where the children used amazing techniques of facial expression while chanting in Gujarati 'My mother, my toy does not take food or drink nor bath nor play with me. What can I do? Oh doll, you good doll, you come and explain to me. Oh little doll, you good doll, we are going to the sky and moon.' The doll said 'No'. The words sound corny but I was intrigued by the miming and accompanying gestures. The next day the older students performed a Garba stick dance while wearing yellow waistcoats and white pantaloons plus large green kerchiefs around their heads and waists.

Shantibhen took me to a rural centre situated in Old Wadhwan town. Formerly women's education was negligible with cases of prostitution leading to suicides by destitutes. The pupils at the centre were kept in contact with village life by attending a nearby village primary school. As at Bal Ashram, the staff assisted in arranging marriages for those wanting it. Also in Wadhwan, I visited an old unfurnished palace built by the local Maharajah. It was a sandstone structure with lovely fluted arches. The bulk of the surrounding buildings consisted of one storey cottages with pantile roofs. The houses were dark and local custom appeared to be that all the kitchens were surrounded by barred windows and doors without external walling.

North Gujarat has an atmosphere all of its own. Called Kutch, it has a separate language Kutchi. With a letter of introduction, I arrived at Mahdapur, a wealthy village as twenty per cent of its inhabitants worked in the United Kingdom and Middle East, so they sent remittances home. Noticing a group of reasonably well-dressed women queuing near piles of bricks, I was told that they were waiting to see if there were building jobs. Women worked on all the building sites as they do in many parts of India and they were paid on a daily basis and of course there was little job security as few were unionised.

In Mahdapur, I stayed with another family with the common Gujarati name Patel. Mrs Patel, as an incoming daughter-in-law had a degree in philosophy and was much better educated than her husband. Although she possessed a Bombay University degree, she did not possess any books. I deduced that the aim of her BA was partly to obtain a husband as many newspaper marriage adverts placed by prospective groom's or bride's families stipulated the level of education required. Thus the husband could say 'my wife is educated'. She was not required to prove it unless she had to supplement his income. No intellectual conversation is expected between husband and wife in most business families. Mrs Patel's husband refused to let her work. Her home was Bombay and she missed the cinema more than anything. Within the marriage, she adapted to the in-laws not vice versa, whereas for her husband life remained more or less the same.

At nearby Bhuj, I visited a tastelessly decorated palace, which had nondescript glassware and hideous English china dogs. Of more interest was a disused bat infested mausoleum near the town centre, which had been built to commemorate sixteen wives of one king who had all committed suicide. In Rajasthan and Gujarat, this practice of collective immolation called Jawar as opposed to Sati, which is individual immolation practiced by widows on their husbands funeral pyres, was historically quite common. The warrior caste Rajput women undertook this mass suicide because they were afraid of being raped by Muslim conquerors. In India, as sometimes elsewhere, a raped woman is often believed to be an accomplice in such atrocities and her shame is greater than if she was dead. A few carved stone figures covered in vermilion stood out amongst the gloom. A nearby building appeared to be the home of a deaf and dumb man who had gone mad. He kept making wild gestures and grunts while his sole pal, a half starved dog dozed.

Mrs Patel arranged for me to visit Mahdapur schools, which because of the overseas remittances were well stocked with visual aids. Then I went to an ashram called Kutch Mahila Kendra, which was a girls' orphanage. It was owned by prominent village figures under a Hindu temple trust. Inside all the walls were bare and a garlanded photo of the founder on the office wall formed a break in monotony. Some of the mothers stayed one year with their illegitimate offspring and then left them forever. A greater form of torture is hard to imagine as there is no way whereby illegitimate children might stay with single mothers in India.

As Mahdapur is near the Pakistan border of Sind, the locals picked up Pakistan television, which happened, in 1980, to be more interesting than its Indian counterpart Doordashan. This was to repeat partly because Pakistan had depended heavily upon foreign aid to set up her television network whereas India had developed her own network with her own technology.

The Patels were followers of the Hindu reform movement founded by Swami Narayan. I went with Mrs Patel to the ornate temple, which was surrounded by forbidding-looking widows dressed in cheap, drab maroon coloured saris. It was the time of the Kutchi New Year. The Patels spoke Gujarati and though settled in Kutch for some generations, did not speak Kutchi because they viewed Kutchi as some sort of inferior dialect. At secondary school, the Kutchi speakers were taught in Gujarati and they were amused when I suggested that schools should give Kutchi some recognition. Some of the school teachers I met in the temple compound looking surprised when I enquired as to whether any of them followed Gandhi's ideas on Basic Education on reference to manual work by pupils. One chimed in 'we employ servants for that". They gave no reply when I asked if all the kids would have servants when they grew up.

I went to the house of two brother artists who designed pictures of Hindu gods and saints for home and temple altars. My immediate impression as I climbed up onto the second storey verandah was that the paintings were gaudy in appearance but closer up they were quite beautiful with strong contrasting colours of dark blue and green against gold paint. The colours of the gods were attractive owing to an embossed effect made by producing tiny blobs of white paint and painting gold over them. The brothers were not hereditary painters by subcaste but had learned the art through family connections.

Leaving Kutch, I travelled south, still within Gujarat to Rajkot where I visited the local branch of the worldwide Ramakrishna Mission. The swami in charge was very welcoming and showed me the ayurvedic and homoeopathic dispensaries. The mission ran a gurukul school and hostel, teaching what they deemed to be the best of Indian values. Their temple was new and built as a magnificent sandstone structure with a conglomeration of forms relating to Buddhist, Islamic and other religious styles of architecture. Inside, it had statues of the Bengali mystic Ramakrishna, a passionate devotee of goddess Kali for whom he worked as a temple priest in Calcutta. Another statue was of his chief disciple Hindu scholar Swami Vivekananda who had attended the ecumenical parliament of World Religions in Chicago in the 1880's. Murals depicting Vivekananda's life were designed by students of the Baroda School of Art. One mural also showed a lake with representatives from different religious groups taking water symbolising the separate paths in search of truth. Afterwards, I had lunch with the monks, then collected two volumes in Gujarati of the sayings of Sri Ramakrishna, and gave them as a gift to my friends at Bal Ashram.

From Rajkot, I travelled by bus to the small Gujarati port of Dwarka and entered Dwarkanath temple dedicated to Lord Krishna who is supposed to have had sixteen thousand wives. Formerly, non Hindus or untouchables were forbidden inside. Once inside, the strangest thing happened. I was informed that all visitors had to take an oath in front of a magistrate swearing allegiance to Hinduism. An obnoxious little man with a nasty piece of paper entitled 'Declaration Form – I hereby declare that I have adopted Hinduism' or 'I have devotion for Lord Krishna' or 'I have faith and respect in Hindu religion. Dated this day of ......' As far as I was concerned, an atheist has the right to enter a religious shrine as long as he shows respect, as only a Superior Being knows the innermost thoughts of humanity. I had a friendly argument on this matter with the temple official who then added that a Muslim archaeologist was forbidden entrance some years back. On signing the bit about having faith and respect in the Hindu religion, I entered the temple and during worship, a conch was sounded and a bowl of water was given a circular movement around the image. This was followed by another circular movement of the sacred fire conducted by the temple priest. The overhanging temple bell was continually struck throughout the ceremony and added to this was the constant beating of drums.

Just outside the temple, I bumped into a little character locally known as Rangoonwalla because he had worked for years in Burma. He was in a depressed condition and suffered from severe rheumatism. He left the United Kingdom because of that ailment and later spent over twenty years in Rangoon in the travel business. At Burmese Independence, he thought he had no future in that country and returned to India. He invited me to his tiny house situated up a narrow alleyway. Here he displayed faded photos of his Morris Oxford car in Burma. It was sad to see his demise. He hated India, especially 'the behaviour of the people'. I had just explained my experiences within the temple and the teasing boys of Dwarka. Rangoonwalla had the tendency, found in some Indians, to glorify the people of the west. He offered me chapattis and lentils and we bussed to

Ocka Point and took a boat to Bait Island to see a temple. Rangoonwalla explained that while Krishna had lived on earth, he founded Dwarka as his capital after he had fled from Mathura (remains near modern Delhi) because he had been attacked by the King of Magadha. Dwarka was a major Hindu pilgrimage centre. Later, I bade farewell to Rangoonwalla.

I travelled along the coast eastwards to Porbandar, the birthplace of Mohandas Karamchand Gandhi, otherwise known as the Mahatma or Great Soul. The sea was grey and Porbander had a rundown appearance. Gandhi was born into a middle class family of merchants. The house looked insignificant as it was surrounded by a large rectangular memorial building with a temple and upstairs museum. The Mahatma would not have approved of the lavish expenditure in building the temple with its huge blocks of marble pillars. The house itself was whitewashed with green painted doors and windows. The place looked bare and the only mark worth remembering was the age old Sanskrit symbol of well being, the Swastika (Sanskrit word Svastika-Svasti, well being – sv, good – asti, he is). The sign was painted onto the floor, supposedly in the spot where Gandhi was born. His wife Kasturba's house stood nearby in a rapid state of decay. Like many local merchant houses, it was tall and narrow with many rooms. It too looked bare apart from a few photos on a downstairs wall. From one depressing place to another, my little rented room facing an even bleaker sea.

Chapter Eighteen

A Portuguese Backwater and a Pioneering Spirit

An interesting bus trip to Una town near the miniscule former Portuguese territory of Diu island. The countryside was of a bleak sandstone appearance with scattered, well-built dry stone walls, which unfortunately were often covered with an awful concrete mixture. Wandering shepherds dressed in white jodhpurs and strange high-waisted cotton shirts, drove their sheep on the roadside. The bus stopped at Harshad village near the seashore and all the bus passengers disembarked and went to pay homage to Harshad Mata, a local mother goddess whose home was in a nearby temple. This little temple had tiled walls with peacock and flower decorations. Outside a solitary vulture devoured a carcass. This area had a good number of flamingoes and there was talk of starting a flamingo reserve in this part of Gujarat.

I spent one night in Una at an awful guesthouse. The walls of my cubicle were made of cardboard, which did not reach the roof. On one side resided some irritating youths who deliberately kept me awake the whole night by attempting to peep over the wall and through any cracks in the door. This was always the risk of cheap lodgings. I always took the precaution of attempting to seal up any door cracks because of peeping toms. I always carried my own padlock and key, as I did not trust many of the smaller lodging houses' staff. Most Indian doors were double with a sliding rod so a padlock could be used anywhere. The managers of this hotel never offered any help even though the disturbance must have kept everybody else awake.

After the dreary little town of Una, Diu was a merciful release. It was green, unlike the parched land in most of Saurashtra. Many men still wore the tight-fitting jodhpurs and short loose shirts gathered above the waist. On their heads, they wore white turbans. Women also wore the same form of dress I had seen in Kutch in the northern part of Gujarat. It was a form of an open backed bodice. Their arms were heavily tattooed in blue.

I introduced myself to a Roman Catholic priest, a distinguished looking man with a goatee beard. Formerly his church had belonged to the Jesuits. He took me onto the roof and pointed to a typical white Portuguese style church, now disused, which was once occupied by Portuguese soldiers. Pointing in another direction, he noted a former Franciscan church, now a hospital. Elsewhere, a former church cum hospital built by St John Hospitallers was now part of a cemetery.

At one end of the gentle coast of Diu stands the sixteenth century Portuguese solid stone fort. This Portuguese stronghold and the rest of Diu were 'liberated' by the Indian troops in 1961, thus all the former Portuguese territories including Goa became part of the Indian Union. There was still a Portuguese patois spoken by some of the Christians. One small boy taking me around one of the churches spoke English, Gujarati, Hindi and some Portuguese. The church was in a dreadful state of decay, especially the once-magnificent plaster and woodwork. The backcloth of the altar depicted Balthazar's Feast and was carved by Portuguese artisans but the carvings showed both Hindu and western influences. There was still an incredible array of statues befitting a Portuguese church. The whole place was covered in dust, giving it a museum-like appearance. The church authorities had requested government aid but without success. The Catholic priest was opposed to the demand for Diu being a part of Gujarat state, which surrounds it. This was because automatically, it would get the status of a village and might remain undeveloped. The Portuguese remnants would become even more vestigial than now within a sea of Hinduism.

The fort battlements held original sixteenth century canons and anti-aircraft guns from the second World War, all going rusty. The small museum near the fort was formerly a chapel and it contained mainly broken slabs depicting various Portuguese coats of arms. One solitary state of Vasco De Gama stood looking somewhat forlorn observing piles of cannonballs long since unfired.

I purchased the English language Indian Express, which had the headlines screaming out 'a German girl marries rickshaw puller'. This German was a former music teacher who spoke no local languages. Hard to imagine what she had in common with a poor rickshaw puller who spoke only Gujarati. Perhaps she married him for a gimmick. A bus ride through the Diu countryside showed scattered flocks of flamingoes and clusters of upright gravestones. The stones had carvings of warriors on horseback. Some were covered in vermilion, reminding me of those sinister figures in the bat-stinking mausoleum in Kutch.

For a small town, Diu had a super abundance of liquor shops, a strange sight because the district was surrounded by prohibition-ridden Gujarat state. Naturally, lots of smuggling went on. None of the local bars looked enticing for me as a solitary female. They were not of the Portuguese taverna style such as I would find in Goa, only full of local yobs. There were a number of walls which had 'up with pot' scrawled on them.

Opposite the island of Diu lies Ghoghla on the mainland. I travelled in a small sailing vessel crammed with women and pots. My companions, the fisher people gazed at me with unsmiling eyes. At Ghoghla, there was a colourful fish market with fisher women selling small crabs, eels, flat fish and tiny silver fish. Walking up one street, I came across an open doorway leading into a tiny dark room crowded with men and women making beedies or country cigarettes, then packing them. Beedies do not have salt petre, so one has to continuously puff on them as they continually go out like western 'roll ups". No doubt, the workers were operating on slave labour wages even by Indian standards and owing to the lack of light, most of them would end up with diminishing eyesight.

Hearing the sound of chanting female voices, I followed and came upon one street blocked by a funeral party consisting of groups of women forming a circle and beating their breasts in time to a song they were chanting. In the centre of the circle on the ground was a woven mat. At intervals, frenzied women threw themselves onto the mat in apparent agony accompanied by continued breast-beating. One advantage of keening as a ritual is that it does allow for open expression of grief and must act as a cathartic, even when assisted by professional mourners. Whereas in countries such as Britain, we are embarrassed to show great emotion in our grief. We have buried the ritual without creating a substitute apart from professional bereavement counsellors.

Further up the scruffy lane, I ventured towards a potter turning his wheel inside a decrepit hut. His wife was firing the clay and in front of her were rows of newly-manufactured vessels, many of them tiny oil lamps for use in religious rituals. In one metal bucket, she had shaped a clay oven. In addition, there was a newly made three-sided oven of the type found in many rural Indian kitchens. Interestingly enough, I had been informed that there was 'nothing to see in Ghoghla' but with open eyes, the traveller can discover anything.

Later in the day I returned to Diu and at its local park, there stood a memorial dedicated to the Indian freedom fighters against Portuguese control. 'In memory of the gallant and brave soldiers of the twenty Battalion, the Rajput Regiment (Jodhpur) who were killed in action on the 18th December 1961 during operation Vija for the liberation of Diu island.'

I met an Anglo-Indian family who invited me to their home. They became cagey when I enquired about their Indian origin, 'all we know is that we have European ancestors.' Considering that the woman who told me this was darker than many Indians were, I thought this an odd reply. What puzzled me here was that one would have thought that the father's side, usually the European side in these cases, would be forgotten because the mothers would have been the ones to, in most cases, keep their children if these offspring were not put in institutions or adopted by others. Many Hindu mothers may well have abandoned any illegitimate offspring but it was hard to get the true facts from them. Their answers would be less puzzling if they were living outside India. On entering this Eurasian household, I enquired as to whether I should remove my shoes. They replied with an amusing expression 'we do not follow these customs.' The couple had a desire to migrate to Australia as many Anglo-Indians have done in the past after India became free. Of course, India was never 'home' even before the British left.

Once again, I visited the dilapidated church, which was beyond repair. It did look as if Cromwell's horses had been stabled inside. The entrance was up some steeply rising steps, formerly elegant, now covered in grass, unloved and forgotten, rather like Diu itself.

I left Diu and departed for the interior of Gujarat on a bus where a half-hearted attempt had been made by state customs officials to search for liquor. I arrived at Tulsi Shayam, a Hindu pilgrimage centre situated deep in the Saurashtra Gir forests of south Gujarat. Its temple was dedicated to Lord Krishna. Outside the main pilgrimage period, the place was deadly quiet. I met a Maharashtrian bus controller nicknamed 'Dada' who hailed from Pune. As he was nearing retirement, he offered to be sent to work in Tulsi Shayam as nobody else would keep the job in this remote area. I noted that it was an excellent job for a man of his age. His English was quite good although he said that for twenty years, he had not conversed in it. He had served under British officers during the war and had picked up the language that way. He finished by saying 'now even graduates in English often cannot speak it.'

I ate at the caste Hindu dharmsala where we all squatted on the floor in long rows with individual plates of course bajra roti (millet bread) and dal (split lentils). This was frugal fare but nourishing. Unusually for a religious country, where food is concerned, the floor was dirty with cigarettes and paper. A peeling picture of Nandi (Lord Siva's sacred bull mount) was pasted on one wall.

I met Dada again and he showed me the tiny Krishna temple, which had a spotlessly clean dharmsala (hostel) for the non caste untouchables or scheduled castes. These poor people had been refused entry to the main caste Hindu temple and hostelry, though as I witnessed, it was quite alright for a cow to pass the dining group unannounced. I decided that the scheduled castes had the best view from the dharmsala and it was only marred by the concrete roof of the modern bus station. Dada lived temporarily in a small room in the bus station surrounded by books and papers plus mosquitoes and creepy crawlies.

I went by bus to Amreli to visit some Gandhian workers at Sarvodaya ashram. Unfortunately I had a long wait at the bus station. In India, railway stations were fine for killing the waiting hours whereas the bus stations often attracted the worse elements of the public. While awaiting the Babapur bus, I was surrounded by a large group of grinning leering youths. One peered right into my face. While sitting on the bench, two of them sat either side of me. A boy on the left began to touch my duffel bag and exclaimed mockingly 'you are foreigner, where are you from?' I replied sarcastically 'Albania'. 'Where are you going?' he asked. The crowd got nearer. One elderly man nearby offered only further grins. 'Do you like India?' one chimed. 'No,' I lied. I became just a little afraid so I leapt into the ticket office and even then, a few bold specimens crept in and continued teasing.

It was a fact that 'Eve teasing' had become a national pastime for some youths. Even Delhi buses sported the caption 'No smoking and no Eve teasing.' They were only poor, cowardly yobs with as much variety as the segments of an earthworm. Just before sitting on the bus, I slapped the face of one of the yobs and only a few days before I had hit the face of two lads at Una bus station. It is strange that individuals who you meet once in a lifetime have to bring out the worse behaviour on both sides! I found myself reflecting upon the smooth-talking convent educated sari clad girls in Indian government air conditioned tourist offices saying demurely 'how do you like our India?' My good humour had not been aided by the fact that at Amreli bus stand, two useless policemen were standing by while I was being teased. They also stood by lamely watching the hordes stampede onto the bus without any attempt at queuing. It was awful when one could not rely on so-called agents of law and order. Even when I got on the bus, two youths continued to bang on my window, and no other bus passengers told them to go away.

With mighty relief, I arrived at the ashram and received a good welcome from the Purohits. This Brahmin name denotes that their ancestors were purohits, hereditary temple priests. They ran an educational institution for scheduled caste children. Meena, their daughter, was a second year BA English student at Bhavnagar College. She only had to read five English books in one year. Her teacher told her 'no need to buy or read a book, just read the notes.' Whatever happened to Renaissance man? They did not ever have to study any Shakespeare. Obviously, standards varied all over the country.

I found that many female students in India were experts in giggling. Superficially, they seemed like the women in Pride and Prejudice but at least Jane Austen's women were often competent in music and painting. I had met many arts graduates in India who never read a book, the main thing students got into the newspapers for was 'mass copying' or mass walkouts, or intimidating invigilators at examinations. Perhaps I was being too pessimistic, things were never too rosy in my own country.

The ashram farm bred beautiful Gujarati red Gir cattle and it owned an enormously handsome bull of that breed. While showing me around, Purohit told me that during the struggle against the British, he spent seven years as an underground subversive after he had blown up a railway line in Lahore (now in Pakistan). When he began the ashram, while clearing all the undergrowth, he killed about twenty eight snakes each day. The snakes only appeared at night.

Purohitji took me by village bus, which was more like a battered shoe held together by elastic. He wanted me to meet an old Muslim scholar of the enlightened school. The distinguished-looking Ismail Dada was that form of traditional scholar who is a rarity in modern universities. He studied at Gujarat College and had both Scottish and Persian teachers. Before going to Pune to study at India's then only agricultural college, he had developed a deep love of literature. He met Bengalis, Burmese and other groups at Pune and he believed that even scientists should know about literature. While discussing the former princely states of what was then Gujarat, he mentioned that the former tiny state of Jafrabad once had a black prince. Blacks were imported from east Africa to Jambura, a small village in the interior of the Gir forest prior to independence. I had seen many black Makranis in Pakistan who were descendants of slaves sold by the Arabs. Historians and others have forgotten the millions of Africans transported to the east.

Dadaji had studied the Hindu Gita in seven translations including Sanskrit, which was unusual for a Muslim. He was a keen gardener and had none of the 'educated mass' dislike of manual work. He showed me his spider lily, date palms and bougainvillea. His own son was lucky enough to be taught by his father and his wife was a Pathan originating from far away North West frontier in present day Pakistan. Ismail Dada was indeed a rare specimen with catholic tastes and like a good scholar, he saw the interconnectedness of all things.

I travelled onto Bhavnagar on a winding route to meet Servas host Arun C Popat, a very pale-complexioned man. Just after my arrival, we went for a walk and came to a temple surrounded by groups of cows while mounds of cut grass were stacked at one end. The temple made money out of selling fodder to the pilgrims who fed the cows. Arunji took me to Vaneeta ashram, a superior type of girls' home run like a boarding school.

The students lived in spartan-looking dormitories and appeared to have no possessions. Newspaper reading was compulsory and this was followed by writing down the main items of news. Not a bad idea.

The local Montessori school was excellent. Arunji's brother taught here. The building was well decorated and there were painted pictures of Krishna as a child and assorted animals. The pupils played with specially designed Montessori equipment combining work and play, having a higher teacher pupil ratio than most primary schools. They performed a folk song connected with Krishna and the cowherds depicted in Hindu mythology. One little girl exclaimed, 'He loved cows.' The place had a relaxed atmosphere, unlike many poorer Indian schools where children were not encouraged to think as individuals, even in the best sense of the term. The Montessori school even encouraged gardening and spinning. It was founded by Sri Gijubhai Badheka, the father of the Indian Montessori system. The main problem for these children in the future would be to find equivalent enlightened colleges of higher education apart from the usual dreary degree mills. The Montessori system stresses mutual self-service rather than the attainment of pieces of paper for the rat race.

Arunji later said, 'You must meet Mannubhai Bhatt, one of our leading Gandhians.' Eventually I came face to face with a tall, skinny man with a crew cut and clad in homespun cotton shirt and shorts. In 1939, Mannubhai, alongside other port workers who were skilled smiths and carpenters founded Shishuvihar, which became a huge children's playground with an open air theatre. He refused all government aid. He too followed Montessori lines and classes were held for older boys in blacksmithery, carpentry and handling electrical goods.

Arunji arranged for me to see Vikas Gruha Rescue Home for Women. Most of these women ended up there via the police in collaboration with neighbours and family. The main reasons involved marital discord and 'moral danger'. The latter applied to the stigmatisation of unwed mothers, deserted women and the frequently victimised Hindu widows. One high caste woman had married an untouchable and they had to flee from their home area. Her husband attempted to return and was murdered. This woman I saw in the dispensary with tattoos all over her arms. In-law, matters were a recurrent problem in arranged marriages, especially between an incoming daughter and her husband's mother. In parts of northern India, there had been an increase in battered wives who had committed the unmentionable crime of not bringing enough dowries to their greedy in-laws. Women could be exploited economically and sexually, of course India is far from being alone in this matter. The dowry system often depended on supply and demand, whoever paid the most dowry within the same subcaste, often got the husband.

Part of the same institution also catered for orphans. Boys could be adopted because they would eventually support a family and a boy's family did not pay dowry. In addition, the religious purpose makes it easier because a Hindu boy, if an eldest son, lights the father's funeral pyre. A daughter cannot do this. Fostering is not popular in India because of its ambiguity and unlike the modern trend in northern Europe, even adoption is rarely publically proclaimed. Families involved maintain secrecy, not only because of the stigma of childlessness but also because of the importance of genealogy. The best that could be done for girl orphans was to arrange marriages for them, even then, they could only marry into low caste families because no large dowry would be demanded since the charitable establishment could not pay it. Finally, a suicide prevention service was also run where mainly women came for counselling.

Arunji dragged me to a Giants International evening. It was a home grown version of the Lyons Club. All members appeared to be self made men, each ready to proclaim themselves as social workers, the most overused term in India. Under its umbrella, cow protection workers and donating businessmen rubbed shoulders. Many of these 'Giants men' claimed a decoration to their name. All sported the usual Indian emblem of affluence, the potbelly. It was a fact that Giants did finance several social service projects but I found something shallow and vulgar about these men. Total philistines. 'Why do you not learn our national language?' one man pontificated. I was attempting to learn Urdu. But he was the type of Indian who would never even attempt to mix into another culture, let alone travel alone for years on end such as I was doing. I was glad to see the back of the conceited middle class bores.

Arunji and family took me by scooter to Gogha, a seaside place near Bhavnagar on the Indian Ocean. To see some of the non- westernised, more stuffy middle class at the seaside was a treat. The women went out in their very best saris and the kids were clothed in spotless clothes. Father was in his favourite shirt, which on no account must be removed in the sunshine. They were unable to prepare themselves for a day at the beach such as a westerner might. No blankets, sheets or buckets and spades or adaptable clothes. Few Indians ate on beaches except fishermen and the more westernised elite. Even Arunji's kids were afraid to get sand in their clothes. My attempts at playing in the sand met with little response. Arunji's wife looked distinctly uncomfortable anywhere near the beach. The day had a good ending when we were all invited for tea and were offered sweet treacle stuff served in saucers.

I bade farewell to the Popats and departed for Ahmedabad, the capital of Gujarat state. 'Brides are not for burning,' declared my favourite magazine India Today. Bride burning was put down as a Punjabi disease. It is true that many husbands are spineless and live under mother's threats but then their wives are often total strangers. So why support one's wife against one's mother? India Today went on to say that in 1975, over three hundred wives were burnt to death, kerosene being a popular way of getting rid of daughters-in-law. Women in India may be insecure until they have sons. The son may be her only safeguard and through him the extended family.

Ahmedabad appeared on first impression to be a fairly clean city. It was founded in 1411 by Ahmad Shah I, a member of a dynasty of Muslim Kings who ruled in Gujarat. The legend goes that while he camped by the Sabarmati river, he noticed that the rabbits on the riverbank, instead of bolting in terror, confronted his dog defiantly. Believing this was a gifted land, on the advice of a Muslim saint, Ahmed Khattu Ganj Baksh, he laid the city's foundations.

I made my way to the Tribal Research and Training Institute. I had a meeting with Sri Haku Shah, the leading worker for tribal interests. He told me that he got his intellectual stimulation from his journeys abroad. He heavily condemned the Gandhian's handling of some of the tribals, for example, barring alcohol and certain modes of dress. I recounted my talk with Voraji regarding his approval of sari-clad tribal women. Haku told me of an incident in southern Gujarat connected with a wooden musical instrument like a saxophone. This instrument was often the focal point of tribal ceremonies and some zealous Gandhians using Hinduised tribals of the Dobru from the Choudhary community, collected these instruments and publically destroyed them. Another thing that vexed the Gandhians was too much mixing of men and women, which upset Hindu orthodoxy.

What the Gandhians, most of whom are born Hindu, were objecting to were not forms of worship but modes of social intercourse. One group concerning the research group was the Siddhis who are negroid in appearance and Ismail Dada had briefly discussed them with me beforehand. As in Pakistan, most of the negroid Indian groups are also Muslims, their ancestors long since converted back in East Africa.

I had a row in a bookshop when I saw that a book I wanted entitled Embroidery of Kutch and Saurashtra was marked at Rs40 and the bookseller demanded Rs200. I told him what he could do with his book. My host, a journalist on the Indian Express who had taken pity on me after I had sent in a letter complaining of 'Eve teasing', said that the bookseller was a self-made man whose business was based on sex magazines. Outside the shop, I purchased some delicious chico juice. Chico is a round fruit looking like a potato and it has a mild coffee taste.

This journalist had spent four years in Canada as a student. As this was Ramadan, the month of fasting, he and his family, as strict Muslims, were up at three in the morning to eat before sunrise. His two sisters spent most of their time in the kitchen area and they must have been puzzled as to who I was. If I had been a boy, they could not have spoken to me even if they had known my language, yet it was acceptable for their brother to speak to me. His sitting room had books on Sufism, politics and literature. His sisters were not educated after basic schooling. This was the Muslim district of Ahmedabad. We went to some mosques, which displayed strong Hindu inspiration, especially in the pillars and ceilings, whilst the bulk of the buildings retained their Islamic simplicity.

Before leaving Ahmedabad, I visited a remarkable organisation S.E.W.A (Self Employed Women Association) started by Ela Bhatt, a truly pioneering spirit. Unfortunately, my interview with her was cancelled as my visit coincided with an election of shop stewards, which accounted for the noise coming from the nearby textile labour building. The self-employed women whom S.E.W.A. was involved with were not the professional fraternity but those at the bottom of the economic heap such as handcart pullers, vegetable vendors, fire wood packers and scrap metal merchants. The executive committee itself had representatives such as fish vendors and used garment dealers. It lacked any mark of elitism.

Ahmedabad had a profusion of handcart pullers, who were usually two struggling creatures dragging a long cart loaded with rags, even concrete. The men or women were always bent double and it was hardly surprising that most of them got severe backache. Even their babies were with them, sleeping in a cradle tied beneath the cart. A thousand women in the city worked as junksmiths who collected iron and wood scrap. I was shown some metal bucket makers in different areas of the town. Used garment dealers constituted the bulk of S.E.W.A's membership. These women with baskets of utensils on their heads roamed in the middle class neighbourhoods to collect discarded clothes in exchange for steel scrap or crockery. After being repaired, these clothes were sold in the markets. S.E.W.A. claimed that the vendors were harassed by the police because of the shortage of space allocated to operate stalls. A number of women pot sellers were victimised by merchants who refused them work after they had been involved in strikes. Many were Muslim women and being in purdah, they were not permitted to seek employment outside their homes. S.E.W.A. began production units for quilt makers, which gave employment to some of the strikers.

Head loaders were brutally exploited, their head loads were carried to and from the wholesalers to retailers. For each trip, they were paid a pittance such as ten to twenty paise. (Rs1 = 10 paise). At the end of a slogging day in the heat, they would get the grand sum of Rs2-3 (in 1980). Female sand carriers were involved in the construction industry. They took sand from the riverbank and transported it on their donkeys to building contractors. The agarbatti (insence stick) industry employed many women to roll joss sticks at home on piece rate.

The S.E.W.A. co-op bank provided services involving credit. In addition, local problems such as difficulties people had recovering gold and silver jewellery from private money lenders. Legal aid was provided for those whose slums had been demolished. Social welfare benefits involved maternity benefit schemes, widowhood assistance schemes and crèches for children of vegetable vendors. There were also 'productivity raising' courses like cattle care for milk producers, upkeep of machines for tailors, food preserving for food vendors etc.

S.E.W.A. was one of the finest organizations I ever visited. It was democratic and gave encouragement to the formation of trade unions. Too many Gandhians were too reactionary to attack fundamental evils within the system.

Chapter Nineteen

From a Man of Letters to a Loveable Fanatic

After a brief rest at Gandhi Nidhi in New Delhi, I departed directly north to Haryana state for a second visit to Pattikalyana nature cure ashram.

One of the ashram's patients was a curious character called Ishwar Chandra, a self-taught man. He had just published a book called World Alphabets and it was based upon seventeen years work. Ishwarji had completed arduous journeys by bicycle across many lands and was only refused admission to Mauritius because he had no return ticket, so a kindly port official gave him a ride around the island on the back of his scooter. He then addressed gatherings in different places and raised money. I believed Ishwarji to be a free thinker but he liked the sound of his own voice too much so I wondered whether he ever learned from others.

Once he taught a Muslim boy yoga and did not care a damn for the more cranky Hindu fanatics who claimed that Ram lived twenty thousand years back. Alternatively, the 'Sanskrit is the mother of all languages brigade?' I added. His pamphlet depicted a photo of himself lecturing behind an old fashioned board with the caption 'I.C. Rahi from India on a study cum lecture tour of the world. Already covered forty thousand kilometres.' He published his own books because 'In India, a manuscript may sit in a publisher's office for years and then appear on the market under somebody else's name.' In 1936, he began his career as a boot polish boy. Certainly, in India, one was more likely to meet a greater variety of characters than in a confessional country such as Pakistan where individual ideas on philosophy and religion were less encouraged.

Razi Sahib invited me for a sojourn in his home state of Bihar for the post Ramadan festival of Id ul Fitr, which is celebrated when the new moon has been sighted. On the train to Muzaffarapur, a tea seller offered us a detailed description on how to cure bee stings. The injured party should gather a fistful of hashish and pulverise it between the palms to extract the juice, and then press it onto the sting followed by rubbing iron (a knife) on the leg. I was actually to get something like this treatment at a later date from an amateur medicine man up in the distant Himalayan foothills.

On the train, Razi Sahib met up with some old cronies and I watched amused at their continual bantering. Whenever anyone cracked a joke, he would shriek with laughter and shake hands with whoever was around him as if to signal the fact of his being a good comic.

On our arrival at Muzaffarapur in north Bihar, we went directly to one of his friend's houses. We were offered attar, which is based on fragrant oils extracted from various plants. In wealthy Muslim houses, this attar is rubbed onto one's clothes. These oils were soaked in a woollen substance and kept in tiny silver pots or boxes. Spirit perfumes were rarely used and they do not last so long.

During the Id-ul-Fitr festival throughout the day, there was a constant stream of visiting by men to each other's houses. Women's participation amounted to preparing the food and they were allowed out at night. The Muslim of either sex during the festival, and at other times, embraced a member of the same sex with a rigidly formal procedure. It was not the casual same-sex embracing that one sees among Latins and Slavs. There was no real touching of the bodies. Each party moved to the left, right and left again while the body was kept generally rigid and hands remained by the side. Then they would stand for a while holding hands. Only close relatives of the opposite sex embraced. Afterwards each guest was offered the favoured foods of the season, which were very sweet. Sevai is a fine vermicelli made of wheat flour and fried in ghee and saffron. I preferred phirni, which is a ground rice mixture served with pistachios, almonds and rose water. In these Muslim households, male guests would be served by either male servants or children of any sex below puberty. The domestic space for women to move around in within each house was limited and usually they were relegated to the worst areas and only men sat on verandahs. Being Razi Sahib's guest, I always sat with the men and was occasionally introduced to females, though knowing these families for years, Razi Sahib had never met any of the women.

I set off by train for a day visit to Vaishali in north Bihar named after King Vishal. It was once a capital of the Republic of Lichavis in the early seventh century B.C. That last 'pathfinder' of the Jains, Mahavir lived in this vicinity at roughly the same time as Gautama Buddha. Vaishali remains include an Ashoka pillar and stupa dating from the second century B.C. A sleepy looking rest house, which received few visitors, was surrounded by thatched huts with walls of horizontal and vertical bamboo poles. Biharis, like their Bengali neighbours are mainly rice eaters and the surrounding fields were growing only paddy.

Razi Sahib told me that before Partition, especially in what was called United Provinces (now U.P.or Uttar Pradesh) many cultured Hindus had consciously adopted features of Muslim culture, especially the Urdu language and its literature, which is mainly poetry. However, the Muslims only adopted Hindu culture unconsciously. The conversation drifted onto what he called 'the arrogance of Punjabis'. He related his experiences of them while visiting his relatives in Pakistan. He claimed that Indian Punjabis were less rough. Later on I heard of a counsellor who was kicked out of his home and lost his business as he had married a prostitute but through willpower had become wealthy again.

Just north of Muzaffarapur district is Champaran area. Here Gandhi began his campaign against British rule by backing landless labourers struggling against exploiting British indigo planters. The Muzaffarapur club was built as a place where these tough planters could come from 'up country' to relax. The building was a fine example of Disappointed Gothic both architecturally and in atmosphere. Razi Sahib was one of the few Indians formerly allowed into the club to play tennis, otherwise Britishers only could be members. Standing in one corner was an upright piano long unplayed. The bar was closed because of prohibition campaigns. An incongruous picture of Gandhi hung above one doorway. The club must have thrived on its weekend sessions of British planters. I was told of one old European hospital doctor, who as a young man had shaved off his wife's hair after accusing her of sleeping with fifty men, including his father and brother. He was expelled from the club!

Razi Sahib was formerly an advocate and he took me to the decrepit lawyers' rooms down at Muzaffarapur courts. The lawyers were not so well paid and looked shabbily dressed in their poor quality thin, shiny black jackets and often yellowing shirts. One chap had broken off to prostrate himself in prayer. Another character was a communist allopathic doctor and Urdu poet with a huge beard who expressed his desire to live in an ashram. All these Muslim lawyers who once worked with Razi Sahib continually teased him of being a Hindu. He often became annoyed with Muslims when in any competition between India and Pakistan, they went out in the streets with their radios on loud and began voicing support for Pakistan. In fact, many objections by Hindus to Muslims were based less on religion and more on the questionable loyalty some of them had to India. Why attack Hindu shops when Muslim fundamentalists attack the main mosque in Mecca? There are, of course, extremist Hindus who query whether any non-Hindus can really call themselves Indian but they are a minority.

Muzaffarapur had the most comfortable bicycle rickshaws in all India. Many of the rickshaw pullers were low caste Hindus with shaven heads apart from the tuft sprouting from the back of the head. For five mornings, I went by rickshaw to the local nature cure hospital. The man in charge was a believer in urine therapy. Drinking one's urine has even been advocated in allopathic/western medicine in its time and urine is well known as an antiseptic when used externally. Moraji Desai, the previous prime minister to Mrs Gandhi, drank a glass of his own urine each day alongside his fruit juices. I came across a book called The Water of Life, a treatise on Urine Therapy by J W Armstrong. This it quotes from a British book called One Thousand Notable Things published over a hundred years ago. This book says that urine can be used for washing external parts of the body and wounds. In 1980 a leaflet published by Shiavambu Auto Urine Treatment Centre in Bombay promised big things. 'The Urine Therapy treatment can cure not only TB but cancer, cataract, deafness, pyorrhea and many other diseases.' From a speech by Prime Minister Morarji Desai regarding massage 'that along with drinking one's urine, massaging is also necessary. Massage the body for four to five days using old urine', or 'if the patient does not get clear daily motion, more quantity should be taken of urine. Cloth pad wetted with auto urine placed on the abdomen can also help to bring motion.'

Walking around Muzaffarpur, I noticed so many donkeys, which belonged to the washermen caste of dhobi wallahs. These donkeys looked better off than the pathetic creatures I had seen in Karachi.

One of my favourite local dishes was curd and chura. Curd is yoghurt and chura is pressed uncooked rice. Together with sugar, they make a delicious meal and Muzaffarpur is famed for this dish. I also drank a local speciality called satu, which is made of ground roasted gram flour added to water.

Razi Sahib insisted that I should meet an eccentric orthodox Muslim Rais or proprietor who formed one of the rural gentry gone to seed. He could only be called a loveable fanatic. Mustaphaji lived most of his time on the verandah of a large house alongside a crumbling red-bricked edifice over two hundred years old. The bricks were cemented together by a mortar of lime and brick powder.

A discussion developed with Mustaphaji about the age of the Holy Quran. It is near sacrilege to claim as Razi Sahib did that the Quran was written down three hundred years after the Prophet's death. Whereas Muslims believe that the book was assembled soon after the Prophet's lifetime, Mustaphaji exclaimed, 'you are all ignorant and the Bible itself is a distortion of the original.' During the conversation we were blasted by music from a crackly loud speaker. It was not the usual film music but religious bhajan (hymns) preparing for the Hindu festival of Durga Puja, which is the main holiday of the year in these parts. It is on the last day of Dasahra festival to honour Goddess Durga's slaying of the demon Mahishasura who had the body of a man and a buffaloes head. Mastaphaji always knew the exact time without looking at a clock. At precisely three quarters of an hour after our meal, he took water and at exactly four o'clock, he ordered tea. I never met any female of his family but I wondered if they were peeping at me from any part of the building.

The steam boat we took on departure from Bihar at Paleza Ghat on the banks of the Ganges, was an old boat constructed in 1890 at Yarrow shipyards in Glasgow. This day, the Ganges was like a giant millpond and white flowers adorned the banks, which gave them the appearance of distant white sands. Immediately beyond the river banks were acres of sugar cane. Hundreds of planters from British days must have stood on these old decks. The vessel was packed to capacity. It looked as if the boat was modelled on a Mississippi river steamer. I am sure it could tell hundreds of tales.

On the boat, I spoke to a man whose daughter was at Patna University in Bihar where she was taking a BA in history. 'Is she interested in history?', I enquired. 'No.' 'Then is she studying BA to get a husband?' I asked mockingly. 'Oh, yes!' He then added that a BSc in chemistry would take work as a police officer, even if he were not interested in the job, because bribes are good, even if pay is not. As elsewhere, a degree is cherished primarily for a job. Light years from the gentle scholar I had met in Gujarat, Ismail Dada. The man went on to tell me when his friend returned from the United Kingdom, he asked him how long English boys and girls took before sex. He had forgotten the answer.

Back in Delhi, Razi Sahib and I went for a meal at a posh Chinese restaurant at the York Hotel. The Indian waiters were smartly dressed lamp stands (probably all BAs) and very mechanical. They lacked any charm and the finesse of an Italian waiter, or the muddled chaos of the comical and less-educated Bengali waiters that I had encountered at the old and charming A.B.C. Chinese restaurant in old Karachi. Once these types of graduates were secure in their jobs, they lost interest. They were unimaginative enough to refuse me the permitted double amount of coffee for one, because I had requested a second cup so that I could share my entitlement to a second coffee with my friend. It was these types of uninspiring and unimaginative middle class specimens that were making India more bureaucratic than need be, one of the disasters of British rule.

Chapter Twenty

Central India, a Brahmin amongst the Tribals

By train to Indore in the central state of Madhya Pradesh. As the night train neared Ratlam, all the lights went out and my carriage halted opposite a locomotive where I noticed an enterprising fireman using his fire shovel to place his chapattis before thrusting them into the firing furnace under the boiler.

At Ratlam station, I purchased Caravan magazine, a rather ungodly socialist paper. It had an interesting quote inside from 1939. The secretary of the right wing All India Hindu Mahasabha is quoted. 'Let the people of Germany and the Führer's government know that Germany's solemn idea of a revival of the Aryan cultural life and the glorification of Swastika were welcomed by religious and sensible 'Hindus of India' with hope.' The secretary went onto claim that when Gandhi spoke against the Nazis, his Mahasabha group said that 'he was only a man who has betrayed and confused the country with affected mysticism.' It is true that some reactionary Hindus held some sympathy with Hitler and not only because Hitler was fighting the British. The misuse of the term Aryan is laughable. Aryan (Sanskrit Arya-Noble) is a linguistic rather than a racial term, though many Hindus do use it in both senses as when they speak of some lighter- skinned Indians being descendants of invading Aryans rather than being related to the older dark-skinned population.

Caravan then quoted the injunction against letting low caste Hindus hear the sacred words of the Vedas 'If ever the word of the Vedas were to fall upon the ears of a Sudra or woman, their ears must be sealed by molten lead.' Then the magazine stated that King Rama killed Shambuk, the Sudra, because he had attempted to study the scriptures. One can quote the stupider points in any world faiths. In fact, a Muslim in Pakistan who seemed to know nothing else about Hinduism quoted the 'molten oil' factor at me. If a magazine in Pakistan had written an equivalent form of religious criticism, the editor would probably have been lynched. Faith is not the basis of India's existence.

In Indore I spent some time with Servas host Jaiswantraiji, an elderly Gandhian. He arranged for Dr Apte, a homeopathic doctor, to show me the city. The doctor seemed a quick thinking man. He was dark skinned and had deep blue eyes, a handsome combination. His home was the Konkani coastal region near Bombay. He had no European blood to account for his blue eyes. In the far north of Pakistan, it is quite common to see blue or green-eyed people but their skin is fairer.

Dr Apte took me by motorbike to see a fabulous Jain Temple, Kanch Mandir, built by a rags to riches man called Huckam Chand. The temple was embellished with masses of mirror work plus frescoes and tiles. The silver fronted door had embossed figures, which gave a gleaming effect. The temple was only seventy years old and the whole place had a multicoloured extravaganza about it. Unlike some modern temples, it lacked vulgarity. The old palace of Indore became a museum. One of the exhibits was a water clock, which consisted of a large bowl of water with a small bowl and a tiny hole in it floating inside the larger bowl. When the small bowl filled up, it sank. Every hour, a mechanical man replaced the newly emptied bowl back onto the water again while banging a gong.

The Visarjan ashram had a decayed atmosphere but Kishore Bhai, its best worker, did active work in the neighbouring jhuggis (slums). I accompanied him to some slums and saw huts made of vertical, thin strips of wood, cloth sacking weighted down by stones. The sacking occasionally covered sheets of corrugated iron roofing. The mud path was crammed full of beggars and some labourers were mending push carts. Kishorji and I were taken into a gloomy hut to see a woman who was moaning in agony while stretched out on a push cart. Her spine was broken because she had been knocked down in a road accident. After three days in a so-called charitable hospital, she was discharged. If that was not enough, a local doctor charged Rs50 for two injections. This was the ultimate in exploitation from so-called guardians in public welfare. What did political freedom mean to such as her?

Returned to Indore, Dr Apte told me that once he had met an Englishman who had remarked on India's backwardness. Apte replied, 'When you people were not wearing clothes, we had the Ramayana epic.'

I remained in Indore but stayed with a Dr P, a naturopath. For some days, I accompanied him to his clinic. The only evidence of there being a naturopathic clinic was a couple of old zinc hip baths. His consulting room was more like a library, which had a number of nature cure classics including John Harvey Kellogg's (the inventor of cornflakes) writings and Dr Lindlar's Theory and Practice of Nature Cure. Both these men had worked in the United States Battle Creek Sanatorium, a naturopathic institution that faced terrible onslaughts from the drug companies, which were threatened by it. It finally closed many years ago.

My Indore visit coincided with the Dasahra festival. According to the ancient epic, the Ramayana, Rama (an avatar of Vishnu) fought the demon Ravana and this was symbolised by effigies of Ravana being burnt on huge bonfires. A number of the more frenzied spectators got 'high' on bhang. Dr P asked me if I wanted to try it so he took me to his clinic and make a decoction of hashish, which is boiled in a small amount of water, then ground in a mortar. To the green paste are added almond, opium, pepper and cardamon. Unfortunately or luckily, he said he had no opium. When all the ingredients were well mashed, he added milk, and then the paste was placed in a bag, which was continually dipped and squeezed through the milk, which took on a light green colour. I consumed the liquid at the clinic after being told that the amount would only have a little effect upon me, and then he added, 'Do not tell my wife.' Four hours after consuming this green liquid, I became dazed, my vision was blurred and I thought I would faint. A strange sensation of a rush of wind came to my ears and I felt nauseous. I decided to lie down. By that time, Dr. P's wife had gone to sleep, so he just sat with me in his front room observing my behaviour! P was a strange man. He spent most of his free time writing enormously long letters to world leaders. As far as I know, he never got any replies.

The Gujarati community in Indore was celebrating Dasahra in its special way. One late evening, I came across groups of men dancing a circular step in a large ring. Some of them were dressed in western fashion, which removed much of the dignity and grace from the dance. Some children performed a Gujarati stick dance, the Garba. Women dancers carried copper pots while dressed in lovely green and red saris. During the ceremonies, P showed me some oriental perfumes, which 'last longer than yours'. They were in fact, essential oils in tiny bottles. These were khus and hinna. Khus is for summer and is cooling and hinna (not henna) is worn in winter and gives off heat. Some people came and offered a sona leaf as a mark of respect, then touched P's feet. To the children, he gave a few paise. Before I departed, the doctor showed me his 'pornographic book' clad in brown paper, which made it look even more suspicious. The book contained the erotic paintings and sculptures of Pompeii.

On my journey to Gram Bharat ashram (Village India ashram) at Tawlai in central India's Madhya Pradesh (MP) state, I crossed the Vindhyas, which are the mountainous dividing line between north and central India and the south. The hills were gentle-looking with a sparse forest covering depleted by humankind. Originally, this part of central India was predominantly an adivasi or tribal region. Sri Trivedi, a Brahmin Gandhian ran the ashram. He was a thin austere- looking man attired in the usual khadi cloth and cap.

It was not long before his Brahmin snobberies surfaced. Most locals were Bhillallah who had Rajput fathers and Bhil (tribal) mothers. Trivedi said, even our Anglo-Indians are superior to the Bhils".' The Bhils tend, like most tribals to be darker-skinned and broader in feature than many higher caste Hindus.

Trivedi's ashram held twenty five acres of undulating land growing cotton, jute and maize. In the local village of Moripura named after a tribal group the Mori, the 'inferior' food of jawar (sorghum) grew in abundance. Ground mats and charpoys were covered with sorghum, peanuts and maize being dried out in the intense afternoon sun. The roofs were red with chillies. These tribals were small peasant farmers tilling only a couple of bighas (one third to two thirds of an acre). Owing to land reform, there were no large landowners in the area such as many tribals still had to face in Bihar or Uttar Pradesh states.

In one of the Mori courtyards, a baby hung in a tiny joli (hammock), which descended from the ceiling. Old baskets also hung from the ceiling but these contained broody hens. Their huts were constructed of clay and wattle with earthen floors. They had an ingenious way of keeping their water cool. The large water pot was placed within a big clay surround, which joined the hut walls. Even in the strong sunlight, the water kept cool. Their granaries were huge, some having circular mud walls with jute roofs. As huts, they stood outside and were used for storing grass. The clay granary bins inside the outhouses stored previously dried mung lentils. Some of the granary storage pots had a twenty year life and they varied considerably in shape. Some were tall and circular while other strange- looking characters consisted of two mud bins joined together as 'man' and 'wife'-with pyramid shaped tops and square bodies. This was certainly an example of man's ingenuity in adapting to nature.

I was introduced to the cobbler whose leatherwork was excellent. The heavy leather farm boots had multi-layered soles joined up with leather nails. No metal was ever used in their construction. Later I met the village headman, a non-tribal businessman of the baniya community. Trivediji, as an enthusiastic Brahmin, refused buffalo buttermilk, as he only believed in cow's milk products. The headman had two wives of which I was only introduced to the second. Both lived in the same house. On a nearby charpoy, a mound of maize stalk fodder for buffaloes was awaiting use.

At the ashram stood a stone carving of the monkey god, Hanuman and Trivedi's father had had a small temple built to house the statue. Just outside it stood a small grove, which is actually called a 'triveni' because it holds three sacred trees, neem (margosa), peepul (figtree) and banyan (fig tree with aerial roots). Another example of a 'triveni' is the confluence of the sacred rivers of Ganga, Saraswati and Yamuna. I was pleased to note that the ashram school had some small tools designed from my past friend Mohan Parekh of Bardoli in Gujarat. On the road near the ashram, donkeys passed weighed down with sacks of earthen pots, a scene which was more Mediterranean than Indian.

Trivediji offered me some tasty food, crispy kakri bread and an unusual local type of homemade brown bread called badti, which looked like a craggy baked potato. As usual, we ate on the floor but the food was placed on very low tables only a couple of inches off the ground.

In nearby Khedi village, we visited the blacksmith cum postmaster's house. The walls were painted with small black paintings of the nag or snake. In this area, they had an annual festival for snake worship.

It was the full moon and my host fasted for the day. For some inexplicable reason, the conversation drifted onto Madame Montessori. Trivediji had visited Italy in 1947 in connection with Montessori. Apparently, while Madam Montessori was in India, the British had put her under detention during the war because Italy was at war with Britain. This was followed by a discussion on sports and Trivedi disapproved of cricket because 'we still want to copy our old masters.' Ashram children played the popular Indian game kibedi'.

Trivedi's own children were married according to local rites. At Gandhi's Sabarmati ashram in Ahmedabad, the Mahatma introduced a cheap kind of marriage. The boy and girl would spin each other's clothes. At the marriage, a few Vedic hymns and a minimum of ritual followed, with the whole ceremony taking only forty five minutes. Therefore, Trivedi's children were married at his own ashram under that system. I noticed his son helping with the sweeping while I visited Trivedi's Indore house. I heard a sad story of a woman whose sari caught fire while praying to a household god, after she had lit the candles.

Trivedi requested me to attend ashram prayers in the early evening. All the prayers were in Sanskrit and afterwards we had a discussion. I asked whether Trivedi had attended a church service while abroad or in India. He said that he had never been for long in a church. Then one of the gathering exclaimed, 'Muslims are so rigid'. I asked him if he had ever read the Quran. He answered by again proclaiming the rigidity of Muslims. I accused him of being as rigid and then he said that Gandhi and Vinoba knew the Quran. I enquired again, 'No, I cannot read everything.

I travelled over the Vindhyas again to the ruined city of Mandhu. Trivedi took me by bus and it passed through one of the old walled gateways. Immediately upon arrival, Trivedi invited me to a picturesque Anglo-Indian style house to meet an elderly archaeologist. Away from Trivedi, he said, 'British rule was good for us.' He had been recently presented with a book on Britain's country houses by a relative of Lord Mountbatten. We sat on the semi-circular verandah surrounded by bougainvillea. The archaeologist explained that his guru had been John Marshall, a British archaeologist. 'Before the Pathans invaded Mandhu in the early fourteenth century, there were many Jain temples. Three hundred had gold domes and they were destroyed.' I was later to see that amongst the ruins, a 'new' stark beauty had arisen. Sanskrit schools had turned into (now empty) mosques. The tomb of Hoshang Shah was constructed of white marble with a huge dome, which became the abode of bats with their characteristic smell. Champa Baori was an incredible four storey well reminiscent of a church crypt with small low arches and pillars. Trivediji, as a strict Hindu, kept pointing out that remains of the original Hindu temples could be seen everywhere. The Pathans smashed the images but retained some stone and marble lotus designs in their starkest of buildings. Inside one mosque, a huge minbar (stepped pulpit) was plainly Hindu in style. Around the mirhab (point facing Mecca) were marble arches removed from an earlier temple. We passed by an old temple where a dreary twenty four hour chant of the epic Ramayana was beginning to drive me mad.

Trivedi and I had deposited our belongings upstairs in the same temple where the chanting was going on below. This was the head priest's room. The bearded priest was a graduate of Banares Hindu University and a Sanskrit scholar. He was treasuring his new acquisition, a book about the nineteenth century German scholars' contribution to the unearthing of India's past. Huge wooden pillars supported the wooden beamed room, which today would be impossible to construct because of their high cost. Hanging from the ceiling were enormous glass bowls that in the past held the light as a handi (chandelier). The priest's furniture was shabby Edwardian reminiscent of the kind of furniture found in the more salubrious waiting rooms of India's finer railway stations. One item of furniture stood out in many ways, the sofa looked and felt like a relief map of India. Over half this upper floor of the temple was covered in maize and some of the cobs had an unusually deep red colour, which stood out amongst the usual orange ones. The walls were covered with familiar coloured pictures of Hindu mythological figures.

Trivedi and I departed for Dhar. The bus slowed down near a shrine before going up the Vindhyas. This shrine was more effective than a go slow sign as the bus automatically stopped for passengers to throw the odd paise! Farm workers were packed inside the bus with their haseja (sickles). Trivediji wore a handkerchief on his head when we set off 'Oh, I am just drying it,' he said. The bus conductor looked very smart. I guessed correctly, unlike Travedi, that he was a graduate 'BA final'. One giveaway was the fact that the boy kept combing his hair like so many of the superficially westernised kids I had seen.

At Dhar, there was a Sanskrit college, which had been transformed into a Mosque. A large store with Sanskrit scriptures was found in the same college compound. I argued with a petty official in order to try to get into the college, which had just been closed. Dhar is chiefly famed for its huge iron pillar dating from the twelfth century and it is believed to be a pillar of victory. Later it was in three parts in an undignified horizontal position.

I returned briefly to Dr P in Indore. A white-bearded Muslim lecturer came to his house wearing white shalwar and kurta and embroidered skullcap. Greetings between a Hindu host and Muslim guest can be a trifling embarrassing, there were no 'salaams' nor 'namaste', they only compromised by greeting each other in English. After his guest had departed, P made a surprising comment for a Hindu, 'Hindus are more dishonest than Muslims.' Probably, the older British rulers would have agreed with that sentiment as they found many Hindus too complex unlike the less complex Muslims and Sikhs.

We ate a sago and peanut mixture with potatoes and the doctor was eating with a spoon. He saw me watching and told me that when Gandhi visited Ceylon, he attended a meal with the British governor. The governor was actually eating with his hands and Gandhi asked him why. The governor replied, 'When you eat with a spoon, so many have used it but only you yourself use your own hands.' The question was amusing because Gandhi usually carried his own spoon whereas most Indians eat with their hands.

Chapter Twenty One

Rock Paintings, Revolutionary
Education and the Forest of Joy

I joined a bus of Hindu pilgrims bound for Ujjain, which is famed primarily as a historical centre for astrological studies besides being an old observatory similar to those at Delhi and Jaipur.

Our first stop was Kshipra bathing ghats. The Puranic legend claims that the Kshipra River appeared from the blood of the forefingers of Lord Vishnu, which were speared by the trident of Lord Shiva. The guide peered down at some ominous ants and declared mysteriously, 'Please be seen', after telling me to leave my 'sooj' behind before entering the Temple. Nearby, some children were playing on a traditional big wooden wheel, which had wooden boxes perched at the end of long poles connected with a vertical pole. The local bazaar had some colourful sights, especially the multi-coloured mounds of powder dye. Donkeys pushed through the narrow lanes laden with quarried stones. I lost count of how many temples we went through and at the end of the day, I had had enough. The most memorable temple scene was a huge statue of the elephant god Ganesh.

Still in the central state of Madhya Pradesh, I travelled by train to Bhopal and rested at the Buddhist guesthouse. Much of nearby Buddhist Sanchi's remains were constructed during King Ashoka's rule in the second century B.C. after Ashoka had converted to Buddhism. The bulk of the monuments were either huge circular stupas containing relics of religious persons or memorial pillars and chaityas (prayer halls). The four big stone gateways at the cardinal points were also stupendous. They depict in bas-relief the Buddha's previous lives, and such symbols, as the Buddha's footprints, the Bodhi tree and wheel of law were common motifs. One Ashoka pillar had an inscription ordaining Buddhists to avoid schism. A local zamindar (proprietor) broke the pillar into pieces to use as a sugar cane press! The lion motif found on many of these pillars became the Indian national emblem. At Sanchi, a gigantic stone bowl carved out of one piece was used for distributing food collected through begging by the monks.

In the museum, I noticed that one attendant was badly scarred by smallpox as his right eyeball was missing a pupil and it was more than double the size of a normal eye. I joked with him and said at least he still had one good eye. A sandstone statue of a meditating Buddha attracted me. It appeared as if it was wrapped in a huge shawl and the texture looked so fine it could have been cloth.

On the bus back to Bhopal, I had to give the conductor Rs100 as I had no change. The man behind exclaimed helpfully 'He will give you the change in one year.' Then the usual nosy questions, 'Are you single, married?' On arrival I purchased India Today and noticed an article 'The Ugly Indian' stating that Indians are unpopular in diplomatic circles in the United States as they are 'overbearing, preaching and bumptious' (1980).

At Bhopal, I stayed with the family of Sri Bhargawa. A man came to the house and explained that his brother and two friends had been wrongfully arrested after some Harijans had complained to the police that high caste thugs had damaged land they had been tilling. Instead of trying to catch the thugs, the police had arrested the complainants. There was nothing unusual in that. A little late, the conversation drifted onto Muslims because I informed Sri Bhargawa that he should not say 'Muhammadan', because Muslims do not worship their Prophet 'They don't?' he exclaimed. I replied that for a Muslim, Muhammad was for them the greatest and seal of the prophets and not a divine being, as many Christians believe Christ to be. 'Why do they go back and forward when praying?' he enquired. Here, he did not mean the prostrations during formal prayer, but the rocking movement that some Muslims make while reading the scriptures. Trying for an answer, I replied, 'Perhaps it helps them concentrate better and that orthodox Jews rocked even more when they said some of their prayers!'

I was advised to visit Bhimbetka, which was frequented by few visitors. I knew of Bhimbetka rock paintings because I had met an orthodox Hindu archaeologist at Bhopal railway station and he told me about the ancient rock paintings. I bussed to one village and found a local character to show me the rock shelter where the paintings were situated. These paintings were simple outlines in white and red, mostly of hunters in hunting postures or ritual dancing. Some of them wore head dresses or other hunting disguises while holding bows, arrows or spears. Others were naked apart from a tail-like thing hanging from the waist to the feet. Other scenes included elephants and the odd pig, another had harnessed horses. The country around the rock shelters was composed of mainly light forest and scrubland. I could visualise generations of hunter gatherers tramping about the place and taking temporary shelter in these rocky enclaves.

I moved to Hoshangabad to visit Servas member Sri Choudhari at nearby Nitya Village. A Hindu, he had been influenced by Quakerism by living at the Quaker college Woodbrooke in Birmingham, England. I had also boarded in that same college while studying for my degree in African studies and Archaeology at Birmingham University. He ran a school for over a hundred scheduled caste girls and wanted to use the Gandhians precepts of Basic Education but had been informed that if he did so, the local state secondary schools would not accept his pupils.

In the evening, Choudhariji took me to the ghats at Hoshangabad. Right up against the ghats stood a very narrow alleyway and nearby the children were playing up by the riverbank floating tiny leaves as oil lamps, which bobbed merrily into the moonlit distance down the river.

The following day I visited Rasulia Friends (Quakers) Rural Centre where they trained science teachers with a more practical method of teaching in that the children were encouraged to ask questions. The Canadians running the school sent their own children to local schools while the Indian staff preferred to send their offspring to boarding schools! I met an American woman who was married to an Indian and she studied allopathic medicine at Bombay University. I offered her my views on naturopathy.

There was not much to see around Nitya village so Choudhariji accompanied me by bullock cart to Itarsi railway station. The little cart was like a small Wild West style covered wagon with semi-circular crisscross wooden strips covered with cloth. The train was three hours late and eventually I got the Amritsar Express, and at some ungodly hour, I disembarked at Bhushaval station where I asked if I could sleep in the railway retiring rooms. On getting the room, a cheeky lad later knocked on my door and said in a slimy voice 'Do you want a friend?'

I went from Bhushawal to Buldana to meet Bhai, a local social worker. My visit concluded with the Diwali (festival of lights) celebrations, which celebrate Lakshmi, the goddess of prosperity. Buldana district was mad with noisy firecrackers while tiny lighted oil lamps flickered in the still darkness. In one house, the worship centred on a picture of Lakshmi. The father knelt before her and continually placed holy food including tamarind before the deity. Everybody was dressed in brand new clothes, and children kept offering me popcorn and custard apple pieces. On one side of the household altar were paintings of many gods. During the prayers, they stood and the first prayer was always to the auspicious elephant god Ganesh, then a prayer to Krishna who protects the cows against the rain god Indra. Finally, they prayed to Lakshmi, not for money but for general prosperity. Around the altar hung lucky mango leaves and outside the door stood sugar cane bundles, a custom only found in Maharashtra state. Many people paint pictures in front of their houses during Diwali and at this house, somebody had painted a lovely blue peacock and placed small oil lamps on it. Another painting had boats with little circular huts around it, giving the appearance of a tropical scene from Kerala much further to the south.

For the merchant subcastes Diwali represents the new financial year. In one Buldana medical store, puja was being said over the new account books. These books were covered with turmeric and banana leaves. In front of the line of account books were pictures of goddess Lakshmi. The streets outside were alive with deafening firecrackers, which they even use days before the festival. Plenty of rockets and sparklers went off. Here they just set them off in the open streets and it got very unnerving.

Bhai took me to a farm with one hundred and fifty acres, which was farmed by three brothers who grew mainly sorghum, sugar cane, guavas and mangoes. All the roofs were red with dried chillies making a colourful scene. Lakshmi is also connected with good harvests. I enquired what happened to the old cows as slaughtering is banned. Their cattle were sold off once their milk declined and nobody would take responsibility for these cows, most of which ended up rummaging in the bazaars or forming semi permanent traffic islands.

At Buldana, Bhai's educational centre was quite radical. They had a conventional curriculum but education was primarily for 'civic sense'. School staff and pupils took part in secret ballot elections and elected a panel of seven who formed themselves into Speaker, Chief Minister, Minister of Home Affairs, Agriculture, Sports, Cultural Affairs and Health. Everyone, including staff, were subject to criticisms (touches of the Chinese Cultural Revolution!) During the fortnightly open general meeting, a student could discuss anything, for example, if a student saw a member of staff spitting on the campus, he had to note the time and date so that the matter could be introduced at the meeting. The teacher must then explain himself. One teacher was criticised by students for eating betel leaf while teaching. Even methods of teaching were criticised. I was told, 'Usually the students are accurate in their criticism and will give a more honest appraisal than the teachers colleagues.' Besides all this, the centre had a 'see and learn' system of teaching. 'Many have not seen a train or the sea, so some groups went to see fishermen on the Konkani coast'. Each child did physical work such as constructing the new school building in the summer from six in the morning to ten in the morning. The majority of pupils were scheduled castes including boarders.

One staff member was an Indian Jewish doctor called Sheba Ezekial, her son was wearing a T-shirt with a Union Jack design on it. At the meal table, Bhai pointed at the shirt and said, 'I see, we are still slaves of the British.' 'Well,' I replied, 'It is better than Raj Narayan's (an eccentric politician) face on the front!' They all agreed. I also said that only in Britain could we wear the national flag on one's 'behind' as we do not honour the flag so much. Bhai replied, 'but here, people are still slaves to British ideas, even when the colonists have departed.' I suppose if we could wear our flag on our 'behind' then it presumed an implicit national self confidence or anti-British patriotism!

During Diwali, we ate special food. A pastry containing fresh coconut called kurunji, also chuki, which is chickpea flour gram plus sorghum and rice mixed into a paste and rolled into long strips, then fried. Fried chura (pressed rice) was popular. Bhai told me of a bullock festival where the animals get a holiday. They are fed with special puran puri, a sweet chapatti mixed with jaggery (palm sugar) gram (chickpea, flour) lentils, and then they are bathed. Many festivals are linked to the monsoon period, as this is auspicious for fertility. Another festival Bhai told me about was Naga Panchami for the snake. Snakes are the farmer's friends as they kill rodents, even children may hold the cobras. As I have stated before, many faiths not influenced by the Judeo-Christian or Islamic cultures respect the serpent as a symbol of fruitfulness. Still, I was happy not to have attended any snake festivals during my travels.

Before departing from Buldhana, I ate a mixture of peanut, garlic, coriander with barley chapattis. After this farewell, I journeyed from Bhusawal to Khiroda and up to Pal village situated in the Satpura range of hills. I was lucky to get a lift in a ministerial Ambassador, a car that is based on the old Morris Oxford but entirely manufactured in India. En route, we bumped into a herd of buffaloes. As a group, they looked a gormless lot of animals. They took their time shifting and matters did not improve when a jeep came in the opposite direction. Only lowly passengers were ordered out of our car to shift these ungainly black beasts and then we came across a herd of cattle, which caused only a minor problem because unlike the buffalo, as soon as the cattle heard the car horn, they fled.

At Pal village, I was introduced to another community. The locals were Bhil tribals and Rajasthani Banjara who were traditionally involved in transportation. Their name literally means 'forest travel,'. Banjara women wore heavy jewellery in the form of clanking anklets to frighten off dangerous wild animals rather than being worn for purely decorative reasons.

Sunitbhai, a small round-faced fellow, ran a nursery residential ashram school. At this centre for 'Agricultural Awakening', camps were run for training in cattle and crop research. Tribals had been introduced also to fruit tree cultivation and cacti were grown to sell to city dwellers. Sunitbhai told me that he was interested in forest conservation and that it was mainly non tribals who were killing off most of the forest and its creatures.

To the tiny post office to mail some air letters, which as usual did not stick properly. Indian post offices had glue available for the job but here the glue had been so watered down that it was useless.

The school at Pal was run democratically but here committee members were voted by a show of hands. Ministers were elected for many roles such as 'kitchens', 'lighting and guest' and even 'prayers'. Tasks took place after early breakfast. The children had many chores, classes and rest periods until ten at night after prayers. Very few English children would have the stamina to survive that day. Every three months, staff and students worked one week together in such projects as brick making, collecting stones, soil construction and collecting firewood in the forests. Adult education schemes ran to home science, nutrition, childcare, sanitation and folk singing. The people were so poor that over forty percent could not even afford a pair of bullocks, so tractors were hired out at a very low rate.

For some obscure reason, I suddenly realized that I had lost the ability to use a western lavatory because of becoming so used to squatting at an eastern-style latrine. Then squatting really is the correct and healthiest posture and man's original and natural one. It had been years since I had used lavatory paper and now I preferred water. It just proves how we are so culture bound.

After an awful overnight journey by slow 'passenger train' from Bhusawal, I eventually arrived at Bhadrak to visit Gramodaya Sangh founded by Sri Mirmira. He had studied ceramics and inspired by Gandhi, he opened an amazing pottery co-operative. A comical Anglo-Indian called Brother Joseph showed me around. 'The workers all work harder because they own and control the place,' he said. However, in 1980 their wage was only Rs 7 an average per day, but then 60 percent of the profits were distributed.

I took a train through the flat uninspiring landscape of eastern Maharashtra state towards the more forested area of Chandra. Here, I was to meet one of the most remarkable men in modern India. Baba Amte was a middle aged Brahmin of serene countenance. His thick white hair had an unruly fringe above his lively intelligent eyes. He was dressed in simple khadi cloth.

Hailing from a prominent Brahmin family, he studied law and while practicing it, he joined the local untouchables in clearing latrines. These latrines were what are called 'service lavatories' which had to be emptied by hereditary bhangis (scavengers). Baba cleaned forty lavatories each day until eventually he obtained the trust of those scavenger sweepers. One day- Baba Amte came across a leper who had lost his nose, fingers and toes. The poor man's eyes were maggot filled and Baba fled away in horror, but he soon returned. Then he decided to dedicate his life to helping lepers. At that time, he did not know that leprosy was hardly contagious. His Brahmin family were horrified but Baba told them that if there is fear, there is no love and without love, there is no God. He took a course in leprosy at the School of Tropical Medicine in Calcutta. Leprosy germs cannot be cultivated in situ except in one species of armadillo and human beings. The knowledge regarding the armadillo was still unknown at that time. Baba bravely volunteered to have the germs cultivated upon him for the purposes of experimentation and nothing happened. He was a sufferer from cervical spondylosis and had several vertebrae removed. Occasionally, he wore a neck collar and used a back support placed around his waist.

What made Baba Amte unusual was that his immediate family were involved in the running of Maharogi Seva Samiti, a leper colony or as it was known Anandwan or 'Forest of Joy'. I had by this time met many so called Gandhians of good character but few of them could inspire their own families to be involved in their projects. One of Baba's sons, Dr Vikas had also inherited spondylosis. He was not only an allopathic doctor but also a master of every trade. He designed looms, made lamps out of medical boxes and fishing traps and used weaverbird nests for lights. He collected old logs and twigs to make elegant traps and lamp stands. Greeting cards were made of bits of cloth and leaves. Outside the planned 'Wisdom Bank', he had placed huge rocks of varying shapes. One rock he had nicknamed Mrs Gandhi. He showed me a selection of wooden pieces, one that held a remarkable likeness to Khomeini ... after being overthrown! The 'Forest of Joy' started from small beginnings. The area had poor cultivable land or so it seemed. Baba began with one lame cow and hundreds of rats, which even ate parts of the limbs of leprosy patients whose nerves had ceased functioning.

Dr Vikas said that Baba had accepted foreign aid and some petty minded people have condemned him for this. The centre had ashram-style buildings all nicely painted. The gardens were fabulous unlike in many Gandhian centres. I was informed that one of Gandhi's less inspired comments was that 'flowers are themselves provocative in that they worked against the attainment of Brahmacharya.' Most of the Sarvodaya workers considered flower planting a waste of time. 'Why do you not plant fruit trees?' they asked Vikasji. This was one of the most beautiful places I had ever seen. Baba discarded such terms as Gandhian and was one of the few social workers to admit some disagreement with both Gandhi and Vinoba. Baba considered Vinoba more as a friend than a teacher. At Vinoba's Wardha ashram, which was quite near Anandwan, the sisters objected because Baba had sat beside Vinoba and not on the floor below him.

On the side of one hut at Anandwan, a message proclaimed,

'I sought my soul and my soul I could not see.
I sought my god and my god eluded me.
I sought my brother and I found all three.'

An assembly hall was the venue for a festival. Outside, groups came and together with the leprosy 'patients', they performed music and drama. One lovely ceremony that was held at the same time was tree planting as part of a wider scheme to help in fighting the depletion of the forests. Saplings were brought ceremoniously on a palanquin and ritually planted to keep an ecological balance in nature.

With the motto 'charity destroys, work builds' there was a healthy atmosphere of mutual self-help rather than the Victorian ideal of 'God helps those who help themselves.' Dr Vikas claimed, 'We produce all except salt and sugar.' I asked about the buildings. Well, apart from the early 1950's, when a small number were constructed at Service Civil International workcamp, those with leprosy had built the rest without any outside help. The lepers had constructed a college called Anand Niketan, which was used for teaching agricultural science, commerce and art to non lepers. They had also built a college for the blind without leprosy where crafts and music were taught. Such an enterprise must be unique in the world in that leprous people built for the youth without leprosy. People without hands and fingers do not have to be passive recipients of welfare to be left on the scrapheap. Even the children of the lepers were schooled here. Leprosy is not hereditary but it can be passed by contact over a long period.

Dr Vikas, although an allopathic doctor, had been involved in naturopathy. He showed me his book on fasting and his hospital had no smells of disinfectant or ulcerated limbs. The place was spotless unlike many hospitals I had seen. As we came out of the hospital, Dr Vikas said, 'Want to see the pet snake?' 'No thanks,' I replied as I disappeared down the path.

A workshop was in the process of being built to be used as repair shops and for tailoring, masonry, plumbing and shoemaking (sandals from worn out car tyres). One machine had a bicycle wheel, which was used for separating the strands of mill made woollen yarn. The yarn was then handwoven, thus it was not true khadi, because that must be both handspun and handwoven but at least they were using recycled materials. The looms, some designed by Dr Vikas, were specially created for weavers with damaged limbs. Afterwards, I was shown a newly renovated bright blue truck.

A little away from the main ashram was a home for aged destitutes. These old people pooled their mental resources and even took on individual lepers to look after. This idea of social responsibility in the older people was linked to the Vanprast stage of a religious Hindu's life. Walking around the home, I passed one old character without fingers and was told 'he is oversexed and nobody will go with him, that part of him had remained active in his old age so he was put in charge of irrigation to keep him occupied!' Female lepers found it hard for themselves to get mates, as they were less able to do some household chores. At a series of hostels called Mukti Sadan, lived a few married couples. It gave them 'the right to love and the capacity to give it.'

The doctor had complained to the Catholic Relief organisation over the wastage of drug distribution. He had continually informed them that Baba's organisation did not require tranquilizers or heart tablets but the relief organisation had continued sending them.

It was hard to get a word in edgeways with Dr Vikas as he had a tendency to ignore questions though he offered information freely without a touch of arrogance. He had that rare talent called initiative and an exploring mind. Time marched on so I had to depart.

Chapter Twenty Two

From Christian Hospitality to the Atheist Centre

The journey to Warangal from Chanda in the forests demanded a change at the chaotic bus station at Karimnagar, where every bus in the vicinity converged. I was now in Telegu speaking Andhra Pradesh state. Buses here displayed the slogan 'untouchability is anti national and irrational'. I asked somebody about this and he replied that is was, 'just an election stunt.' Then I noticed that already some of the signs were beginning to wear off the sides of the buses. I had to wait two and a half hellish hours at Karimnager. Finally, the bus came but the stampede for the door was so great that I had no earthly chance of getting on. Eventually, I got a bus to Warangal and it too arrived late at night. Some Christian fellow passengers invited me to a small 'hotel' (in India, any little café could be called hotel) where we ate samosas. I felt constipated after having eaten nothing but unripe bananas in the last few hours. I spent the night with the Christian family in their little house, just outside Warangal. They asked me if I wanted to join them for prayers. They were local followers of the American Baptists. 'The Lord Jesus is our saviour, so we must help others,' they claimed. Perhaps they thought I was a practicing Christian. Mr Thomas was a very dark-skinned clerk, his grandfather was a Hindu. Next morning, we ate a south Indian breakfast of upma (semolina fried with pulses and peppers). I was very thankful of the hospitality of the Thomas family.

I got a cycle rickshaw to the local nature cure hospital, which was situated amongst a typical Andhra scene of huge rocky boulders that sat scattered in clusters all over this plateau. The newly-built hospital had twenty beds. At the crack of dawn, a loud speaker blasted the place out with religious music in Sanskrit, a nerve-shattering experience. The only place available for me to sleep was on the examination couch. I asked them to remove the dirty covering, which had once been a white sheet and the even filthier mattress underneath was only fit for burning. In other ways, people could be obsessively clean, as for example when I was told not to take a morning drink before brushing my teeth. In south India few would touch a tumbler of water with the lips, the cup being poised a couple of inches above the mouth and hopefully (in my case) the water arrived at its correct destination.

Above my sleeping place was a photo of the former Prime Minister, Moraji Desai, looking very sanctimonious indeed. It was amazing how many homes and institutions one went into and found photos of the Indian politicians. Even a friend of mine who had been imprisoned by Mrs Gandhi had still kept her photo on his wall. Perhaps he was displaying an underlying tolerance of a part of the Hindu character or maybe because Mrs Gandhi was of Nehru stock thus of sound mind.

I went for daily walks past the washermen caste bashing their client's clothes on stones by the riverbank. After washing the clothes in the murky water, they were then put to dry on any available ground. It was enjoyable to watch washermen at their tasks until you remembered that one of the items of clothing might be yours! In some areas, wooden boards were used to beat the clothes. Whatever way was used in washing, it was rather destructive to clothes. Most of the time, I washed my own clothes because I wanted them to last as long as possible.

I arrived in Hyderabad in time for the tulsi plant (sacred basil) festival. At Secunderabad, a suburb of Hyderabad, I ate at an Irani café. Like some of the Iranian cafés in Karachi, Pakistan, it had the ubiquitous notices 'stay healthy by eating less' and 'truth is the highest form of religion'. A touch of theosophy there.

On arrival at the Gandhian centre Raj Bhawan, I bumped into a crowd of middle class, saried women carrying ghastly plastic bags, who were demonstrating with placards plastered all over with slogans in Telegu letters. They were demanding nationalisation of the wholesale trade in essential commodities; the banning of the export of vegetables and a judicial enquiry into atrocities against women. The demonstration involved over one thousand women and they looked a rather unrevolutionary lot in their garish saris.

I travelled eastwards within the State of Andhra to Vijaywada to meet Sri Lavanam, a social worker in charge of the Atheist Centre. Lavanam was a jolly broad-faced man whose father, Goraji had become a follower of Gandhi. Goraji, a Brahmin, had denounced religion outright and coming from an orthodox Hindu family, he and his wife were outcasted and lived like outlaws. They had several children who all ended up working for Goraji's creation, the Atheist Centre, that in reality operated as an ashram without a religious foundation.

I arrived at the centre in time to attend a ceremony for the opening of a balwadi (kindergarten), which was to be addressed by a Parsi woman Minister of Education. The majority of the gathering consisted of children and true to form, the minister arrived an hour and a half late for the opening. The poor children had already been seated cross-legged on the ground for one hour before the meeting was due to begin. I appeared to be the only person to be perturbed by the ubiquitous Hindi film music blasting out from a loud speaker. Lavanam gleefully informed me, 'Indian culture is loud'. Eventually, the minister arrived wearing a fashionably-styled sari and coiffured hair adorning her very pale-skinned face. Just as a contrast, I suddenly thought of the black skinned nomads I had seen squatting around a Hyderabad bazaar the previous day. It was too much for the minister to apologise to the children for her late arrival. In India ministers were expected to be late. There was no entertainment by the children and adults performed all the dances and mimes.

The following day marked Goraji's birth anniversary. The local bishop visited the Atheist Centre and Lavanam had a typewritten list of Sunday services held in Vijaywada made out for him. Perhaps Lavanam's atheistic tolerance was the result of actually living in a Hindu cultural environment. Lavanam liked to attack charlatans who bamboozled gullible villagers in such matters as taking a bowl of rough rice and placing a stick inside the bowl and after a little shaking, lifting up the bowl of rice by the stick. These tricksters also use magnets and pictures of gods.

One fellow visitor to the Atheist Centre was a character whom I nicknamed the 'Godless Baba'. He had a dark round smooth south Indian face with a heavy white beard. He decided to expose the most famous living holy man in India, Satya Sai Baba who had a large centre near Bangalore. Baba told me that his family had been threatened by some of

Sai Baba's devotees. Baba's brother Dayanand had accompanied him to the centre. By profession he was a painter cum screen printer who had studied at the Theosophical Centre at Adyar near Madras, and obtained an 'MA First Class' at the Tagore Centre of Shantineketan in Bengal. Some students had asked Dayanand how much he had paid for his degree. Strangely enough was the fact that his teacher had come to him and asked how many marks he wanted in his final exams! Dayanand replied, 'Just pass me' and got eighty percent. Dayanand was handing out a booklet he and his brother had published against Sai Baba and one part of it that did amuse me was the comments on the holy man's physical appearance. His unusually large frizzy Afro hairstyle was indirectly referred to as African and 'primitive'.

One of Lavanam's workers took me to Mudarum to see one of the centre's projects with the 'cobbler untouchables'. There I gave my usual talk about English rural life to the assembled school. About the classroom doors were the keynotes of Victorian moral education, which Indians were so fond of, such as 'Good thoughts lead to good habits, manners maketh the man and the greatest talkers are the least doers', and 'Speech is silver, silence is golden.' A Canadian Baptist had provided a communal radio, which was situated in a separate hut in the centre of the village. One cobbler family had a brother in America and exclaimed, 'Many Indian boys marry American girls.' Then I enquired how many Indian women married American men.

The cobbler untouchables were being encouraged to take up fishing and one of the fishing nets I was shown looked like a Gladstone bag. It had two holes at the front and back and collected about ten kilos of fish, which could be sold for Rs 40. The huts of the Harijans (a term preferred by the workers) were made of bamboo and the roofs of sugar cane foliage. Untouchables always lived on the periphery of Indian villages because of their supposedly higher polluting factor. Pigs are usually kept by groups belonging to this community because swine can live on any rubbish, so cost nothing to maintain. In fact, pigs kept the areas cleaner than they might otherwise be. Most families in these very poor communities lived in nucleated rather than extended units and few had more than half an acre of land per family.

I was proudly shown a new statue of the untouchable or scheduled caste leader Dr Ambedkar. The statue was of a very fair man and it stuck out in contrast to the blacker than many African faces around me who, unlike many other groups, all had magnificent white teeth. One boy asked, 'Do you like our black skins?' and another very dark man told me confidently that Dr. Ambedkar's skin was 'red'. I was also told of some acrimony that had arisen because the government had allocated some houses for Hindu Harijans but excluded members of that community, which had converted to Christianity. Perhaps the government thought that the converts had some monetary reward as 'rice Christians'. Buddhist converts were ok.

Mudanum formed the centre of the freedom fighters' struggle in this area during the 1940's when Gora was active in the movement. His son Lavanam and family had continued the fight for economic freedom for the oppressed as political freedom was meaningless if it only benefited a post-colonial elite. One way of fighting caste had been for the Atheist Centre to encourage intercaste marriages. It was only this measure that would eventually eradicate caste. Even though Lavanam's family were atheists, they were still Brahmins by ancestry and I believe that he and other members of his family had married members of lower castes than themselves.

Lavanam lent me a book by a British woman, Ms Tyler who wrote My Years in an Indian Prison. She had been imprisoned by being wrongfully arrested because her Indian boyfriend had been involved in the revolutionary Naxalite movement for agrarian reform. In the prison the inmates looked after a beggar child. Because of its large belly, it was nicknamed 'Minister'. The fat belly reminded them of the bloated paunches of government officials who, unlike the child, had never known malnutrition.

The coast of Andhra Pradesh is frequently hit by cyclones and the centre was heavily involved in rehabilitating cyclone victims.

In Guravada town, I met Gora's brother and he informed me that prior to independence, many Muslim tanners in neighbouring Vijaywada had fled to Pakistan causing unemployment among the local untouchable cobblers.

The bus journey to Bhimavaram passed harvested paddy fields, palm trees and bullock carts crammed with rice and fodder. At Bhimavaram, I stayed at one of India's oldest nature cure establishments. Dr Vankat Rao of Hyderabad had studied here but all I saw was fifty acres of land going to rot. An elderly man told me that he had wanted to start a residential gurukul establishment run by retired people in the Vanprast stage of life. Another character claimed to be teaching Andhra's state language Telegu and Sanskrit. Everything was happening but naturopathy.

En route back to Vijaywada, I purchased a copy of the south Indian English newspaper The Hindu. An Irani consul had answered a barrage of criticisms about Khomeini by exclaiming that Khomeini should be compared with Mahatma Gandhi. Perhaps the consul thought that Gandhi had held the British leaders as hostages and arranged mass tortures in India's jails!

Back at the Atheist Centre, Lavanam organized celebrations in connection with Gora's birth anniversary. Instead of the usual Indian neck garlands made of flowers or tinsel, we used garlands made of vegetables, which were eaten the following day. Gandhi would not have approved of anything more.

Lavanam described the former Criminal Tribes in India. In Vijaywada area, there had been a number of these tribes whom the British had legislated against. Their anti-social activities were transformed into new subcaste duties. Often they were employed by certain Kshatriya (warrior castes) to spy on the latter's enemies. The British discovered that crime amongst these groups was a hereditary occupation unlike in areas, which might be plagued by banditry or 'dacoity' where the criminals were breaking the law by individual choice. British authorities established settlements for these groups that did not repent and the missionaries in charge were often given magisterial powers. Many of these settlements were little more than open air prisons. A vicious circle usually developed owing to the past records in crime of these people in that non institutions would give loans or jobs. In 1950, the Criminal Tribes Act was scrapped and the concerned groups were labelled 'Denotified Tribes. Unless the parties concerned migrated to new areas, it was hard to see within a genealogically-conscious country how such labels could ever be forgotten.

Sadly, I departed from the Atheist Centre and the effervescent Lavanam to go further south towards the Coramandal coast, but first a little eastwards to Vishakapatnam on the coast of the Indian Ocean.

My only bad memory of the Atheist Centre was waking up one morning at three o'clock and lying quietly with my hands behind my head when suddenly I heard a little scuffle and a rat bit one of my fingers. Luckily, it did not draw blood, so I was not poisoned.

At the port of Vishakapatnam, I stayed with a Jain family of drapers who a few generations back had migrated from distant Rajasthan in the far west of India. In the large compound, the joint family consisted of five brothers, their incoming wives and their children. My host Hiralal kept asking me, 'did your parents give you permission to travel?' A rather preachy man, he said, 'we look after our old people, not discarding them as in the west.' I ate separately from the rest of the family, which supported an organsation against cruelty to animals. After a while I felt that I needed to get away from the constricting Jain circle, so I walked to the seafront passing the fisher folk sorting out their dried fish on the sands.

It was arranged for me to visit Prema Samajam, a leprosy asylum. I found a number of the leprosy patients were educated but still ostracised by the community at large. Some of them were playing chess and other board games. Books and newspapers were scattered about in various stages of dilapidation. The atmosphere was congenial. One patient was working as a male nurse. I wondered if patients came voluntarily for refuge, but most were referred to the centre by their families and only a few invited themselves. There was little rehabilitation but the place did offer warm and friendly sanctuary.

Another centre contained an orphanage but the babies had not come from unwed mothers, rather from parents who had just been widowed and were unable to cope. There stood a house nearby for destitutes. This was a most depressing place. All the truly decrepit bodies were lying motionless on their beds. There seemed to be no communication between bodies, the poor wretches had been deserted and left to die by their families. Discarded like old rags, mainly because of poverty though a few hailed from middle class families. Nobody visited or talked to them, just their basic needs were catered for. I forgot to ask my moralising Jain host what he thought of this unhappy place, which was so dingy, even by Indian standards. Apart from bed boards, there was no furniture or cushions. A few maintained their dignity by working at a printing press.

To cheer myself up, I went to Simhachalam or Lion Hill. After one hour's walk, I witnessed a lovely view of a lake surrounding a temple. The water now looked stagnant but formerly the pious pilgrims would have bathed in it. Cashew nut trees grew profusely amongst the hill terraces thick with pineapple groves. Down in the temple, the devotees heads were being shaven for tapasya (penance). 'What do they do with the hair?' I asked. I was informed that the temple got good money for women's hair, which is particularly excellent for wig making. This was, once again, all good godly business. A huge sculptured lion stood at the temple gate. The man lion Narsingh is the fourth incarnation of Vishnu.

Before departing from Vishakaputnam, I visited a borstal and mental hospital. The borstal was entered through a green metal gate, which faced the prison and was noted for its incarcerated Naxalite revolutionaries. On either side of the borstal gates were giant paintings of Buddha and the elephant god Ganesh. Most striking was the expanse of red beaten earth, which competed with the vividness of the neat rows of rich green shrubs. Boys were playing badminton, the bulk of them aged sixteen to twenty years old. The borstal also held eye catching paintings of Hindu deities such as Saraswati who was the goddess of speech and music. The boys had painted all these lovely pictures. Besides the paintings, inscriptions on the walls proclaimed 'Keep good company or none' or 'Every child comes with a message that God is not yet discouraged of man' and 'Love cannot be forced, cannot be coaxed, it comes out of Heaven unmasked and unspoilt'. In the office hung a picture of Satya Sai Baba, the woolly-haired guru, with the caption 'Flowers are the sweetest thing that God ever made and forgot to put a soul into'. Many Hindus would dispute the fact that flowers or any plant did not have souls.

The boys went to borstal for offences, which could be punishable by imprisonment. They were mainly illiterate on entrance but were taught the three 'R's', some even sat for matriculation. They were taught agriculture, gardening, plastering, carpentry, irrespective of caste background. Nobody knew of my visit in advance and I was extremely impressed with the atmosphere of constructive learning. This was definitely more pleasing than any equivalent institution in Britain.

Hiralal, my Jain friend, was the only one of his family to involve himself in social work. He told me that he had to marry off his five daughters, and then afterwards he would be a free man. He was opposed to the dowry system but the Jains are big business people and it would be a rare future family of in-laws who would welcome any of his daughters without a huge dowry.

I went to the mental hospital with some of his sisters in true woman bountiful style to deliver fruits for patients. I met the lively western-trained woman head psychiatrist. She was plump with short hair and an American accent. When she took over the running of the hospital from her predecessor, she sent many chronic lifelong patients back into the community in order to concentrate on those with acute illnesses. Perhaps some of the chronic patients had ended up in that awful home for destitutes. In the unit for addicts, one of the doctors was addicted to morphine. Another patient came from Afghanistan. The criminal section was unfettered unlike at Jaipur, but they were kept behind bars in the admission unit. During my visit, all the doctors were on strike. This superintendent was a good-humoured woman in spite of her troubles. The Jain sisters that accompanied me admonished the woman psychiatrist in my presence regarding the hospital diet, which included meat. 'Why don't you stop it?' they enquired. The doctor replied, 'this is a government hospital, we cannot.' Once she was asked to take in some lepers and she exclaimed, 'We have got enough garbage already.'

Within the hospital, women were kept in separate compounds to men by being segregated by a big metal gate. In the outpatients unit, one minion was scribbling out prescriptions non-stop. Women were queuing up for electric shock therapy used for depression. In spite of her comments about the lepers there were a number of chronic patients staring vacantly into space while seated on some of the verandahs. One could see that perhaps they would have a negative effect on the other patients but it was hardly productive to take an 'out of sight out of mind' policy. I met a few of the social work students who came for three month stints, seconded from Andhra University. Just before leaving the hospital, I planted a coconut tree sapling.

The bus to Ellamanchalli, a small town to the north of Vishakapatnam, was packed and I joined over thirty other passengers standing in the gangway. After my arrival at yet another institution of social welfare, I was taken for a meal in celebration of a marriage of two tiny dolls made by some young girls in care. The dolls were blessed on their heads with uncooked rice and wore beautiful clothes as 'bride and groom'. A visiting Hindu priest 'married' the two dolls.

The next day, I went to Allapadu, an untouchable fishing community. These were highly-skilled people. For constructing traps, horizontal poles were fixed to two vertical poles. On the main horizontal pole hung strips of coconut fibre weighted with stones. Along the same pole, they fixed strips of bamboo, which also formed the basis of the net, then they wound the fibre around it by bringing strips of coconut coir forward towards them and vice versa. Whole families were involved over six month periods in producing these nets, by making the tiny strips of fibre twist into twine. Ingenious little doors allowed the fish to enter the net! The fishermen's huts were made of bamboo walling and the roofs were of palm leaves. These scheduled castes were no longer at the mercy of interest-grabbing money lenders. These usurers formerly demanded Rs 10 for every Rs 100 lent out. On the way back to Ellamanchalli, the bus passed numerous washermen emerging from a river bank carrying enormous bundles of washing on their backs. In the same river as the clothes had been washed, small boys were washing buffaloes with straw. A few long, rough wooden boats were scattered by the river bank. They had cabins made of palmyra thatch, possibly vulnerable to heavy leakage, no doubt.

At Ellamanchelli, I was the guest of Sreenavas Rao who was connected with an animal welfare organisation. He showed me a photo of a buffalo being milked with its tail shoved up its rectum, at the same time it was foaming at the mouth. Not a pretty sight. Afterwards, he showed me another untouchable colony of temporary palmyra thatched huts where women were making mats of woven palmyra leaves to be used as meal plates.

After bidding farewell, I departed for the south east state of Tamil Nadu.

Chapter Twenty Three

In the Land of the Tamils

Caught the Coromandel Express to Madras and had to kick my way through to get off, otherwise I would have detrained in the far south of Madurai.

I travelled from Madras onto Kanchipuram. This was the ancient capital of Vijaynagar's past rulers including the Pallavas, Cholas and Rajas. The area of Kanchipuram and its environs are occupied by numerous temples. The district forms part of the fertile Coromandel coastal plain, which has a semi-tropical atmosphere allowing a profusion of coconut and toddy palms to grow.

The Dravidian temples have their own style of architecture. They are richly sculptured, especially the gopurams, which are tall pyramid- style structures of several storeys high. The elaborate carvings include Hindu saints, legends and representatives from the major Hindu pantheon. The chariots made of wood are locally known as raths and they can only be found in the south. Each major temple has its chariot or temple car and they vary in size. On certain festivals, they are decorated and pulled by devotees along the streets. These Tamil temples have several internal shrines and a pair of these will be for the main god and his wife. The section called the kalyana mandapan is the marriage hall, the images of the god and goddesses are united in wedded bliss during several marriage ceremonies held at various times of the year.

I then travelled to the seaport of Mahabalipuram, which was built by one of the Pallava rulers in the seventh century. Against the deep blue sea, handsome temples cut out of solid rock project themselves. The sculptured buildings are a mixture of Buddhist and Dravidian influences. A panel of bas-reliefs depicts the descent of the Ganges from its Himalayan source. If that theme does not prove the unity of India, I do not know what does. The Ganges sculpturing was in juxtaposition to a multiplicity of gods and animals. Stone raths stand, which are named after the Pandavas who feature in the ancient Hindu epic the Mahabaratha. Right on the beautiful beach of Mahabalipuram stands a 'Shore Temple' dedicated to Shiva and Vishnu. Unfortunately, the temple scene was plagued by leather chapal (sandal) sellers who kept moaning 'business bad'.

The elephant god Ganesh is very popular and in these parts, he is better known as Subrahmanya. Stone statues and small carvings are everywhere in profusion in Tamil Nadu. I purchased two small figures of Ganesh whilst in Mahabalipuram as he is supposed to be a bringer of good luck. Amongst all the buying and selling, one fellow proved himself a Christian by suddenly thrusting out a tattooed arm holding a crucifix.

Before departing from Mahabalipuram, I visited the crocodile park, which had plenty of warnings such as 'Keep away hands' posted at strategic places on the cages.

Compared to Bombay, Delhi and Calcutta, Madras is a small provincial city as the capital of Tamil Nadu state. It has some handsome railway stations ranging from the white-domed Egmore to the clock towered central station. Along its tree-lined streets, there seemed to be more child beggars than I had seen elsewhere. It was in Madras that I first heard of the eccentric atheist leader E.V. Ramaswami or Periyar (Tamil for leader), as he was better known. He was an apostle of the Tamil anti Brahmin and North Indian cultural supremacy movement. His portraits show a grey bearded and bespectacled old man, I began to wonder if he was ever young. ('Negative atheism is what you will see,' I was forewarned). At his former headquarters, this dead atheist was rewarded with a memorial fit for a saint. A huge hand holding a burning torch created out of handsome black marble was his memorial. The museum consisted chiefly of gifts presented to Periyar such as a silver chair and silver plates, which I could not imagine he made much use of. The bulk of the permanent exhibition proclaimed his life in photos, though there were again, few of him as a young man. One painting showed him holding up a stone image of the elephant headed Ganesh poised so as to smash it. A good example of 'negative atheism'.

The rationalist who took me around the place was simplistically dogmatic, claiming, 'only fools believe in God.' The organisation functioned mainly as an anti-Brahmin movement. It was, in connection with this movement, strongly opposed to what it felt was too much domination by north Indians. Many Tamils believe that even some Tamil Brahmins originated in North India. Regarding the racial issue, it is true that many south Indian Brahmins are paler-skinned and have less broad features as compared to their southern brethren. Periyar attacked the Brahmins as house and temple priests ie. Purohit and Arcaka respectively and from this stance, he made general attacks on all religions, especially Hinduism because of its connection with the caste system. Interestingly enough, Periyar attacked the Brahmins as Aryans who transmitted Sanskrit Vedic culture. Connected to this latter point was a problem dear to Tamils more than other south Indians, and that was the pressure of the Indian ruling group based in New Delhi to make Hindi, one of the North Indian languages, albeit the dominant one, to be the national official language for all India. Because of this, the more extremist Tamil elements, including Periyar, when he was alive, advocated a separate country Dravidastan. His self- respect movement was based upon all these prejudices.

Periyar also campaigned against the ban on untouchables' admittance to temples and the prohibition against non Brahmin Tamils entrance to the central edifice of Hindu temples, the garbha griha. The Vaikom Satyagraha was an active campaign against untouchability leading to the passing of the Temple Entry Act in which Gandhi co-operated. Vaikom is a town in Kerala, formerly Travancore State where there were rigid laws regarding untouchability in and around the temple area. Periyar caught onto the anti caste feelings and in 1924, Vaikom was used to start a Satyagraha or passive resistance campaign. This was eventually successful in opening the temple to all Hindus. Periyar continued his campaigns into the wider political area by being involved in the Justice Party where he exclaimed that 'Home Rule is Brahmin Rule.'

In old Madras stood the oldest Anglican Church in India, namely St George built in 1680. It was connected with the East India Company. The nearby museum held little interest for me with its display of arms, military costumes, coins and medals. In the national state museum, there were magnificent collections of stone carvings depicting Hindu mythological themes. I found the bronze castings too sombre and cold. Bronze was never one of my favourite mediums of artistic expression.

On Sunday I walked up and down the long Madras beach. Only fisher boys were swimming in the shallow waters of a deep blue sea. The fishing boats are called by the Tamil word catamaran, which denotes wooden planks or logs strapped together. Larger and better- built plank boats had wooden strips sewn on top of each other with leather. Dotted along the beach were triangular Palmyra fishermen's huts. Most of their women were scattering their fish about on the sand for drying. They made all attempts at begging from me, their hands being thrust out and back to their mouths and stomachs. A few others attempted to sell shells.

Afterwards, I walked over to the High Courts and Law College built in handsome Indo-Saracen style. This contrasted visibly with the look of mediocrity on the faces of most of the students. Downtown Madras centres on Mount Road, which still sported the elegant old department store of Spencer's. Inside this Victorian, gothic edifice was a show of lovely wrought iron work on the ceilings. The top floor only held a collection of cheap oil paintings. The smell of fresh Madras coffee pervaded the atmosphere. Apart from the oil paintings, Spencer's was quite a classy store.

On Sunday, a group of Australian 'born again' Christians or 'Reach out for Christ' brigade at St Thomas Anglican Church, waylaid me. I followed them to a flat belonging to some Indian Christians. One of the Australians, an ex-architect, told me how he had lived the good bachelor life in Sweden and had caused two abortions. Then he 'found Jesus'. He informed me, 'The Muslim God is hate as he destroys unbelievers.' After the meal, we all touched each other addressing everyone by their personal names. Was the Australian ebullience just a form of phony sincerity? Back at St Thomas Church, I had witnessed some of them being involved in the process of exorcising evil spirits or devils. 'By the name of Jesus, I command ...' The poor victims always looked as if their heads were about to be parted from their bodies.

Another area in the old city was Armenian Street where, hidden away, was the Armenian Church. Here lived the remnants of that much-persecuted nation the Armenians, most of them were pensioners so the community still lived only in name. Their church was now virtually a museum piece and looked after by a rather nervous woman who lived in a flat on the church roof. She behaved as if she was seeking refuge away from the world. An aura of bitterness enveloped her. She had an olive complexion and short hair and her angry face told me that she still hated all Muslims. Inside the flat the walls were covered with yellowing newspaper cuttings about her community. The last group photograph taken of the Armenians of Madras, showed them alongside the former Armenian Bishop Vaharis Constantiaris in 1949 when he was their Madras bishop. This bearded figure was also hooded and robed.

The Armenians settled in Madras about 1702 and they acquired land on what was to be the future Admiralty. Then the community sold out to the Portuguese East India Company who ordered the Armenians to be evicted from what was named "white town'. Later, when there were forty Armenians in the vicinity, they built a new church.

I left the Armenians and a friend from the Madras YMCA where I stayed showed me a home for the mentally ill. It was full of boys who had been rejected or run away from their parents. Many had been found by the police on streets or trains. Sympathy was often lacking for them because of belief in karma or rebirth. Very few took the children back home. Their behaviour might hinder marriage chances of siblings. Also I was told that in south India incest was often blamed for mental problems. In Tamil Nadu state there seemed to be a higher number of uncle-niece marriages. Also several social workers included 'brain fever', polio and 'falling down wells'. The government had donated to the home in 1980 and activities such as sheltered workshops made it more lively than equivalent places I had seen in Britain.

By bus to Vellore to meet Dr Benjamin at the Church Missionary Community Development Centre. Their New Life Centre was involved with leprosy patients. In their pig sty, I spied the healthiest Yorkshire breed of pigs in all India. In 1980 the Christian hospital still dominated this pleasant town of Vellore. Dr Benjamin showed me some village projects involving women's self employment. Home manufacturing of sisal grass mats, baskets and various palm leaf goods. Everywhere, women were hand threshing mounds of jawar (barley) in the middle of the roads.

A letter to the Madras paper The Hindu claimed that to 'walk the streets of Madras with a bottle of whisky in my hands is a serious offence but if I were to let loose hell over an area of one square kilometre right from sunrise till midnight with loud speakers planted all around creating noise that would be fine. This appears to have become part of our living and serves no function.' No function, be it political, religious or social is complete without a loud speaker. The writer went on, 'if only the amount of noise we make were an index of our religious fervour, political maturity and social etiquette, then I should think we should lead the world.' These were my sentiments exactly. The loud speaker is the modern curse of India and especially when Hindi film music is its chief offering.

Moore Market sold everything from spare parts to old gramophones. A red bricked archway edifice towered over the tiny kiosks below. A visit there was followed by a detour to the Tamil town of Tiruvanamelai, where the holy sage Ramana Mahashi formerly lived. His photographs showed the gentlest persona imaginable, with bright intelligent eyes set in a small bearded face. En route to the ashram, my cycle rickshaw passed three huge wooden temple chariots. Their carvings depicted the usual complex Hindu mythology.

Within the holy man's ashram compound were about twenty four westerners of varying ages. One English woman went there for six months each year. Arunachala Mountain shot up behind the ashram but not oppressively. Climbing up the mountain, one got a magnificent view of the old Dravidian temple complex dominating the town. Ramana Mahashi had a wonderful affinity with wild life and he could rightly be called the Indian St Francis. The ashram was too crowded for my taste, I kept longing for my little refuge far away in the Himalayan foothills of the Sivaliks.

Briefly leaving Tamil Nadu for Bangalore, I went to meet a new friend Sri Menon, who ran a welfare centre for girls called Vallabh Niketan ashram. Menon was a well meaning but naïve apologist for not only the Soviet Union, but also Stalinism in that he believed Stalin's atrocities to be exaggerated. Certainly, he was correct in condemning mindless modern systems of education. He thus established a 'Friends World University' with students scattered in many countries. He advised his students to understand India and not necessarily rush to the west but study other Asiatic countries such as Japan.

One of the ashram evenings during my visit was put aside for a poetry recitation session. These were always more lively affairs than their western counterparts as the audience deemed it their right to join in with appropriate exclamations of 'Wah Wah' ('Bravo! Bravo!') These exclamations occur after a witty turn of phrase or lilt in the voice. A lot of clapping takes place but it does not seem to interfere with the performance. Most of the poetry was in the north Indian languages of Urdu or Punjabi, some religious and often romantic. Some thought the Punjabi poetry was a bit earthy judging by the type of laughter going on. Unlike the Muslim and Sikh poets, the Hindus recited in Hindi or Telegu as the latter tongue is the language of Bangalore because it is situated in the state of Andhra Pradesh.

I had a long, interesting bus journey to Satya Sai Baba's world famous ashram at Puttaparthi. The countryside was stacked with low- lying but rugged hills. Sheep were dotted about the landscape but the prettiest sight was of the little gatherings of bullocks with brightly coloured rugs on their backs. This formed part of the local festival to give thanks for the service of these animals to man. This was just the kind of festival that attracted me to parts of Hinduism. The bullocks looked majestic in their rugs, which probably covered some rather scrawny bodies. Some animals were on the move while others were resting along the roadside. The poorest farmers covered their animals in sacking.

My immediate impression at Sai Baba's orderly ashram was of better-heeled Indian and western disciples. There was less of the lean and hungry look of some of the western disciples of Rajneesh with lots of mothers and children about. One woman from Trinidad looked at my sceptical face rather sadly and said in a voice of deep foreboding, 'You did not get darshan (view of Baba) darling?'

Sadly, I did not even have the opportunity of seeing Baba as he came and went without anyone knowing. From his photos, he was a striking-looking man with a massive Afro hair cut on top of a gentle brown face. He appeared to be always dressed in an immaculate silk or cotton kurta and pyjama dress.

I moved into a new concrete hostel with bare unfurnished rooms. I paid only Rs 3 per night. Luckily, I carried some light blankets with me. My neighbour had lived here for five years and came from Australia. This middle aged woman had left her family behind to be with Baba.

The first evening, I was not allowed in the temple because my body, including my head was not sufficiently covered. I had never been refused entry because of clothing into any temple. I was wearing loose fitting trousers and an equally loose shirt but with bare arms. The next time I was lucky. In Hindu fashion, the congregation sat cross-legged while chanting Sanskrit prayers. Women on the left and men on the right but not segregated as in many mosques, where women are often forbidden entry.

Whatever criticisms have been made of Satya Sai Baba, it cannot be denied that he had financed many educational institutions, which were remarkable for their good standards within a sea of mediocrity. It was his aim to revive study of the ancient Vedas. Where the Vedas are properly taught, it can take up to seven years to learn these texts by heart. Traditionally, they were memorised by chanting so that the exact sounds would be transmitted in Sanskrit to prevent misinterpretation. At Puttaparthi, the ashram had a model dairy. Alongside the dairy, there was a beautiful statue of Krishna as a young man and cowherd in his typical posture as flute player standing beside a radiant sacred cow.

On the return bus to Bangalore, an aristocratic looking Bengali woman who may have come from the ashram, suddenly began to discuss Punjabis when she exclaimed, 'These Punjabis have spoilt everything ... a rough lot.' She hated Delhi and was non committal when I mentioned my liking for Chandigarh, the then attractive modern town in Punjab.

I returned to Madras for Christmas and stayed again at a YMCA, which was as usual, situated in a handsome old colonial building in suburban Madras. From there, I attended the Church of South India's own church of St Andrews. Its name and manner of service informed me of its former links with the Church of Scotland as Presbyterians had been amalgamated into the Church of South India, which is part of worldwide Anglicanism.

An Indian Christian family invited me for Christmas lunch of biryani. After the meal, a wealthy Jain visited the family to offer religious greetings, and then he departed on what looked like a fourth-hand scooter that coughed its way out of the front gate. My host told me that the Jain worked 'non-stop'. Nevertheless, as a typical 'Marwari', he just 'wants to make money'. Marwar is a region of Rajasthan and the term 'Marwari' describes business communities who originally hail from that area. Marwari was often a term of abuse for these people implying that they are crafty. Some months before a row had broken out regarding a Gujarati dictionary, which gave the derogatory meaning to the regional word.

The Scots minister of St Andrews invited some of the YMCA guests to his manse for supper and here we drank wine. Because of prevalent teetotalism in the 'dry' state of Tamil Nadu, many local Christians did not even approve of communion wine, so during the service, little cups of what looked like blackcurrant juice were distributed in Presbyterian style around the seated congregation. I had not eaten English food for years so I relished the cold meats and baked potatoes.

The Theosophical Society held its annual gathering at the internationally-famous headquarters in Adyar, a suburb of Madras. The centre is well situated in several hundred acres of ground and places for worship representing the major world faiths, which are situated in the gardens. The Christian Church was being represented by the little known but tolerant Liberal Catholic Church. The Theosophical movement encourages the study of comparative religion and science. It also seeks to investigate unexplained laws of nature and mankind's latent powers. People arrived from all over India and abroad for the conference. I was befriended by a Sikh who was also a member of the Paris based Co-Freemasons, which is a branch of freemasonry allowing female membership.

During a meal, while discussing my travels over India, a delegate from Varanasi exclaimed that although Kashmiris were fair-skinned, they were rather dirty. 'We tend to think because they are fair that they would be cleaner.' A little later in the conversation, a Parsi woman informed me regarding south Indians that, 'despite their skin colour, they have some fine points.' As a generality, it was believed by north Indians that south Indians were less aggressive and better educated. To some extent, this could be true.

Before moving into regular lodgings for my ten day stay after the conference, I shared a straw hut with a couple of Germans and generally amused them when discussing my exploits. I suppose that I found that I could relax in a way that I would not allow myself to do, even in front of my closest Indian friends. I always felt that Indians would be questioning enough because I was a women who normally travelled alone.

The Theosophical conference coincided with a series of open lectures given in Madras by the sage Krishnamurthi who was formerly connected with the Theosophical movement and was discovered by Annie Besant, the British social reformer who attempted to develop him for 'Messiahship'. Krishnamurthi was always speaking against submitting to authority in the form of the traditional guru chela relationships, but he found it hard to escape that predicament with his own followers. He was a handsome man with a calm, beardless face and an Oxford accent. He would always interrupt his discourses and look at some character in the crowd and say, 'you are following all this?' His main theme had a Buddhist flavour when he spoke of desires imprisoning the mind. More challenging was the point he made that we should try and look at objects without making opinions, even when looking at a tree, we should forget its name. During one dialogue towards the climax, Krishnamurthi blurted out to somebody 'For Christ sake, are you listening?' The Indian students in the crowd were habitually interrupting Krishnamurthi.

A Muslim Theosophist (a rare species), spoke on meditation at seven in the morning in the tiny mosque garden back at the headquarters. He stressed that in meditation, one must not force the mind. In Hindu imagery, he discussed the 'Boundless Ocean', which is unconscious of itself. That we were (before birth) drops in the ocean without sensation of separateness between the ocean and ourselves. Then there was a desire in the ocean to manifest itself. Waves emerged and through a wave comes a bubble. The journey of the bubble goes through the mineral-animal-human kingdoms. Thus in the centre of all of us is that drop of water, that bubble. The soul within us is connected with the whole ocean. In meditation, we should not initially be conscious of the big ocean, only the bubble. The bubble then becomes disentangled from mental and physical impression. Finally, we must become one with the ocean and the cycle goes on. The imagery was heresy for a regular Muslim mainly because of Islam's belief in the duality of God and Man.

A north Indian friend had given me a letter of introduction to a Gujarati woman called Kusum Bhen who lived at the international centre in Tamil Nadu, namely Auroville. Auroville was an attempt to construct an international city of world peace via the teachings of the guru Sri Aurobindo and the Mother (a French disciple of Aurobindo). The main ashram was based in the former French colony of Pondicherry.

My host, Kusum Bhen had been requested by the Mother to look after the tiny Ganesh temple. Inside this temple, Lord Ganesh was carved in shiny black stone. Kusumji would lovingly clean out the temple and daily garland, the tiny statue with fresh flowers. A wealthy proprietor formerly owned the land where the temple stood. The Mother was requested to find someone to look after the temple, so Kusumji was asked. At first, she took on the task solely for the Mother but later she did it because of her devotion for God in the form of the elephant-headed bringer of good luck and learning. By the time I left India, I nearly became a devotee of Ganesh or Ganapati as he is sometimes called.

I lived in one sector of Auroville called by the optimistic name Promesse. During my stay with Kusumji, the Tamil Pongal festival was about to begin. At four in the morning, an enactment of an ancient temple drama was on record and blasted out all over the landscape via the ubiquitous loud speaker. Each day ended with the pair of us walking to the tiny temple of Lord Ganesh. Kusumji would light a tiny clay oil lamp and perform the fire ritual, the idea being to light the light within ourselves. The temple bell, which is situated near the entrance of most temples, was rung in order to wake up the God and ourselves.

Before bed each evening, Kusumji practised on the harmonium. 'This is for my old Age,' she claimed. The Indian harmonium is a square wooden box with piano keys at the front and a back that is open and shut while playing. Somebody told me that Mr Nehru had wanted to ban the harmonium but I never discovered why. Perhaps he found the sound monotonous.

Auroville, which claimed to be a haven of peace, was a centre of squabbling inactivity compared with ashram projects I was to see in Pondicherry, while staying at the Ashram's International Guest House for only a few rupees per night. While there I obtained meal tickets to eat at the main ashram restaurant, which was situated in a large French house with a towering ceiling and huge handsome shuttered doors. It was a clean and well-ordered place. There were tables and mats for those who preferred eating on the floor. One ashramite thought I looked underfed because he kept catching my attention for second helpings. I thought it best not to be too greedy because of the ever watching eyes of Sri Aurobindo and the Mother whose enormous photographs looked down on the diners.

The ashram had a main building constructed around the burial remains of Sri Aurobindo and the Mother. Otherwise, its projects were scattered all over the town of Pondicherry, which lies on the south east coast of India. The ashram schemes ranged from handmade paper making using bamboo waste, rags and sugar cane waste. The ayurvedic pharmacy, which held a variety of tablets with extravagant names such as the 'power pill' which 'strengthens the brain and heart' besides slowing down ageing. Then there were 'gas pills' and 'appetising pills', also 'Sonaswami milk purgative brings easy motion'.

I kept bumping into a French woman who called herself 'Auroculture'. She collected flowers from all over the world and dried them. She then turned them into compost in order to create new matter to 'raise consciousness'. This was her way of purifying the atmosphere. Her husband was Iranian and was absent during my visit. She invited me to her room and told me she had lived eight years at Pondicherry and only twenty people had been allowed in her room, so I was very privileged. She invited few people because she did not like to 'disturb the vibrations'. Her room was full of pots enclosing compost of the purest kind. She was incredibly diligent as she showed me educational visual aids for mathematics teaching, which she had designed. Humbly, she claimed that the ideas came from the Mother. Unfortunately, she had had trouble getting these aids accepted by teachers, even in this so called enlightened atmosphere.

Sri Aurobindo's educational method taught in its school was exam free. Learning here was based upon the child's self-discipline. For more than seven hundred children, they had four hundred teachers. The pupils could opt for any course of study from French to beekeeping. The classrooms were lovely with the tables and chairs arranged informally.

Auroculture explained some of the difficulties with members of the Sri Aurobindo Society who lived away from the ashram, 'People with big cars who do not understand us.'

One day I went for a walk along the beach and an Indian family requested me to photograph them using their camera. They stood to attention in front of the modern concrete building, which could have been anywhere, the position of the sun had nothing to do with their choice. I enquired as to whether they disliked the sea, and then they started giggling so eventually I told them to stand with their backs to the sea and face the sun. This episode amused me because in Pakistan, one of my hosts showed me a photograph of two women standing to attention in front of two broken television sets. One wonders about middle class aesthetic taste. It is true that many people could not relax in front of cameras, thus their facial expressions reminded one of the stern postures encountered on Victorian–Edwardian photos.

One day, I met Vijay, a teacher at the ashram school. He said that all the children belonged to the resident sadhaks (members of the ashram). For some incomprehensible reason, he informed me that the teachers did not wish to exchange or share ideas with their brethren at Auroville. One 'Aurovillian' had been to Vijay's house and 'he took notes and never looked at me.' The ashramites also believed that many of those living at Auroville to be hippies or dropouts. They claimed that such people had not read Sri Aurobindo's writings.

In one house, I met a man called Richard who was a Yorkshireman with a French accent. To crown it all, he hailed from a neighbouring village of my birthplace near Huddersfield, Yorkshire.

I departed from Pondicherry whose whole existence revolved around the ashram complex and took the train southwards back into Tamil Nadu to the small town of Puddokotai. The prime reason for my visit was Sarma's Nature Cure Sanatorium.

How unlike the western idea of a sanatorium, it was just a group of straw huts huddled together in a little compound. Immediately after my arrival, I was offered a tasty drink of ragi, which is a malt drink made of millet. Another popular drink of the area was a lovely tonic made from fresh ginger. My host's father who had been a lawyer and a frequent sufferer with stomach ailments, had founded the centre. A fellow advocate suggested German naturopath Louis Kuhne's method of treatment with special baths and improved diet. The elder Sarma experimented with this method and his problem departed. Unlike many nature curists, Sarmaji was opposed to steam baths because it put 'too much pressure on the heart.' He was also opposed to the Hyderabadi school, which advocated drinking quite large amounts of water in order to cleanse the body of impurities. Sarmaji said that this overworked the kidneys. 'Diet is the main thing and fasting should be for about a week.'

Sarmaji in common with several Brahmins, introduced as part of their nationalist movement, the Anti Vaccine campaign with allopathic western orthodox vaccines being viewed as 'filth'. He advised me, while travelling around India, to offer to do 'non-violent enemas' for the public. 'All you need is a stainless steel or anodised aluminium can, which will carry half a pint of water plus a tube of a metre in length.' In India, it was quite usual for people to mix Imperial and metric measurements. People would speak of a place being so many kilometres and in the next breath speak of a direction being so many furlongs.

Sarmaji told me of his European visit. Many of his hosts, he said, misunderstood vegetarianism. Somebody informed him vaguely that 'any beast that does not have hooves can be included.' At one place fish had been specially cooked for the Indian guests. Sarmaji and company practically existed on milk. Luckily enough, they were not vegans who refuse all animal products, including milk and cheese.

The second day of my visit was the start of Pongal harvest festival, which takes place in January. It is a Tamil festival equivalent to Holi in north India. As with many Hindu festivals, Pongal offers an opportunity for spring cleaning ones house. Houses are plastered and whitewashed. Rice flour designs are made of Hindu themes on the ground both inside and outside buildings. Sarmaji's wife cooked the glorious pongal, which is rice mixed with milk and coarse sugar jaggery and cooked in a huge handleless pot. When the pongal was cooked, she cried "Pongalo Pongal"! ('Hail Pongal!') The rice pudding was delicious.

The following day of the festival, I woke up to find Sarmaji's cow already garlanded after being washed. On this day, the animals get special attention. A less fortunate animal was a small bullock, which came hurtling past Sarmjai's front entrance because it was being chased by children trying to grab at the rupee notes tied to its horns. This was all part of the festive spirit of Pongal.

Sarmaji's son was a photographer who had photographed former Prime Minster Shastri and the then-leader of Pakistan, Ayub Khan, when they met in Tashkent. Ayub Khan was an extremely tall Pathan while Shastri was a tiny Hindu. I reflected that it was hard to believe that once the fiery Pathans of the North West Frontier Province of Pakistan belonged to the same country of India as the predominantly dark-skinned gentle Tamils of the deep south of that country.

The preferred mode of dress in Tamil Nadu was to keep the chest bared when not wearing a white cotton shawl, together with a white lungi skirt. For women, Tamil Nadu is sari country but there seem to be hundreds of ways of wearing this garment according to caste rules.

The food I ate was simple vegetarian fare. At breakfast, I was offered idli, which is a steamed white cake made of rice flour and black gram pulse, utma was the semolina dish with chillies and peas added. Coffee is the predominant beverage in Tamil Nadu and it is usually served in metal tumblers. Sarmajis sanatorium forbade any tea or coffee. Another south Indian favourite was dosa, a huge rice pancake filled with vegetables and eaten with fresh coconut chutney. All 'Madras Hotels' (cafes) would serve these dishes in many parts of India.

By bus to Kodaikanal, a small hill station of seven thousand feet up in the eastern ghats, not too far from the dusty, dirty but glorious temple city of Madurai. The bus wound upwards at a reckless speed. On arrival, I felt goose pimples on my arms as the temperature had dropped considerably.

I stayed at a small hotel in the centre of the bazaar. This market consisted of one main street which cut the town into two parts. The ubiquitous Kashmiri shopkeepers were well represented. For these Muslims, a new mosque was being constructed. Kodaikanal was far less commercialised than many better-known hill stations and far superior in scenery to its more famous counterpart on the western ghats, Ootacamund. English-style cottages dotted the hillsides, their most noticeable characteristic being the lack of any barred windows.

Walking along the beautiful lakeside, I bumped into an Indian professor of maths based at Alberta University in Canada. He was a Brahmin and a fanatically anti-American pro-Indian nationalist. He told me, after inviting me back to his hired cottage, that the Americans dominated the whole of Canada's economy, even his university. He took me for a nice meal at the Old Carleton Hotel where I had steak and cheese soufflé. Because of an absence of guests, the hotel was freezing, as the authorities could not afford to heat it up, so I took my after dinner tea while shivering in a blanket. Afterwards, we went for a lovely walk overlooking miles of terraced hills. Luckily, there were still dense carpets of virgin forest. My friend was a keen amateur ornithologist who continually lectured me about how the 'white man' had destroyed more flora and fauna than any other human group. The following day he took me for a ride in a taxi but all I remember of it was that every ten minutes, we would stop at fresh coconut stalls.

On arrival at the city of Madurai, I went to the home of Servas member Sri Pandian who worked as an advocate. He had a small dark fine-featured face and he was a Brahmin. I remarked uncritically upon the dark skin of the Tamils. 'But some are beautiful,' he exclaimed. Who said that colour had anything to do with beauty?

The Dravidian style of temples found in Tamil Nadu are amongst the richest to be found anywhere in India. The city is a mass of lavishly sculptured stone buildings. Nine large towers of gopurams surround the Great Temple built in the seventeenth century. A related temple dedicated to Siva's consort Minakshi (a locally name for Parvati). The most memorable scene was the huge pillared stone corridors, amongst these pillars stood tiny traders' stalls or kiosks selling everything from baskets to plastic images of Lord Ganesh, a scene reminiscent of Balthazar's Feast. Any moment, I expected Jesus to step out and chase away the moneylenders. One huge hall had been transformed into a tailors' centre. Rows of treadle machines stood in front of the pillars and facing these tailors were rows of cloth merchants. One chap lay sleeping on his counter, the next man was sitting cross-legged staring into space. Voices exclaimed 'What what'' or 'Indian pyjama' and something that resembled 'pudum' and 'abam'. In one of the temple compounds, tiny children begged. A German girl told me how she had had her bag snatched. I gave her a few rupees.

Dendrolatry (tree worship) of the sacred tree Sthalavriksha is old in Tamil Nadu. There are also images that honour the Vilva trees and sacred Tulsi plant. Siddha herbal medicine is prepared and poured over some of the images. It is believed that ethereal changes take place owing to astro-physical elements within the substance of the images!

One of my host, Pandian's neighbours was a Christian woman from Sri Lanka and she invited me to her house. She disliked the orthodox Hindu neighbourhood and one Brahmin boy she had invited for lunch exclaimed 'you Christians like fish and meat.' She too had visited Kody (Kodaikanal) and materialistic locals had murmured, 'Why go to Kody there is no life there.' This woman liked to play cricket but because of social conventions, she was only able to play the game inside her compound.

I visited Gandhi Museum and got the usual teasing from boys in the park, though 'Eve teasing' was not endemic in south India as in parts of the north. They kept demanding 'Give me stamps'. I ended up slapping one. Back on the streets, there seemed to be a surfeit of giggling females who found me highly amusing. In the museum I glanced at a book by Nehru's secretary Sri Mathai called My Days with Nehru. Mathai claimed that he was pursued by white women who he found were fond of dark skinned men!

Sri Pandian took me to one government rehousing scheme for Tamils who had left Sri Lanka. These Tamils had refused to take Sri Lankan citizenship as they were Indians by birth so they were expelled from Sri Lanka without their hard earned cash, which was their payment for working on tea plantations.

The housing colony consisted of tiny rectangular brick houses with red tiled roofs. The inhabitants wore ragged clothes. One man exclaimed to me 'wait' and appeared again with a dejected and undeveloped nine year old albino girl. She was regarded as a zoo like specimen. They requested that I should 'take her to England' because she does not like the sun'. They had played on her strange appearance and kept her retarded. She was not originally mentally handicapped but now she acted as if she was. I gave them my opinions of their treatment, via my interpreter Sri Pandian and told them that although they had not been deliberately unkind to the girl, they should let her take on little tasks about the place and not be continually shut away.

Srinagar houses and workboats, Kashmir

Shah Hamadan Mosque, Kashmir

The author in the Persian gardens

Ladakhi 'Tibetan' group, India

Chorten (Stupa) Ladakh, India

Punjabi Jat farmers, India

Tomb Shah Rukn Multan, Pakistan

Hunza, Pakistan

Local houses Hunza, Pakistan

Chaukundi Tombs, nr Karachi Sind, Pakistan

Bal (children) Ashram in Gujarat

Gir Bull, Gujarat

Statue of Dr Ambedkar with 'scheduled castes' Andhra Pradesh,
South India

'Pongal' Festival, Karnataka, South India

Backwaters Kerala, India

Dakshineshwar Kali Temple, Calcutta

Chapter Twenty Four

To the Land of Serendipity

I travelled by overnight train journey to the port of Rameswaram on the southernmost tip of India in order to catch the ship to Sri Lanka. The 'Rameswaram Passenger' arrived at its destination about four in the morning, just in time for everybody to argue with a sea of cycle rickshaw pullers. As the saying went, 'the boat journey to Sri Lanka is one big hassle.' The 'passenger train' was packed to capacity, so it had been impossible to sleep and just a few stations prior to Ramaswaram, the train was invaded by some noisy, pushy characters who ignored dozed voices from my carriage crying 'reservation!'

I just managed to reserve a room at the Indian Government Tourist Bungalow, which was beautifully situated on Ramaswaram beach. From the window, one could see groups of saried women splashing about in the shallow waves, for once, they were not being bashful.

The next day the boat departed for Lanka. The journey would be only three hours long but the queues began at seven thirty in the morning. My immediate problem was that the Sri Lankans refused my Indian rupee notes, partly because I did not have a certificate stating where I had received them. Two English travellers came to my rescue and exchanged my rupees for German marks, English pounds and US dollars! Getting rid of the Indian notes was like ridding oneself of persistent bindweed!

Before we joined the main boat, all passengers climbed onto a dilapidated wooden vessel, which was steered outwards to the large ship.

'What time does it go?'

'No definite time' came the helpful reply. It was supposed to leave at one o'clock but it actually left at half past three in the afternoon. Remember that I had queued since half past seven in the morning. The arrival time at Sri Lanka was six thirty in the evening but those of us travelling second class disembarked at quarter to ten in the evening. The Ceylonese returning home held a precious commodity called plastic buckets. I had never seen so many in my life, perhaps there was a scarcity in Lanka. While we were queuing to get off the boat, it was the Indians or Ceylonese rather than the westerners who kept jumping the queue. Strangely enough, nobody complained. At Sri Lanka's Talaimannar railway station, there was a mad rush for Sri Lankan rupees.

The Sri Lankan authorities tended to regard all western passengers who travelled by boat rather than plane as degenerate hippies or potential drug smugglers. The 'boat train' to Colombo departed at the correct time of ten thirty pm regardless of the time of the incoming boat. While we were queuing for the currency, everyone was murmuring 'Oh, it won't go on time, they never do.' Well it did, leaving about one hundred of us stranded on the crummy little station. The café was pathetic and we accosted an unhelpful station master who paraded us into a large metal garage-like structure, so we spread out on the floor. We made the usual jokes about 'welcome to Sri Lanka'. There was constant chattering and clattering the entire night. I met up again with the German girl whose money had been stolen in the Minakshi Temple back in Madurai.

I decided against going direct to Colombo, so I took the first train at five am bound for Anuradhapura. The wooden slatted seats were filthy, at the front of the carriage, a dingy sign said 'Reserved for Clergy'. The clergy in question were Buddhist monks. Matters were not in my favour when I had purchased the wrong bananas from some Tamil stallholder, they tasted woody in texture. On throwing them out of the window, in the direction of a couple of goats, I was amused to see that the animals ate the skin and left the contents!

At Anuradhapura, I spent a few days at an awful cheap hotel, which was the sort of place that when one took a bath in the roofless compound, one had to be constantly on the alert for leering kitchen boys. Most of the guests as foreigners were less than complementary about Sri Lanka – as opposed to India. 'They are always staring and mocking at foreigners'. 'Yes, that is why we are leaving,' chimed in another group.

Anuradhapura has a history of well over two thousand years, as it was one of Sri Lanka's ancient capitals. A 'daughter' of the sacred Bo-Tree or peepul of India's Bodh Gaya is planted here and it is supposed to be related to that Bo-tree that Gautama Buddha meditated under. Around the particular tree are some of its descendants.

Local versions of Buddhist stupas are the dagobas, which are bell-shaped coverings of reliquaries. They are scattered about the ancient site. The only remains of the Brazen Palace, which was really a monastery, is a huge group of stone pillars about twelve feet high. Besides other monastic ruins are pokunas, which are either sacred bathing tanks or storage for drinking water, probably a mixture of uses. Nearby, just outside the centre of Anuradhapura is the rock temple in Isurumuniya. The temple, like many of its counterparts in India, is carved out of solid rock. Inside is a large statue of a seated Buddha.

I took a bus to Mihintale, which is a famous pilgrimage centre owing to its connection with Mahinda who is believed to have introduced Buddhism into Sri Lanka from India. The centre of focus being a stone bed called Mahinda's Bed, situated in a tiny cell. The central hill of which it forms a part is dominated by a large dagoba, which is approached by steep steps forming part of a huge complex of stairways that lead to scattered temples.

I visited Sigiriya and its Lion Rock with a German boy who had been sleeping in my hotel dormitory. Sigirya rock rises abruptly above the surrounding forests. It has a steep ascent but one is rewarded at the summit. There are exquisite frescoes painted on the rock surfaces. The gentle faced bare-breasted females are adorned with fabulous head dresses and elaborate hairstyles. Their fingers exquisitely poised, holding flowers and trays with exotic fruits. All the figures are adorned with necklaces. These frescoes date from c 500 AD. At the foot of the steps are gigantically carved lions feet with only the paws remaining.

There were so many German visitors to Lanka that German became the second foreign language of many people who met visitors. One local saw my camera flash and yelled 'blitz!' 'Oh no,' my German friend said, 'It is too crazy, I cannot stand it!' The problem was that many German visitors came in convoys of coaches and thus spoiled the atmosphere around them. Such groups were hardly noticeable in a huge country like

India but in Lanka, they appeared to take over some places. My German pal discovered his countrymen on some occasions and exclaimed 'I am a New Zealander'. The joke backfired back at the hotel when a local man asked him about New Zealand cricket! We could not contain our laughter. The hotel provided excellent 'hoppers' (rice pancakes) and buffalo yogurt served with jaggery (brown sugar).

Kandy is a delight to the eye, it has a heavily wooded setting centred on a small artificial lake. The Temple of the Tooth is situated on the lakeside with a backcloth of wooden hills. Its striking red tiled roof over-layed external walls of stuccoed paintwork. Immediately beside the temple was a tortoise filled tank, which was crossed by a small bridge with two stone elephants alongside it. The 'sacred tooth' in question is claimed to be one of Gautama Buddha's. It has been in Sri Lanka since the fourth century AD but the Portuguese insisted that they had removed it to Goa in the fifteenth century and destroyed it. The Buddhists claim that the Portuguese only destroyed the replica.

I missed one of the elephant parades during my Kandy visit because of a minor attack of sunstroke caught on the heights of Sigiriya through dehydration and too much sunshine. Luckily, I was staying at a pleasant guesthouse situated in the forests. Their food was excellent as they served gigantic bowls of fruit salad and buffalo yogurt plus chocolate cake made especially for the foreigners. Owing to illness, I was off eating and shared a room with two selfish foreign women who kept me awake all night. I was sick and had headaches.

One day, I struggled down to the British Council reading room and avidly read the New Statesman. British Council reading rooms were often so cosy that it was easy to fall asleep in their armchairs.

The sign on the bus to Nuwara Eliya hill station threatened a Sri Lankan Rs 200 fine for smoking inside the vehicle, needless to say the driver was puffing away quite merrily. On arrival, I visited Hakgala botanical gardens, which had a delightful background of a fertile mountainside planted with shrubs of cypress and rhododendron. There was a chilly atmosphere as the sun was full of inhibitions. The garden was beautifully kept and I nearly missed it as the bus conductor initially refused to take me to the garden, as it was an 'express bus', so I enquired at the bus office and the official therein ordered the conductor to drop me there. Of course, by the time

I actually had got on the bus, it was packed to capacity so as usual I had to stand crammed with others. The ticket collector deliberately avoided demanding a fare from me even when I asked him twice. Maybe he had a twinge of guilt.

Nuwara Eliya had a handsome half-timbered English style Hill Club that was originally a hunters' club. I ate a costly lunch, half of which I left as my appetite failed me. A waiter wearing white gloves was serving. I ate with knife and fork, the first time for a couple of years. Hanging over the dining room fireplace was a portrait of Queen Elizabeth II. That is all I remember of it. One of the drawing rooms had a selection of black and white prints of Hogarth's 'Industrious Apprentice'. Without a fire burning, the place looked empty and the deep armchairs appeared permanently unused. I picked up one Country Life magazine, which was dated 1946. On the way out of the building, I passed a group of noisy French tourists, perhaps it was they who had filled the womens' washroom with awful paper handkerchiefs.

Later, I walked to the Pedro Tea Estate, which was situated just outside Nuwara Eliya. The Pedro Estate tea plants were sown before the sun set on the British Empire. Tea plants may last one hundred years. Normally, they are pruned every five years. In 1975, the estates were nationalised. During the manufacturing process, about forty five percent of the tannin is removed. Pedro Estate made seven grades of tea, one of which was labelled 'Super Dust'. This was a familiar sight as I was such a frequenter of basic teashops. It took twelve to fourteen hours to remove moisture from the leaves before they were twisted and fermented as the leaves oxidise. Afterwards, the familiar aroma coupled with the brown colour appeared in about one and a half hours. The majority of the work force were Tamils, in fact, it seemed the Tamils appeared to be the hardest workers on the island rather than the dominant Sinhalese.

It was strange, after India, to see alcohol sold almost anywhere. There was none of that feeling of alcohol not being quite respectable that existed in India, even in areas without prohibition. Women here could drink in most places without feeling cheap. I sampled some local arrack, which tasted more like whisky.

Off to Colombo and I found that the zoo was one of the best I'd seen. Any place would have been superior to the zoo in Karachi where animal teasing thrived. The indignity of man on animals. All the cages in Karachi had 'Do not tease the animals' signs, but that did not stop the young ones indulging themselves in that vice.

I stayed at the YWCA, which was situated in an old decayed rambling Dutch colonial mansion. The roof was in the process of being retiled. In the centre of the entrance hall was a richly-carved Dutch table covered with intricately carved animals. A capable, energetic stout Tamil woman ran the place with a rod of iron. All her co-workers were Tamil. She offered me a hearty condemnation of the behaviour of western, especially German girls who 'appear to pick up any local boys.' The excuse offered was usually 'Well, I met him and he said he would like tea.' Then our Tamil woman added, 'You British keep your old traditions', as if to apologise to me. The food was good, plain English fare with a choice of fried fish or beef and two vegetables plus a pudding.

The old Portuguese port of Galle is situated on the south west tip of the island. It was an important stopping place for vessels between Aden and the Far East. Galle had a lovely white mosque, which served the fairly large local population of Tamil Muslims. The mosque may once have been a Portuguese church. A lovely Tamil Muslim family ran the guesthouse. How unlike Pakistan, where it was harder to find a small hotel where it would have been possible to sit and talk to the entire family owning the establishment.

In Galle descendants of Arab merchants married local women and produced mixed populations. Some were part Dutch including today's Burghers. Galle's Dutch Reformed Church was well-polished inside. In true Calvinist style there was a dominant pulpit but no altar.

I bussed to Matara by the sea. Unlike north Tamil-dominated Sri Lanka, the south was lush green landscape. At Matara I stayed in the old part, the 'Fort', with a Sinhalese family in an old house. The household was Buddhist-Christian. I told them about the Lankan nationalist who I had stayed with in Colombo. He claimed the Christian missionaries had used force when they first came to Lanka. My hosts dismissed that as 'rubbish'. The experiences would be mixed.

I went on a winding bus trip up the mountain to tiny Ella situated near Haputale. It offered a magnificent view from the rest house. For a change, there were no tedious tea plantations dominating the view, only lots of turpentine trees and other deciduous shrubs.

At the resthouse was a German with a cockney accent. He had been a squatter in the East End of London! We took a walk past the tiny Ella railway station, which reminded me of a scene out of the Edwardian story The Railway Children. I walked to nearby Dowa temple, which had rows of Buddhas and two much larger horizontal Buddhas behind glass cases. One forthright monk asked me what my age was. We swapped experiences and finished having a discussion on the effects of taking hallucinatory magic mushrooms.

Polonnaruwa was another ancient capital of Sri Lanka but in later times it was deserted. The ruins were scattered about amongst forest and scrubland. One spot had a huge reclining Buddha cut from solid rock. Nearby was a figure of a sitting Buddha and a large mournful statue of his closest disciple Ananda. There was another gigantic standing Buddha about a mile away, in fact the whole area must have been full of them prominently situated amongst the forests. There were some Hindu-style buildings called Siva Devale constructed from granite where perhaps a tooth relic may have been kept. One large brick temple had both Hindu masonry and included statues of Buddha. The remains of the royal buildings could be seen at the Audience Hall and Council Chamber. The most memorable thing was a large stone lion, which supported the throne. There were countless other ruins too numerous to mention here.

My month in Lanka was coming to an end, so I returned to Colombo only just in time to catch the night train back to Talaimannar port in the north of the island to get the boat back to India. Joining up with other travellers, I found that Colombo railway station had no food in the canteen and on the way north, there were no food sellers to be seen anywhere. It was something unimaginable in India. Our tempers were not aided by the miserable-faced policeman who kept walking up and down the train looking at the poverty stricken foreigners as if they were all drug addicts.

At dawn, we arrived at the little port. We few foreigners were so famished that we gobbled up some awful greasy parathas fried in coconut oil and cooked in a nondescript Muslim stall. We then walked two miles to the cheap guesthouse where we all swapped experiences and wrote letters home. On the ferry back to Rameswaram in India, I was amused at the sight of a scraggy looking western woman sat in a bedraggled sari eating her food with chopsticks. What a ridiculous sight.

The fondest memories I have of Sri Lanka were of the little terraced rice gardens that you would come across by chance on long walks. Also, the peaceful faces of the older colossal stone Buddhas that are found all over the place and look as if they will be there for all eternity.

Every one of my fellow passengers was glad to be back in Ramaswaram. I walked around the town with an eccentric Korean boy who had been a student for some years in Belgium. The two of us laughed all the way to Madurai on the train journey, this being my third sleepless night in a row.

After staying the next day with Sri Rasa, a new advocate friend, I took the bus up to Tenkasi in the eastern Ghats. Tenkasi borders on the south western state of Kerala. My destination was the 'Good Life' ashram" at tiny Sivasailam in Tirunelveli district of Tamil Nadu.

The ashram consisted only of the family of Sri Krishna who was a slightly-built, black-skinned Tamil with a long shaggy beard and longish hair falling in ringlets, but receding on the forehead. At the teaching post at the small school of nearby Ambassamudram, he wore a drab uniform of homespun khaki coloured cloth. At school, he taught his own difficult language Tamil. Out of school, Krishna felt relaxed in a white lungi and shawl.

Krishna was a fruitarian in that his diet only consisted of raw fruit, most of which was grown in his tropical garden, which included coconut, bananas, guavas and papayas in abundance. Within this narrow but healthy diet he consumed mostly coconut. His wife still ate cooked spiceless food and his four year old son looked tough enough on his mainly raw fruit diet. I think his mother occasionally sneaked some cooked rice into the boy's mouth. Two vegetarian Australians were also visiting the ashram, as they were keen to experiment with a raw fruit diet. We three guests visited Krishna's school one day and after a two mile walk from Sivasailam, we caught the train to Ambassamudram. At the school, the rest of the staff was amazed at how we could live on a fruitarian diet. Krishna, like many Indians had a tendency to view things in black and white when discussing a factor such as diet, the effect being to put people off even experimenting with the diet. While discussing the matter with some of his female colleagues in the staff room, he kept talking about living in an ashram and repudiating worldly desires. The net result of such talk is that in general, people continue in their usual patterns. In this case, the fellow teachers associated fruitarianism with austerity. Krishna continued to lecture everyone even after his colleagues began chorusing 'fruit is expensive' to which he replied 'but you buy saris and jewellery.' 'Surely it is not necessary to be an ascetic in order to eat more fruit!' I exclaimed.

At the school, the children continually asked us questions about our families. I reciprocated and discovered that they were mainly the sons of tailors, carpenters, Hindu priests and farmers. One tailor's son spent the bulk of his free time helping his father in his shop. I asked them what aspirations they had and amongst the replies were film director, film actor and medical doctor.

Krishna walked with the three of us to a small hill town called Padamasam, which is noted for its red-faced monkeys. We visited a philosopher friend of his who lectured us on the Hindu concepts on diet. Hindus often classify food into sattvic, rajasic, and tamasic. This graduation is linked to degrees of nourishment and qualities of goodness or harmfulness. It may refer to food that is considered pure such as fruits and vegetables (especially raw and unfried). This sattvic diet is linked to spirituality and light and is symbolically linked to that part of the body above the waist and ultimately the Brahman. Rajasic food or rajas are linked to passions, physical energy and strength. Foods included with this category are meat, eggs, onions and garlic. Thus in some areas of India, widows are denied onions and garlic as they are believed to stimulate the passions. No such rule exists for widowers! Tamas relates to lethargy, darkness and stupidity. This is linked to the body below the waist, bodily secretions and darkness of the mind generally. Foods included here would be pigs meat, very oily food and carbohydrates. Ultimately, these gunas (categories) are linked to caste, the latter category supposedly categorizing sudras and untouchables. In one sense, there may be some truth in the philosophy in that certain foods will have this or that effect on the body and mind and even may have an intergenerational influence but it cannot be so clearly compartmentalised in relation to such factors as caste. Many of the Vaishya caste have a close diet to Brahmins and share some of their values though not necessarily the ideal of intellectual refinement. In addition, it is the low caste group that does all the heavy backbreaking work, so where does lethargy enter?

Our philosopher friend went on to explain the Hindu concept of the godhead from the remote Brahma, which as an idea may border on atheism to the multiplicity of images of the eternal energy with its male and female aspects.

My preferred Hindu image is that of 'Nataraj' or the Dancing Siva surrounded by a ring of ever burning fire. Siva is the Lord of the Dance and represents here the three divisions of time-past, present and future as they relate to man, but in divine terms, they are fragments of one time. The fire represents destruction and recreation. While the right hand reassures, the right food destroys a dwarf representing man's ignorance. The extended left hand of Siva directs the left foot to rise out of the abyss.

Krishna's friend fell for the cliché of the tolerance of Hinduism. Hinduism is, as he claimed tolerant in that it has less of a rigid body of revealed texts and laws. It tends not to persecute others in the name of religion. Many Hindus will state, for example, that Jesus was a good man and that he may be one amongst many reincarnations of the godhead. So if a Christian wishes to approach the truth via the path of Jesus, then that is alright but if a Hindu family member were to become a Christian, then they could be expelled from that community. The reason would be less to do with an intolerance about Christ but more a disapproval of Christian ways of life, which would necessitate a rejection of Hindu values. Many Christians are believed to be unclean, meat eaters, hence their lifestyle is questionable.

On returning to Sivasalam's Good Life ashram, I perused the small library in my sweltering whitewashed upper room, which was approached by a steep external staircase. I found a book entitled Raw Eating by an Iranian Armenian called Arshavir Ter Hovannessian (Aterhov). He was a fruitarian and categorically claimed the propagation of raw eating as the noblest and the most humane work in this century. The author's daughter's photo hung on one of the whitewashed walls. The caption underneath it read 'the forerunner of the real and perfect human being of the future ... the first raw eater of the twentieth century ... his daughter who has never consumed a single morsel of cooked food or any other lifeless material in her life.'

Krishna told me that formerly, he had experimented with meat diets whilst living in Madras, but he concluded that a fruitarian diet improved the mind. Although he was a slightly-built man, he managed on one occasion to out-walk the two tall Australians. From two o'clock in the morning until ten o'clock at night, he would whenever possible walk many miles. Even his cat and dog had boundless energy being addicted to coconut and rejected animal milk. The large dog even ate bananas, including the skins. Krishna also rejected the use of soap but like all orthodox Hindus, he would take his daily bath. He constructed a special trench latrine in the open and kept telling we guests to observe the dietary change in our stools. Our daily diet was composed of dried oranges, dates, plantains, sesame seeds and coconut. All but the dates were grown in the garden. Krishna only ate a tiny meal at night time and he was aiming for a sole coconut diet, which he admitted finding hard to achieve. Like all nature curists, he ate only when hungry. At least his wife did not have to spend hours on cooking his food and his fuel expenses must have been minimal. In this part of Tamil Nadu, wood was the main source of fuel. Cow dung could be then used as fertiliser instead of being squandered on fuel.

The Iranian author Aterhov advocated the eating of sprouted cereal grains and pulses. These grains have to be soaked for so many hours and then kept where they may breathe and sprout. The pulses have to be occasionally rinsed in clean water to prevent fermentation. The resulting product is tasty, crunchy and nutritious.

In the aforementioned book by Aterhov, Krishna had written in the section on honey 'do not steal the bees food, he works very hard to make it, it is meant for the bees and it is not man's food, nor is any other product from animals … for sweetness, use dates, raisins, etc.' Thus spoke the true vegan. Afterhov even advocated the eating of wax but he claimed that the cravings for cooked food were not hunger but were sensations stimulated by poor cells already poisoned! He added 'any attempts to use fire in order to improve the quality of the natural, faultless foodstuffs created by Him for human consumption is tantamount to doubting His supreme wisdom.' Afterhov blamed cooked food addiction ultimately for breeding wars and massacres in the world. Then followed an attack on the Turks for killing half of the Armenians and driving out the other half. Pretty extreme stuff.

The German naturopath Adolf Just wrote another book in the library called Return to Nature (Paradise Regained). Its contents were products of nineteenth century German nationalism and romanticism. One message said 'Many female troubles including hard labour would not occur if women did not wear drawers. A terrible monster has found refuge in the wardrobe of our girls and women. The corset is an instrument of torture.'

Just was also opposed to swaddling clothes for babies. 'Even the savage nations know it is correct to use moist earth for wounds and skin troubles.' The book continued in this vein and I departed from Sivasailam suffering from mental exhaustion.

I headed towards the southernmost tip of India to Kanyakumari formerly known as Cape Comorin. I stayed with an acquaintance Sri Ravi and his family whom I had met at the nature cure conference at Ullhasnagar near Bombay. On the train southwards, I purchased the Indian Express and the headlines described nine cases of human sacrifice in Bengal's Cooch Behar district. A father had axed his four children, all less than seven years of age, to propitiate Goddess Kali. Another case was of a Saddhu from Bangalore who throttled some babies to collect human blood by which he hoped to gain tantric powers and cure those suffering from chronic ailments and ironically, to bless childless couples with progeny and drive away evil spirits from the demented! The journalist ended his article 'it's a crying shame on our society.'

Ravi lived in Kanyakumari district in the village of Aramboly. The Tamil village had straight streets of terraced houses raised above the ground. My host's family belonged to one of the leading Brahmin groups in the area. He showed me his copper plate, which had been awarded to all the freedom fighters against the British and he had a freedom fighters' pension of Rs 200 per month from the central government. He was hard to imagine as an active freedom fighter. For a Tamil, he was tall and slender with a shock of grey wavy hair and deep-brown skin. He always wore a white homespun collarless cotton shirt and lungi. He accompanied me to Nagercoil and its snake temple before seeing the Gandhian centre, which manufactured agarbhati or joss sticks.

I was disappointed by the seafront at Kanyakumari because it was full of cheap modern cafés and hotels. Mrs Gandhi had correctly advised not to build on the actual beach at nearby Ramaswaram port. The Mahatma once said that the rock, which today houses the famous temple, was an 'unequalled sight in the world'. Now, a pretty exaggerated claim. Marco

Polo had sailed past Comori, which is named after Kumari, the virginal aspect of goddess Durga. Kanyakumari became famous owing to the nineteenth century Indian Scholar and holy man Vivekananda who founded the worldwide Ramakrishna Mission. Swami Vivekananda had fasted three days on the rock without both food and water. His statue is made of black marble and stands in a handsome octagonal pillared enclosure, also constructed in black marble. Before departing back to Ravi's home village, I tasted neera juice from the palmyra tree. After fermentation it becomes 'toddy'. In 1980 prohibition reigned in Tamil Nadu but in neighbouring Kerala state, 'toddy shops' abounded.

Ravi's family occupied the whole of one street in Aramboly. From the outside, each house looked small but once inside the rooms were quite large. Each room had bare mud floors and a roof supported by wooden pillars. In many traditional households such as this, there were no furnishings apart from a few mats and cushions. To repeat, in India even educated people of a certain, perhaps Gandhian influenced philosophy would deliberately opt to live in houses of a basic traditional character including cow dung mud floors, which are cooling to the bare feet in hot weather. Many people advocated health reasons for using cow dung but can it be scientifically proved to be more efficacious than buffalo or goat dung?

Chapter Twenty Five

The Land of Coconuts and Backwaters

The state of Kerala is a narrow strip of land situated between the Arabian Sea and the western ghats. It is divided into the long Malabar Coast and the hills of the ghats. These hills guarantee plenty of rainfall to Kerala, especially in the monsoon season, which in this area lends itself to luxuriant vegetation of coconut trees and plantations of coffee, tea, rubber and pepper.

I stayed at the Gandhian centre in the coastal town of Trivandrum and paid only Rs 5 for my room in their guesthouse. I requested a visit to a fishing village called Adimalathura, which had about eight hundred families. The majority working as day labourers and fishing but only ten percent of them owned their own outriggers. Amongst idyllic scenery, poverty is masked, especially when the village huts are sandwiched between coconut trees and a vivid blue sea.

The local Gandhians were trying to encourage the growth of village self-government as the bulk of the villagers had been for generations indebted to money lenders. This is often how people become bonded labourers in that their ancestors may have borrowed just a few rupees but over the generations, the interest on successive money has accumulated. Money lenders have been the curse of much of rural India, even in 1980 at least seventy million people were classed as bonded labour. Initially, for this project, the Trivandrum Gandhian centre locally paid Rs 32,000 to the usurers. The former proprietors gave coconut trees to the families who then paid back the loan over a long period. I left the village and waited at the bus stop. When the local church bells tolled, all the Christians turned towards the church and crossed themselves.

I made a brief visit to the Trivandrum museum, which was situated in a handsome building constructed in the architectural style of Kerala with layered red tiled roofs, the bottom roof overhanging a verandah. The museum's outer walls had black diamond shapes embedded into a red and pink mud and brick background. Trivandum itself was well situated on the seacoast but too sprawling and modern for my taste. It was dominated as the holy city of Ananta (Vishnu) by the temple called Padmanabhaswamy, which had an unusual horizontal gopuram towering over the city.

At the Trivandrum state tourist office, I found that the sole occupant was a hopelessly uninterested official with a BA degree who was too satisfied with himself now he had his job. I ticked him off afterwards because he never warned me that non-Hindus were banned from the inside of most of Kerala's major temples. At Padmanabhaswamy temple with its horizontal red roofed gopuram, in the temple yard, I noticed the sign 'Only Hindus Allowed'. Meanwhile, a priest tried selling me some carved sandalwood images, so I replied, 'no temple, no buy, our money is good enough for temple but not our bodies.' Obviously, there were many non-Hindu Indians who could get by pretending they were Hindus just for the benefit of getting into many temples, and Sikhs have always been allowed in most temples being considered by many Hindus as another version of Hinduism.

For a break, I set off to the peaceful nature cure sanatorium at Nalanchira run by the Indian Christian Bethany order of the Imitation of Christ. The brothers belonged to the ancient Syrian Christian faith, which claims apostolic origin from St Thomas who is supposed to have been martyred by a Brahmin near Madras. Formerly, the Bethany brothers, in common with many of their faith, used the ancient Syriac script in their services because they had, and maybe still do have connections with the church at Antioch. Prayers are said in the very difficult native language of Kerala; Malayalam. The Bethany brothers' church in common with many local churches, had no seating apart from a few mats for the congregation to sit cross-legged on the floor. The only item that I remember in the church was a locally-made silver fan with little bells on it, which one of the brothers brought out to show me. Afterwards, I was given a spice-free meal of gently boiled vegetables with unpolished round grain brown rice, which I ate accompanied by the handsome bearded head of the sanatorium.

I spent an entire day at nearby Kovalam beach and treated myself to a huge steamed tuna fish and vegetables costing Rs 10. The beach was lovely but scattered about it were bare-breasted women gathering the usual core of leering Indian men around them. These westerners then had the nerve to complain about local boys when they went out of their way to attract them. I preferred to enjoy coffee and gossip in a couple of thatched beach huts and cafés that were scattered on the sands.

Kerala should never be visited without a long slow journey through the kayals or backwaters. These backwaters comprise the coastal intersections of rivers and lakes and these in turn are connected by a network of canals. The backwaters are of various depths and are consistently surrounded by swathes of coconut trees with tiny palmyra huts and white churches dotted about amongst the foliage.

I started my seven hour passenger boat journey costing Rs 7.50 from Quillon and terminated it at Alleppey. Leaving the Quillon backwaters, there were enormous Chinese fishing nets splayed out as if waiting to pounce on some unsuspecting creature of the deep. Constantly the small motor launch passed country boats locally-known as vallems plying up and down with goods of all kinds. Some of the boats had semi-circular roofs of plaited straw matting and were operated as punts. Villages appeared scattered or dispersed rather than nucleated in Kerala. Along the river banks were always lots of laughing children eagerly waving at us. The only sedentary figures were white painted statues of Christ or St Francis standing with outstretched arms.

On arrival at Alleppey, I travelled on through more backwater lagoons or lakes on the two and a half hour boat journey to Kottayam. Far more fun than doing the journey by bus. Here the backwater kayals were more open and generally less scenic than nearer the coast. At Kottayam, I travelled by bus to stay with Mrs Cellin, a Keralan woman who ran a local nature cure hospital. She was from a Christian family and her mother still wore the traditional local Christian type of white sari, which is arranged like a fan at the back. Like most Keralans who afford it, her long black hair was nourished daily in large doses of coconut oil. Unlike north India, the women of the south prefer to decorate their hair with beautiful flowers.

How different from the cowering covered heads of Rajasthan and parts of Pakistan.

Her tiny hospital was situated in the most peaceful surroundings imaginable. She only had a couple of steam baths and spinal baths in the compound. Most of the patients were treated through fasting and special diets. In this area, alongside the usual tropical fruit of coconut, papaya. and the like, there were large variations of bananas or plantains. Some shops sold only this fruit and local varieties included red-skinned sweet bananas, yellow fibrous ones, which were inedible if uncooked while others were delicious little semi-oval shaped ones.

I took a bus to Ernakulum, the capital of the former state of Cochin. Very near the bus station, I found an excellent Indian style lodge, which I thought would be the best place to stay while sightseeing in neighbouring Cochin and its port. Cochin is really a clustered group of islands, so I travelled about on an old battered boat, which took me to Gundu island, famous for a well developed coir co-operative where doormats and all and sundry were woven with coconut fibre. The coir workers were paid Rs 5 per day. The buildings here and in many parts of Kerala were covered with graffiti including Communist Party slogans and hammer and sickles. Communist rule in Kerala had created a state with the highest literacy rate in India and managed to get the birth rate under control.

Decided to visit the old Jew's Town. These Jews are broadly divided into black and white Jews. The black Jews originally came to India in circa 587 BC, many of them from Yemen and they have intermarried with other Indians. They have their own synagogue but I visited the synagogue of the white Jews who came to India from Baghdad in the 16th century and before. Their small synagogue has a lovely floor of individually painted blue and white tiles imported from China. I was shown some copper plates in which grants of privileges of land for Jews were made by former rulers of Malabar. Hindus in India never persecuted Jews and the only persecution that they suffered was around 1560 AD when the Portuguese introduced their inquisition into their territory of Goa to the north of Cochin. There are some Iraqi Jews in Bombay, a few in Calcutta and Pakistan and others are termed the Beni Israel (the sons of Israel). Faber-Kaiser in his book Jesus Died in Kashmir, claims to have met people of Jewish descent in the mountains of Kashmir. Kashmiri traditions state that Moses came to Kashmir and was buried there, the tomb being situated on Mount Niltopp, which is supposed to have been venerated for about three thousand years. There are some local names in Kashmir called Muqam-i-Musa (the place of Moses). Faber-Kaiser met the tomb custodian Wali Reshi whose family claim to have guarded the shrine for nine hundred years. These Jews hold an adjoining area Yusmarg (Meadow of Jesus) sacred because they believe that Jesus fulfilled his mission on earth to search for the Ten Lost Tribes of Israel.

Cochin's St Francis Church was built by the Portuguese, being the first European church in India. Vasco de Gama was originally buried here. Inside the church, in line with the aisle were two huge wooden punkas (fans), which had to be operated manually by the dying breed of punkawallahs.

A Dutch friend I had met on the boat decided on an evening at the ambitiously entitled Cochin Cultural Centre, which was housed in a simple rectangular thatched structure. There were only two of us in the audience. We watched a form of martial art fencing called Kalaripayatti. It was pretty amateurish stuff, just a teacher with two disciples, one of whom was deaf and dumb. Then a speaker who explained some of the intricate gestures of the Keralan classical form of dancing called Kathakali. Before the entire evening's performance had begun, we had crept behind the stage and watched the brilliant dance make-up artist at work. The two dancers wore elaborate multicoloured headgear and heavy voluminous costumes. The performance of Kathakali classical dance always uses incidents from the ancient Hindu epics of the Ramayana and Mahabharata. The facial expressions and hand gestures, even as displayed by these amateurs had to be seen to be believed.

Characteristics displayed included anger, hate, envy and love, all performed in the most subtle manner. The musical accompaniment was a couple of drums and cymbals. The most pathetic part of the entire evening's performance was the fact that these artists were small fry and slogged away on performances for several days at a time with little reward. For that evening's performance, the make-up had taken around three hours and underneath it, one could see the sweat pouring down their faces. For all their efforts, there were only two of us present to witness the spectacle, which was a shame.

I decided on a visit to the temple town of Guruvayor near Trichur. What a mistake on my behalf. One was not only made unwelcome by leering youths and rows of disapproving bethreaded Brahmins dressed in Keralan mundu, (small dhoti) but also by the fact that the temple was closed to non-Hindus. The atmosphere was awful though I had no fear of violence. It was here that I understood for the first time, the erstwhile British rulers incomprehension of a given type of Hindu Brahmin. What impenetrable faces! Opposite the main temple entrance stood two long rows of terraced housing and on each step sat a sullen faced Brahmin. The only useful piece of information I gleaned was that this was one of the first temples to open its gates to untouchables or scheduled castes. How these downtrodden folk must have cowered beneath that impenetrable Brahmin façade. These faces represented a religion that did not seek to convert but was confident in its own self will to survive.

From Trichur town, I caught a bus to Palghat, which is a typical Keralan village with houses scattered over a broad acreage. The Tribal Research centre existed more as an ideal than a reality. However, the journey was not a complete disaster as I made my way to the delightful Malampuzha dam and gardens. The garden was fairly modern in design but it had been influenced by the Moghul cum Persian style of garden found in Northern India. The scene was only marred by a series of hideous electric lamps.

I travelled to Kottakkal, which was the centre of Kerala for the ancient Hindu system of medicine ayurveda, although the bulk of the local population was Muslim. Even small Muslim girls wore the local Islamic dress consisting of a blouse and lungi plus a loose veil, which made them look like Christian nuns. Muslims in Kerala are called Moplahs who are descendants of Arab traders and local Indians. Like their northern co-religionists, their Arab ancestors converted some local low castes to Islam through the old trading networks rather than by conquering as contestants for political supremacy.

Upon visiting the Arya Vaidya Sala Medical Centre, I discovered that Yorkshire TV and Alan Wicker had preceded me. P.S. Verier was considered the saviour of ayurveda. He was the first person last century to organise the treatment of patients under the Ayurvedic College and hospital as a charitable trust. Students obtained a Bachelor in ayurvedic medicine upon successful completion of their studies. Quite a number of allopathic – western orthodox – doctors also studied here. At the time of my visit, I was informed that there were a few Arab and Danish patients. The Indian government financed a clinical research ward in which there were twenty beds for those suffering with peptic ulcers. Another ward specialised in various types of ailments including snakebite and other poisons. All Verier's textbooks were written in the classical language of Sanskrit and Mayalam, the language of Kerala. Verier also did much to revitalise a stagnant Keralan culture, so he encouraged classical Kathakali dance and the theatre.

Ayurvedic medicines are either herbal or mineral based and the college ran its own herb garden. The process of manufacturing the medicines appeared complicated. Inside the processing plant next to the college were massive mortars and pestles for grinding all kinds of substances. Huge mixers resembling domestic cooking appliances contained a multitude of herbal concoctions. These stood alongside huge bowls filled with some weirdly colourful decoctions.

I was lucky to get good cheap and clean accommodation at the local dak bungalow built in the old colonial style. For these few days, I just ate from cheap tea shops or bought fresh fruit as no food was forthcoming at the rest house but at least I had the luxury of my own bathroom.

Chapter Twenty Six

New Dawn Village and a Friend of the Trees

While still in the Muslim district near the western part of Calicut, I visited Servas member Sri Rama who lived in the hills of Ramnatkara. He and his wife had set up a Gramdan (village gift) centre called Navodaya Danagram (New Dawn Village gift) in this rural backwater to create the Gramdan ideal of a village owned and run by its population.

All the local adults voted in the Gram Sabha (parliament) which met once every three months. They elected a committee to discuss various matters and the most positive result was that even problems that would normally go before a court, were dealt with at local meetings by the Peoples Court. The land itself was owned collectively. However, the land plots could be transmitted from father to son without being sold. The cultivators were taught to see themselves in Gandhian terms as trustees of the land rather than viewing their plots as a commodity. Some of the ground was undivided common land. All the adults gave one percent of their income to a common fund. The bulk of these rural poor were scheduled caste who later adapted well to their new economic freedoms.

The only blot in the vicinity was a loud speaker, which constantly spewed forth film music during a marriage party. Sri Rama explained that in his view, the loud speaker was the poor man's way of proclaiming his new freedom as far as 'nobody can stop me'. For example, not long ago, at an untouchable scheduled caste wedding, that community had to remain silent because they were so despised. In 1980 nobody would dare ban the music, the music being more a proclamation than a mode of enjoyment.

The hills were a mass of coconut and cashew nut trees. In 1951, under Vinoba's Bhoodan movement, a wealthy landowner donated over seven acres to the untouchables. Under the Gramdan movement, the families retained all rights in their land except the right to sell, mortgage and lease it. All these rights were assigned to the village council, which operated on a consensus rather than majority vote principle. As with much of the land gift ideal, landowners willingly donated their most useless land. So Sri Rama and his workers terraced the hills in an area where terracing was not the local tradition. Acres of tapioca, coconut and cashews were planted. Thatched huts were replaced by ones constructed in stone. In addition, with voluntary labour, good wells were sunk. Fifty families were initially involved in cultivating the first hundred acres.

If members wished to leave this Gramdan village, they got the market price for each coconut tree (Rs 100 in 1979). Many of the villagers were also day labourers such as stonecutters and agricultural labourers for other landowners. In India, land represents financial security and there was fear of relinquishing title to the land, claimed Sri Rama. Because of government policies, New Dawn's 'Basic High School' had to offer the conventional curriculum so Gandhi's ideal of Basic Education, which included an acceptance of physical work and the dignity of labour, was relegated to one daily period where students worked in the school's two acres of land. The produce grown was then sold in the school's co-op store. In winter, the children learned book-binding and they had to sweep and clean latrines. In their holidays, they had to carry out public maintenance projects and run mock parliaments. I wondered if there was any relaxation. Entertainment was organised amongst themselves.

I visited the community's school for primary teachers' training and the students asked me questions on Mrs Thatcher and how many languages were spoken in England. One loud-mouthed fellow asked me 'what do you like or not like about Kerala?' I told them my views, including my thoughts on loud speakers. On the latter subject, I got little support 'Nobody can afford tape recorders, so hire loud speaker, we like it.

Tuned into the BBC World Services programme Outlook and heard their India correspondent Mark Tully being questioned on whether Gandhi's ideas live on in India. Unfortunately, he discussed only politics and excluded all the various village schemes that operated all over the countryside in the Mahatma's name.

After the kind hospitality of the gentle Sri Rama and his kind wife, I departed for Cheyvoor.

Chevoor had the best Tribal Research Institute in south India. Here, I talked with the heavily-bearded anthropologist Dr Mathur. He was a social worker and told me that Kerala had developed a pension scheme for agricultural workers. In 1980 a farmer in Kerala could not employ new labour without consulting present farm labourers already employed by him. The Communist government in Kerala had certainly made some far-reaching reforms and it was true that within Kerala, one rarely heard of brutal behaviour by landlords such as was still common in states like Bihar and Uttar Pradesh. In Kerala, most of the land was freed of absentee landlords, many of whom had been connected to the older ruling families of Travencore state.

While I was staying with Sri Rama, he told me to visit one English woman social worker who had, much to his disgust, converted from Quakerism to Roman Catholicism.

From Nandi Bazaar, I climbed up to Asha Niketan, the small settlement where she lived. What a view! Carpets of coconut trees and a deep blue Arabian Sea. Sari-clad Chris lived in these delightful surroundings with mentally handicapped children and adults. In one house, many of the children were microcephalous. She told me that their parents had been unobservant in that they had only noted odd behaviour patterns rather than the fact that their children had small heads, and that the two problems might be connected! She said, 'One boy ate stones and suffered from large stomach worms.'

Chris offered me some delicious pancakes made of ragi (millet) and wheat. What a cheerful environment, how different from the often gloomy Victorian buildings or even modern 1960's ones that were used to house disabled groups in Britain. A good climate and lush vegetation allows so much scope to those running such a community. In nearby Calicut, I spent the night at Gandhi Bhawan and slept in the office dominated by a picture of Gandhi hanging forward on a chain from the wall. Behind the picture was a huge bird's nest, which I am sure Gandhi would have approved.

From Calicut, I travelled by bus to the hill station of Ootacamund or Ooty as it is affectionately known. What a delightful trip! The bus passed groves of coconut trees on top of the undulating slopes and amongst them were scattered red tiled houses squatting in the densely- packed foliage. As the bus climbed up the western ghats, the deciduous shrubs and trees took over the landscape. Instead of uniform evergreen, there were differing hues from silver to some monotonous tea plantations, which carpeted the ground in their uniform height. A few female tea pickers with baskets on their backs tied by a rope supported from their foreheads were returning home after a hard days' work.

The bus engine began to hiss badly and half the passengers fled to the front of the bus attempting to get off, thinking there was going to be a loud bang! The driver and conductor scrambled off, headed with an array of cans for a nearby stream, and scooped up water for the steaming engine. The uphill stretch was too much of a sweat for the heaving clapped-out bus. At Ooty, I headed straight for a Persian Bahai café. A sour-faced, pale-skinned Iranian woman stood by the till. The café was empty. On the walls were the Bahai principles regarding the Oneness of Mankind. She mumbled miserably, 'What do you want?' I replied 'Can't you make me smile? You are a bad ambassador for the Bahai's because not even in the worst Indian restaurant run by Indians would one get such surly treatment.'

On Palm Sunday I attended St Stephens of the Church of South India. I suddenly realised that the bulk of the regulars sat in the back pews whilst I was saddled amongst a group of grey-uniformed private school kids, all busily engaged in pulling apart and reassembling their green palm crosses. In England it would be rare for me to attend such a service, perhaps I just wanted to reaffirm my identity or heritage rather than a religious urge.

Grey, gloomy clouds stalked my return from the botanical gardens. In the bazaar were lanes of jewellers and pawnbrokers. Many migrant Kashmiri traders inhabited squalid dwellings near the central market whilst neighbouring Tibetan traders sold cheap woollen clothes down another alley.

Back at my hotel, a dark Anglo-Indian insisted on telling me that his son Chris was fair like his mother. It was a pretty dreary establishment altogether. In fact, I lodged a complaint about the mice or rats, which were scuttling about on the floors all through the night.

I went from Ooty for the day by bus to Kotagiri in the Nilgiris Hills. Kotagiri's surroundings reminded me of a lion's mane that had been severely attacked. This once forested area, now terraced, had a strange barrenness about it. The only plant that thrived in these parts was tea.

On my way back to Ooty bazaar, I passed a tiny crippled hunch-backed tot, which had been just deposited helplessly on the pavement with a begging bowl. In Pakistan, I had read of horrific stories about children being deliberately crippled in order to be used as beggars. Often they would be kidnapped and never be heard of again.

Some new houses were being constructed in Ooty and I noticed that many had 'dolls' perched by the roofs. These 'dolls' ranged from poles draped in rags with a head made out of an upside down pot, to huge rag dolls. I had forgotten that I was back in Tamil Nadu and this Tamil custom allows house building to go auspiciously to keep evil spirits away.

Near the south west of the old state of Mysore (now Karnataka) is the hilly region of Coorg, a former princely state. The people of Coorg are a martial community by tradition and are known as Kodavas. I ascended the unspoilt forested hills by bus, which only just struggled up to the largest town Mercara. The passengers had been delayed for two and a half hours owing to several burst tyres. The scenery in Coorg was far more impressive than the much publicised, but denuded Nilgiris around the overrated Ooty. The hillsides here were covered in a lush green carpet of rice fields, orange groves, coffee plantations and cardamon fields. Against the green shrubbery, the town of Mercara displayed a maze of handsome red tiled roofs and whitewashed walls surrounded by fields of red soil. Bourganvilia in this district grows in profusion. It was strange how so few people visited this area.

Coorg is famed for its clear honey so I purchased some from the local co-op store. At what is known as the Rajah's Seat, one got a fabulous view of the steep serpentine roads below. In the distance, one could just see the Tibetan refugee settlements, some of which I passed on the bus route. The Indian government has settled thousands of Tibetans on local land. Quite a number have settled in the higher regions of Karnataka state.

The Kodavas of Coorg tend to be quite tall and very fair-skinned. The women wear the sari in quite a distinctive style. The sari looks like an apron at the front because the pallau, instead of being draped over the left shoulder as it is usually done, is brought over on the right from under the left arm. Married women wear a head dress tied in a knot at the back of the head and hanging down the back.

The Rajah's tomb is in Muslim style with central domes and minarets. This old fort's compound holds a former Protestant church later transformed into a delightful museum. Its best exhibit as far as I was concerned was a Vahara boar in the form of a bronze mask. Vahara is one of the reincarnated avatars (incarnations) of Vishnu in the form of a boar.

Before departing from this very clean town, I decided on an evening walk to Rajah's Seat. The route was spoilt by the usual brand of cheeky effeminate youths. What a relief to come across two rugged Tibetan faces in the park. Tibetans never bothered women travellers.

I visited nearby Chettalli coffee and orange experimental centre. Some orange trees live for fifty years and coffee trees can last for thirty seven years. I was offered a tasty meal at the staff rest house, during the meal the subject turned to the sacred basil plant tulsi. If it is worn around the neck as a mala, it prevents evil upon the body. My hosts told me gleefully that sesame seeds increase male fertility.

By bus from Mercara to Mangalore where I had to change buses for tiny Mulki in the district called south Kenara. Scenically it was closer to Kerala in its tropicality than to the drier northern areas of the same state of Karnataka, directly to the north of Kerala.

At Mulki, I was met by Gandhian Sri Babu who was a tall, lean bespectacled man. He ran a school and I was requested to attend a function for opening a new classroom. The Indians constantly overdo speech making and the small children looked bored to tears whilst they all sat rigidly cross-legged on the floor. Why do the speeches have to be so serious? There was no effort at making the children laugh. A flag raising ceremony followed this speech.

A marriage party came down the road by Sri Babu's handsome old house. The usual film music interspersed with a ghastly out of tune trumpet. The bride was bejewelled and blue-saried while the bridegroom wore a horrid pink turban with a fan at the front and a long drape down his back. Babuji, standing alongside me, chipped in, 'The man likes to see the lady before accepting.' 'I expect she is too modest to look up to her prospective spouse?' I murmured knowingly.

I purchased my favourite political magazine Sunday, which included the comments 'Want to get a first class in your B.Com exam from Calcutta University? Then don't study, just buy the question papers.' In the Calcutta bazaars, the going rate for a question paper was Rs 200.

I presented Sri Babu and family with the honey from Coorg. He told me, 'We only use it for medicinal purposes'. I think that I ate most of it with my tasty breakfast cakes of jack fruit ground with rice flour, a truly regional Karnatak dish. They offered me the usual south Indian breakfasts of idli, a steamed ground rice and black gram cake and savoury semolina upma served with peas and green chillies.

I spent a day in Mangalore where I visited St Aloysuis College chapel, which had magnificent frescoes depicting the life of Jesus and St Aloysuis. The frescoes had strong vivid colours without vulgarity. Many of the ceiling frescoes had quotes from the Bible beneath them. An Italian priest originally painted these hundred year old frescoes. Mangalore town had no suburbs, just a juxtaposition of villages with lots of greenery outside the town centre. I went by bus to Ullal and Surutkul beaches, which were huge expanses totally empty of visitors with the occasional small huts of matting together with sleeping fisherboys basking in the midday sun. At Surutkul was a beautiful engineering college but because of its situation, its students had a rather lonely existence.

My visit to Sri Sati, a member of 'Friends of the Trees', coincided with his local temple's chariot car festival Ratoatsava, which is an eight day annual event. The Mukli temple is dedicated to Goddess Durga and this deity, which, during the festival is taken out of the temple everyday in a different direction in order to bless her devotees. Flowers are distributed to everyone and the Hindus walk around the temples inner sanctum five times.

At night outside the temple compound, I saw the mind boggling spectacle of the very heavy gold and silver image being carried up and down in a long gap between two lines of people. Those at the front carried huge torches lit with coconut oil, which emitted a ghastly smell, one torchbearer was continually refuelling his torch with a sponge drenched in oil. The centre of attraction was balancing the image for a considerable time. He rushed up the steep wooden steps of an enormous temple chariot decorated with mango leaf bunting and bamboo. The chariot was perched at one end of the rows of spectators. Then masses of humanity dragged the temple car over very uneven ground for nearly two kilometres.

Sri Babu belonged to the Shetty subcaste of business community found in south Kenara. Their local dialect is Tulu, which is unwritten and not taught in schools. The state language of Karnatak is Kanarese or Kannada.

Nearby Mukli is the town of Udipi, which is famed for its export of Udipi restaurants to other parts of India. Sri Babu took me through Udipi to Manipal in order to visit a Dr Pai's educational institution aided by public donations. At nearby Karkala stands a monolithic statue of Gometeswara of the Jains. It was erected in 1432 AD Moodabidri, which is also in the same district, has a Jain Thousand Pillar Temple that we visited after a spell in the dry fish market. The walls of the temple were stone panelled with tiny sculptures of arches, animals and dancers. At Moodabidri's general market, the locals displayed an ingenious local product of boat-like structures, which protected against the rain. They reminded me of beetle-shaped Irish curraghs planted on mens' backs. These rains protectors were made of palm leaves and framed inside.

At Udipi, we visited the Krishna temple of Kanakadas (local scheduled castes). For four hundred years, untouchables could not worship here and the Brahmins on one occasion pushed the outcastes to an obscure part of the temple. The story goes that the image turned on its own towards the untouchable Kanakadas. Today, the windows on that side are called Kanakadas windows. While we were at Udipi, the chief minister of Karnataka was visiting the locality to give a speech at the Sanskrit College. The temple elephants were decorated with huge coats and two large man-made figures were being carted around. Apparently, they were bodyguards of the temple god. Sri Babu showed me the swamis' tombs of Vrindavan, meaning peaceful garden. Unlike ordinary mortals, many swamis are not cremated but buried. In front of the temple image were beautiful silver embossed figurines on a wooden door. Above them stood a silver painted Vishnu lying upon the many-headed primordial serpent Sesha. The image looked snug inside, surrounded by tiny clay oil lamps. In the temple vicinity, lucky little Brahmin boys were getting free meals.

At the Sanskirt College, I sat through vociferous speeches by non-Sanskirt knowing politicians advocating Sanskrit in all schools. Just like somebody suggesting that Latin or Ancient Greek should be made compulsory in European schools.

After departing from Sri Babu, I went from Udipi to Jog Falls. On the way, the bus water tank leaked four times, so eventually we had to change transport. On the next bus, an old toothless woman was crammed in with three squawking hens with their legs tied. I stayed at a simple hotel for Rs 5. I found myself yearning for fried eggs, bacon and tomatoes! I settled for an Indian omelette, which although greasy and tasty always look as if they have been under a steam roller.

I travelled on toward Mundgod to visit Tibetan refugees at Ganden Monastery. At the bus stop were clusters of Tibetans. Years ago in 1968, these refugees settled in Karnataka state. Not one of them stared at me, what a change! Without my asking, several of them offered help with my luggage, and one woman heaved my bag onto her shoulder. There was nothing servile about these Tibetans. On arrival the Indian passengers pushed through the Tibetans. Some Tibetan monks insisted on taking my bags. I was too embarrassed and insisted on carrying one. The mind boggled at the thought of any Hindu Swami or equivalent offering help in the way these monks did.

The familiar deep rhythmic thud of Tibetan cymbals, last heard by me in distant Himalayan Ladakh, arrested my thoughts while approaching the reconstructed Ganden Monastery. This monastery or gompa was formerly one of the great monasteries of Tibet prior to the Chinese conquest. The monks who fled brought what they could with them. The present monastery in the unlikely surroundings of southern India is only a shadow of its former glory. Inside the prayer rooms, the sight and aroma of butter lamps assaulted one's senses. The butter sculpture consisted of many delightful designs and colours. Stacks of long narrow books of the Buddhist scriptures were stacked on top of each other. These were the Tibetan books with hard wooden covers and loose sheets covered in Tibetan calligraphy. The Chinese claim Tibet as part of China, but Tibetan is totally unlike the major Chinese languages and the script bares alos no relation to Sanskrit. The books themselves were stacked in loose jackets of embroidered cloth. On the floor were rows of cushions for the monks to sit on.

I had a clean simple room in the monastery guest house. The food was tasty with lots of spaghetti-like noodles and huge dumplings stuffed with mutton. Unlike Indian food, the dishes were spiceless. The Tibetans relied heavily on tsampa (barley) in their native Tibet but in Karnataka, they used a variety of cereals.

One gentle-faced monk, Tashi, who spoke beautiful English, took me several miles away to two other small settlements. At one settlement, the verandahs were filled with groups of Tibetan women and girls weaving carpets with traditional vertical looms. These rugs were delightful, my favourites being those using various hues of the same colour, a theme that has always interested me. Some rugs depicted plants and dragons. They trimmed the pile with some very antique-looking instruments and used large scissors for creating a relief effect in separating the colours on each rug. Often up to three workers were employed on single carpets. The atmosphere faintly reminded me of the carpet factory I had visited in Albania. There too, the labour was intensive and the Albanians used hand looms but they were working in a dark, gloomy factory.

Passing by some fields, I noticed two monks pulling a plough. These refugees had cleared the forest in order to plant maize and rice. Tashi had spent four years at the Tibetan College at Varanasi (Benares) and he learnt Sanskrit. He told me that in religious discussions, he met too many Hindu fanatics with closed minds, though a closed mind is not really in the nature of Hinduism, as it might be said with Protestant fundamentalists. Tashi said that oft repeated phrase 'We Tibetans feel closer to westerners than Indians'. He said that the Smithsonian Institute of Anthropology had recently filmed at Mundgod during the Tibetan New Year. They came especially to film the Tibetan oracles.

Tibetan Buddhist methods of debate were curious and to an outsider, they looked extremely taxing for the participants. Small groups of six or more monks (including boys) were busy occupying themselves in heated but amicable discussion. One or two of them asked questions at high speed to the rest of the group with the aim of developing the analytical faculties of the mind. One saw a mass of gesticulating, shouting and hand-clapping participants. To make a point, a monk stood and raised one hand and brought it down with a heavy thud against the other. They had four sessions of debate a year and each could continue for some weeks. This tradition of monastic college education hails directly from Tibet. The young boys were 'incarnate boys' and believed to be avatars of previous lamas as they learned quickly. A special group would gather information about previous incarnations. Occasionally, the boy could choose the artifacts or belongings relating to the previous life he lived. A past lama may have said that he would be reborn at a given place or date. The debates went on for six hours each day.

At night time, a cool breeze and thunder came warning us of impending rain. The next day, some of the monks took part in an energetic noisy folk dance. Here, there were no fat monks equivalent in bulk to some of the obese Hindu swamis. Tashi told me of one black American who had converted to Tibetan Buddhism and lived at a nearby monastery, becoming a brilliant debater in Tibetan philosophy, speaking Tibetan of course.

In one section, Tibetan boys were bent over their scriptures and learning by rote. Others were studiously working at their calligraphy in Tibetan characters with special dip pens. In one corner of the guest room, one of the monks would come in daily to work at the butter sculpture. This was done in cold water with flour to prevent matting. The monk was in the process of carving floral lotus designs and painting in bright colours. The butter was boiled first and then cooled and it stank!

The original Ganden Monastery in Tibet was built in 1409 AD and it had two colleges, Jangtse and Shartse. Nearly two thousand monks lived in Jangtse. When a monk completed his study, he was examined by the Dalai Lama, plus his tutors, through rigorous debate. Monks from the other monasteries of Drepung and Sera could examine him. Only three hundred of the three thousand monks from Ganden escaped to India. At first, they were in Buxa refugee camp in Bengal before they moved south.

Inside the main part of the monastery stood a statue of the future Buddha in gold leaf. In addition, there were statues of past lamas, including the founder of the monastery Je Tsong Khapa Lobsang Dakpa. Huge thankas or hand-painted cotton scrolls on wooden frames adorned the walls. Now Drepung, Sera and Ganden Monasteries are situated in Karnataka, the former Mysore state. Gyudto College Monastery is far away in Arunachal Pradesh deep in the Himalayas. My old Tibetan pen friend Lobsang Tseering lived there.

Before I departed, the monk who made the butter sculpture came to my room and gave me my regular flask of salt and butter tea before embarking on a new batch of sculptures from dough. He sieved flour and water as if he was making bread and then kneaded it vigorously before transferring it into brick size blocks and triangular wedges, which he placed in a pattern on a tiny table. Another block turned into a tower shape then later, like the others, it would be painted after placing a little pattern on it. Before departure, I was garlanded Tibetan style with a white scarf. What wonderful hospitality.

I arrived at Hubli and headed for my new friends, the Ram family at Sarvodaya Mira Mandali. These Brahmins were all members of the orthodox right wing, Rashtriya Sevak Sangh. Hindu gods adorned the house including a picture of the bull Nandi, Krishna and Ganesh. One room was put aside as a shrine room 'where we go after bath'. In their garden, they grew great clusters of tulsi, the sacred basil.

I ate with most of the family (Hindu wives often eat after the menfolk) on the kitchen floor. They sprinkled water on the food and in a clockwise direction around the tali (platter) itself, and over a nearby tulsi plant in order to purify everything. Then we ate sample amounts of vegetarian dishes. It may have been a tulsi festival because kumkum (red powder) was put on the plant itself and then prayers were said over it. Kumkum was placed upon my forehead and two pieces of khaki cloth were given to me.

My host took me to the local Lingayat community at Inamvirapur, a hamlet of three hundred people. It had been helped by Gandhian workers and the state government. The small brick houses with red tiles had been built by the state government. Behind them were some older huts, which included accommodation for cattle and buffaloes.

In the 16th century AD, Busaveshwar founded a sect called Lingayats for low caste Hindus and untouchables who were deprived of common social intercourse. Lingayat members wear a linga around their necks and they in turn have become in Indian fashion, an intermarrying subcaste. Four acres, which had been put aside for cucumber growing, looked healthy enough. A buffalo gave birth but showed less care for its young than the cow I had seen giving birth at Ramantkara. Some village industries were about to be started with the help of bank loans. Ram showed me a model dairy he owned, and then he bored me with his continuous moralising.

At night, we returned to old Hubli where I witnessed the preparations for the September festival for Lord Ganesh, the elephant- headed god. One local family had a little workshop crammed from floor to ceiling with models of Ganesh. There were rows of unpainted brown images. Some of the finished specimens were in all the colours of the rainbow. I told those present that the images painted blue and brown looked awful. 'We like that,' they chorused. At the end of the festival, all those images would be immersed in water (sea or river) and then new ones would be made. Certainly image makers will never go out of business. Each Ganesh image sold for Rs 12 or less.

Sri Ram, a former bookseller who had opted to return to village life, being a man of extremes, totally condemned city life. He was keen to start a type of kibbutz, even though he knew little of the Israeli system, but he had written to the Israeli consulate in Bombay for advice!

By bus to Hampi, I noticed that many of the cattle had their horns painted bright red with tassles hanging off them. Only two passengers were on the bus. The top of it was loaded with huge rolled up straw mats, which were deposited there from a waiting horse and cart. Half way to Hospet, a box of snuff packets fell off the roof and an argument followed. By now, more passengers had got aboard but then they all got off again and gleefully watched the argument. I sweated alone on the bus. The countryside became very dreary as we moved out of the lushness of the south of the state towards what I would call the 'backwaters' of Karnataka with its abundant scrubland and cacti.

However, Hampi was beautiful and lush, with lots of bananas and coconuts. Hampi consists of the ancient capital of the Vijayanagar kings who were dominant in southern India around the fourteenth century. The ancient town grew around the river Tungabhadra where there is only a small dam. Hampi's remains are magnificent in their decay. Many were smashed by Muslim invaders. The ruins seemed desolate amidst this rocky terrain. A huge Ganesh looked forlorn in a handsome dark bat-infested sanctum. Its trunk was broken but that was compensated by the elegant pillared hall surrounding the image. The elephant stables were enclosed within an Indo-Saracenic style of domed roof and arched entrances. A stone chariot majestically stood. Its wheels were made separately and they moved on stone axles. Their bas-reliefs represented women riding on parrots. The man lion incarnation of Vishnu stood gigantically. Hewn out of a single granite boulder the entire statue was very mutilated, though enough remained to show a huge mouth and glaring eyes. Above the image was a sculpture of Sesha, the multi headed snake, which supports Vishnu on the cosmic ocean.

Amongst the many monuments in varying degrees of dilapidation were the baths, which formed part of the former palace. Nearby, an aqueduct with earthenware pipes took water to the rectangular granite reservoir. Hampi seemed to have become popular with western hippies and a number of small straw-matted tea shops had sprouted into existence amongst the ruins to serve the new clientele. Most of the Hindu visitors stayed in cheap hostels run by the temples.

I went by bus to Badami to visit the temple caves. They are situated in huge rock faces, which look down onto a sandstone mosque and some Hindu bathing ghats. From a distance, I could hear the rhythm of the washerwomen beating their clothes down at the ghats. Badami was once the capital of the Chalakyas dynasty. In one rock- cut temple, Jain images were grouped in panels of varying sizes. The Siva rock-cut temple held two huge carved Vihara boars and a magnificent man lion. An amazing sandstone fort towered directly above. Monkeys were busy delousing themselves. How different north Karnataka was from the coconut-filled southern areas of the state. Mud-bricked, flat-roofed houses abounded. These reminded me of the poorer parts of the Punjab and Uttar Pradesh. This was bread rather than rice country or so it looked. The poorest people lived in mat and thatch huts. Here the poverty was not softened by lush scenery.

On the return bus to Hospet, some of the local women wore fabulous clothes of multicoloured patchwork with mirror embroidery. Instead of saris, they wore blouses and skirts. The blouses were backless. These women were covered with huge white ivory bangles, which covered the entire arm. Some wore chunky silver jewellery and cowrie beads. I guessed, it turned out correctly, that they were migrant workers from the far west of India near Pakistan called Kutch in Gujarat. Their dress had more in common with Pakistani Sindi cloth than any local dress of Karnataka. The trouble was that the ubiquitous sari was gradually replacing these more localised clothes, which could be splendidly colourful.

My next port of call in Karnataka was Bijapur. I was lucky to get a room at a comfortable Indian government tourist bungalow. Bijapur scenery is bleak but its monuments, though of a matched bleakness, are truly handsome and dot the horizon as one enters the town. The former rulers of Bijapur were of Turkish stock. The Gol Gumbaz (Round Dome) is a mausoleum of Adil Shah, a 15 century ruler. This hall is the greatest domed space anywhere and is larger than the Pantheon in Rome. There is a whispering gallery but all I heard was everybody trying everything but whispering. The main body of the building is square with towers at each corner. Since Mandu's Pathan architecture, I had not seen such starkly handsome buildings in one town until now. The Jama Masjid (Friday Mosque) is yet another gloomily-handsome arched building, but it is purely the gigantic proportions of these buildings that first catch the eye. Not until I reached Lucknow did I encounter equivalent structures again. Sunday market was quite lively but the streets of Bijapur were mainly patrolled by pigs.

Before departing for Goa, I stayed with a new friend at nearby Kolhapur. This used to be a major sugar cane producing area. He was listed in the Indian Who's Who. A philanthropic man who had made money from converting wasteland into sugar cane production. He also manufactured cement pipes. He always proclaimed 'I am not educated, my brothers still live in the village.'

Formerly, Kolhapur was a princely state ruled by a Maharajah. The palace was full of his memorabilia, which appeared to be mainly slaughtered animals. Huge portraits of his family in the form of the males of the species and a surprising few of the women, dominated the walls. The most delightful objects were small birdcages made of porcupine quills and gorgeous elephant saddles with silver peacock designs. The Maharaja was a descendant of the famous Marathi conqueror Shivaji, the most famous symbol of the Hindu warrior caste.

Chapter Twenty Seven

A Respite in Goa and Bombay

I caught the 'Vasco Express' night train from Miraj to Goa. It departed from the starkness of north Karnataka and at about six o'clock, I awoke to the lushness of Goa in the form of a sleepy little station called Dudh Sagar, set amongst dense deciduous forests nestling in the hills. The train stopped for a short while and an Indian fellow passenger returned to my carriage after unsuccessfully trying to obtain a cup of tea exclaiming, 'Rough people, they all pushed for the chaiwallah's six cups.' If that was not enough, he then discovered his pocket had been picked and ripped out!

Panjim, the capital of Goa, had the left over atmosphere of Portugal. Goa was freed from Portugal in 1961 by Nehru's forces. Even though the monsoon was about to descend on the area, Goa constantly retained its greenness with coconut trees and dried-up paddy fields dominating the scene, plus mangos in profusion and cashew nut. From cashew, the Goans make their most precious alcoholic drink feni, a gin like substance. The mango is good enough without being turned into alcohol. In India, it is known as the queen of fruits and in my first year in Karachi, I ate so many mangoes that the skin on my arms blistered. Locals said that mango creates heat in the body. When eating so many, I should have neutralised them with milk or water.

Walking in downtown Panjim, I entered the Cappuccine café, a delightful place with tables covered in checked cloths. It was run by a well-contented Christian family who operated behind the bar that was backed by an array of alcoholic drinks, such a strange sight in 1980's India. How pleasant to come and sit in a café and sup white wine or ice-cold beer without feeling like a lower form of animal life. In fact, there were tiny bars and tavernas all over Goa. I sampled the very rich oily and pungent Portuguese pork chourisso sausage, which was awful. This was the home of pork vindaloo, which was another throat-searing experience.

Most of the Catholic Christian women wore shortish skirts and the old women had stern expressions, which matched their tight-fitting grey dresses, looking as if they had stepped out of long ago Lisbon.

A couple of times, I went to a Hindu restaurant and ate a thali meal, which was a large tray-like dish filled with a variety of vegetables and rice. Once a local couple joined me. The wife ate rapidly while her husband ate nothing. 'I am fasting until ten am tomorrow,' he said. He was honouring elephant-headed Ganesh's birthday.

I spent a fortnight staying with Ali Noor of Gujarati origin now living in Margoa. Some years back, I had met Noor at a conference of Gandhians. He had requested me to stay with his family when I came to visit Goa. His family were Khojas or followers of the Agha Khan. His daughter, formerly called Zeenat, had become a Hindu on marriage and was now called Geeta. It is unusual for a Muslim or even Hindu girl to disobey her father and not only marry out but change religions. Her husband was a meat-eating Saraswat Brahmin.

The family offered me a mixture of Goan and Gujarati food. Each day, the cook would make kanji a Goan cum Keralan dish of boiled whole speckled brown rice and water. This was very simple but nutritious and surprisingly tasty. Everyday Noor took me to the fish market at Margoa and the fish included small shark eaten as a curry with rice.

Photos of the young Agha Khan adorned the Noor's old house. The founder of Pakistan, Mohammad Ali Jinnah's ancestors were also Khoja's and originally hailed from Gujarat.

When Dad was out, his daughter Geeta told me that, to her thinking, Goans were inhospitable. 'They never invite each other into their houses. They will chat on the street but not visit each other.' I also developed the same opinion. Geeta's husband was a car mechanic and belonged to a low subcaste of Brahmin, but his family was very hospitable though they might have been Gujarati in origin.

She took me to a Hindu marriage in her husband's family. Apparently, the bride's parents had opposed the match because, although the partners to-be belonged to the same subcaste, they worshipped the same household gods thus the proposed union was viewed as a form of incest. Ideally, within this group, families should worship separate household gods!

The marriage was held in a shabby schoolroom, even signs of a maths lesson remained on the blackboard behind the couple! All the guests sat behind school desks. Geeta and I had come along with the bridegroom's party but the bride's family boycotted the wedding, apart from one sister. One of the bride's brothers had threatened to kill the groom. The white lungi-clad priest was unshaven and straightened the curtain separating the couple who later walked around a small fire seven times, during which handfuls of rice were thrown at them. The Divine Fire is ritualistically lit to invoke the Gods, especially Agni (Fire God) to witness the marriage and bless the couple with good luck and fertility. The priest advised the couple on their duties to one another and their families. The Saptapadi (seven steps) is the most important part of the ceremony. With the seven steps, the bride's gotra (clan) changes to that of her husband's, so now she leaves her family and any children she may have become her husband's family property. The ceremony is a form of rebirth as the bride changes her old name and is reborn into a new gotra. Both partners make the vows, and then the ceremony is over. For Muslims, the marriage is purely a contract but for Hindus, marriage is a sacrament.

After the marriage, we went to the market. The fish market was run by the Gaura community who are Christian, and Geeta insisted on their honesty. We purchased miniature white shark fish. Nearby were huge pyramids of dried red chillies and ground orange-coloured tamarind. Walking home, we purchased some jack fruit seeds, which were quite tasty.

I spent one day in Velha Goa (Old Goa). It was here in 1510 that Alfonso de Albuquerque and his Portuguese fleet came. He fought the local ruler Adil Shah of the former Bijapur state. Old Goa had become mainly a ruined town where bourganvilia and coconut trees survived amongst the handsome churches, which were far from being ruins.

The church of Bom Jesus (Good Jesus) is dedicated to the infant Jesus. The outside walls have had their lime wash removed and in between the stone carvings are columns of brick. Inside as in all these Portuguese churches, one is immediately in awe of the richly-gilded altars. The main altar at Bom Jesus has a gold figure of the child Jesus and above it a larger statue of St Ignatius Loyala, the founder of the Jesuits. Equally lavishly baroque in style are the splendid wooden carvings and paintings. The wooden pulpit is extremely handsome with a mass of sculptured figures that is Hindu in its eroticism. A smaller chapel has gilded twisted columns and floral decorations of wood, and it is in this chapel that the sacred relics of the body of St Francis Xavier are kept. The saint is also depicted on several paintings including one where the King of Bango in Japan is interviewing him. Others show him praying fervently for the ending of the plague and kissing an awful ulcerated wound of a hospital patient in Venice. Parts of his body are kept in a sarcophagus made of jasper and marble. The inner silver coffin formerly held the long-preserved body but now the mummified remains are held in a glass casket. The remains are showed only on special occasions.

When I first entered the church, I deposited my sandals inadvertently by one of the doors as I had become so accustomed to discarding sandals at non-Christian shrines, that I found myself repeating the habit needlessly. After looking around the church, I had some difficulty in locating the correct entrance and my sandals.

The largest church among the group is Se Cathedral, which has eight side chapels along the aisles plus six altars in the transept. The façade is lime-washed apart from the stone surrounds of the windows and doors. Much of the interior is also lime-washed, which makes the gilded altars and wooden screens and pulpits look extremely handsome. Near the cathedral was once the Palace of the Inquisition, which had its own prisons, none of this remains today, only the knowledge that the Dominicans introduced their form of intolerance into this beautiful place.

I also visited some of the other churches, including the Church of St Francis of Assisi, which besides the frequently indulgent baroque features has a large statue of St Francis of Assisi and a huge crucifix. Underneath the two figures are inscribed the three vows taken by the saint: 'poverty, obedience and humility'. The life of St Francis is depicted on either side of the altar on some paintings on wood depicting the life of the saint.

In the centre of Old Goa stands a commanding statue of the 16th century Portuguese poet Luis de Camoens. My visit coincided with preparations being made for his fourth centenary death celebrations.

Prior to visiting some of the beaches, I went by bus to Pilar seminary. It belongs to the Indian Order of St Francis de Xaviour. The monastery is situated on a hill with a magnificent view of the river Zuari. Priests come here to study from all over India. I spent some time with a young guitar playing priest called Father D'Cunha. He helped young people and spoke to me of the increased divorce rate amongst Christians.

I left Pilar for Aquada Fort, which historically was linked to the Goan freedom fighter movement against Portuguese rule. The Portuguese in the fort imprisoned many Indians.

The father of 'Goan Nationalism' was Tristão de Bragança Cunha whose writings were published in a book called Goa's Freedom Struggle. For his activities, he actually spent several years as an exile in Portuguese prisons. In fact, he once said that in Portugal, learned people could only be found in the jails. The civil disobedience movement to liberate Goa from the Portuguese was launched in 1946, only a year before India attained her independence.

I went by bus to Bondla Forest, which is an animal reserve. The forest had a magnificent bison and many wild boars. I fumed at one parent who would not control his boy who was throwing stones at one unfortunate pig. Another bunch of idiots were teasing the peacocks where a notice was pinned up 'do not tease the animals'. This was a depressing experience. I returned to Panjim and walked past the Cobweb Hotel. It looked as if it lived up to its name. At Goa Museum, the most memorable exhibits were rows of portraits of dark glum-faced Portuguese governors all displaying the confidence of empire.

I went back to the Capppuccine café and met an American girl called Mandi. One Belgian girl had spent twelve years travelling. Mandi had lived eighteen months on Calangute beach. She told me that she had fallen asleep on one bus and had woken up to find a man's hands placed firmly on her chest and he was pretending to be asleep!

I spent a few hours at Maem Lane, a small resort. The Hindi film music drowned out any rural sounds that might have been present. Later on in the day at sunset, I arrived at a nice spot called Dona Paula, which overlooks Marmagoa Harbour. Here stands a memorial to a young couple who had committed suicide. She was the daughter of a Portuguese counsel and she wanted to marry a Goan fisherman, her parents opposed the match.

At Colva beach, the fisher folk by their outriggers were squabbling with trawlermen over a five fathom fishing limit. I sat with a German visitor in one of the regular dilapidated beach cafés. He had been to Sri Lanka some months previously and was refused an extension of his visa. The authorities told him, 'we like tourists who come for three weeks, spend a lot of money, then go, not you!' We watched the fishermen unloading their outriggers, which were filled with tiny silver fish and shrimps. Scrambling around the boats were groups of women sorting out the catch. Walking towards one of the boats, I noticed crowds of people waiting to pounce on a rejected-looking sea snake. Somebody then told me that trawlermen were cutting the outrigger crews' nets.

Noor took me to a lovely old Goan house at Margo, which was inhabited by a well known Hindu Konkani writer called Ravendra Kalekar. He was sitting comfortably on his huge verandah, which formed part of a quadrangle surrounding a small garden. He said that about thirty three percent of the Goan community was Roman Catholic, the rest being mainly Hindu and a few Muslims. The Christians use some Portuguese and English words but most of them also spoke Konkani, a language that is closely related to Marathi, the major language of neighbouring Maharashtra state. There was a fervent debate going on about whether Konkani was a separate language or just a dialect of Marathi. Kalekar was a big supporter of the separate identity of Konkani and he disputed that it was only a dialect of Marathi. Konkani is a musical and less literary language than Marathi. Kalekar was a member of the Maharashtra Gomantak (Goa) Party. The bulk of the Goans prefered to remain Goanese rather than be absorbed into the already gigantic Maharashtra state. Some Hindus opposed this and I was not too sure of Kalekar's views. Before leaving this beautiful haven, Kalekar showed me his fine old library and the masses of coconut, cashew, banana and areca nut trees and shrubs.

The Christian servant of the Noor family named C, had given me an introductory note to her brother Jim, a toddy tapper of Palolen village deep in the south of Goa. The bus passed hilly ranges of increasingly denuded forests. I was deposited at the village, which on first appearances was a few huts huddled together. I spotted Jim sitting with a group of fellow toddy tappers in an open-sided hut. He rented his tree and with only a small sickle and much agility, he climbed the tree and arranged the pots to catch the trickle of palm juice, which when fresh is called neera, and only when fermented becomes a gin like toddy. The only thing that frightened me at Palolen were the awful growling dogs. Otherwise, the other main non-human inhabitants, which abounded everywhere in Goa were pigs. He took me back to his hut and I noticed that the palm leaf-thatched roof was almost touching the ground. The mud walls underneath were almost hidden and crumbling secretly. He offered me beer and fish curry. This was followed by coconut feni. I felt slightly guilty because of Jim's generosity, as he could not have been making much money from one tree, which he rented for Rs 5 a month and had to pay Rs 5 excise duty per month. Hens wandered in and out of the hut and at one moment, an enormous sow popped her snout in the doorway and plodded off in a very superior manner. For a moment, I thought I was witnessing the effects of alcohol. Before departure by bus, I walked to the tiny semi-circular beach studded with almost horizontal palms bowing before the sea. Returning amongst the beautiful scenery, one could see that the entire village was dilapidated. Its inhabitants were unskilled and unemployed. 'Any jobs in Germany?' asked Jim. For much of the day he lay idle, lethargy seemed suited to this tropical haven.

I returned to Noor's house. One of the marriage adverts in the local English daily caught my eye. 'Goan Catholic Brahmin boy wants girl caste non barrier.' The bulk of the Christian converts in India came from the lower castes of Hindus, very few high castes converted.

At Baga beach to the north of Goa, I managed to get sunburn. At St Anthony's Tavern, the menu tempted me with roasted pigling. The problem was that in order to eat a pigling, it had to be specially killed. I just did not fancy sentencing a pigling to death. In Goa, the older English word pigling was used rather than piglet. In Goa, the pigs are a dirty lot, it is they who are the scavengers of the lavatorial domain.

Back at Panjim, I stayed at Goa Lodge after having left the Noor family. The lodge only cost Rs 10 per night but all the beds were in cubicles situated within a dormitory. Everyday, I visited Cappuccine Café and on one visit, I met a local eccentric who was part Portuguese who tried his hardest to get off with me. Perhaps he was trying to impress me by saying how much he hated the Indians.

I bussed to Calangute beach. The driver nearly ran over one respectable-looking aesthetic middle aged European who yelled out, 'you bloody bastard, I am Jean the Belgian!' The poor bus driver was bewildered. Goa seemed to be full of long-stay Europeans who felt they owned the place. Thankfully, at this time of the year, most of the western drop-outs had ventured away from Goa to far north Manali up in the Himalayas so that they could collect plenty of cannabis. In the pre monsoon season, Goa was fairly quiet.

Anjuna beach was preferable to Calangute, here there were many purplish-tinted rock formations and scattered palms, enough of them to offer some shade. The few western youngsters told me, 'the Indians (tourists) are spoiling it, they come here to see the freaks.' I walked over to a Tibetan café and ate vegetables and noodles. The Tibetan's dearest possession appeared to be a 1980 edition of the American National Geographic. Inside it were lovely photos of Tibet, recently opened to foreigners. The old woman kept exclaiming 'Lhasa' every few seconds. I wondered if she would ever see it again. Their teenage son had long hair and he tried to sell me a Tibetan dagger, leather bag and embroidered belt. During my meal, one German boy came shuffling by shouting 'I need money'. He appeared to have sold everything but himself. A less pleasant character was a German person with bald head, droopy moustache and earrings. He wore a glittery waistcoat without buttons and attempted to get work in the poorer than poor Tibetan café. One Indian hippy from Kerala sat smoking his chelum (pipe) filled with hashish. A few middle class Indian tourists came by in the late afternoon and started discussing a French boy's camera. The boy said, 'Indian tourists do not want to buy camera, they just bargain for the sake of it.' One German girl appeared in Rajasthani dress, which consisted of a heavy embroidered skirt, a backless bodice, earrings, a nose ring, scarf and heavily- bangled arms. 'Anything to sell'. Her ethnic costume was handsome enough though many Indians would think she looked like an idiot. Most of these poverty, stricken people of Europe would sit all day in cafés sharing smokes and experiences about life's troubles. One foreigner said she had earned Rs 50 in Bombay as a film extra. Apart from my episode with bhang, the only time I smoked pot was in the Karachi law courts when one lawyer offered it to me in the form of a cigarette. It only made me drowsy.

Later at the disreputable Starko Café, which was the venue of some very dubious looking motorcyclists, I heard about the 'Birmingham Mafia'. When Bali became a tourist centre, many of the former tourists there brought back motorbikes and some operated as informal taxis in Goa. They were also drug carriers and frankly, I wanted to stay clear of them.

Before leaving Goa, I travelled by bus towards Betul beach in south west Goa. Thankfully, it was an area free of foreigners. On the bus, I was lucky to meet one Goan family from Bombay. After leaving the bus, we managed to find a tiny outrigger, which was only a glorified dugout canoe. This took us across a creek to Betul beach. We nearly capsized en route back. On the banks of the creek, dried fish were spread out in the shape of individual fans. The Goan family were unable to understand Konkani clearly, because this was their first visit home for years. They shared some cold sausage with me. Dogs, pigs and chickens were also keen to share our food. We also swilled down the food with kaju, cashew feni.

After one month in Goa, I took the steamer Konkani Shakti for a twenty four hour journey north to Bombay. Before the last lot of passengers got off the ship, half of the ongoing passengers had got on, what chaos! I found myself a space on the deck as all the wooden slatted seats were already taken. Unfortunately, an awful Italian girl who I had refused to buy a drink of lassi a couple of days back was sitting near me. When she saw me, she leapt up and explained to the bald-headed German drop-out whom I had already met on Anjuna beach, that I was the one who had refused to buy her a lassi. She instantly abused me, then spat in my face and knocked off my sunglasses. In front of all the Indian passengers, she looked a fool while I remained calm. A group of Goans were squatting nearby on the deck and they invited me to sit with them. 'If she makes trouble, one of our boys will sort her out.' For the entire trip, her two small boys stuck their tongues out at me whenever they crossed my path. These Goans plied me with bread and sausages plus feni. Only a few seats away sat some very orthodox bearded Muslims who must not have thought much of the screaming drugged Italian. Later on in the evening, the Italian girl picked a fight with a local boy much to everyone's amusement.

At twelve thirty am, as if in one sudden movement, at our end of the ship came bed bugs. We all bashed as many as we could as they were entrenched in the ship's timbers. 'I zink ve should burn zis side of ze ship.' suggested one German boy. I doubt if the planks had been cleaned for years, they would not get the chance to be washed when one lot of passengers climbed on board before the previous lot disembarked. Eventually, I fell asleep on the lap of one good fellow after further hours of chat. He was an anglophile Goan and was enjoying 'the first intelligent talk for four years'. He was disillusioned with his own country and could not get agitated about national languages.

A passenger told me more about the dispute between the small fishermen and trawlermen in Goa. It was partly an inter-family dispute. The small mechanical boats were just called trawlers but they could only effectively fish in shallow waters, which was where the older outriggers went. The outrigger Ramponkars agitated for their five fathoms rule and the present government backed them plus the church. The Ramponkars attacked and burnt some of the mechanical boats and in return, they had their nets destroyed. The new government declared a five kilometre zone for the outriggers. Their trawlers trade union went further (in 1980) and imposed fines from Rs 500-2,000 on any outrigger union members who talked, visited or even attended weddings and funerals of mechanical boat operators!

During the early hours, as the steamer passed the distant tiny coastal villages, their remoteness reminded me of Norway's fishing villages that clinged to the coastal wharves.

I arrived exhausted in Bombay where I stayed in Dadar with a handsome dark skinned Marathi woman called Shami. She worked as a librarian at the Khadi Gramudyog. (Khadi and Village Industries Centre). Her flat was part of a forty year old block of tenements. It was solidly made and dingy but once inside, her flat was quite cosy. The entrance to the tenement was situated by the local market.

The following day I went by electric train to Borivli to the north of the city. I then took a bus to Kanheri caves in Salsette island, which are part of a rock-cut temple complex. From a distance, the caves appeared a little sinister, cut into dark rock faces. All of them are Buddhist and they date from late BC. One cave had rows of pillars encircling a huge sixteen foot dagoba, which contained relics beneath it. Large statues and innumerous carvings of the Buddha lurked in all corners. There are numerous colonies of caves near Bombay but I was too tired to see them.

Shami often, in common with many high caste Hindus had a disparaging view of up and coming members of the scheduled castes. A touch of caste elitism would often creep into her comments about those newly-liberated people. She believed that over the generations, untouchables had become genetically poor stock and because of that, culturally impoverished. The cultural impoverishment was hardly surprising if a given group had been physically malnourished for hundreds of years. She then went on to attack the quota system whereby the government services were required to allocate a given number of jobs to 'Backward Castes' (an all embracing term including tribals, untouchables and sudras). 'These people on reserved jobs, even in our office, dominate too much and they cannot even pronounce the language properly,' said Shami.

I commented on the fact that a leading scheduled caste politician had recently visited Benares Hindu University and had touched one statue of a secular notable. Some orthodox Hindu students then poured cow's urine over the statue to 'purify' it. Shami did not seem so perturbed by this action. I asked her if whether her views were reminiscent of Nazi Germany. "No, the Jews were highly intelligent,' she replied. At its level, the argument was not so much different though she was a little shocked by my comments.

On visiting her workplace, I met a former minor film director and classical dancer. He had requested me by letter, to purchase some kaju feni whilst in Goa. That day, I brought the alcohol hidden in my bag, feeling pretty sheepish while passing the homespun-clad followers of Gandhi. When he and I were alone in our office, I presented him with the bottle. 'At least you know our culture, one other foreigner just put it straight on the desk without warning me,' he said. Alcoholic drinks are taboo for anyone connected with Gandhian philosophy and institutions.

I went by electric train to Pune. The Bombay district commuter trains were really good. On the train, I sat with two respectable middle aged Jain women who were followers of Rajneesh. They hardly fitted the Indian stereotype of the gurus' troubled disciples. These women wore chains around their necks with small photos of the thickly- bearded Rajneesh dangling over their sari blouses.

I stayed at the Pune home of a Sri G, a teacher of transcendental meditation. I had previously met him on a visit to Pune when I had slept in the Gandhi prohibition office in the company of Razi Sahib.

At Pune, I found a wonderful museum called the Raja Dinkar Kelka Museum of Treasures of Everyday Art. Raja was a diminutive eighty six year old with boundless energy. He had collected antiques and objects of folklore from all over India. His collection included inkwells, nut cutters (designed in the form of romantic figures, instruments, animals) and lamps. There were fabulously-carved doors from Rajasthan and Gujarat. Windows with lattice-work and carved pillars. I loved the fish shaped silver paan boxes for keeping areca nut and accompaniments.

My next family belonged to an orthodox business caste. Sri A lived at Jalna in Maharashtra state. During my visit, he was busy arranging the marriages of his two sisters. That is the responsibility of a brother to his younger sisters if their father has died or is as in this case, socially incapacitated. The girls in question had been awarded BAs but their degrees were primarily for obtaining a husband. In the orthodox business community, women were not always expected to earn a living. I did meet some male members of the family the two girls were marrying into. They owned a draper's store and, on the day I visited, were clad in long white kurtas and dhotis while sitting cross- legged surrounded by bales of cloth. Some male representatives of their family came to meet one of the daughters in her own home. She sat on the floor and never once looked up at the visiting males, including her future husband. That would be considered 'bold' and unattractive. A woman often looks submissive, even if she may eventually rule her future household, as she gets older, especially if she has sons. Afterwards, I enquired as to what questions were asked at the meeting. The husband to be had asked her name and where she studied. 'Did she ask anything?' I enquired. 'Oh no, no,' he chuckled.

Sri A offered a dowry of one lakh (100,000) rupees, jewellery and clothes for one sister. His family were an example of social mobility. He had started out as a simple farmer and now he was a seed packer and distributor. Unfortunately, he was one of those moralising characters that one meets a lot of in India. 'Our families are much closer than in the west.' I agreed with him, but I said that it was often at the cost of any individual freedom. Could his sisters' bodies be considered their own? I doubted it. I hoped that for their own happiness, they would produce sons while they themselves would totally submerge their own identities with their husbands' families. 'In our community, one who becomes rich must help his family, when my sisters are married, my duty has ended,' he explained. We had an argument over reports of bride burning in northern India. He claimed that reports were exaggerated. I did not claim that it existed in his community or region of central India. Bride burning in 1980 was mainly restricted to Delhi and the Punjab amongst the greedy of the socially mobile.

A annoyed me when, looking well fed, he told me how he could live off 'chapattis and fried chillies for five years as we are simple people. How many Indians have told me that? We argued again over Sanjay Gandhi whom he much admired. The best thing about Sanjay as far as I was concerned was that he advocated tree planting and kindness to animals awaiting slaughter. He was far too zealous over the slum clearance projects in Muslim old Delhi. 'A' then lit the spark when he said, 'All Muslims should leave India, they cannot and do not act as Indians, if they are poor, it is their own fault.' As I saw it, the Muslims did create trouble for themselves when some of them appeared to be more interested in happenings in the Middle East (or West Asia as the Indians correctly call it) than in Mother India. For example, when Iranian Muslim terrorists attacked the main mosque at Mecca, some Indian Muslims went on the rampage attacking Hindu shops. I have already mentioned this and the fact of supporting Pakistan against India in international competitions. Therefore, when A was speaking against Muslims, he was not so much attacking their religious beliefs but that they were anti-national. He had no Muslim friends. Later on, he went onto his favourite theme of Mrs Gandhi's emergency rule. 'We needed ten years- dictatorship and Sanjay's anti communism. Sanjay would not have favoured his mother's friendship towards the Soviet Union.'

Jalna is near Aurangabad and A kindly arranged for me to stay with a Punjabi family friend of his there. In Jalna I visited the Bibi-ka-Maqbara, which is a mausoleum of Aurangzeb's wife Rabia Daurani. Aurangzeb was the most orthodox Muslim ruler within the Moghul Empire. The place was a mass of crumbling plasterwork. Near the Punjabi family's home was Marathwaada University. Some people wanted it renamed after the untouchable leader Ambedkar. The usual student riots had occurred over the matter.

I thought how beautifully simple Aurangzeb's tomb was. Its surroundings were more ornate, but that was due to Lord Curzon who got permission from the Nizam of Hyderabad for the more florid enclosure. Nearby, the Panchakki water wheel was well situated near the shrine of a Sufi saint Baba Shah Musafir of the Chishti sect or brotherhood. The water wheel was used for grinding corn and often free foods were distributed from there.

After leaving Sri A, who for all his controversial arguments, did give me fine hospitality, I departed for Shirdi, the sacred home of Sai Baba (the Afro-haired guru Satya Sai Baba, claimed to be his incarnation). What a dirty, vulgar place! Did someone mention spiritual solace? I stayed in a cheap, dingy but clean lodge in a room without a window. Outside, a continuous din went on in the streets with temple bells clanging, loud speakers blaring and a never ending array of gaudy holy pictures being sold. How inappropriate, for the Sai Baba pictures with such a calm face under his clipped white beard.

I spent the next day at the ancient Buddhist caves of Ajanta. Dated around 200 BC, there are twenty nine caves and obviously I managed to see a few of them. They are full of frescoes using local pigments spread over rock surfaces caked with layers of clay and cow dung followed by lime plaster. Once the entire walls of many of the caves would have been covered in paintings. In one of the main viharas (assembly halls) the giant Buddha has according to the position of the light, a smiling, contemplative or serious expression. Paintings in the caves depict scenes ranging from the royal processions with elephants, horses and soldiers to the life of Buddha. The chaityas (Buddhist prayer halls) are equally splendid with handsome rock-cut pillars, statues and stupa reliquaries.

The caves at Ellora consist of thirty-three Buddhist, Hindu and Jain shrines and unlike Ajanta, they are best known for their sculptures than frescoes. They date from the earliest Buddhist caves from the fourth to seventh century AD, until the twelfth century Hindu complexes. The whole of Ellora is carved into the hill slopes of volcanic stone. By two huge sculptured elephants stands the Sivaite Kailasa temple. Inside it is a special shrine for Nandi, the bull vehicle of Siva. Near the entrance are walls with rock-cut galleries supported by columns. These galleries support statues of Ganesh and some goddesses. There are many shrines and relief panels cut into the walls of the lower courtyard, which is under the Nandi shrine. The whole of Ellora is magnificent in its proportions and the mind boggles at the organisation of labour involved over the centuries until its completion.

I went by bus from Nasik to Bombay. The passing scenery was lushly green, as now the monsoon had broken. This is an area full of pathetically poor tribals and many of them were selling fruits and berries in leaf folders at the bus stops. Once in Bombay, the bus passed through the shanty shacks made of all and sundry from corrugated iron, plastic bags, sheets, boarding, hessian, wooden strips to red tiles. How they survive in the monsoon, it is hard to imagine. Salt pans reminded me of Karachi and these were followed by dirty drab apartment blocks, which loom up from nowhere in all this flatness.

Chapter Twenty Eight

Travels in Punjab, South to Dacoit Country

Back to dear old Delhi and north India after nine months continually on the move. Travelling alone is at once exhilarating and mentally exacting. When two travel together, each person can always release his or her feelings, for even the smallest frustrations, whilst alone, a continual bottling up process may take place. That does not mean that one does not continually meet local people on the move but that offers a separate experience rather than a shared cultural response.

In New Delhi, I revisited my old haunt Gandhi Nidhi near Rajghat. The centre backed onto part of the old city walls and now there were monkeys clambering about the ruins. Walking for about ten minutes towards Delhi gate, one passed low caste Hindu squatter huts slightly hidden amongst the scrub near the Gandhi Museum. The main luxury was pig's meat. How these poor swine hated the pre monsoon heat. Why do people speak of sweating like a pig? The fact is that they sweat only a little. I always felt at home near Delhi Gate because I would frequent the south Indian restaurant tasting such delicacies as upma and masala dosa. In Britain, Muslim Bengalis or Bangladeshis own about 70 percent of the so-called Indian restaurants. They do not cook the simple Bengali food but mostly a form of Punjabi cooking and hardly any vegetarian dishes.

In the canteen at Gandhi Nidhi, a scholar of Indo-European languages, Acharya Dhamendra Nath took me under his protection. He understood seventeen languages within the 'Aryan' group. He had formerly worked at Tehran University and had presented a book of his to the Shah. One night he took me to a famous Hindu Pathan restaurant Moti Mahal, famed for its tandoori food. A tandoor is a clay-based oven and this form of cooking came primarily from Iran or central Asia to the North West Frontier Province, now in Pakistan. Prior to Partition in 1947, tandoori cooking was hardly known in what is now India. It was introduced by Pathans and Punjabis, so to see the sign in a British restaurant 'Bengali Tandoori' sounds quite comical. 'Moti Mahal' was quite a simple outdoor restaurant but it attracted the very rich and those with little income. I just ate chicken tikka and nan bread.

Dhamendraji told me that Nehru's response to eating chicken with a fork was that it was like making love to a woman through an interpreter! Looking at the waiters, I thought that a Hindu Pathan seemed a contradiction in terms. In pre-Pakistan days about seven percent of the Pathans were Hindus. In 327 BC Greeks campaigned in North West India but at that time, the ancestors of today's Pathans would most likely have been Buddhist. Today, it is hard to image the Pathans as anything but Muslims. Their stark austere countryside and their sharp facial features fit a severe iconoclastic faith such as Islam. On looking at these tall waiters with their long faces, I kept asking myself, are they really Hindus? For a moment, I had forgotten the tough Hindu Rajput warriors or sons of Shivaji for that matter!

I travelled from New Delhi to Jullunder City, set in the flat plains of the Punjab. Punjab was a Sikh dominated state, though the Sikhs themselves formed only about 56 percent of the state's population in the 1970's. On the bus, the Sikh driver and conductor were continually teasing each other in their bluff Punjabi manner. After the gentle rains, the greenery sprouted amidst the parched cracked clay. The women in their shalwars and kurtas looked plump with more heads uncovered than in many other areas of the North Indian plains. My fellow passenger was a Sikh whose brother lived in the United Kingdom but had planned to retire in India.

I picked up a horse and tonga and arrived for a six week rest at Ladowali Road's Vidhwa ashram (widow's ashram) which was initiated by Lal Rajput Rao, a political philanthropist who was aware of the humiliation of widowhood for many of India's middle and high caste Hindu women. In the 1930's and 40's, he campaigned for better treatment of widows. Originally, many women were employed by the ashram as tailors and cooks. During my stay in 1981, there were only a few widows present.

One woman was in her mid-thirties and her husband had been killed in a war against Pakistan. Another widow had lived at the ashram for twenty five years, she now worked as a traditional midwife. One very old woman had been widowed at the age of five! While a widower of any age could remarry, the opposite was the case for a widow, no matter how young she had been widowed. It was if she was damaged goods. Many widows either remove or smash their bangles and other jewellery to discontinue being attractive. They often wear drab clothes and generally remain the Great Uninvited One. Thus to be offered sanctuary in an ashram could be viewed as a refuge offering personal dignity.

I met up with an old pal of mine whom I had not seen since I had been at Vinoba's ashram at Maharashtra in central India. Piaralal Sharma was a man with boundless optimism to match his face, which forever turned to infectious laughter. He took me to Simla by bus and we visited the tribal communities within the area who were under the jurisdiction of Adijati Sevak Sangh, (Tribal Social Service). Originally, the Kinner, Gaddi and Gujjar tribals had been nomadic. According to Piaralalji, a dedicated Gandhian, they existed by selling alcohol and their women. Now they were being encouraged to plant orchards of apples, peaches and plums. At night, we ate a very frugal meal with another Gandhian stalwart who wore a huge woollen shawl and spent the entire meal preaching against spicy food.

What a labyrinth of streets within the Simla bazaar. As in most hill stations, Simla's bazaar clambered up the steep hillside below the more Anglicised areas here dominated by the Mall. Some of the bazaar houses were six storeys high and they looked as if they were propping each other up. They hovered oppressively over the passerby. Many of them were flimsy wooden structures with metal roofs. The Mall with its half timbered houses with steep roofs above the shop fronts reminded me of a dormitory suburb in the south of England. During British rule, Indians were banned from the Mall. In 1981 there was no traffic on the Mall and the people walked in an orderly fashion keeping strictly to one or the other side of the road. In the hilly regions, mules were the main pack animals but occasionally one saw human pack horses. One man I saw walking down the Mall was bent double with an almirah (cupboard) roped to his back, while another carried mounds of bricks.

Piaralalji was friendly with a woman socialist member of the Himachal State legislature so both of us stayed at the MLA (Member of Legislative Assembly) Guest House. To be a Parliamentarian in India is not always an envious position. They suddenly find themselves surrounded by 'chumchas' (spoons i.e. people wanting favours). We were kept awake until the early hours by those characters pestering, whichever MLA was present.

Piaralalji took me by bus past Narkanda, just north of Simla to a small town called Thanadhar to visit a Rajput woman called Mrs Stokes. At Thanadhar, we sat waiting for a bus in a drapers' shop run by a very fair English looking Rajput who plied us with tea. The last cup of tea I had in Simla was in the house of a miserable Punjabi character called Dehle. Piaralalji and I had climbed some rickety stairs up to this incongruous follower of Gandhi who kept his daughter in purdah. The poor girl came into the room where we were seated, trembling while holding a tea tray. Her face was covered by a dupatta (shawl) and she nearly went flying. What a change from the real Himachal women of Thanadhar, how handsome they looked in their headcloths, woollen waistcoats, collarless shirts and long woollen skirts. Most of the locals were Gaddis and numbers of Tibetan refugees were in the area. Prayer flags fluttered over their shacks clustering on the hillsides. In the bazaars, they sold rubber shoes, shawls, cheap suits and their usual woollen sweaters.

Before visiting the Stoke's residence, Piaralalji and I made for the so called rest house. Here, there was no water, electricity or food and the lavatory was blocked. We ordered an oily dalda meal from the bazaar, dalda being a dish concocted out of a combination of pulses. The view compensated for the hospitality. The Sutlej River could be seen struggling on its way. At night, a surprising number of lights shone in the mountain villages, which by day were barely conspicuous. I always liked the hill people, excluding the Kashmiris. They had craggy faces rather than the smooth faces one finds in plains Indians. A number of them had a slightly Mongoloid appearance and best of all, they rarely stared at foreigners even though the region had few tourists. They spoke a variety of dialects roughly classed as Pihari (hills) and related to Hindi. Some local words were cheess, (water) pipli, (chillies) shuli shuli (slowly) and hando (go). Quite different from standard Hindi.

Mrs Stokes lived in a beautiful old house in the middle of a valley thick with apple orchards. Her circumstances were unusual in that her late husband was an Anglo-Indian. Her proud Rajput family had strongly opposed the marriage. Her father-in-law had come to India in 1908 as a missionary from the United States. He studied Hinduism while in India in order to argue his case for Christianity and ended up converting to Hinduism, even if to many Hindus that was impossible. Mr Stokes studied Sanskrit and married a poor Christian Indian girl. She was introduced to him by his cook but forgot any grand ideas of starting a Christian ashram, so he just remained a prominent social worker and set up homes for the deaf and blind. She told us of the difficulties in getting local leaders to continue similar work in abolishing child labour. 'Many labourers have become too dependent upon their employers".

The elder Stokes had introduced English Cox's apples into the region but they were too sour for local tastes hence they had been replaced by Kashmiri ones. Most of the labourers employed in the local orchards were Nepali. 'Locals are not interested, though some do seasons work," we were told. A few of the old British who had left, had introduced for local consumption green China tea, but it never became a popular drink and the estates had long since gone.

Mrs Stokes loved gardening and her passion was making exquisite miniature designs with pressed dried flowers. Piaralalji pointed to a photo of her husband on the wall 'a pukka Gandhi wallah'. The photo showed a handsome man clad in homespun cloth, the uniform of many a Hindu nationalist.

I bade farewell to Piaralalji back in Simla. I was offered a lift by jeep belonging to the Forestry Board down to the lower-lying town of Nahan in the Himalayan foothills. Here I stayed with Shyama Sharma, the local M.L.A. (State Parliament member). She was a tough, affable woman whose slight build belied the underlying strength. In Nahan, she lived unmarried in a joint family with her mother and siblings. As with many joint intergenerational families, the family compound was a series of rooms surrounding a central courtyard. Most of the rooms had the usual Indian farmhouse design including beamed ceilings and windows with internal wooden shutters. Shyama, because of the nature of her job, rarely got any privacy and like all Indian politicians was plagued with requests for assistance at all levels.

Her bachelor cousin Ravi, took me to see the old fortress-like Nahan Foundry, founded in 1874 by the then-ruler of this once tiny princely state, Maharaja Shamsher. The foundry became famous for its manufactured cane crushers. To my amazement, some of the old lathes which were still in working order hailed from near my home town Huddersfield at a village called Liversedge. I was told that they worked better than the modern Indian ones. How many wrought iron railings and stoves had been manufactured here? Ravi said that there was still a real demand in these hilly areas for iron stoves, one real gem was lying on my pathway out of the factory. It would have done justice to any Victorian cum Edwardian kitchen range. What a splendid looking foundry, the entrance had turrets and an arched Gothic façade.

Shyama arranged for my accommodation at the local M.L.A. rest house, a dak bungalow-type of colonial building with large verandahs under a steep overhanging roof. Every night, I smelt the lovely Rat-Ki-Rani (Queen of the Night) flower, which only came out at night. Here at Nahan, I first heard the cuckoo since leaving England and the sound made me a little homesick for the English countryside. My last night was disturbed when a bat flew in and joined me in bed. Thank God it was not a snake!

I returned to Chandigarh in the Punjabi plains and visited some African Kenyan students who wanted to meet me because of a letter I had had published in the Hindustan Times.

'Sir, The book, World Resources and Trade displays an appalling lack of knowledge by the so-called educated people regarding Africa.

Anthropologically, there is no meaning in terms like 'black race'. The 'small stature' and references solely to central Africa imply that the authors have latched onto some archaic commentary on the pigmies, a hunter-gatherer people.

The African people have a great wealth of oral tradition, religious beliefs, (many extremely complex) a variety of indigenous political institutions and ranges of economic development in the form of complex trading patterns, manufactured goods of the past in the form of gold and bronze work, etc. Even hunter-gatherers such as Bushmen, have a very detailed knowledge of flora and fauna etc.

All peoples have innovators in any given society but they are always a minority. Africa was never a blank state or 'dark continent' waiting to be discovered – yours etc.

Josephine Scholes

Gandhi National Memorial Fund. Rajghat, New Delhi'

One of the Africans called Anyona had been studying in India for five years and hated it. A number of African students studied in India because many of them lacked better qualifications for the admission into their own universities. It was also much cheaper in 1980 to study in India than in most of the African countries. Part of the Africans' prejudice against Indians owed much to their experience of Asians in their native Kenya. There the Indians had been overall, quite wealthy and led segregated lives from the Africans. Although Europeans had been aloof, many of them did socialise with Africans unlike the Asians. On arrival in India, many of the Kenyans were amazed to see Indians doing menial jobs and pulling rickshaws and they found the country very cheap after Kenya. I explained that many immigrants to Britain had been very surprised to see white people sweeping the streets and working as station porters.

Their lives in India were extremely boring. In the pre-monsoon season (the monsoon had yet to reach Punjab), it was too hot to go out and apart from that, there was no social life on the university campus. The Indian students rarely invited them home and such fixtures as international clubs were unheard of. Another problem was that most Indian girls would not date the Africans or even their own boys. Nevertheless, even amongst the Africans, there was little socialising such as between the Kenyans and Nigerians or male and female. Some Nigerians had married Anglo-Indian girls. They all told me that they related with the more down to earth Tibetans. Anyona told me a story about an African student in New Delhi who fell off a bus and suffered mild concussion. Nearby were a group of Sikh taxi drivers who just stared. After a while, a Tibetan came and took the student to hospital. One local newspaper article described the grouses of overseas students, which included being cheated by rickshaw pullers and having difficulty getting accommodation with some local families who objected to foreigners eating meat and eggs. They also complained of hostels with overspiced food and restrictive rules.

On a later visit to the Kenyans, I was invited for a meal with some of their friends. The house that these students rented was kept by them spotlessly clean. During our meal, the Indian proprietor walked in. Immediately, she started nosing around in their kitchen and asking personal questions. She was not unfriendly, just curious. One of the African boys exploded and said, 'Oh these Indians, one day they will have to leave Kenya, they do not mix and they are uncultured.' The latter was the type of expression that many Indians used for Africans! Another Kenyan added, 'They never say please or thank you'. In true Indian fashion, the nosy proprietor picked up all their ornaments and asked the price and whether each item was foreign. By this time, one of my hosts was on the verge of a brainstorm. Anyona exclaimed, 'When we came here, we were shocked to see Indians doing manual work, the way they carry on back home.'

What a tragedy that travelling to India had been for them such a negative experience, they learned little about Indian culture and the Indian students had not gained anything from their overseas brethren. Even Mrs Verma, my dearest friend, would sometimes say, 'These negroes are noisy'. We all make generalisations, which hopefully we drop after meeting a wide variety of people. I attempted to show the Africans that not all Indians were good at business. The state of Maharashtra was the most industrialised state in India but the top business people there were mainly Gujarati, Sindi or Punjabi whilst the Marathas were not especially famed for their business acumen. Those Indians who had gone to east Africa had been mostly from these successful groups. However, many formerly did menial work like building the railways, and opening stores in remote areas.

Before leaving Chandigarh staying with the Verma's again, I paid twenty three paise to view the extraordinary Rock Gardens. An energetic low-level public employee had dedicated eighteen years of his life to collecting junk including broken pots, crockery, bottle tops, broken glass bangles, bottles and tiles, which he used for designing the garden. The entrance to the garden consisted of handsome pebble walls. Passing amongst green bushes, were banks with model figures made out of all the junk. The monkey god Hanuman with his army of monkeys, also camels and bullocks made of bangles, girls dancing, sitting and fighting made out of broken cups and saucers. The entire garden was so aesthetically pleasing. The French gave the creator an award but the Indian government had been unforthcoming in 1980.

Chandigarh also boasted a pleasant botanical garden. Inside the hot house, several unfortunate cactus plants had come face-to-face with some talented students who had scratched their names on the less prickly surfaces.

I left Chandigarh to return to the widows' ashram at Jullunder. The youngest Sikh widow told me part of her story. Before marriage, she had only been educated not further than primary level. When widowed after one of the wars with Pakistan, she decided to educate herself. She took a diploma in tailoring and made it to teachers' training college. At the ashram, she managed to make a living from private tuition and tailoring.

Every day I used to frequent the Sikh teashop across the road from the ashram. An elderly Sikh who had been fourteen years in the United Kingdom came into the shop and invited me to Amritsar to see the Golden Temple. The following day, he and two of his pals took me in their Ambassador to Amritsar, a very dreary-looking town with masses of cycle rickshaws occupying every available space. Amritsar is one of the industrial centres of India. Sikh temples or gurdwara all have common kitchens where free meals of blessed food 'Karha prasad' are offered to travellers both Sikh and non-Sikh. People made contributions in cash and kind. In the central hall of the Golden Temple, groups of mahants (priests) chant for twenty four hours in turn from the Sikh holy book, the Guru Granth Sahib. Drums and harmonium accompany the chanting. The mahants and visitors sit cross-legged within the temple. Visitors bustle in and out continuously having purchased food and flowers to offer for blessing. A large water tank or pool surrounds the gurdwara. This in turn is surrounded by sleeping accommodation and kitchens. My host invited me to bathe in the sacred pool but I declined. They said that it takes forty eight hours to read the holy book without pausing. Each reader spends about four hours chanting in rotation. The non-stop reading is done for the people in their names. Individuals deposit money with the temple authorities and then reading is arranged for them. A man may wait two and a half years for his turn to come!

The bulk of the Golden Temple or Hari Mandir, to give it its correct name, is encased in gilded copper. The walls have embossed designs of flowers and sacred writings in the Punjabi Sikh Gurumukhi script. The immediate successor to the Sikh founder Guru Nanak, Guru Angad produced this special script for writing down the hymns of Nanak. This aided the development of a separate Sikh identity from Hinduism even further. The lower parts of the temple walls are of white marble inlaid with Petra Dura work. Inside the temple, we were offered prasad made of wheat atta (flour) ghee and sweet supari. The priests keep some of the food to distribute to the poor. All sexes must cover their heads on entering a gurdwara. In the cloakroom at the Golden Temple, I borrowed a dupatta (thin shawl). The shoes have to be removed far away from the temple, and then visitors have to walk through a shallow pool of water to cleanse the feet.

On leaving the temple compound, we visited the Sikh Museum. The whole of Sikh history as depicted in the museum seemed to consist of battles. There were many gory paintings of Sikhs being tortured by various oppressors, usually Muslim. One martyr was shown on a wheel chopped in two. Suddenly, my host yelled out, 'There is one of your countrymen, a white man, you want to speak to him?' He could not understand my embarrassment.

How odd the gentle-faced Guru Nanak looked amongst all these pictures of aggressive looking Sikhs. The Sikhs only became more military-minded at the time of their tenth guru Guru Gobind Singh in 1699. They had suffered severe persecution by Muslims. Their new identity was distinguished by five Kakkars, Kesh (uncut hair) Kara (iron bangle) Kanga (wooden comb) Kirpan (an iron-handled knife) and Kachh (short pants). Guru Nanak preached against idolatry and the caste system for his Sikhs (disciples).

Though there were many discontented Sikhs in India, they had as a community been one of the main beneficiaries since India became independent. They were hard workers in common with many other Punjabis. There were few Sikh beggars, and the only rickshaws that they operated were motorised. The majority of Sikhs hailed originally from the Hindu Jat community. They were mainly owner occupying peasant farmers. Before Partition, the percentage of Sikhs in West Punjab (now Pakistan) and east Punjab (now India) was roughly half of their community on each side. Mohammad Ali Jinnah, the founder of Pakistan, invited those Sikhs living in what became Pakistan to stay on. The Sikhs refused to live under Muslim majority rule for historical reasons, so the west Punjabis joined their co-religionists in the eastern part of the state where they replaced a mostly Muslim population who fled to the west of the Punjab. The bulk of the Sikhs' holy places are in Pakistan and the Pakistan government maintains the shrines. All non-Sikhs are forbidden access to them but parties of Sikhs travel there from India.

In relation to the language issue in the state of Punjab, in the past and later, many Hindus did not complain so much because they were more pro- Hindi, the national language, or saw their own Punjabi, if they happened to be Punjabi speakers, as a language for home use rather than a vehicle for educational advancement. Sikh priests or religious scholars mainly use the Gurumukhi script for Punjabi and many even literate Sikhs cannot read it. By all means, let the schools teach in Punjabi as they can in Telegu or Tamil in respectively Andhra Pradesh and Tamil Nadu states.

They (Sikhs) also complain about Hindu moneylenders. So do many Hindus. The Sikhs also have their own subcastes of moneylenders because they, in turn, had maintained this occupation when they converted from Hinduism, as did Sikh Aroras and Ramgarhias, who are not part of that majority Jat peasant stock forming the Sikhs. Also, a character such as the Hindu Arya Samajist reformer Swami Agnivesh has for some years been campaigning for the most deprived in the Punjab, the tribals. They have migrated from poverty stricken states such as Uttar Pradesh and Bihar, often to arrive in the Punjab to be exploited by Sikhs and some Hindu. These tribals work as labourers in field and brick kilns. Many are in effect bonded labour. They are the poorest who have gained the least in free India and there are millions like them whom top castes often look down upon. When untouchables have converted to Sikhism, the mostly caste-free religion, these Mazhabis (untouchables) achieve some freedom but are still socially and economically underprivileged within the Sikh community. The Mazhabis were amongst those Sikhs who shouted least for Khalistan.

On my return journey to Jullunder with the three Sikhs, we visited a number of places. Beas is the centre of the international headquarters of the reformist Hindu-Sikh inspired Radhaswamis. Their establishment was situated amongst beautiful grounds and nearby was a nature cure hospital founded by the Maharani of Beas. The hospital had forty beds and the latest massage equipment in the form of a type of roller. The centre was beautifully situated in a part of the old palace. Bags of sprouting pulses were hanging everywhere in the hospital compound. On the walls were photos of some patients including a few foreigners. Each patient paid about Rs 1.50 and the treatment was free.

My three Sikh acquaintances suffered from what I would call a lack of curiosity. It was their choice to visit Beas. On arrival, they got out of the Ambassador and were about to make a rapid exit, so I requested to know for what purpose they had come to visit. Was it only to claim that they had been there?

After Beas, we stopped at a number of Sikh farmhouses and drank beer and awful Indian rum. One of my bald-headed Sikh companions removed his turban because he was sweating profusely. Another Sikh who had accompanied me the whole way to Amritsar and back, was either too shy or too proud to speak to me, though I realised that he understood English well, but he made no effort in helping to translate for others.

Our little group visited the Sikh manager of a textile factory, which manufactured a rather flimsy and gaudy variety of dupatta. All the machinery was German. In the upper-storey cutting room, there were rows of dexterous workers. The chemicals used in some manufacturing process made my eyes stream. There being no ventilation, I enquired about any air conditioning and was informed, 'it is only needed for the machines'. The manager's office had the usual tasteless furniture and plastic flowers, which were popular amongst some new middle-class groups, and excellent air conditioning.

Back in Jullunder, I said farewell to my Sikh friends and left for Batala to visit some south Indian Servas group who belonged to the Syrian Orthodox Church from Kerala. They were employed as teachers in the local Christian college and I found them hard to communicate with except on a formal basis. In fact, in the whole of India, I found the people of Kerala the least open in conversation. The language situation had nothing to do with the matter.

I decided to visit the home of the Ahmadiyya Muslim sect's 'Promised Messiah' in Qadian, situated in Punjabi district Gurdaspur. Nearby Batala was a Muslim town prior to 1947. Only desolate Muslim tombs reminded one of the facts. Some Ahmadis stayed behind to guard the monuments. But today, the main centre of their community is district Jhang at Rabwah in Pakistan. At Qadian, only three hundred and thirteen members remained after Partition to mind the shrines. In Qadian, there were over one thousand Ahmadis, some of them converts from Hinduism. Ahmadis were about the only 'Muslims' left in Indian Punjab. The problem is that other Muslims do not include them in their category of Islamic. This is because when the community was established in 1889 as yet another sect of Islam, their leader Hazrat Ghulam Ahmad declared himself the 'Promised Messiah'. Muslims are obsessed with the concept of the Finality of Prophethood, meaning that Muhammad was the final prophet. Ahmadis claims that Muhammad was the last law-bringing prophet and that their 'Messiah' was a different kind of prophet, more a renewer rather than a transmitter of new laws. In Pakistan, they have suffered from groups such as the Jamaat-i-Islami Sunni fundamentalists who derogatorily call the Ahmadis 'Qadianis' as do other orthodox Muslims.

The bulk of the Ahmadis are middle class and fairly well-educated, very few of them are illiterate. Many women are well-educated. Westerners are wrong to assume that all hijab-wearing women have no power. Islamic law allowed Muslim women to have property in their own name long before some of their western counterparts. There was never the concept in Islam that a woman, once married, sacrificed all rights to property in her husband's name. But as a by-product of the segregation of women, it was rare to see women in Muslim communities involved in jobs bringing them into regular contact with men, such as office work. Pakistan has far more women doctors than Britain and many of them own and run their own private clinics whether they observe purdah or otherwise. Many female patients only want 'lady medics'!

During my visit to Qadian, I stayed with a delightful family, my host being an allopathic doctor with five daughters and no son. One of his married daughters bestowed her first son upon her own father. Qadian like Rabwah attracted a number of overseas Ahmadis who had been converted by one of their well-established overseas missions. I met some African students from Sierra Leone (where an Egyptian had introduced the sect) and we had a good discussion. Most of these students had to spend seven years studying Islam including Arabic and often Urdu.

Back in Jullunder, I attended a cultural centre called Rashewar Kala Sangam. Walking around the classrooms, I noted an almond-eyed flute player taking a class. One Brahmin accompanying me claimed snootily that Punjabi was a vulgar language. It is true that Punjabi has rarely had a strong literary tradition because many of the Punjabi top poets recited in Persian or Persianised Punjabi. The best Punjabi, it is claimed, is spoken in Lahore in Pakistan.

After the cultural centre, I was taken to the local Doordarshan television studios. One man told me that he wanted to produce Urdu programmes, presumably to beam to nearby Pakistan. Later, the National Cultural Association invited me to a cultural concert for a merit award because of my interest in Indian culture. The ceremony was held at the Skylark Hotel in central Jullunder. During the presentations (there were six of us), one character condemned hippie culture and western pop music. I doubted if he had ever ventured to hear western classical or folk music. The old joke was recited about the Indian who spoke to an Englishman about the superiority of Indian culture and the Englishman retorted that the only Punjabi culture was agriculture. That reminded me of Gandhi's famous remark when asked what he thought of English civilisation and he replied that it would be a good idea!

I stayed a night with my friend Mr Verma's brother in Ludhiana. He and his family lived in the 'principal's residence' at one college. My main memories of the visit were the high ceilings and deserted fireplaces to be found in their home. Their ancestors were lawyers from Pakistan Punjab where they originally held land. They were very hospitable and unlike Mr Verma, they were still meat eaters who belonged to one of the higher caste Punjabi Hindu groups where meat eating was quite acceptable.

I had a five hour bus journey from Jullunder to New Delhi where I stayed as usual at Gandhi Nidhi. Time for relaxation and letter writing. I shared a room with two young vigorous Australians. Their mouths fell open when I told them that I had been travelling on the subcontinent for over three years and had many months to go before returning home. Their complaints about India were the usual ones echoed by travellers. They referred to individuals poking about in one's belongings and asking the price of each article. 'They never let you finish an answer to a question.' One Indian student had told them 'You Europeans smell'. The Australian had replied, 'Well at least we wash in clean water, not in rivers filled with shit.' They had had their passports stolen and the same day the girl had had her bottom pinched by a young lad standing beside his 'educated-looking' parents. The Australian boy then yelled at the parents' 'why don't you bring your son up properly?' The boy went on, 'I was a pacifist before I came here.' They had had an unpleasant visit to a Sikh family where they claimed they were practically kept as prisoners. The Sikh's mother did not drink but she kept implying in a crazy manner that the Australian girl was her son's girlfriend. The Sikh boy then announced, 'We drink only to get drunk'. Eventually, the Australians managed to get away. 'We liked the Nepalis because they were straight, honest, they do not laugh and stare obliquely at you like many Indians,' they said.

In some ways, these experiences seemed pathetic, but as a foreigner one could find certain truths with many of their comments. Yet one had to fight against getting too negative because of these unfortunate occurrences.

Leaving Delhi I took a bus on the Agra road to a village called Jamna near Sikandra to stay with an elderly man named Raavi. The village was built around a simple temple. To approach the village one passed through a once-handsome, but now decayed arched doorway that displayed an Islamic influence in a predominantly Hindu village. The village looked asleep when I arrived in the early afternoon. Two years previously, they had suffered severe flooding and the mud- walled huts inside the sturdier outer walls appeared to be sinking. Sri Raavi said that he wanted to start up his own school. He seemed very keen to learn about the minority languages spoken in Britain.

For some nights, I slept in a nearby swami's homeopathic dispensary, which was perched on a hillock offering a commanding view of the village. A small goat would intermittently rub its back on my charpoy, but at night, it slept in a cave shelter together with Sri Raavi. The cave was a partly man-made shelter. Raavi told me that he got telepathic messages occasionally while living as a cave dweller. I did not question him further on the matter.

There was a long train journey back into Madhya Pradesh state to Morena district in the Chambal Valley, which was famed for its dacoits or bandits. I had met the agile Gandhian Subha Rao back at Gandhi Nidhi and he had invited me to visit his ashram named Gandhi Seva ashram at Joura Village. Most of the local dacoits were not hereditary bandits but became dacoits on an individual basis. Subha Roa got involved with the dacoits and took many of the youths on to his youth camp. In the 1950's, the Chambal Valley was notorious bandit country. The area has low-lying rather sparsely wooded hills but they offer good hiding places for men on the run. The bandits were casteless unlike those groups formerly classed by the British as Criminal Tribes. Subha Rao got some of them to surrender their weapons alongside their lifestyle.

Subha Rao looked a trim figure with his khaki shorts and upright walk. His ashram had a slightly militant Hindu atmosphere. On October 2nd, Gandhi's birth anniversary, the ashram held a march and through loud speakers, the national anthem was sung with full voice. The local Bal Mandir School, numbering over one thousand pupils turned up for the celebrations. We all marched through the big village chanting 'Jai Hind' ('Victory to India') and singing some patriotic songs. Back at the ashram, mass cooking was taking place to feed all the kids. Huge holes were dug for the fires and cooking pots crammed with rice and lentils were placed therein. Subha Rao enquired which ashrams I had visited. Perhaps he was waiting for me to mention the notorious Rajneesh ashram near Pune. When I answered, 'Widows' Ashram in Jullunder', his face dropped. Later on, I told him about the other places.

In 1960, twenty of the legendary Man Singh gang surrendered in front of Subha Rao and Vinoba Bhave. Unarmed Sarvodaya Gandhian workers had approached these dacoits. There were later surrenders in 1972 when the Chambal Peace Mission was founded. Mohar Singh, another notorious bandit had a reward for two lakh rupees on his head. Upon his surrender he said, 'I plead guilty to all my sins, please pardon me, I did it as I was in the dark, now my eyes are opened, and my future life will be dedicated to the service of all.' He then placed his rifle before an image of Gandhi and Jayaprakash Narayan (a famous politician cum social reformer affectionately known as J.P.) who gave Singh a copy of the Holy Scripture the Baghavad Gita. Over five hundred bandits surrendered handing over three hundred and fifty guns. Many of these youths were later trained in oil crushing, weaving and agricultural jobs. Voluntary workers came from all over India to help. Land was distributed to the landless and Subha Rao would always tell them, 'Every saint has a past and every dacoit a future.'

I was not too sorry to leave the area as I felt an undercurrent of menace about the district, that was not helped by the fact that many locals carried rifles with them when walking in the fields and elsewhere.

I travelled by bus to Gwalior to see its magnificent fort. By Indian standards, it is not so old, dating from the sixteenth to seventeenth centuries. The Man Singh Palace forms part of the fort and has blue enamel walls depicting tigers, elephants and peacocks. All royal women were kept in purdah in their zenanas (womens quarters) and they would watch the dancers while hidden behind screens. Because of fear of invading armies, provision was made for a form of emergency sati. When widows die collectively, it is called sati johar. A huge forty foot pit stood perhaps in silent remembrance. Everywhere there were doorways leading into the zenana but they were kept small so that invading soldiers would not get through.

Two temples within the fort were called Mother-in-Law and Daughter-in-Law! The former being dedicated to Lord Vishnu, the latter to Lord Siva. The Muslim invaders, especially in the form of the iconoclast Aurangzeb had most of the stone-carved images covered in awful white clay. Luckily, the statues were not smashed on this occasion and the British were able to renovate the temples and their images. The Muslims had turned one of the temples into a madrassa (mosque school).

I cannot remember how I got to Khajaraho except that it was not by plane. Perhaps by train via Jhansi where I did stay with a family who lived right in the middle of the bazaar in the crumbling district called Manak Chowk.

At Khajaraho, I shared a Rs 3 room with a decent Australian girl. While visiting the temple complex, she had purchased a large bronze tara, a Buddhist figure depicting male and female elements. She also talked a lot of rubbish about 'my yogi' and the usual.

The exquisite Khajaraho temples have been well described elsewhere. They are chiefly famed for the incredibly erotic statues and friezes on the temple walls, sex in every position under the sun including bestiality. My favourite temple was the Vahara Temple dedicated to the boar incarnation of Vishnu. The enormous stone boar was itself covered in a mass of tiny carved figures.

A brassy Swiss woman owned one of the costlier looking hotels. All the hoteliers looked as if they were in a conspiracy to over charge foreign visitors. One was continuously pestered by cheeky little men trying to sell 'naughty photos' of temple images.

In the evening, we foreigners all sat gossiping. One English boy started preaching about all Indian milk being contaminated by 'Bovine Tuberculoid'. I replied that if that was so, then I should have gone down with TB ages ago. I took a walk in the actual Khajaraho village near the Eastern Block group of temples. The huts were long and low and mud walled. The roofs were made of red pan tiles, which are a common feature of village huts in Madhya Pradesh. Many of the walls had rings of cow dung drying out to be used for fuel. Cow dung insulates the houses in winter. Some jet setters must have been in the vicinity because a few of the many shaven-headed but tufted Hindu boys kept asking me for chocolate. How could I tell them that I had not had a block of chocolate for several years? I did buy a non-commercial wooden cowbell for Rs 5 after admiring one, which was being worn by a bullock.

I returned to Jhansi and immediately travelled to Orcha with an old acquaintance Panditji. Orcha is a historical place, which most visitors miss. It has two fifteenth century palaces. The lovely old rest house offered a lonely but grand view over masses of forestland, which was formerly inhabited by tribal hunters. The tiny stone balconies of the rest house looked vulnerable on the huge expanse of wall, which was being taken over by nature. The environment was returning to the wild. Panditji said, 'The Hindus go (to Orcha) only for the temple, not the architecture.' The river Betwa cut through the village and alongside the river stood dark, sinister-looking mausolea, giving Orcha the atmosphere of a ghost town. At the end of the day, Panditji drunk from the river, which shared its waters with the goats.

Afterwards, I returned to New Delhi to start yet another journey to the Himalayas.

Chapter Twenty Nine

Festivities in the 'Valley of the Gods'

Overnight bus northwards from Delhi to Kulu in the Himalayas. The bus passed through Haryana and Punjab then into the state of Himachal Pradesh. At one thirty in the morning, herds of buffalo and sheep appeared and pushed around the bus in isolated groups with their drovers attempting to commandeer them through the painfully narrow roads. At eight in the morning after a twelve hour journey, the bus bumped its way into the small town of Kulu. It was October and I was here to celebrate yet again the Hindu festival of Dasahara, which went on for ten days held to honour Durga triumphing over evil in the form of the buffalo-headed demon Mahishasar. In the Kulu Valley, Durga is locally named as Raghunathji. Kulu is known as the 'Valley of the Gods' and each village has representations of the deity called devatas. These devatas are represented by amazing masks of silver or brass, which are only displayed on the major festivals. During Dasahara, these devatas are carried in decorated palanquins. Processions pick up the crowds as they move along. The biggest procession takes place on the seventh day when fires are lit for burning effigies of that symbol of evil Ravana who was destroyed by Rama. Some of these palanquins are carried for miles over the undulating roads and the shoulders of the bearers must ache terribly on the long journey. The first sounds of the procession are heard shortly after dawn when all one can hear is an eerie drumming coming from afar. The accompanying musicians play brass instruments, which are often massively proportioned. They look and sound culturally Tibetan rather than Indian. Huge brass u-shaped trumpets and drums feature in the processions. As the seventh day passes, the passage of the devata must become more uncomfortable owing to the swaying of the palanquin by often semi-inebriated bearers. All around them are folk dancers, usually men in tough woollen Himachal dress consisting of colourful woollen caps, loose trousers tight at the ankles and coarse top coats, which are tied at the waist by woollen kamarbunds. The dancers accompany the palanquin following a slow rhythmic step and they intermingle with all the other pujaris (devotees).

Like most Hindu feasts and those of medieval Europe, these festivals are also fairs. In Kulu, many little stalls sold a variety of goods. Earthenware pots of all sizes and shapes were strewn on the ground. Large woven straw creels rested in piles and were used by the rural folk for carrying anything from dung to rice on their backs. Amongst the more important items were heaps of straw mats, trays lining the roadside. Sellers huddled around in small groups smoking clay pipes. Colourful Russian life-size puppets performed amongst the stalls. The puppeteers stood immediately behind each puppet. Elsewhere, some comedians mimicked TV actors. Visiting Russians were garlanded with Kulu caps and shawls. An accordionist singer accompanied one Sikh flautist.

My Indian army family friends who had briefly resided with their mother at the widows' ashram in Jullunder had requested me to visit their army friend at Raison, a small village between Kulu and Manali. Captain Sharma lived in a lovely old house amongst Kapoor Orchard, formerly a British-owned apple orchard.

In this region, all the rural houses were built of stone but they all had handsome wooden windows and overhanging jetties. Dry stone walls surrounded most of the fields and gardens. Locally grown maize and special rice that survive well in dry cold climates were developed in the district. At this time of the year, many roofs were covered in orange maize cobs, which stood out prominently against the blackened wood of the houses.

After a tasty breakfast of coarse maize bread, Captain Sharma's son took me by motorbike to Manikarn, which is famed for its sulphur water springs. What a glorious journey! We passed the banks of the River Parvati, which joins the River Beas under a bridge where poll tax is collected, the Beas being one of the five rivers by which Punjab is named. The surrounding peaks were snow-capped and there were many mossy, steep paths trickling to apparently nowhere. We passed women bent over double, carrying huge bundles of cereal on their backs. Himalayan babies are also carried on the back whereas in the plains, the babies cling to their mother's hips like little water pots. Many of the Himachal folks were beginning to wear large rugs wrapped all around them. The European overcoat had not taken on in India around the time I was there.

Manikarn is primarily a Sikh shrine. Guru Nanak, the Sikhs' founder, plus the Hindu deity Siva, are supposed to have visited this place. The two sides of the Parvati are linked at Manikarn by a suspension bridge and on crossing this, the little group of buildings is dominated by a Sikh gudwara. In common with other gudwaras, this temple also has a langar (common kitchen) for distributing free food to devotees. I went in with Captain Sharma's son and everybody sat cross-legged in rows. The food was simple but tasty and very nicely served.

Quite a number of French and Italian hippies wearing local dress had perched themselves like unwelcome crows about the place. The police had recently raided Manikarn for drugs and twelve Europeans had been arrested. The Sikhs had eventually resorted to refusing them free meals because some of them had abused their hospitality. They looked a pretty miserable lot, always uncommunicative, unless they wanted money.

The hot sulphur water reaches 98 degrees celcius at one point. A number of pilgrims were bathing and the more resourceful Indians had placed little bags of rice to cook in one corner of the bubbling water. Close by some bread was leavening. Pots and pans were lying around. The water was so hot, even in the cooler reaches of the spring that I still could not keep my hand in it for long.

Many of the rooftops had pumpkins and gourds of every shape and size drying in the sun. It was strange to think that the pumpkins had originated in the distant Americas alongside so many other vegetables.

Along Manikaran's narrow streets, the odd character would step out asking, 'Do you want charis?' the local term for hashish. The area is also known for its magic mushrooms and thankfully, I was not offered any.

Back at Raison, in Sharma's house, I had an attempt at hookah smoking but was unsuccessful. Here, ninety per cent of men and fifty per cent of the women smoked. In most parts of orthodox India, women rarely smoke unless they are from the lower castes. Prior to Partition, many Muslims lived in this area and in 1980 there were only one to two percent in the Kulu area. Because my hosts were high caste Punjabis, their women did not smoke. Culturally, they belonged to the plains rather than the hills.

Before departing to Manali for a few days, I was cooked a local dish batura, which consisted of rolled leaves of yam and mixed vegetables. This I ate with country bread and local pink-coloured rice with a concentrated texture.

I took the jam-packed bus northwards to neighbouring Manali. It was surprising the number of local women who suffered from travel sickness on these bumpy, winding Himalayan bus routes. I always found the buses too rough to cause nausea. My main fear was of the bus disappearing over the side of a hairpin bend.

Manali was concentrated on one main street and much of it held a profusion of Tibetan cafés. After taking tea, I walked to Vashist, which is famed for its hot springs. The village was perched up a steep hillside. Its temple I found to be worth the trek. It was a charming stone building and each stone was individually carved. Nearby, I heard the sound of heavy metal rock music coming from a long row of traditional, stone cum wooden houses. Apart from Goa, Manali is the other Shangrila of the western hippies. Cannabis grows like grass in the neighbouring hills. Many of Vashist's and Manali's shops were actually run by enterprising Punjabis rather than the locals, so when hunger called, I was served with tiny fried puris rather than the coarser rural breads. Punjabi cuisine has spread to so many lands and often is the sole representative of Indian cookery.

Nearer to Manali, I went to the Devi temple situated amongst the evergreen deodar trees. The temple reminded me of old Norwegian wooden stave churches, partly because of its pagoda-like appearance as these temples are only found in the Himalayas. It had intricate carvings embellishing the porch and doorway. Footprints of Devi, the goddess were inside, the surrounds of it being garlanded, and above the door hung the skeleton of a deer.

Then it was the final day of Dasahara, when a buffalo is sacrificed and beheaded. The meat is eaten by the local chamar (leather worker) group of untouchables. I did not stay in Kulu long enough to witness the spectacle.

While in Manali, I spent a couple of days in a hotel. To begin with, I paid Rs 30 for an awful but clean room where the double bed took up nearly all the available space. The next day, I moved to a cheaper old place to a room offering what must have been one of the best views in Manali.

I took a bus to the Rohtang Falls and passed gangs of road workers melting tar in huge barrels, which seemed an awful job and it must have got bitterly cold up there in winter.

Back in Raison, I spent my last day in these parts just strolling around. I came across a field of okra. The cows were busy munching the okra leaves, a herdsman told me to try the raw okra, and I found it quite tasty.

I returned to Delhi. After resting at Gandhi Nidhi, for a change I went by luxury bus to Agra. The trip included staying at a good hotel. Upon the Delhi-Agra highway, the traveller passes little towers every two miles, which are Kos Minar. The Mughals built these as milestones.

On first seeing the Taj Mahal, one feels obliged to think of something original to say about it, to explain one's first reactions. Mystically stark. I hope that my perception was not influenced by the increasing haze of pollution that was gradually eroding the monument.

The Taj was commissioned in the seventeenth century by Emperor Shah Jahan as a tomb for his queen Mumtaz-i-Mahal (the Elect of the Palace). In front of the Taj is a long watercourse set in a formal Moghul garden and the Taj is always reflected in the water. The walls of the Taj are built of white marble from Makrana in distant Rajasthan. Apart from the white marble trellis work, I was most impressed by the variety of precious stone inlays depicting flowers and arabesque work plus Arabic calligraphy with writings from the Holy Quran.

The Taj is more Persian than Indian. One wonders why it should be more famous than the magnificent often ancient Hindu temples of south India. Perhaps the Taj appealed to a more iconoclastic Protestant English eye than the complex mythological sculptures found in stone temples. One demands far more understanding than the other.

There are many splendid buildings in Agra including Akbar's mausoleum built in red sandstone like the Red Fort in old Delhi. Agra fort is built of sandstone blocks and has the usual towers and turrets. Within its walls are a variety of Moghul buildings, including the Jodabhai Palace and Diwan-i-Khas (Hall of Private Audience).

Before leaving Agra, I visited a traditional workshop. Bow string lathes were busily employed in shaping semi-precious stones or alabaster. These workmen were practising the centuries old skill of manufacturing inlay work. One example of the enamel work showed about sixty separate pieces in one flower.

Nearby to Agra stands the handsome mausoleum at Sikandra for the tolerant Emperor Akbar who lived at the same time as Elizabeth I of England. But unlike Elizabeth, Akbar tried to observe the best aspects of the major religions, which is quite unusual for somebody born a Muslim. Inside Akbar's tomb were lovely examples of mirror work. Precious stones and tiny shaped mirrors were embedded in the walls. The mirrors danced against the light when the local guide lit up a torch.

The Moghul ghost town of Fatehpur Sikri is quite magnificent. The city was inspired by Akbar because originally the site was inhabited by a saint of the Sufi Chisti brotherhood called Chishti Salim who had prophesised the birth of a son to Akbar. The buildings are predominantly Islamic in style but with Hindu influences. The town became deserted primarily because the water source dried up. All that remains is a deserted complex of palaces, forts and mosques.

While remaining in the state of Uttar Pradesh, I journeyed by train to Jharkand near Mirzapur. I came to visit a Servas friend at Banwasi Seva ashram. The district is a forested tribal area in the Kaimar ranges in the Vindhyas, which form that vague dividing line between north and central-south India.

During the 1952 famine, food had to be dropped by helicopter. A permanent relief centre was initiated by the chief minister of Uttar Pradesh and Delhi's Gandhi Nidhi to serve the tribals. The ashram land was acquired through the Bhoodan movement. Eventually they were granted well over two hundred acres of forest land in Gouindpur village. They started with five workers plus a dirty well. In 1965 to 1967, another famine occurred. The ashramites changed from purely relief work and progressed to employment projects. The jungle was cleared and earthen reservoirs built for irrigation. 'War on Want' helped with an agro-industrial project. The local soil was difficult to work on, as this was hard and shallow with a low water retention rate. Only millets, a little rice, pulses and oil seeds were grown later. An agricultural workshop repaired machinery and they produced hand tools and oxen drawn implements. There were smithies, carpenters, tailoring, tanning, brick making, rope making from forest fibregrass, sugar making, lime making and sericultural production. They even had their own residential schools plus barefoot doctors on the Chinese model.

The gram kosh (village aid system) was maintained by a small contribution from local villages. The ashram operated credit services for seeds, bullocks, artificial insemination and so forth. They even had a village assembly as a form of local democracy. There were many such schemes going on in rural India unlike rural Pakistan and many other similar impoverished communities in other countries.

While at Banwasi, I slept in a lovely single-storied building with a huge verandah. I always loved verandahs.

From Ranakoot to Varanasi by bus. The road was dusty and the bus was windowless so as usual we were all covered in sweat and dust. As compensation for this misery, the bus passed an interesting procession of drummers surrounded by celebrating bystanders as we neared Varanasi. A fearsome, black-skinned statue of the goddess Kali sporting a lolling bloodthirsty red tongue was being carried on a palanquin through one village. The goddess was heavily garlanded and sumptuously dressed. Her tiger mount was being carried separately. It was the festival of Durga Puja, which is a very important festival in Bengal and areas such as eastern U.P. and Bihar, which are not too far away from that state.

On first appearances, Varanasi, the name for Benares but in ancient times known as Kashi, appeared chaotic. Cycle rickshaws crowded every street and their tingling of bells rang in the air. Cows happily threaded their way about munching yesterday's leaf dinner plates plus threaded garlands, which soon became litter. I took a bicycle rickshaw to Benares Hindu University, which had twenty thousand students of which ten thousand resided in numerous decrepit-looking hostels boasting the usual barred prison like windows. A pseudo Hindu architecture prevails on the campus. The massive white tower of Birla Temple looked as if it aimed for high ideals. On visiting the museum, I headed directly for the Moghul paintings. My favourite picture depicted the ladies of the harem spraying each other with gulal, a purplish liquid used in celebrations during the Holi festival. The campus was enormous, covering several square miles.

On the rickshaw towards my Shi'ite Muslim host, Maulana Dr Rizvi, I reflected upon the journey to Varanasi. The Kaimar Ranges had changed to scattered woodlands and immediately within the Gangetic plain of which Varanasi forms a part, this scenery was replaced by tedious scrubland and paddy fields with a yellowy-green colour,showing that the paddy was about ready for harvesting.

My arrival at Rizvi's residence coincided with their Shi'ite Islamic festival of Muharram. It commemorates the martyrdom of the Prophet's grandsons Hussein and Hassan.

Dr Rizvi was the head of the university's Persian and Urdu department. He looked the archetypal Islamic scholar with Muslim beard, (no moustache) skull cap and wearing the collarless sherwani jacket with tight trousers. He was an unfanatical man who revelled in Persian and Urdu poetry. During my visit he spent much of his time seated cross-legged on his bed. Near at hand was his spittoon shaped like an hour glass to which he would spit out a reddish residue including betel leaf mixture. This scene was accompanied by hawking or clearing the throat, a sound I never became accustomed to. On my first day, the Maulana took pen and paper and wrote down the main parts of my life. He seemed utterly surprised at the amount of travelling I had been able to do.

The following day, he took me to his department and I met a few of his students. What an uninspiring group. For most of them, their study of Persian was just a degree, not a subject to take great interest in for the rest of their lives. After graduation, they would never open a book again in Persian. What a tragedy, for even if a man becomes an engineer or bus driver, he should still be able to draw mental refreshment upon special subjects by which to enrich his life. Perhaps that sentiment belongs to an ideal world.

Later, I walked through the leafy overgrown gardens of the Theosophical Society and noted that their library was donated by one K. Pepper of 'Ancient Irish lineage, a lady who married a Major Tibbit of Lahore and who converted to Hinduism, the religion of her previous lives.' I met an elderly English woman, Miss Morns who lived in Dr Annie Besant's former house. Inside, the rooms were dark but cool. The centrepiece of one was a highly polished writing desk.

Varanasi is famed for its eighteen ghats (stepped slopes), which stand on the bank of the River Ganges, which is popularly called by Hindus, Ganga Mata (Mother Ganges). The first thing that struck me about Varanasi was that in spite of its longevity, one does not see so many really old buildings. This is because, as I found out later, Turkish Muslim invaders destroyed so much of it during the thirteenth century. Five of the ghats are known as the Panchtirath, which are holy places especially for bathing. The Ganges, which rises in the Himalayas, is linked to Siva because the Himalayas are his chief abode. Thus owing to the increase in popularity of a divinity in the form of Siva, the river increased its sanctity. The Ganges represents the movement of life, or movement from the motionless, unmanifest cosmic reality. Certainly much of the prosperity of northern India depends on the Ganges as does Egypt upon the Nile. Hindus believe that the river offers physical and moral purification.

The cluster of ghats faces its opposite bank, which has no buildings, only sand banks. The ghats are places wherein votive offerings of all types occur. Some ghats were donated by members of particular communities, others being in the possession of Bengalis or south Indians. Foreigners cannot help noticing the burning ghats with the twenty four hour fires busily cremating bodies wrapped in shrouds. Prior to burning, these bodies lie around waiting their turn. I had attended one cremation of the Scotsman, Mr Coates of the British thread making family. He was given a Hindu cremation as the former head of the Theosophical Society. Compared with a British funeral in one of our crematoria, I found the experience in India far less depressing.

Quite a number of people must live on the houseboats, which were moored in different parts of the river not too far from the ghats. On one boat ride that I took down the river, groups of washermen were as usual pounding their clothes as if in a frenzy. One man washed his buffalo as if he had all the time in the world. Silently, a dead dog floated by.

Remaining with my Muslim host, I spent one day alone at Sarnath where Gautama Buddha gave his first sermon after he had obtained enlightenment at Bodh Gaya. He had learnt that his five former companions were staying at Sarnath so later he explained his teachings to them.

Amongst the Sarnath ruins, the artifact which interested me most was the remains of one of King Asoka's pillars. Asoka who lived in the third century B.C. had converted to Buddhism after being involved in too many wars. He first sent missions to the Far East and Sri Lanka. Upon this pillar was an edict exclaiming that monks and nuns who create schisms in the sangha (order) should wear white clothes and live separately. Strange to think that the famous Chinese traveller Huien Tsang (A.D. 640) had also seen this particular pillar and other pillars and stupas then in existence. Also at Sarnath is the beautiful lion capital (now India's national symbol), which had a metallic look about it. To think that it is much older than our Norman cathedrals. It has a lotus-shaped base. Four lions sit back to back with a wheel between them. Below that, four wheels separate an elephant, horse, lion and bull. The wheel symbolises the Wheel of Life as described by Buddha. Sarnath also includes monastic ruins including monks' cells amongst its ruins.

The next day, I travelled to Bihar's Bodh Gaya after a six kilometre ride by cycle rickshaw from Gaya railway station. Bodh Gaya offers a fine synthesis of Buddhism past and present. The Japanese, Thai, Chinese and Tibetans all have temples here. They live and pray in their beautiful new temples amongst the ancient ruins. The old Mahabodhi Temple is magnificent. It has a huge narrow pyramid- shaped tower with handsome carved stone niches. On top of the tower is a round stupa-like structure. In the sunken gardens around the temple are many small stone stupas.

Towards dusk, saffron-robed monks queued up by the Mahabodhi Temple bringing plates of good food including rice, fruit, bread and milk to be given as offerings. The monks certainly looked plumper than the poorest of the community around them but they were not obese.

Close by the old temple stood a huge coloured prayer wheel. In one nearby room, a monk was ironing his robes with a fearsome-looking coal iron.

I managed to obtain a letter of introduction to the Japanese temple at Rajghir. This letter had been kindly given to me by the only Indian Buddhist I had ever met, called Sri Maharatha. His ancestors were members of one of the subcastes within the Hindu Kshatriya caste as was Gautama Buddha.

The only Japanese I saw who were not monks were a group of Japanese drop outs with long hair and beards who were hanging around some of the local tea shops in Bodh Gaya.

The garden ponds around the Mahabodhi Temple were filled with rose and purple lotus. Added to that was a good reflection of the temple glimmering in the water. Outside the same temple's main entrance, worshippers prostrated themselves many times on special wooden boards. It is a more energetic prostration than that found amongst Muslims and to an onlooker, because of the amount of time spent on it. The performance looks more like a form of rigid exercise than prayer.

From Bodh Gaya, I travelled to see a Gandhian worker at an ashram for scheduled castes. Dwarkaji Sandrani worked in the Bhoodan movement. Within this area of Bihar, the Land Gift policy had distributed four hundred and fifty thousand acres to half a million families. The government and the Naxalite Marxist revolutionaries had between them given about two hundred thousand acres away. The Naxalites forcibly removed the land from its former owners often by killing them. Bihar had the worst record in India for oppression and violence plus lack of social reform. Unfortunately, as Dwarkaji pointed out, corruption and bureaucracy had bogged down the whole process of land redistribution. It is not possible to just partition land. Much depends upon family size of recipients, quality of irrigation and the fertility of the land itself. It should also be put down in writing. In this poor part of Bihar, bonded labourers needed to be educated to new responsibilities. To be landless one day and receive land the next after generations of oppression. Oppressed people know only a little about account keeping. Dwarkaji said, 'It is hard to get selfless workers, often the families are so poor they have often lived for months on roots and leaves.'

The ashram taught gardening, cooking and Gandhi's ideas on Basic Education, taught in their gurukul. Residential schools were deemed important for joint living and serving.

Some of the local land was donated by the Bhoomidar caste of Brahmins. Dwarkaji added, 'Vinoba Bhave was not a good organiser, more an inspirer.' Much of the land had been donated during and following his thousands of miles foot marching or padayatra.

Dwarkaji added, 'Foreigners ask me, you give visitors tea, not the kids. Well, I reply, when they go back home, then they will demand tea which they cannot really afford, so why make expectations too high?' Glancing at the smallest children, Dwarkaji said that most of them were betrothed at about seven years old within the traditional system. 'But we will marry them when they have left at about sixteen years.' Because of poverty, there was no dowry problem, so girls in these poor households were considered less of a bind than they would be amongst the middle classes.

I departed from Dwarkaji and before going onto Rajghir, I had to return to Bodh Gaya. There I visited the Bodhi Tree when all was quiet. This sacred fig tree is a descendant of the original tree under which Buddha received enlightenment. It had fallen down and two saplings of it were planted at two places. Ashoka's son, Mahinda took a cutting of the original tree south to Sri Lanka and planted it at Annuradhapura, an episode I have already referred to.

The hilly town of Rajghir was one of the dirtiest towns I encountered while travelling in India. Luckily, all the religious buildings were in the cleanest district and never was there such a discrepancy between the sacred and the profane. Fortunately, my hosts at the peaceful Japanese Buddha Sangha were situated in a tranquil area. The monks were members of the Nichiren sect, which represents a militant asceticism. A number of the monks had badly scarred arms, the head monk, the Rev Narimatsu told me that burnt incense sticks are placed horizontally on the arm, the skin then blisters and breaks, creating a bad-smelling liquid. This process is repeated several times. It takes a hundred days to heal and then the wound is treated with white and green parts of an onion. I could never see the point of this form of mortification any more than the activities of medieval Christian flagellants. What of Buddha's concept of the Middle Way?

The urbane Rev Narimatsu took me up to their peace pagoda on Mount Ratnagiri. The Nichiren sect have built peace pagodas in many countries, including one at Milton Keynes in England. We ascended the mountain by chain lift (the then Prime Minister Moraji Desai had recently done the same journey). On the mountainside, brick remains of Ashoka's stupa, stood looking forlorn amongst the healthy looking forests. Rev Narimatsu pointed to a piece of land in the valley below and said that he wanted to build a world peace centre and a university. He was also interested an Hindu ayurvedic medicine and wanted to encourage it. The mission of the sect's leader Guruji (Nichidatsu Fujii) was to spread Buddhism back to India.

I had a few happy days of wholesome food with the monks. On the long table set in a verandah, the central plate was always filled with noodles. At the start of each meal, a small amount of the vegetarian food was set aside as an offering. Their diet included, alongside the normal Indian fare, imported salty seaweed biscuits from Japan. One monk exclaimed, 'I enjoyed fish and chips in England'. Not many orthodox Hindus would ever admit openly to having ever eaten fish or meat, even if abroad. At the end of their meal, they would pour water onto one plate. Transfer that water with any food remains to another used utensil and so on, then clean their cutlery, if any, with the same water and finally drink it. I preferred the Tibetan method of licking the plates clean!

At Mount Ratnagiri, Rev Narimatsu had shown me their little retreat. Hidden away inside it was a delightful Japanese rock garden with running water. The retreat had tiny rooms, including a beautiful guest room for when 'Guruji visits'. It had the atmosphere of a shrine. I was given permission to stay a few days up in the mountain but I declined the offer. Before leaving the mountain, Rev Narimatsu had presented me with a tiny silver Tibetan prayer wheel.

I found the prayer meetings at Rajghir a little tedious. In their little prayer hall, the faithful sat on floor mats and were each given fan drums on which to thud out rhythmically the matra 'Namu myo ho ren ge kyo'. (This refers to the jewel in the lotus theme). There were two huge barrel-shaped drums, which were hit with two large sticks whilst the drummer sat in front of his drum, as do the Kodo drummers. The altar at one end of the hall was set in layers and had photos of Gandhi and Guruji on display. Worshippers came in and prostrated in front of the altar while the mantra was being chanted. After that they received prasad (blessed food). Then immediately they would join the rest of the congregation (if any) and bang their fan drums. Towards the end of the prayer ritual, the monks chanted from prayer books and the Rev Narimatsu would rhythmically tap a hard wooden circular block drum and intermittently tap a metal cylinder, which echoed.

The most embarrassing moments for me were all the bowing that went on with the Japanese. When does one stop bowing?

I went to Bargaon village in order to see the ancient Buddhist University of Nalanda built in the early fifth century A.D. Ten thousand monks once populated it. The traveller Hiuen Tsang lived there for five years. Apparently, about eighty percent of the students used to fail their exams and personality and behaviour of the students were all taken into account. I would not hold out much hope for today's students under such a system. Nalanda was in ruins but there were monastic cells and temples. Turks who used the university as a fortress destroyed most of the buildings. It is terrible to think of those great minds being slaughtered.

Before leaving rural Bihar, I went to Jayaprakash Narayan's former ashram Gram Nirmas Mandal. J.P., the pacifist socialist built the ashram in Nowadah district in a tranquil area. J.P.'s ashram house was now kept in memory of his lifestyle as a museum. A couple of uncarved walking sticks, white cotton khaki bed linen and a straw flower basket were the chief items. Wall murals depicted a folk dance and Christ's walk to Calvary. The hut was open-sided and it reminded me of a large verandah. The view from the hut was a mass of heavily- forested mountain ranges. Wild pig still damaged crops, even bears and tigers were occasionally sighted. The local people were mainly tribal.

Before departing for a more industrialised area of Bihar, I went by a private local bus and tum-tum, a type of horse-drawn, barrel-shaped, straw-matted, covered wagon. I then travelled by bus towards Shambarti Khadigram, another educational Gandhian ashram. This place was historically connected with J.P. Only children willing to undertake manual work were taught. A few of them were sitting spinning on the verandahs. I arrived in time for the rice threshing, which was done mainly by the scheduled caste people living on the ashram. The government had allocated land and money for housing.

I arrived at the dirty coal mining centre of Dhanbad, which is situated en route to Calcutta. I greeted my friend, the gentle Sikh Mr Bhardwaj whom I had met at the Madras Theosophical Society Conference. He was employed as a colliery manager and naturally, he arranged for me to go down one of the mines. Before being kitted out with a helmet and a belt with a lamp attached, he showed me some colliery maps exhibiting the different seams. Most of the miner's earned about Rs 2,500 per year (in 1980). Often, whole families would be employed in different jobs connected with mining but women did not go down to the pit. Most of the local labour was tribal.

Down in the mine, I noticed that the seams were supported with wooden props and disused mines were filled with sand. I only went down about two hundred and eighty feet. The lowest level in that pit was one thousand feet. The ventilation was better than I expected but some of the seams were very hot. I remarked how broad the seams were as I only had to bend my head a little. 'Oh, we are impressed by how hard your miners work in those very narrow seams,' he said. Thank heavens these were not too narrow as I suffer from slight claustrophobia.

Mr Bhardwaj's family were delightfully friendly. They had a lively little puppy called Jackie. None of their Hindu neighbours relished the idea of a dog peeing all over the house, especially in the kitchen. Indians (apart from the wealthy) are not accustomed to allowing or even having pets in their houses because they are polluting. My host was a Punjabi exile in Bihar and his wife told me that (as true Punjabis) they consumed more milk than all their immediate neighbours put together. Their breakfasts consisted of rich fried stuffed parathas and curd or chutney. How good to taste carrot pudding again. Punjabi food is very rich and owes more to Muslim and Persian influence than Hindu.

Mr Bhardwaj had become a vegetarian, unlike many Sikhs. The Theosophical Movement had influenced him and he was also a Co-Freemason. He asked me if I would like to be nominated as they allow women to join. I said that I would prefer to read more on the subject of Freemasonry. He was shocked when I told him of an anti-Masonic pamphlet I had picked up in Pakistan. The pamphlet had played on anti-Semitism and today masonry is banned in Pakistan as in many Muslim countries. I remembered one of the poor quality photos in the pamphlets as it showed a formal dinner where masonic participants were partaking of some alcoholic beverage. An accompanying blown- up photo zoomed in on the bottle, it was whisky. Freemasonry must be bad news.

With sadness, I left my friends and departed by an overcrowded passenger train to Calcutta where I decided to spend Christmas.

Chapter Thirty

Christmas in Calcutta, Exploring Lucknow

On arrival at the jam-packed Howrah station in Calcutta, I commandeered myself towards the exit, still yearning for my lovely Sikh family in Dhanbad. How easy when one is travelling alone to succumb to not so much home comforts, but love and affection.

My immediate task was to find Servas family Dasgupta. He was a bookseller dealing in language books ranging from Sanskrit to Tamil. College Street Market was my destination, so I boarded one of the famed Calcutta trams, which was thronged to capacity with humanity. I never did get a ticket, as the ticket collector was unable to get into the tram. He was to be seen hanging on the outside alongside some unfortunate passengers. I found myself squeezed in at the end of the tram. How to get out? Suddenly, College Street Market appeared. The nearest passengers pointed at a conveniently broken unbarred window and grabbed hold of my duffel bag while I just managed to crawl out. Without their help, I would have ended up at the opposite side of Calcutta.

Dasgupa's publishing house was to be found in a tenement block hiding behind a group of market stalls. What a dreary dump. I felt depressed as I had only just heard of the death of John Lennon via the BBC World Service. Being alone, there was nobody to commiserate with and I did not bother asking Dasgupta if he had ever heard of the Beatles, why should he care?

Sri Dasgupta was a lean-looking man attired in white kurta and dhoti. He lived in the suburb of Bhawanipore. I shared the bedroom with two female members of his family. They did not know English and I knew even less Bengali. That first evening, I ate a hearty meal of fish and rice, the Bengali staple diet followed by jaggery date palm brown sugar. Many high caste Hindus will eat fish, especially if they come from Bengal or Kerala and still consider themselves vegetarians. One man actually believed that fish was the 'vegetable of the sea'. Well, it is possible to believe anything if you want.

I intended to spend Christmas in the Salvation Army hostel at Sudder Street, which was one of the cheapest and cleanest digs in central Calcutta. It was based just off the Chowringhee Road, one of Calcutta's main thoroughfares. There, I shared a dormitory with a Japanese girl, a French girl who worked with Mother Teresa, also an English girl who had worked in an Icelandic fish factory. There was a Dutch girl engaged to a Burmese and studying Bengali at Calcutta University. Later on, the Dutch girl and I had an argument over whether the Nehru family of Mrs Gandhi were really Brahmins or not. She insisted that they were not and she was the only person I met to deny Mrs. Gandhi's Brahmin ancestry. In fact, she was on the verge of a mental breakdown. I doubt if I could survive being a long-term university student in India with all the upheavals that go on between students and staff, especially in politically active Bengal.

In the evenings, groups of us would try the various Chinese restaurants around the vicinity of Free School Street, which was situated at one end of Sudder Street. Unlike English Chinese restaurants, the waiters were Indian but the bulk of the clientele were Chinese. Calcutta has a large Chinese community and they dominate in the shoe trade. One can order any style of shoe to be made by hand in Calcutta. My only direct contact with the Chinese was at a beauty parlour where I paid Rs 50 for a facial.

On Christmas Eve I attended a beautiful carol service at the Anglican Cathedral. The bulk of the congregation was either Indian or Anglo-Indian with a sprinkling of Europeans. Calcutta, during British times, once had the biggest population of Anglo-Indians. Since independence, many migrated overseas, including Australia.

On Christmas Day, I attended a more sober service at the Scots Presbyterian church (probably St Andrews), which had a Bengali minister the Rev. Sen. Sober suited Anglo-Indians ran the entire church. It had no altar, only a dominating pulpit. During the service, the church elders sat grim-faced at the head of the church facing the small congregation.

After the service, one elder called Mr Simpson told me that his mother was Anglo-Indian and father a Scot. 'I call myself Scottish.' Then he added, pointing at a fair-skinned military-looking man, 'Life was better under the British.' I told Mr Simpson that I had attended the Cathedral and he muttered that it was 'too cliquey down there'. Many Christians, not only Anglo-Indians, seemed to live in a limbo existence in a twilight world. They could not come to terms with their place of birth, especially the Eurasians. Using the term Christian here, I am really referring to Protestant Christians rather than the Goanese Catholics and older Christian groups of Kerala.

I spent a few hours at the Victoria Memorial cum museum, which stands handsomely near the maidan (parade ground). Queen Victoria still sits upon high as a confidently pensive woman who listens silently. Inside the museum were some lovely paintings from the seventeenth and eighteenth centuries that viewed India in romantic hues, favouring scenes of the Himalayas, Ganges and temples all generally lacking signs of public squalor. The museum itself was in a spotless condition. Then I found that it had been spruced up for Prince Charles' visit. What a contrast to Calcutta's main museum, which was drab, dusty and dark.

At the Red Shield Salvation Army hostel in Sudder Street, guests from all over the world would congregate. They ranged from an American who had studied acupuncture in China to an elderly English couple who had spent thirty four years as missionaries in Kalimpong, high up in the Himalayas. They had adopted a Tibetan boy with the Dalai Lama's permission and were a couple still obviously in love, a delight to the eye. They were not too inspired by Indian officialdom and remarked on their visit to Writers' Buildings (West Bengal Secretariat) witnessing clerks with their feet on desks sitting amidst rows of dusty files. The 'Writers' once were clerks of the East India Company.

Other guests whom I met over the usual breakfast with weak tea were an Irishman and his children who worked with Mother Teresa. One of his offspring was rather blasé about the poverty. Other foreigners included Iranians such as representatives of the much- persecuted Bahai's, plus Armenians and Dutch. The Salvation Army generally does a grand job but it is amazing what prejudices may leak. The wife of the major in charge overheard a conversation at my table and she chipped in with her Scottish voice 'The Muslims are a dirty people'. What a fatuous generalisation. However, I have met several Hindus who would agree!

A Scots girl called Pat appeared in my dormitory. She had three months vacation as she worked as a stewardess on one of the boats that travel through the Scottish Hebridean islands. She took me to the Calcutta Marine Club and there we met an old Devon sea captain who had worked on the Scindia Line. He was enjoying a pleasant retirement living at the club having his own servant. He told us that few British merchant ships came to Calcutta these days (in 1980) and that most of the vessels that did were Greek and Yugoslav.

Pat and I travelled a little way up the Hooghly River to Belur, which is the headquarters of the Ramakrishna Mission. The mission is a Hindu-based organisation, which is heavily involved in much educational cum social work. The Hooghly River (in Calcutta, it was no longer called the Ganges) that day looked hazy with overhanging yellow smog accompanied by the sight of several fires burning on the river banks. After the mission, we visited the fabulous Bengali-style Dakshineshwar Temple with its large overhanging roofs. It is dedicated to the popular deity, the goddess Kali. At this temple, the saint Ramakrishna (whom the Mission is named after) served as a priest. He was an ecstatic devotee of Kali.

I took the Coramandal Express night train to Puri on the east coast of Orissa state, south of Bengal. I nearly ended up travelling the whole journey south to Madras as I had terrible problems getting off the train at Puri because passengers who were getting on there were blocking the exits.

On arrival, I went to Jagannath Temple. This name of God means in Sanskrit 'Lord of the Universe' and is the origin of the word juggernaut used in England for huge lorries. Non-Hindus were forbidden entrance. Therefore, I took a cycle rickshaw to Puri, which has a splendid beach. I found a cheap hotel and saw a variety of poverty-stricken westerners frequenting the ubiquitous tea shops near the beach.

I took a bus to Konarak Sun Temple, which is magnificently shaped as a huge stone chariot of the Sun god. The place had been going to rack and ruin until the British archaeologist John Marshall rescued it. The temple dates from the eleventh century A.D. The intricately carved chariot wheels are amazing for their scroll and filligree appearance added to carvings of erotic couples and other mythological scenes.

I returned to Calcutta by train and only just obtained a seat, so did not manage to sleep. The main temple of the Goddess Kali in Calcutta is based at Kalighat. It was an interesting spectacle because on entering the temple, I noticed a sadhu upside down with his head buried in the sand. I do not know how long he had been in that position. Inside the temple, the red-coloured goddess Kali image stood confidently with prominent golden tongue and staring eyes. The eyes of the goddess represent past, present and future. Calcutta is named after Kalighat and like all temples, the site had a constant hub of activity about it. At four pm, the beggars got free rice. In that category was included all castes and western hippies. A buffalo was sacrificed once a year and goats daily. This meat was given to scheduled castes. Local Brahmins do not eat meat, though many eat fish. The temple chopping block had only gruesome bloodstains to remind one of its daily tasks. What a lot of shoving and pushing to get near the image. A nearby sign said 'Beware of pick pockets'. To a non- Hindu, the whole atmosphere of being pushed around appeared unseemly. I gave Rs 10 towards the beggars rice. 'Now they will have rice in your name'. Within the compound stood a 'Barren Tree' where women went to give thanks for children or pray for them. The tree was raised up on a pedestal, babies' heads were shaved, and their hair offered before the tree. Then mothers tied the pieces of hair on string and placed it around small stones, later tying the whole lot onto the branches.

One day, Congress I and the Communist Party (CPI) held demonstrations in downtown Chowringhee. The crowds surrounded Writers Building and set fire to a mini bus. Many people were trapped for hours in the New Market (a Victorian building) while I took refuge in Sudder Street. Bengalis have always been amongst the most politically active citizens in India. They were even prominent in the nationalist movement. The Communists had dominated the political scene for years in this state but they had not achieved the social and economic successes, as had their counterparts in Kerala.

I had an unfortunate visit to Calcutta zoo only to see filthy litter and bear baiting. I witnessed a middle class visitor surrounded by a group of giggling morons picking out the hairs off a bear's face. The bear's cage was just a drab concrete slab with bars. A white tiger seemed humiliated by its depressing spectators. No doubt, the bear baiter would not hesitate to inform me pompously that he was a vegetarian!

I went with Pat to one of Mother Teresa's centres in the Lower Circular Road. A queue of people stood outside awaiting their Christmas hampers. Many, I thought did not look particularly poor by India's standards. I did not see Mother's face, but she passed on one side of me touching my arm and whispering a gentle 'Hello'. Her Home for the Dying was really dealing with the destitute. About fifty percent of the inmates would eventually go back to the streets to die. Here, there was no attempt at rehabilitation. Inside the hostel were rows of beds and rice bowls, nobody had any belongings. One foreign nun was cleaning sores and another, a crucifix. Yes, a social revolution was needed, but there must always in any society be room for true love for every individual that Mother Teresa and her nuns represented.

The film Pickwick Papers was on at the British Council but I did not get round to seeing it. At Kathleen's Bakery in Free School Street, I purchased mince pies, plum cake, and afterwards some delicious cheese at New Market. This was my first English cheese for over three years.

Some years previously, I had seen a programme on the Granada TV Series Man Alive, one programme about Major Dudley Gardener, an ex-British army character who had worked for the Salvation Army. He was an enormous man with a gigantic beard and an equally large leg through suffering from elephantitis. He fed hundreds of poor people daily at the Salvation Army's centre on Lower Circular Road and every night without fail, he went out in a van with his adopted Indian son to take gruel to the poor. Pat and I asked this fearsome-looking character if we might go out one night with him. That same night, the van travelled a radius of over thirty five miles. At scheduled stops, a little orderly queue would appear. Major Dudley refused to serve any of his gruel unless there was perfect order in each queue. In his manner, he was the bluff Victorian paternalist, yet considering the terrible leg, he never stopped working in twenty five years. Hundreds jumped trains from all ends of Calcutta to get the free meals, which were served each day at Lower Circular Road. Major Dudley had a grudge against Mother Teresa's publicity. He thrust two printed papers about his life into our hands. Sadly, we said goodbye to this frustrated extrovert.

Before leaving Calcutta, I pretended to be a Jew in order to get permission to enter the Jewish Synagogue. The Jewish Community in

Calcutta was small compared with that in Bombay and Kerala. The synagogue caretaker was a non-Jew and he just let me wonder inside the main part of the synagogue, which I did with my head covered.

En route back to Sudder Street, I noticed the lean-to shacks around the entrance to that street. These shacks were inhabited by seasonal workers from the rural areas. By the standards of Calcutta, they were far better off than the pavement dwellers who had little to keep them from the elements.

On Christmas Eve an awful band came to the hostel playing or murdering Christmas carols. From my dormitory, we paid them baksheesh just to get rid of them. Later on, we held our own carol service after the free Christmas dinner that the Salvation Army gave all its guests. It was a good meal and much appreciated. The meal was followed by an Assamese choir consisting of tribal girls. A local magician came and put on a good show. For one trick, he poured milk into a magazine and waved the still, dry paper at the audience, then poured the milk out of the same magazine.

Unfortunately, on Boxing Day breakfast, all the guests had the 'runs'. We discovered that one of the cooks was dishing out the Christmas pudding by thrusting his presumably dirty hands into the pudding bowl.

I took the overnight train to Lucknow to meet a Mr Rizvi. The train arrived on a cold, foggy January morning but luckily, Rizvi was there to meet me. I was bluffed by the auto rickshaw pullers who kept the two of us occupied while attempting to pick our pockets. 'They are vagabonds and worse when they work in threes,' said Rizvi.

Rizvi came from a mixed Christian and Shiite Muslim ancestry. He never hesitated in telling me that the local Shias were aristocratic and educated unlike the Sunni Community 'who are dirty'. That same night, a curfew was still in force in Lucknow because of trouble between Sunnis and Shias.

The building of the University of Lucknow was quite imposing, though shabby. It was built in the early twenty century in mock Mughal style or should it be 'Disappointed Mughal'? Lucknow's market was jammed with cycle rickshaws and one day when Rizvi was taking me by rickshaw, we nearly went head-first in a collision. I remember one resting rickshaw puller who stretched his legs out on to the cross bars of his bike while playing a sweet sounding flute. Apart from cycle rickshaws, there were numerous bullock carts crammed with green bananas. The bazaar stalls were stacked with the usual varieties of food, especially gur, the unrefined sugar that stood in huge blocks.

I spent a period of four days living right in the middle of the bazaar with a family of an orthodox Hindu business group called Agrawal. They were pulse flour mill owners and they all lived in a joint family compound. Six brothers and their families lived under the same roof. The father and one uncle lived upstairs. Altogether, fifty people had their living quarters here. My host was a rather uncouth looking man who was born into wealth but acted as if he was a self-made entrepreneur.

On my arrival at the compound, three sisters-in-law came to inspect me, asking me the usual questions regarding family, marriage and my purpose or 'mission' in India. Mr Rizvi had given me a European cake, which I offered to Sri Agrawal. When receiving it, he looked hesitant and then he enquired if eggs were included in it. I realised that Agrawals were vegetarians who also refused eggs in any disguise. Very bravely, Agrawal gingerly ate one slice. Suddenly, we were interrupted by a sound from the bazaar outside the window. It was a man on a bike who was yelling through a megaphone attached to his vehicle. He was advertising films.

I asked Agrawal if all the sisters-in-law cooked on one hearth as a true joint family should, or individually. 'Formerly, they all cooked together but wives kept arguing, so now they have separate hearths,' he said. Agrawal's wife was not cooking during my visit. She seemed permanently to be hovering in their sitting cum bedroom in a type of limbo. She was menstruating and Agrawal said she was thus 'unclean' so had to keep her distance from the kitchen. This belief, of course was common in many countries of the world and still is even in parts of southern Europe.

Agrawal was one of the middle brothers and the relationship between himself and his brothers' wives varied according to their age. Whenever he took me along the corridor to his younger brothers' apartments, immediately upon entering, their wives would cover their heads with parts of the saris and look shy and rigidly nervous. None of them ever initiated real conversation with the elder brother-in-law. However, association with the elder brothers' wife was different. Here, the relationship was known as the joking one. The eldest sister-in-law was confidently relaxed.

Her boldness was assisted by the fact that she had sons and displayed itself in that she was careless in covering her head. All daughters-in-law must be respectful and obsequious in front of their fathers-in-law in orthodox business community households especially. These women hardly ever met people away from their families and even within their compound; their relationships with kin were hedged around with so many restrictions. The women, when not menstruating, took it in turns to clean the little household temple, which was situated in the compound. No doubt, when one of them is widowed, the unfortunate individual will spend much of her life in that small room.

At night, Agrawal and his immediate family all slept in one room. With so much money, I asked why they all slept together. I know that it was a common custom in much of India. 'I am afraid of giving rooms, people demand things, want radio, etc, and we do not want independency demanding this or that. We cannot read, will not educate our girls above tenth class, as dowry has to be paid for each. If she is too educated, she will expect graduate husband. Then husband's family will want big dowry.'

Considering his wealth, Agrawal was typical of a certain type of Hindu. He was meticulously obsessive regarding bodily cleanliness and his house was regularly swept and swilled out by one of his daughters, yet the entire compound could have benefited from a few gallons of colour wash. The décor reminded me of a prison cell. The only spark of joy was a tiny, arched niche by my bed, which had a little painted holy picture and an oil lamp within it.

Agrawal accompanied me by rickshaw to the ruined remnant of the Raj, the Lucknow Residency, dating from 1800. Inside the crumbling edifice were paintings depicting the siege of Lucknow and the Residency buildings in varying stages of decay. The most memorable painting was of the smashed billiard room with the torn and broken wooden shutters, which partly obscured the views of distant skirmishes. The silence around the park and palms seduced the mind away from the atmosphere that must once have prevailed during the last hours of the Residency. 'Old Views of Lucknow' were an equally enchanting collection, all the scenes having that hazy quality, which one finds on many prints of that period.

Lucknow's museum employed a selection of highly uninformative guides. All the labels were in Hindi. Yes, I know this was India, but what about Tamil speakers in the south, not to forget Telegu, Malayalam and Kanarese linguists? The people who wanted Hindi as the main national language were those from the Hindi speaking heartland of the Gangetic plain. The most interesting objects in this state museum were huge trumpet-shaped brassware and carvings of snakes. There were large doors with exquisite carvings, not unlike those I had seen on houses in far away Gujarat and Rajasthan.

After the museum, I was taken to meet a teacher of one of the major schools of classical dance called Manipuri. The teacher hailed from the Manipur region of the former North East Frontier. Unfortunately, it was not possible for me to see him performing his dance techniques.

Agrawal was keen for me to see the Women's Protection Home but we were refused admission to the actual building, though we sat in the garden. Here they helped prostitutes under the Suppression of Immorality Act. The committee arranged their marriages and the government gave Rs 500 for each girl. Some of the prostitutes operated from home, others from brothels. One former inmate became a probation officer while most did the usual things like sewing and literacy schemes. Under Lucknow's former ruler, the Nawab of Oudh, concubines were famous because many of them (as in China) were well-educated, being versed in poetry and dance alongside other refinements.

A friend who asked to remain nameless took me to the prostitutes area of Lucknow. One seedy little lane was called Phul Wali Gali (Lane of Flowers) while a neighbouring street was Chaval Wali Gali (Street of Rice). The majority of the prostitutes were Nepalese and all worked from brothels. They had left their families and the majority had thus forsaken any chance of marriage. The last ruler of Lucknow, Wajid Ali Shah had three hundred and sixty five wives, one for each day of the year, going well beyond the Islam's permission for four wives. Many of the marriages would have been used to form alliances with disparate families.

In one house, the Madam, a dark Bihari told me that some women went with men for as little as Rs 3. Fifty percent of the money was deposited for the collective household needs. The girls I saw were quite well-dressed. On Chaval Wali Gali (Street of Rice) one could see the girls peeping behind wooden shutters. The approach upstairs was by rows of steep, stone steps. The girls ranged from twelve years upwards. One

Madam asked me in Urdu 'Can you get me a husband?' She had only six girls living with her. The least demanding job for the girls was purely posing for their clients. Three middle-aged clients came into one of the tiny upper rooms all wearing head cloths, baggy trousers and cheap shirts. Down in the street outside, a chap was squatting while selling bangles. As we passed through the door, a young girl passed and offered herself to both of us free of cost!

At this part of my visit to Lucknow, Agrawal, without any explanation, claimed that I was a spy for Pakistan. This information he told Rizvi and Vinod, another friend of mine. The only result of this was that he made himself a complete fool. Some years back in Karachi, Pakistan, I became involved in a row with Zubaida, a woman lawyer of poor character who worked at the law courts there and accused me of spying against Pakistan. Later, she apologised as nobody believed her. People on the subcontinent often see conspiracies against their countries.

Lucknow is famed for its Shia Muslim mosques and huge Imambaras, which are buildings used by Shias to carry tazias (biers) in the festival of Muharram. These monuments are very imposing. The Great Imambara of Asaf ud Daula was built in the seventeenth century and is a labyrinth of corridors. I found a guide who was a terrible tease and as a challenge, he told me to find my own way out. He continuously lit matches, and then burnt bits of paper in order to find his way around the huge edifice. One enormous hall was over one hundred and sixty feet long and fifty three feet broad with a huge vaulted ceiling. These internal structures had an amazing capacity to carry sound. After other visitors had departed from the building, my guide rushed to the other side of the hall, leaving me in the darkness clinging to one of the pillars. I spotted him in the distance and suddenly I heard him tear some paper and strike a match. All around me were crypt like archways and as my eyes became used to the darkness, I saw my guide prancing about the pillars on the opposite side at the same time as whispering from that distance. The effect was that both the lighting of the matches and the sound of his voice appeared as if they were coming immediately from my side or behind me. It was spooky. Many of these Muslim buildings have architectural tricks built into them.

The outwardly gloomy Jama Masjid (Friday Mosque) is another huge structure. Inside, it has surprisingly delicate paintings in blue depicting fruits, especially grapes. The building has three huge domes and two minarets.

My journal states that I met one Mr Saxena who had been to Britain and met Mr Enoch Powell, the MP who had campaigned against further Asian immigration. Saxena believed that Indians were undermining the British economy. He reminded me of an eccentric lawyer I had met in Karachi's law courts who proclaimed against further immigration into Britain because the foreigners were 'spoiling your race'.

I decided to go for a walk through the bazaar to meet one of the famous names in Indian naturopathy, a Sikh gentleman with the predictable name of Dr Singh. He ran a so-called 'college' and offered courses for some unmentionable fee. His surgery did not look up to the usual standards I had seen in nature cure hospitals. It was full of junk but his book on the Philosophy of Naturopathy was quite a good read as it ranged in topics from the ancient Greeks to Germans of the Romantic Movement, such as Sebastian Kneipp and his treatment by water and herbs, and Louis Kuhne's Unity of Disease and Facial Diagnosis.

In one house I visited, I was shown a lovely paan-dan box, which had little subdivisions for holding betel leaf mixture. All paans include betel leaf and areca nut, lime paste, cardomans and a sweet mixture called supari which is used for sweet pan. The leaf turns the mouth red and the substance is often spat out onto the streets, leaving a revolting sight. Paan Kiosks can be found on streets in every town. One buys them rolled up in the leaf, which is pinned down by a clove and they can be carried around for days before the substance dries up.

I read an awful story in the papers about a girl in Calcutta who had been bitten to death by a scorpion. She was on a tram and a scorpion crawled up her leg and because of modesty, she did not yell. This reminded me of a true story from Karachi. Two women went by motor rickshaw to a sugar cane juice seller. They drank their sugar cane and returned to the rickshaw. When they returned home, the rickshaw driver found them dead in their seats. It was discovered later that the sugar cane juice crusher had accidentally crushed a poisonous snake alongside the sugar cane.

I visited Gujarat state for a second visit. In Ahmedabad, I stayed with a Servas family of Parsi descent called Medora. There were two thousand Parsis in Ahmedabad and they were descendants of Zoroastrians who fled

Iran from Muslim persecution in the tenth century A.D. Those in both India and Pakistan are a well-educated community. Their sacred fire, they brought all the way from Iran via their old communities such as Aden, when there were not enough of them to maintain a viable community. This fire, they claim, has never gone out and burns in the fire temples which can be found in several parts of India, Iran and there is one still in Karachi. Mrs Medora told me that the first Parsis to come to India landed in Gujarat where the local Hindu kings allowed them to practice their religion as long as they adopted local names, language and dress and went about unarmed. Thus, the name Gandhi is a Gujarati Hindu name for a grocer, but Mrs Gandhi's husband was a Gujarati Parsi whose family must have originally taken that particular subcaste name.

Mrs Medora was unusual in that she refused to have servants because they 'beat the clothes too much and break the china, apart from using too much cleaning stuff.'

The Calico Museum was necessary for anyone going to Ahmedabad. The textiles therein were exquisitely arranged and magnificent in themselves. The museum was situated in an old Gujarati house with fabulously carved sturdy wooden doors. Upon entering, a maze of luscious fabrics hit the eye from harem tents to Gujarati door hangers. One tiny piece of Indian cotton cloth had come from a fifteenth century site in Fustat in Egypt. The idea for the textile museum came from one of the local calico mills within the textile town of Ahmedabad, which wanted a 'company museum'. The British had deliberately destroyed the native textile village industry, which in areas such as central Gujarat was well developed. The British taxed cotton exports and flooded the market with cheap mass produced goods from Lancashire.

Mr Medora took me to a rich village, which owned a huge gobar (cow dung) gas plant. The biogas plant was used by several families who collectively owned it. Medoraji hoped that they would not fight over the gas from the communal plant. I had seen several gobar gas plants before. They had all been individually owned.

For a few days, I returned to see my old friends, the Patel family of Bori village, in what was once India's richest cotton growing district. This district of Broach is still of course a major cotton area to which I have already referred. Bhikubhai Patel took me to visit an old pal of his at Nikova village. The village had a lovely pigeon house locally called Kabutar Khana. A special village committee provided grain for the birds. The Kabutar Khana was a large, decorated three storied octagonal wooden structure and it had carved wooden figures, reminiscent of those found high up on the wooden verandahs of the older richer Gujarati houses. The nearby Narmada River took on a misty appearance in that late afternoon. A boat appeared carrying fodder grass, branches and twigs for firewood. A lonely, banyan tree stood stranded on an island in the middle of the river. Tradition states that this sacred tree was planted by Kabir in the early sixteenth century. Kabir was a religious and social reformer who hailed from a low caste weaving community. He attacked the most corrupt aspects of institutionalised religion, especially the Hindu caste system.

Bhikubhaiji requested me to stay a few days at Nikora with his friend, a nature lover nicknamed Bapuji (respected father). On enquiring about the village communities, I was informed that the stone masons were all Muslims while the carpenters were Sudra caste. We sat on the verandah and Bapuji began discussing locusts. Apparently, they appear about every thirty years and breed under the sand dunes. In climatic cycles, the wind lifts up the sand and when the swarms come, they hide the sun and cover everything. It must be an eerie experience, certainly one I did not want to witness. Bapuji then went on to tell me of this brother who lived alone. Following the ancient Hindu ashrams (stages of life), he now lived a Vanprast stage where he took up social service for the community.

The far south of Gujarat borders on the tiny ex-Portuguese colony of Daman. There, at Phansa on the coast of the Arabian Sea, I visited the amazing Tata Institute for the Blind. The character running this mainly agricultural centre was a typical aesthetic Brahmin who was constantly attired in homespun khaki shorts and shirt. The adult blind who come from all over India and Sri Lanka gave the appearance of having normal sight as one could see them hoeing and digging ditches around the vegetable gardens.

In the evening, a Hindu companion at the guesthouse narrated a story about a man who offered his cow as collateral for a loan of one crore rupees (ten million). When the bank manager looked puzzled, the hopeful customer explained that Gau Mata (Cow Mother) had thirty three crores of gods within her! I never knew whether he was successful. We discussed the point that traditional Hindu wives rarely called their husbands by their personal names. Apparently, the Hindu nationalist Tilak made his wife feel awkward when once she was asked of the whereabouts of her husband, she replied 'the stick is gone'.

My fellow guest offered me a ride on the back of his scooter for the 140 km journey to Bombay. I felt filthy on arrival at Bombay but it was good to see an old friend, a solid personification of Hindu Marathi culture. The market life in this vicinity of Dadar was as usual bustling with activity.

While in Bombay, I checked on the possibilities of going to Pakistan on the British India steamship the Dwarka. Unfortunately, it had sailed a few days before. Now it is a part of history. Its known eccentricity attracted me, the captain even grew potatoes on the top deck. So once again, I took the mail train from Bombay to Amritsar. From New Delhi, the train slowed down and appeared to stop at about every station until the border town of Wagah.

Chapter Thirty One

To Pakistan, Sects Tombs and Saints

At last, a country where nobody objected to torn rupee notes! The Pakistani luggage examiner offered me a cup of tea, which was gratefully received.

On the train to Lahore, for this my second visit to Pakistan, I struck up conversation with a Lebanese journalist called Talib. He had interviewed both Khomeini and Mrs Gandhi. He began describing Khomeni's domestic life, 'he even does the washing up'. It is funny how these tit-bits of information interest one about the famous.

Standing in the queues at Lahore station were enormous Pathans in sombre-coloured cloths, all of them having close-cropped hair to match their unhappy looking faces.

At the bus station, I caught the Sargodah bus, which went close to the Ahmadiyya headquarters at Rabwah in central west Punjab. Looking at my fellow passengers consisting of mainly Pathans, I thought of how masculine these young men looked. What a change from the gentle-faced Indian youths I had become accustomed to seeing. A woman clothed in a black burqa sat next to me. She was a nurse working at Lahore's Muir Hospital. Before marriage, she had travelled abroad. Like many Sunni Muslims, she did not accept that the Ahmadis were true Muslims but I told her that she should go to Rabwah and keep an open mind.

The bus stopped for tea and one boy offered to get me tea and samosa. I gave him fifty paise as a tip. The beggars here appeared to get a better deal than in India. I was surprised to see passengers handing out several rupee notes, while in India they mostly got ten or twenty paise coins. One beggar, with a leprous stump thrust it into my face. I rarely saw a local person being rude to beggars, though occasionally they were shouted at.

I had smuggled in an Indian magazine and in it, I noticed a quotation from one famous Swedish actress, 'Indian men are crude, immature and conceited'. I understood exactly the type of man to which she was referring, but it was rather a sweeping statement.

I noted the solitary hills of Rabwah amongst the tedious flatness of Punjab. The bus in which I was travelling was government owned and it was strange to see the extremely garish private buses and trucks of Pakistan again. The outside of these vehicles especially buses, being covered with chrome or silver plate and rather un-Islamic pictures with animals and plants of unimaginable shapes. It is true folk art and shows fine workmanship. All the paintings are so psychedelic that they look as if they have been done under the influence of the ubiquitous hashish.

At Rabwah, I took a tonga (horse and cart) to the guesthouse. On arrival, a servant looked at me and said 'Salaam Aleicheim!, I am thirsty, I am hungry?' Later on, I was given a tasty stew and enormous chapattis made of the tastiest wheat only to be found in Pakistan.

At Rabwah students from many countries spent seven years studying Islamiat (Islamic studies), Arabic and Urdu. During my second visit, I met a number from West Africa and Mauritius. In one discussion, they spoke of evidence in the Bible for Prophet Muhammad's 'coming'. Here, they referred to the blessing promised to Ishmael (Acts 3.24), the prophesy in the parable of the vineyard (Mathew 21.14) and so on.

I was already familiar with Ahmadi beliefs because in 1977, I had attended their international convention when staying with a family of a local homeopathic doctor living in Rabwah.

In their interesting library, they held books on many religions, including the Encyclopaedia Judaica. One strange American publication that would have done credit to Protestant fundamentalist Ian Paisley, was Romanism A Menace To The Nation by Father Crowley. It was published by the Menace Publishing Company. It describes the escapades of numerous priests in the Chicago area circa 1912. These priests owned dens of prostitution, saloons and such, and used such quotes as 'Rome's thirst for American blood'. One prostitute charges a priest with her ruin.

Irish immigrants are portrayed as 'short on religion and long on graft', recruiting young girls into slavery as nuns. It was a book that could not be missed. Let us hope they had other, more positive books on Roman Catholicism.

The most interesting Ahmadi book was a huge tome called Jesus in Heaven on Earth by Nazir Ahmad. It was published by England's oldest Mosque at Woking, Surrey, which is actually one that belongs to the Ahmadiyya sect. The book examines evidence relating to Jesus' search for the Lost Tribes of Israel in India, it even includes an extensive list of Kashmiri, Pakistan and Afghan place names that have linguistic parallels in the Bible.

The library at Rabwah possessed a rather dotty book from the lunatic fringes of Hinduism entitled Hindu Superiority and the Hindu Colonisation of America. Amongst its claims are that Chaldea in Mesopotamia (Iraq) is a corruption of cul (family of Deva), that Saxons were Sakas (an ancient Indian tribe) and the Scandinavians were descendants of Hindu warrior castes. The Norse epics were directly influenced by the Vedas. Saturday comes from Saniwaram (after Sanischar, the god that cleanses), Wednesday from Boudhawaram (Boudha changed into Oden or Woden) that the Druids were Brahmins and so on.

While at Rabwah, I met Mr Rafiq who was the former imam of the Ahmadi's London mosque. His daughter Bushra had been brought up in England and like any kid of her age was fond of pop music. As a teenager in conservative Rabwah, even though only here for a vacation, she was not allowed out even for five minutes unaccompanied and did not like wearing the traditional black burqa so instead she covered herself with a chador (sheet), which resembled a checked tablecloth. A relative of hers had married a Yorkshirewoman, 'She even calls my Father 'luv'".

The Ahmadiya group have a well-run Foreign Missions Department and thus have missionaries in many countries, especially in the west. Needless to say they are banned in the Islamic countries. Somebody showed me some photos of the Swedish community's mosque. The community's most famous member was the Nobel Prize Winner in Physics, Abdus Salaam. I expect Pakistan was more than a little embarrassed at having their then UK-based citizen member of this persecuted minority receiving this award. I was shown photos of his prize giving dinner where he was seated next to Swedish Princess Silvia wearing a dress with a very un-Islamic low plunging neckline. All these pictures were of Ahmadi men only, as their women remain in purdah. Included in one group photo was an ex-Protestant pastor from Poland, now an imam! Another photo showed a Yogoslav convert who was training to be an Ahmadi missionary in Yugoslavia. One Pathan sitting beside me said, 'India is the land of banias, they persecuted us'. I added that there were some Pathan Sunni Muslims working as moneylenders in India too. The Ahmadiyya community have been persecuted in Pakistan to a much greater extent than in India. It is other Muslims who are threatened by their success, not the Hindus. When Ahmadis are in Saudi Arabia, they pretend to be 'conventional' (Sunni) Muslims. Saudia Arabia has banned Ahmadis from Mecca stating the official line that they are not real Muslims.

An Ahmadi friend invited me to Chiniot, a neighbouring town in this Punjabi district of Jhang. It is a place noted for furniture manufacturing and it was one of the dirtiest towns I had seen on my journeys. The streets were crammed with donkeys, and oxen pulled carts of chunky rock salt. This reminded me of a visit to a small, Karachi grocers whilst in my first year in Pakistan. Asking for salt, I was handed a large block of rock salt. Chiniot's open sewers were as delightful as medieval towns in Europe must have been. At least here, they did not throw out garbage from the upper floors onto the streets below.

My friend was keen to introduce me to an old shopkeeper, Mr Latif from Amritsar in India. All his relatives had been slaughtered at Partition by Sikhs, a community he disliked. 'Sikhs are rude,' he claimed. I bumbled in about 'faults on all sides'. He did not think much of Hindus, as 'Hindus do not fight'. He had obviously forgotten the Rajputs and Shivaji.

The furniture in the bazaars was made of local wood 'equivalent to Burmese teak'. There were lovely huge headboards, mirrors, screens and chairs. After Rabwah's open spaces, Chiniot seemed cramped and congested.

Chiniot's sixteenth century mosque had lovely floral designs and its marble pillars were from local quarries. The wooden palace was now in a dilapidated state and the owners long gone. It was inhabited by poor people, perhaps they were the original family servants. It looked like a mausoleum with its dark, wooden arched windows and collapsing balconies. On its marble floors, women were washing their clothes. This was truly decayed magnificence. While its floral patterns were peeling off, at least the mosque had been restored.

On one narrow lane, we passed a man busily embroidering silma sittara, which is a form of embroidery using originally gold thread but later a cheap, gold-coloured substitute. Further on the lane, I passed a former Hindu temple, which gave me a queer feeling.

During one conversation I was told that the northern Pakistani town of Sialkot not only makes medicines and sporting goods but exports bagpipes to Scotland and Halifax in Canada's Nova Scotia.

The bus back to Rabwah was a private one having a tin plated interior with a heavily embossed surface. Huge Arabic religious calligraphy decorated the sides. Pictures of the sacred black stone Ka'aba at Mecca hung at the front of the bus near the driver. Coloured glass birds were also dangling from different places. Two-toned horns were popular in Pakistan. The first few chords of Never on Sunday were a popular tune on Karachi mini bus horns. Once at Rabwah, I was glad to get off the red plastic-covered seats, which were horribly uncomfortable in the heat.

As the saying goes, 'Dust, heat, beggars and tombs are the few specialities of Multan'. Multan lies in lower west Punjab province and reminded me of Sind to the south. Sind too has a multitude of saints' tombs and is predominately a flat, sandy and salty place. Many of the Sindi and Multani tombs are built using the beautiful blue Hala tiles. The tiles were manufactured in Multan and Hala. The tomb of Shams-i-Tabriz, a Sufi saint, offers a magnificent view over the starkest khaki-coloured city I had ever seen. It was a flat horizon with not an undulated piece of land in sight. Multan is dominated by the blue tiled dome of the shrine of Shah Rukne Alam, the eleventh century patron saint of Multan. The fort was later built around this tomb and much of its tilework in blue and white includes shishagiri, a name implying that the designs are partially made from mirror fragments.

I stayed with a high caste Muslim family called Koker Noon while in Multan. Islam, unlike Hinduism is not a caste based religion but in northern India and Pakistan especially, names are important on a social rather than a religious level. There is a distinction between the descendants of those claiming Arabic, Turkish or Persian origin called

Ashraf communities, with some people actually using that as a personal name, and converts to Islam from often low caste Hindus called Ajlaf communities. These are not strictly family names but families may claim that they belong to the first major category. The name Mian is strictly outside this category as this family name denotes converts from high caste Hindu Rajputs, as the name is also found amongst Rajputs. More religious distinctions relate to those families claiming descent from Fatima, the daughter of Prophet Muhammad. The males can use the title Syed before their personal names. Shaikh is a family name and means a venerable leader. These names should apply to those of pure Arab descent but they are found in all Muslim countries. Those called Qureshi claim descent from the Prophet's Qureshi tribe. Siddiquis claim descent from Abu Bakr, one of Islam's earliest caliphs. Pathans or Afghans use the name Khan, though not all Khans share that origin. Most of the above groups would claim to be Ashrafs.

In Pakistan (and elsewhere) they may retain a local name, such as the past ruler of Pakistan, Zulfikar Ali Bhutto. The forenames are Arabic but Bhutto is pure Sindi. The founder of Pakistan, Mohammad Ali Jinnah again has Arabic forenames but his surname Jinnah is Gujarati in origin as he belonged to the Khoja community who follow the Agha Khan. Some Muslims claiming Persian descent, especially some Khojas or Ismailis will retain Persian names such as Jamshed and Feroze, which are names commonly found within the Parsi community. A confused Bengali (probably an Ajlaf) pointed out his problem to me when on arriving as a refugee to Pakistan, he noted that several official forms said 'caste?' He said that in Bengal there was no such thing amongst Bengalis. This was because only a few Bengalis would be considered as Ashraf, most of whom would be the former landowners, although they too used honorifics such as Mufti and Syed.

My hosts, the Koker Noons had a colour television, which was the first I had seen since leaving the United Kingdom. I have commented before about Pakistan's advanced television technology, all obtained through foreign help as opposed to India's then go-it-alone policy. I watched an all-women discussion group, although they were all traditionally attired, not bothering to cover their heads like the women newsreaders.

Mrs Noon took me to see some of Multan's crafts. I was disappointed as all the pottery was of poor quality and the blue painting on the outside practically crumbled in one's hands. I preferred the colourful lamps made of camels' bladders. 'That's pottery!' cried my polished host, pointing at the most tasteless stuff I had ever seen. All the handicrafts were junk, especially the cheap paintings and felt pictures of the holy Ka'aba. I asked about hand-woven cloth in Pakistan. A shop in Chowk Bazaar had some khadi but to be true khadi, the cloth must be both hand-spun and woven by hand. Quetta in Baluchistan is justly famed for its marble and the green onyx ashtrays and lamp holders can be found all over Pakistan. My sole regret was that I was unable to go to Peshawar's copper and brass bazaar. The quality there is much better than Benares brass wear, which always looked cheap to me.

What a hassle over the train to Karachi. In India in 1981 very few foreigners or middle class Indians travelled first class, but in Pakistan, it was expected. I booked a sleeper, which was costly but clean. Two other women shared the carriage and one endlessly chanted the ninety nine names of Allah on her rosary. As Sind is so dusty, the window was kept shut and it got too claustrophobic. To cap it all, the door got jammed, probably because the religious women kept opening and shutting it too often. We sought help by banging on the wall and a man eventually opened it. Never was I more delighted to get to Karachi, for I had spent twelve rather unfortunate months there some years earlier.

In 1977, I had come to Pakistan as a voluntary worker with The Salvation Army. This amazing organisation worked in eighty four countries and in Pakistan is known as Mukti Fauj (Liberation Army). A number of souls still think that they are connected with the British Army. Their tiny centre was situated bang in the middle of old Karachi's centre called Sadar. Opposite the centre's main gates was Karachi's most prestigious school, the old Grammar School. The most famous landmark surrounding the centre's compound was dear old Empress Market, which had a rat-ridden Victorian edifice as its central building with handsome arched doorways inside. It had steep pyramid-shaped stalls of fruit and vegetables perched perilously vertical with the vendors sitting cross-legged on high. Most of the local traders were followers of the Agha Khan and photos of the young leader were displayed alongside many of the stalls. At one end of the market was what looked like an ancient arched roof café where one could obtain the most beautiful yogurt or curd as it is called in Anglo-Indian. The yogurt sat in huge earthenware dishes and I would greedily ask the grimy yogurt maker for some of the skin, which covered its entire surface. Outside the main building, the market stalls straddled all over neighbouring streets and past the local tiny post office where stamps were always franked with the slogan 'Think Pakistani, buy Pakistani'. I always loved the markets of the subcontinent, though haggling can be a strain after a while.

The chap in charge of the local Salvationists, Major Darrell was an abrupt but likeable New Zealander. At six thirty in the morning prompt, he would be hard at work in his office with its door marked Territorial Division Karachi, or wending his way around the traffic-crammed streets. He must have known every back alley better than many of the locals. His wife was an affable plump Canadian woman who often dressed in the local white sari uniform of the Salvation Army. Another important member was a Pathan convert to Christianity called Major Maqsud. The bulk of Pakistan's Christians are converts from low caste Hindus, though some have converted from Islam like Maqsud. My Urdu teacher, Aga Atta was such a Muslim convert. A tall and military-looking man, he disliked Muslims intensely. 'The only good Muslims are the Ahmadis'. He later introduced me to the Ahmadiyya community.

I went to Pakistan as a recently qualified social worker but there was no job ready for me to take on. The community centre, from which I was supposed to operate, was still being built. It was situated in a squatter area of Karachi called Azam Bustee nearby to Isa Colony (Isa-Jesus) another squatter district whose habitations were becoming permanent with the government's gradual acceptance of their existence. These colonies could not all be classified as really squalid, shanty towns, though many buildings lacked the basic amenities. The squatters in question were mainly Punjabi Christian Chuhras with a minority of Muslim Pathans. The Christians were originally farm labourers in the Punjab but after Partition, the land was increasingly subdivided amongst incoming Muslim east Punjabis, who required less labour. The Christians fled to Karachi. These squatters were nearly equivalent to some of the out caste Hindu sweepers of India. They themselves were divided into 'dry' and 'wet' latrine cleaners. It was with this sweeper colony that I worked. There were about seven hundred thousand Pathans who had migrated since Partition from the North West Frontier to humid Karachi. Some of them had a bachelor life and practised a 'homosexual' lifestyle whilst in Karachi, I was told. This partly explained the presence of both men drivers and boy ticket collectors on Karachi minibuses. In Karachi it was hard for them to meet women. They had travelled alone to the big city.

I shared a nice flat in the Army's compound with a Welsh midwife member of the SA but we clashed from the start because of personality differences. The overseas Salvationists were quite an open minded crowd. It was the Pakistani converts who were the most narrow minded or rigid as are so many converts. The midwife and nurses worked in the clinic below the flat and for some weeks, I worked in the dispensary handing out allopathic tablets to what seemed like an endless procession of customers with worms or gas. Handing out carminatives became second nature.

Later on, every day I travelled to the bustee by yellow minibus and if lucky, I would squeeze myself onto one of the two places reserved for women at the front. Usually, I had to request any man occupying the womens' seats to depart to the back seats. It always amused me in Pakistan that when segregating men and women on minibuses, the women always ended up by being pushed up against a big burly Pathan driver. Perhaps these drivers like some servants were implicitly supposed to be asexual. I could not contemplate how many jokes were made at my expense on the minibuses. Ordinary Karachi buses had a metal grille dividing two thirds of the bus for men and one third for women. Too bad if all front seats were empty. Women still had to scramble for back seats. The young Pathan ticket collectors employed on the minibuses or buses would stand on the open door of the waiting or moving buses, hanging out at all angles, calling the destination using all kinds of pronunciations.

En route to the increasingly open-guttered lanes or galis of Azam Bustee, the minibus would pass the richer environs of Mahmoodabad and the Parsi colony recognisable because of its Tower of Silence where the dead bodies were placed to be eaten by vultures to avoid contaminating the earth or sacred fires, thus inhumation and cremation are forbidden them.

Major Darrell deserved a medal for getting the community centre off the ground as anyone familiar with the subcontinent cannot but be aware of the bumbling bureaucracy, much of it inherited from British rule. Part of the centre was to be a youth club and hostel for needy boys. Next door was the school, which had the worthy legend "Enter to learn, leave to serve" above one of the doors. Mrs Bernard, a lean looking woman was the headmistress and we got on well. Another teacher, a tousled haired man called Joseph, invited me to his simple room and warned me of the coming Armageddon due in the 1990's. As in India, these Christians are tolerated but I always felt them to be an insecure and unconfident community.

My job, with the help of my munshi (assistant), a dark round-faced south Indian Madrassi called Gladys, was to check up on absentees from the school sewing class. I enjoyed visiting local homes but became frustrated with the job because Gladys was lazy and disliked tramping about the muddy lanes, having dreams of sitting in a nice, cool office. Worst of all, she refused to translate clearly what the individual members of the families were saying in reply to my questions. I was actually being taught Persianised refined Urdu, which did not especially assist in my conversation with families speaking an earthy Punjabi.

The most colourful characters in the bustee were the Khwajasara (eunuchs). If this does not sound a contradiction in terms, they were hereditary eunuchs. Certain families would traditionally castrate some male members depending upon the number of children. Three of them used to perform near my munshi's house. They would dance in the traditional female dress of shalwar and kamiz with huge bells above their ankles. They were heavily made up and their other adornments besides bells included bangles and rings. Only one of the eunuchs could have passed as a woman. The others looked grossly masculine with heavy shadows on their faces. They were accompanied by two fellows playing the harmonium and dhol (horizontal drum). A few of the locals joined in the fun.

Gladys' neighbour was a masseuse without formal training but was experienced enough to earn hundreds of rupees oiling the limbs of wealthy Arabs who were domiciled in nearby Mahmoodabad colony. It is quite common to see Asians massaging each other in public. One time when I arrived at a friend's flat with a headache, immediately two girls gave effleurage strokes on my forehead.

The social work proved to be unsatisfactory, partly because I felt that a local person could have done my job, and also I found that living in such a tight Christian community rather suffocating. Even with the European Salvationists there was a reluctance to learn more about other faiths. Mrs Darrell had informed me on my first visit to Pakistan, 'In this country, women are nothing'. One evening I was delayed in the bustee and on arrival at Empress Market in the dark, I suddenly felt a multitude of hands descending on my rear. Then I empathised with Mrs Darrell's remarks.

I began to make a new circle of friends. My Urdu teacher introduced me to some Ahmadiyya Muslims (or Qadianies as they are called locally). My acquaintance with that community just before Christmas coincided with their big international assembly annually held in Rabwah in the Punjab. I stayed at the lovely house at P.E.C.H.S. (a housing colony) belonging to a major in the Pakistan army. Major Ahmad took me later to Karachi Cantonnent station to board the northern bound train to Rabwah. He introduced me to a bearded, fair-skinned Pakistani called Khwaja Wajahat Ahmad. He was the most jovial man I had ever met. For the journey, he was accompanied by his wife and an adopted daughter. They were later to give me hospitality in their small utilitarian flat in Karachi's Al-Azam Square, near the highway to Hyderabad in Sind. My clearest memories of Al-Azam was the sight of hundreds of goats being sold for the feast of sacrifice called Bakar Eid, the commemoration of Abraham's offer to sacrifice his son Ishmael.

On December twenty fourth the train to Rabwah traversed a greener looking Sind, now the monsoon had passed. Normally arid, Sind suffers from high salinity. Unlike Punjab province to the north, Sind is very poor. Its population before 1947 had a sizeable Hindu sector, but most Hindus fled to India during the upheavals. In India, the word Sindi has connotations of wealthy businessmen but in Pakistan the opposite is true. The image of the Muslim Sindi is twofold, as either he is a poverty-stricken, unenterprising landless labourer, or a wealthy conservative traditional landowner such as a Bhutto or Pir Pigaro. That is not to deny that there are not middle class university educated Sindis, there are, but at present they hold little power in modern day Pakistan. Unlike their Hindu Sindi brothers, these various Muslim Sindi's rarely migrated abroad or to other areas of the subcontinent. Regarding Punjabis, there was no distinction in stereotype between Hindu, Sikh or Muslim as they are generally described as hard-working and thrifty. The same image applies in both countries.

During the night the open reserved compartments were used by different groups of travellers who would just squat on the floors blocking the way to the wc. The western style lavatory was an unfortunate introduction as everybody just squatted with their dirty feet on the seat. Westerners make a fuss over lavatory paper but as long as water is available, then there is less need. Most people carry their tiny water pots for their ablutions. By now, I could drink unboiled water, unlike many Europeans, so I had little difficulty with water obtained on the stations. Luckily, I managed to avoid sleeping in the womens' compartments because women in purdah disliked opening any windows and there were usually too many squealing kids.

On arrival at Rabwah, I was placed with a homoeopathic doctor and his orthodox Ahmadi family. The household was affluent but unrelated males and females were kept strictly apart. Their house had separate entrances for men and women. In fact, they occupied different worlds. This segregation of non-related males and females excluded the category of servants. The doctor's family employed hereditary servants in that the parents of the present servants had been employed by the parents of my host. Thus, it was quite normal for example, for an adolescent male servant to be present amongst the female householders of any age. Perhaps the servant, like the minibus driver had become culturally asexual or maybe the servants were loosely considered part of the joint family. Thus in this family, unlike some newly rich Pakistanis, there was not that aloofness towards their servants. I often saw the servants and employers' children playing together, including watching the television in the private parts of the house, rather than just in the public domain.

A western female travelling alone had to become used to people asking very intimate questions at the first instance. It was strange how the menfolk who kept their women in purdah rarely shy of addressing any questions to strange foreign females.

During the Rabwah assembly women and men walked on different sides of the road. I was one of the few unveiled females. Most women were sweltering in their black nylon burqas. Some women had a veil all over their heads but others showed only their eyes. Ideally, a Muslim man or woman should cast down their eyes if passing one another. Of course, this rule is kept mainly by the women. To the onlooker, a woman in purdah is just a shapeless blob. The older style burqas made their inhabitants closely resemble shuttlecocks. From within the burqa, a woman might flirt in her mind. Whereas a western man likes to show off his woman, eastern men often (not just Muslim) prefer to keep women for their eyes only.

Another kind of segregation occurred on the first morning of the assembly. The males and females were segregated into their respectively enormous multicoloured roofless 'tents'. I felt as if I was sitting amongst a crowd of black crows. My neighbour was a black American convert to the Ahmadis. With the keenness of the converted, she defended the use of the veil and told me of another Ahmadi in America who went to court in order to defend her right to drive a car while veiled. Next to her sat a white girl from Fiji while the only representative from Britain was a veiled brown-skinned girl with an upper class English voice.

While sitting in our section, we could hear voices of different nationalities over the loud speaker emanating from the mens' area. I asked why they, in turn, did not hear female experiences about conversion from our 'tent'. 'In Islam, a man should not hear womens' voices unless necessary, because men become more disturbed when they hear voices of women!' I never could get used to spending my time only with women.

What happens is that as an outsider, it is possible to break cultural prohibitions because one is not culturally important.

In spite of the fact that Ahmadi women observe purdah, they are often as well educated as their menfolk. All earning members pay Zakat, which is a tax towards the community's social and educational projects.

Chapter Thirty Two

Travels in Sind and Far North

Back to Karachi with Khwaja and family. There I spent a tedious month at their flat in the dreary surroundings of Al-Azam Square. Somehow from then onwards, I became a prisoner of Karachi. It was easy to develop too much reliance on others. Pakistani people often made empty promises, often well intentioned. These promises related to getting employment and going places. Khwaja was always a true friend and he suggested that I work for him at a basic level selling pencils. He worked in the cement business and had a poky office in an old building off Frere Road in old Karachi. I accompanied him to a couple of salubrious offices, and received nice cups of tea without selling any pencils. I would presume that most of the businessmen who saw me believed that I was Khwaja's 'bit of crumpet', even though this was not the case. My most useful task one day for Khwaja was to pretend to be an irate customer who did not have her correct amount of cement. The following day Khwaja got his cement.

At the end of January 1978 I transferred to the even drearier lower middle class neighbourhood of Al-Noor. Here, I lived in the same building that housed the Ahmadiyya mosque, which itself was situated within the community's own hospital compound. The chief doctor at the hospital was Dr Hashmi, a woman who like her daughters, never left the compound without covering her face, fully veiled. Perhaps Karachi looks better through a veil. Her two eldest daughters, themselves strict Ahmadis, were quite ambitious. One wanted to be a psychiatrist and the other a gynaecologist. The youngest girl informed me that in England the girls get married as soon as they leave school. This was a strange comment from an orthodox Muslim girl. I replied that many working class girls did but girls that were more educated delayed. I refused to get into the argument about whether or not Ahmadis were Muslims simply because as I saw it, in their daily lives, they were as any other conventional Muslims. One myth, common in the west, says that Islam forbids education for women. It is true that over the centuries many Muslim women have been refused education, as have their Christian counterparts. If they are denied education, then this is due to custom rather than religious edict. The Hashmi girls spoke excellent English and were far more confident than many English girls of similar age were. They were not shy and fully supported purdah. I attended a pre-medical exam party at their house where only women were present. This was a local form of 'hen party'.

About this time, I met Mr Adwan, head of Karachi University's social work department. We became good friends and he arranged for me to see some social work projects within the city. He had been a student in Canada. This studious looking man enjoyed taking me to Chinese restaurants. A neighbour of his at the university was Professor Moiuddin, head of the Bengali language department. He was a refugee from Bangladesh, as were all the Bengalis. Later he proposed marriage, even though he already had a wife. It was through him that I met my dear friend, Mufti who came from an old landholding paternalistic zamindar family in what was the former East Pakistan. Mufti would always comment, 'I have lost my flag'. He had been strongly opposed to the Bangladesh movement and had fought against Mujibar Rahman's forces by aiding the Pakistan army. Later, he fled to (west) Pakistan but he was never to feel at home with non- Bengalis.

Mufti looked a Bengali, he was fairly dark-skinned though quite tall with slightly mongoloid eyes and high cheek bones. He appeared the intellectual, being skinny with longish hair and spectacles. His favourite pastime was sitting in cafes, smoking king-size foreign cigarettes and talking about Shakespeare. Like many Asians who have not met western ruffians, he had an idealised picture of the civilised Englishman. He was a permanent student at the 'varsity', (a common term on the subcontinent), yet he was extremely down to earth and very reliable. He always kept time, a rarity on the subcontinent. Yet he argued about politics, being sympathetic to the right wing Jamaat-i-Islami. At that time, they were big supporters of General Zia. Mufti admired that party's religious leader

Maulana Maududi (Maulana is a title for a religious scholar) and he shared with his other followers a dislike of the Ahmadis. Like others of his ilk, he always felt groups were plotting against Pakistan, being even suspicious about the Rotary Club.

In Birmingham, prior to my visit to Pakistan, I had found an Islamic bookshop and acquired a book by Maryam Jameelah called Western Civilization Condemned by Itself. Maryam Jameelah's 'portrait' was on the front page of this bigoted book published in Pakistan. The photo was hardly enlightening as all it showed was a fully veiled woman dressed in a burqa. It could have been anyone. I suppose it was aimed to prove what a good Muslim she was.

Maryam Jameelah was born into a liberal New York Jewish family and her real name was Mary Marks. As a teenager, she had entered into a correspondence with Maulana Maududi and eventually came to Lahore where she met him. Later, a marriage was arranged for her and she became the second wife of a Pathan. She (unlike many Muslims) was an avid supporter of polygamy. She writes with the fanaticism of the converted, condemning all western art, music and literature as being decadent. She even attacks such customary minutiae as the sometime western dinner party custom of seating a man between every woman. Also, the correctness of eastern lavatories (which I tend to agree with) and the dirty habits of westerners.

I must have been the only person in Karachi who was friendly with members of the Ahmadiyya community and of the Jamaat-i-Islami, as both groups hated each other. Some Ahmadis 'accused' me of letting the Jamaat-i-Islami friend Mufti, spy on them because he would visit me in the flat next to their Mosque. From my own experience, I would have chosen the Ahmadi group above many others including the Jamaat-i-Islami as being a sound healthy community. Luckily Mufti did not share many of the views of fanatics like Jameelah. In fact he was extremely fond of one of her bugbears, Eugene O'Neill the American playwright, even though he wrote so much about often degenerate alcoholics and prostitutes.

After going on holiday to Lahore with friend Mufti, on return I found my things packed, so I had to get new accommodation. The Ahmadis had given up any attempt at converting me to their sect and they wanted the room for a missionary. They had thought I had left for good but at least they remained on good terms with me.

The following day, on the minibus going to central Karachi, I found myself sitting next to woman advocate called Zubeida. She was attired in the usual advocates outfit of black jacket and trousers plus white cravat. Her face was heavily made up and her hair was longish but at the front, it formed a heavy fringe, which was partly obscured by a black scarf. We chatted and she presented me with a card saying, 'Here is my card and come to my office tomorrow'. She then arranged for me to stay with a family in Nazimabad, yet another suburb of Karachi.

The next morning, I stood at the minibus stop where the ticket collector sung out 'Merreweather Tower', referring to the tower built by the British. Passing the old building of Denso Hall on Frere Road, I got off the minibus at the law courts and found myself standing on the street amidst a clacking group of male typists all occupied in typing up legal letters for illiterates. The advocates' offices were situated in Noorbhai Jafferji Buildings, which were built in the sandstone colonial style of Karachi. These buildings were named after some Parsi bigwig. Inside the place was Dickensian, the wooden steps looked as if they were about to collapse into a dirty courtyard. These steps led onto wooden verandahs, which in turn led into offices entered though the wooden swing doors one associates with cowboy saloon bars. Zubeida worked in a senior advocate's office. I was introduced to a number of lawyers and in all the time I went to the courts, I never really discovered what work she actually did. Her jovial neighbour Mr Zaidi, who took a fancy to me, was always involved with labour compensation and had a room stacked with fusty law books going back to the year dot. I had a two day job with him having to write out Chief Martial Law Regulations, which bored me silly. The best thing about the place was the small kiosk below in the street, which sold glasses of thick iced banana or mango juice. Zubeida would often offer me the rich oily food that she would order the office messenger or peon to go and get from one of the local Iranian restaurants frequented by lawyers in this area of the city.

Zubeida had a reputation for being miserly because she never went anywhere and when a group of us went to Kolhri Lake in Sind, she was bored stiff after one hour. Therefore, she departed back to Karachi with her friend while I remained behind with the handsome moustached Pathan friend who wanted to marry me and keep me in purdah as his second wife. His main vices were whisky and smoking. He kept begging me to go to North Yemen as his wife while he assisted in constructing the new airport at Sana'a. I fancied Sana'a, but unaccompanied by him. My final image of him was when I refused his marriage proposal. I noticed him gently crying. He would always say, 'damn your books, I will burn them.' Later, we returned to the city by taxi. I did visit him several times at his house with another friend while his wife was away. All I remember was a huge horned head of the markhor, a mountain goat, which is found in the mountains of North Pakistan, hanging on his sitting room wall. He had hunted it on one of his regular shooting parties up in Chitral area. The markhor eats snakes and its spittle is used locally as anti-snake venom.

Kolhri Lake was famous as the site of the grave of a pair of lovers who died in the seventeenth century because their marriage was forbidden by their families as they belonged to different clans. There had been a clan feud and their suicides ended the feud, so their bodies were buried together by the shore of the lake. The graves were later submerged, as Karachi required a larger lake to provide its water.

Another place of interest I visited in the environs of Karachi in 1978 was Mungho Pir. It is a sacred grove with hot springs and a crocodile-filled tank. By its very nature, it is a pre-Islamic holy place or at least Hindu in origin. Murray's guide informs us that the Muslims in charge of what is also a holy pir's (saints) tomb, will actually kill goats for the amusement of visitors who would like to see the crocodiles fed. Luckily, there were few other visitors on that day and nobody seemed to think that I wanted this grisly job performing.

To the west of Karachi, along the Makran coast of Baluchistan was the glorious beach at Gidani. It had the only quiet beach that I encountered, in that the waters were safe and it was free of peeping toms. While I was with the Salvation Army, we had gone there on a day's outing. I was the only one who went swimming. The Pakistani nurses just sat on the beach looking uncomfortable in their shalwar and kamizes, dressed up as if they were going to a party. Later, I sunbathed in the nude high up on some rocks.

On the Makrani coast lived the fishermen who had African blood and originated as slaves from Muscat in Oman. It would be much later, on a visit to the National Institute of Folk Heritage in Islamabad that I bought cassettes of Bilwal Beljium, an Afro Makrani.

I transferred to a house in Najimabad.

Bhai was a big hefty-looking man with pouting lips and heavy-lidded eyes but his wife Sureya was a sallow-faced wisp of a woman. I felt sorry for her as she rarely went out of the house although she was not especially restricted. Some months later I became friendly with a woman teacher who lived practically opposite Bhai's house. Like many school teachers, she lived quite simply and offered me what is considered poor man's food, sweet potato, which I relished. Her sister had suffered a terrible misfortune as her young daughter had recently been brutally murdered by a gang. The girl had been kidnapped and tortured. The story became national headlines. The family of this girl was very rich, owning a cigarette factory. Unlike my friend's simple dwelling, theirs was a huge modern house and completely soulless. It had lots of marble and unlived-in furniture. It looked as sad as its owner did. Grandfather had gone senile and he lived in splendid isolation up on the fourth floor. Could one ever forget the torture of an eleven year old daughter?

There had also been a murder in Bhai's family because his brother had been murdered by an in-law, his wife's. An uncle had died through political activities. During my stay, his wife's repulsive young brother, an ardent member of the Awami League Party, stayed in the house and one night, he climbed through my open window onto my bed, so I kicked him out of the room. Bhai was very pro-Bhutto and once he had flown the banned Peoples' Party flag on his roof.

After leaving the Salvation Army contingent, I met only one foreigner, a Scotsman called Harry Jackson who was emplyed by Coates Patons, the cotton thread manufacturers. He was a bachelor and of striking appearance with his handle bar moustache and gentle Scottish accent. He had spent years in Africa and Turkey and hoped that he would finally be posted either to Latin America or the Far East. Muslim countries like Pakistan were not popular postings. Wherever Harry travelled, his West African tropical birds would accompany him as part of his baggage and he would just let them run loose in his house, which was situated in the posh Defence Society colony. He invited me a few times to the lovely old sandstone building that housed the ex-British Sind Club, the most exclusive club in Karachi. In spite of the grand building, it served mediocre food. Quite a number of the richer Pakistanis would go there, including some of the old Bhutto clan. The newly rich Pakistanis got a better welcome at the Gymkhana Club.

I went to the Gymkhana Club and Yacht Club with one of Zubeida's cronies. In her usual fashion, she had arranged for me to meet Iqbal and we went to the Yacht Club by a small boat from Menora Island. A ruling had been recently introduced that Pakistani Muslims were forbidden alcohol. Iqbal felt humiliated because he could not go to the bar and buy the drinks. It was maddening to see hypocritical Saudis elsewhere in Karachi supping away at a beverage that was refused their co-religionists because they were Pakistanis. How must a Pakistani Muslim have felt while watching a foreigner buying drinks in his own country when he was forbidden? Pakistani Christians would occasionally write letters to Dawn, the English language newspaper, to complain about their difficulty in purchasing alcohol. Pakistan still had some old breweries to the north of the country. Murree Breweries was the most famous and it was perhaps still owned by Parsis.

Iqbal was, by Pakistani standards, a middle aged bachelor. He lived with his mother and, like many of his ilk, had been too heavily indulged in. His friend Zubedia had arranged a party at her cousin's house. Most of the guests were newly rich young lawyers and their wives. All sons and daughters of muhajirs (refugees) who had fled to Karachi at Partition from areas in India such as Uttar Pradesh. (then United Provinces). The party started at eight pm and in true Pakistani style, everybody just sat around the walls waiting for something to happen. Men and women were not separated but everyone sat stiffly waiting to be entertained. There were no refreshments until the ghastly red sherbet appeared at about ten forty five pm. Later on, there were heaps of biryani and rice, the usual party fare. During the party, I suddenly felt depressed, homesick and pretty alien. Zubeida organised a game whereby we all had to take turn in singing. The best singer was a traditionally-attired Pathan who sang to the audience who gave their appreciation by exclaiming 'Wah Wah' (Bravo! Bravo!) at every available moment.

That feeling of alienation overcame me on another occasion, causing me to weep. While living with Mr Khwaja's family, I always met a group of Ahmadi men in Shehzan Restaurant (owned by one of their members) in Victoria Street. Their community leader, the Amir who was also a trader, would meet his male friends for coffee and cakes after leaving the nearby mosque belonging to the sect. They were extremely hospitable to me and we had several theological discussions and on two occasions, I went to the mosque. Unlike in many orthodox Sunni communities, the Ahmadi women could attend their sects' mosques even though they had to remain hidden on the upper storey. On one occasion, I assembled upstairs with the burqa- clad women. At the front of the upper storey, there was a wooden panelled partition, which had a tiny door from which many female eyes would peep and observe the men and imam (prayer leader) down below in the main body of the mosque. How beautiful so many mosque interiors are and yet women, at the best, remain hidden behind a screen, often in a section resembling an attic. Unlike a Christian or Hindu ceremony, it is hard for a non-Muslim to participate in Islamic prayers because of all the prostrations and other bodily movements that go on. I just sat behind and watched while a sea of backs ascended and descended. It was at this time that I sobbed silently, just a feeling of alienation.

During the time of my visit, the Theosophical Society, that world-wide movement, which embraces many world faiths, though heavily influenced by Hinduism and Buddhism, still survived amidst the sea of creeping Islamisation. The leading lights in the Karachi theosophical movement were the Parsis. Their main spokesperson was a white- skinned elderly Parsi called Mrs Gool Minwalla. She was an excellent speaker and very active. Dara Feroze, the secretary of the local branch based at Jamshed Memorial Hall on Bandar Road (now M Ali Jinnah Road) in old Karachi invited me to his house and for the first time in Karachi, I met members of what I would call the old pre-Partition Sindi elite. This family was not representative of a muhajir (migrant) middle class, which now dominated positions of power in Karachi after they had left India. Feroze was a Persian name and some generations back their ancestors had migrated from Iran and intermarried with local Sindis. Their old house was stacked with traditional wooden furniture often richly-carved and not a plastic flower in sight.

The family were probably only nominally Muslims as Dara's mother told me they were fourth generation Theosophists! Dara and his sister were followers of Hindu teacher Satya Sai Baba and they invited me to hear some of Baba's recordings on cassette. While I was listening to the tapes one Friday afternoon, we could hear the loud bellowing of the imam from the nearby mosque while he was preaching one of his sermons. Dara exclaimed, 'Why do they have to shout so loud?'

Dara had turned to vegetarianism in line with many theosophists, though rare behaviour for a Muslim. How isolated such people must have felt in Pakistan.

Everybody lived in their own little world but some of us were permitted to cross the boundaries of various little worlds. I was temporarily within the world of the Theosophists, the Ahmadiyya community, the Jamaat-i-Islami, the Christians and the law court crowd plus the philistines of Karachi's migrant community.

Mufti obtained a job while he was still enrolled for an MA course in English Literature at Karachi University. It was in the Sylleti language department of Radio Pakistan. Sylleti is the language of northern Bangladesh. On one of my visits to the radio station, a cheerful-looking producer walked into the room and enquired whether I could do an American accent. I followed him upstairs and he showed me a rather corny script of a play to be transmitted on Radio Pakistan about travellers on a hijacked aircraft. I actually rewrote a few of the lines. I then recorded several lines of the script and sounded quite authentic. A few weeks later, my few sentences came over the Radio Pakistan airwaves. Unfortunately, I was not paid for it. Mufti told me that the pay was so poor that they felt too embarrassed to give it to a European woman! Anything would have been welcome, even if they had paid my rickshaw fare! Another producer suggested that I audition for a news reading job on the radio but I was too scared and did not wish to remain too long in Karachi.

Towards the end of my stay in Karachi, I had an argument with Zubeida, my lawyer acquaintance, who I accused of using everybody. The other lawyers claimed she was a 'tout' and like everybody else at the courts, she paid bribes just to oil the wheels of officialdom. She was a woman who liked to find out about everybody's private lives but refused to betray any confidences of her own. She was unmarried in her early forties and lived alone, which was unusual for a conventional Muslim woman. Zubeida was obsessed with her ghastly, unruly dogs, rumours abounded in the courts that she slept beside them, and I told her this in an argument with her after I had accused her of using her work mates. She then tried to get me for anti-Pakistan activities and nobody would believe her, so she only made a fool of herself. Several men had told me how 'evil' she was and that I should stay away from her, but in spite of everything, she was usually kind to me whatever her motives and I will always retain some affection for her – and perhaps using people is a two-way affair. I occasionally 'used' her when it suited me.

Karachi had too many opportunists. I had heard so many men who exclaimed, 'he is my fast friend', then the next time, they would add, 'he is a number one cheat'. Several migrants had told me secretly, 'Pakistan is no good' or 'I made a big mistake leaving India'. However, some did say that a Muslim could only function in a majority Muslim country, however imperfect.

On leaving Karachi, the only places I missed apart from the old city centre were the British Council Library and Mufti's favourite haunt, the old Victoria Café. I was glad to get away and escape everyone's clutches, including my last employer Noor, who had taken me on in his import-export office in Liaqatabad (or Laluket) district of Karachi. His main job had been to export cheap labour to the Arab countries.

I took the train northwards through Sind, after a touch of green had softened the otherwise barren landscape. The only plant that had appeared to thrive in Sind was the date palm. Date groves could be seen scattered around impoverished huts. The Sindi populace was quite oppressed under the numerically dominant Punjabis who formed over half the population of Pakistan. Karachi, which before British rule was only a Sindi fishing village, sank under the weight of refugees from India and their descendants. Even their language dominates. Before Partition, little Urdu was spoken in what is now Pakistan. Urdu was the mother tongue of the migrants from Uttar Pradesh and Bihar, otherwise it was a literary language for educated Muslims alongside Persian.

On my journey northwards, a communist from Sind sat opposite me and spoke quietly against the regime. Sind gave little support to General Zia, himself a muhajir. Except Ayub Khan, the rest of Pakistan's former leaders were natives of the region. Perhaps that was one reason why Zia was pushing through the Islamisation, if only to justify a separate state for Muslims. If Pakistan remained secular, then why create a separate state for Muslims?

The train sped northwards and amongst the final glances of Sind was Bawalpur station, where they sold their awful local pottery, Kaghazi, which looks like brown plastic.

I bade a temporary farewell to Pakistan.

On my second visit to Karachi, I reacquainted myself with a few old pals. Mr Khwaja, the Ahmadi introduced me to an elderly suave character called Mahmud Ali Beg, a former polo player whose horse had died of a twisted gut. We three went to the Boat Club built in 1881. The rowing boats were constructed by local Sindi labour (some of the ancient traditions of the Indus remained). Eton College Boat Club had offered this club financial backing.

Aged seventy, Ali Beg had a commanding appearance, sporting a military-type moustache and blazer. From the club house, we had a fabulous view over Karachi port and the club's own garden was colourful in spite of the obviously creeping salinity.

Later in the day we went to the Fleet of the Admiralty building and I heard a discussion about the advantage of going into farming. There were the usual complaints from capitalists about Ceiling Acts and government interference with business.

Ali Beg still felt humiliated about the recently introduced overall ban on alcohol in the clubs. Even foreigners had to buy either tomato juice or oranges. 'Club membership is on the decline', he lamented. At least everybody still had a sense of humour. At the club I had been told the following story. 'A sorrowful sparrow decided unwillingly to fly south in the cold season. His wings froze and he fell in a barn. A cow shitted over the sparrow and a cat rescued the bird from the cow dung and ate it. The morale of the story being, those who cover you in shit are perhaps your friends and those who pull you out of it may not be.' Another joke was 'Khomeini asked God, 'when will Iran get better?' The reply came, 'After you are dead'. The same question was asked Zia, 'When will Pakistan get better?' He replied, 'After I am dead!''

I also heard about the Englishman who had buried his dog. Years later, a cult of one pir (holy man) developed. The Englishman visited this holy place to discover it was where he had buried his dog. In India, the main butt of jokes were the Sikhs whilst in Pakistan, it was mainly the Pathans. The Pathan jokes always related to their tendency to bisexuality whilst living away from home, so I was informed.

By train to Dokri village in Sind, which was the nearest spot to the ancient Indus site of Mohenjodaro (The Mount of the Dead). The train took ten hours through dusty Sind, the little huts made of straw matting, and mud had still that dilapidated appearance. How did Mohenjodaro die? Did the Indus change its course? Was the area invaded? The ruins were fighting a losing battle against salination owing to a rising water table, which had increased because of the new canal system.

Near the ancient site, there was a dreary modern guest house where visitors could stay but I preferred to sleep at Dokri railway station, a few miles away and let the station master fuss around me. The poverty-stricken visitors stayed at the station. The station master kept his own little visitors book, which he requested me to sign. The next morning at six am, I took a tonga to the ruins. The previous night, I had been locked in the waiting room for my own safety.

The inhabitants of five thousand years ago managed to keep a clean city. There were shutes for rubbish, rubbish bins and drainage channels covered in bricks, offering better facilities than could be found in many modern Asian cities. At Mohenjodaro, the major buildings were the Great Bath with its glazed tiles, which might have had a sacred purpose as do the temple baths in India. The Granary even had a floor which was ventilated by air passages. One of the later monuments was a Buddhist stupa from around 200 A.D. The site has many wells, one of them oval shaped so that two people could draw water. Nearby along the roads, one could see dumpy bullocks pulling carts with wheels of exactly the same design as those seen on the delightful clay toys, which could be viewed in the museum. Chessmen, marbles, dice and so forth were also seen there. I liked the seals designed with portraits of handsome bullocks and oil lamps plus the ubiquitous mother goddesses, which are found on most ancient sites. At the Dokri level crossing, camels would queue up and in one of the nearby fields, a small rectangular prayer space could be seen.

I also noticed these prayer spaces further south at Kotri near the railway lines.

I returned to Karachi and walked in some familiar spots in old Karachi, including the street with the unqualified dentists and tables covered in false teeth. Karachi had its Chinese dentists and their surgeries could be recognised in the centre of the markets by gruesomely forbidding pictures of a grinning face with enormous teeth.

How frightful the Russian women shoppers appeared in Empress Market. They looked like fat frumps in ill-fitting dresses. Bohri Bazaar, which is close to Empress Market is a maze of streets. The Bohris are a minority Muslim sect. Another Muslim group, the Memons have their own mosque. They are not strictly a sect but a community who speak Gujarati and hail from one geographical locality in Gujarat, (India). Opposite Empress Market, down crumbling Napier Street lived the old established Goanese Christian community. My friend Imelda Tellis who worked in the Salvation Army dispensary lived in an old tenement named Bismarck Buildings. The Goanese women were always clothed in old fashioned European garments and lived in a separate world from Muslim Pakistan. Imelda lived with her aged parents who existed in a shabbily genteel poverty-stricken world of their own.

My old pal Mufti took me by minibus to distant Orangi Township on a Friday to visit his home with the family of simple refugees from Hyderabad India. After donning his white embroidered skull cap for private Friday prayers, we sat down in the courtyard for a tasty meal.

For old time's sake, I went by minibus to visit my old work place in Azam Bustee colony. In one of the streets I visited, charpoys were strewn all over the place and somebody was delving in their big steel trunk filled with clothes. In many Indo-Pakistan houses, metal trunks serve as cupboards. More houses were electrified as the squatters were being gradually recognised by the authorities. The Christian Punjabi sweeper Chuhra's with whom I had previously worked, still suffered a form of spatial and social isolation. I also reflected on how many Gujarati Hindu sweepers there were in Karachi, they had remained after Pakistan was formed. One would always recognise them in the street because of their gaily-coloured saris amongst the drab burqas and shalwar kamizes. I had forgotten that my cook at the Salvation Army centre had been a Gujarati Hindu.

Somebody told me that the term Muhajir literally refers to those migrants who had given up everything for the sake of Allah. Judging by many of the folks I had met in Karachi, it could well be said that some Muhajirs were those folks who grabbed everything in the name of Allah. The rich migrants who live in Defence Society and Mahmoodabad employed the Punjabi sweepers who still had to support relatives back in the Punjab. Many actually hid their sweeping occupations from these relations because the job would be seen as a downward step from tilling the land.

In order to get to Thatta in Sind, I caught a bus from the dirty Lee Market, which is famed for its prostitutes and smugglers, as smuggling was big business. beedi leaves were brought here from the Indian border of Kutch and hashish could be obtained everywhere. In the bus station at Lee Market, I noticed a tufted-haired Hindu (his tuft was on the side of his head) wearing a green gown with anklets and bangles all up and down his arms and legs.

Thatta was once a seat of Islamic learning. It became a mass of dust-blown ruins. It is true to say that in Sind, the dead are better accommodated than some of the living. Shah Jehan mosque at Thatta is magnificent. It has some of the most elaborate blue tile work in the whole of the subcontinent. Sind as a province is so stark but the Sindi dress is very colourful. They did not wear saris or the Pakistani national dress, the Punjabi shalwar kurta but the long heavily-embroidered mirror work skirts and shirts. Red and blue are the popular colours. In Hyderabad, I did manage to purchase a lovely Sindi-Ajrak (colourful cotton) shawl, which was used by men and women. On the bus going to Thatta, the women had huge junky silver jewellery and coins pinned or sewn onto their garments.

Near to Thatta is the largest necropolis in the world at Makli. The tombs vary from the magnificent to the mundane, all the result of countless battles over the centuries. As at Chaukandi tombs, many of the canopied grave stones with their perforated filigree work and corbelling displayed a rich mixture of Hindu and Muslim art. The lotus and the sunflower are common motifs alongside carved Arabic calligraphy and female tombs have pendants, anklets and bracelets carved. Makli encompasses an area of six square miles. Over a million may be buried there.

Another day, I took the bus to Bhit Shah, the home of one of Sind's Sufi saint poets Shah Latif. I had travelled via Miani forest where in 1843, the British defeated the Talpur rulers and conquered Sind. The bus stopped quite a distance from the handsome blue tiled tomb and I got a lift on the back of a knife sharpener's bike. His sharpener was fixed to the front of the cycle.

Blue, turquoise and white tiles framed the arches and courtyards of the shrine. His urs (death anniversary) was celebrated like a major festival. Local shops sold garlands and gaudy pictures of the Ka'aba. Inside the mausoleum, the tomb was covered in green satin within a carved wooden screen.

The bus back to Karachi passed a number of black Makranis or 'sheedis' as they were known locally. They did not appear to suffer much discrimination and they spoke the same Makrani dialect of Baluchistan as any other native of the area. The bus was crammed to the eyeballs with old women chewing paan, everyone wearing their embroidered smocks and large Baluchi bracelets.

The following day, I bussed to near Bambhore and walked two miles to the seashore where there is the seventh to thirteenth century historical site. At Gharo Creek there is a stone building at a point, which was originally the mouth of the river Indus. There was only a trickle of water. Nearby were the curious remains of a Siva temple where there were carvings of dancers with pots on their heads. During the Islamic period of the eighth century, the place was fortified. The Bambhore mosque remains are part of the earliest known mosque on the whole of the subcontinent. It has some Arabic inscriptions in kufic script dated to 727 A.D. One stoneware storage jar at the site museum had Chinese characters on it. Formerly, this was a big trading region and the Arabs sought to control it once Sind had been conquered. I got a lift back with some Japanese visitors for a little while, and then they overtook one of the glittery private buses. I asked to get on it and they stopped it for me to get on. They all sat there amazed as if going on one of the local buses was the pits.

Back in Karachi, a Pakistani woman spoke to me in one of the shops and explained that Sindi Muslims were improvident. This was hardly surprising when they have been so long exploited by Waderos (Sindi country barons). Perhaps they were less a cohesive community than the

Punjabis or their fertile mighty proprietor-free countryside of nucleated villages.

I took a very slow train to the interior of Sind to see Sehwan Sharif, the burial place of Sufi Saint Lal Qalandar. The mountains of Baluchistan loomed up on the left of the railway line as the train plodded northwards. On arrival, I put up at the local guest house. In a local café I met some Afghan refugees. One of them offered me money later for sex and I declined reluctantly. Opposite the tea shop, a handsome camel stood with carpet designs clipped into its hair. 'That's a camel', one bright local informed me. As I examined the markings on the camel's back and neck, squeaks of laughter came from another tea shop across the bazaar. The tolerated village idiot appeared. Many of the Pathan lorry drivers who overcharged their Afghan brothers (Pashtu Afghans are called Pathans if born in Pakistan) were refugees from Kabul.

I wondered over to the shrine of Lal Qalandar, also noted for its blue and white tilework. In the dark, crowded atmosphere of the shrine, I noticed an enormous man over eight feet tall. I later discovered that he got his name in the Guinness Book of Records as the tallest man in the world. He wore a loose kurta and white shalwar. He was the guardian of the tomb, occasionally giving us lesser mortals a paternalistic pat on the head. Families from all quarters of Pakistan squatted and slept in the cloistered compound. During the saint's melas (festivals), thousands of people visited here. Two miles away at Lal Bagh, there were sheltered gardens and more tombs. These tombs were surrounded by flags and draperies, one just offered ones salaams and received the blessings. Returning to the central tomb at Sehwan Sherif, I enquired about the guardian and was told that he ate twelve naans and one kilo of meat each meal. He was maintained by donations. The tomb was protected by a silver-coated, foliage-embossed cage.

At the end of the day, my tonga walla broke the journey en route back to the government rest house for charris (hashish) and requested me to join him. I did, but declined a smoke.

On the Indus riverside near Maachar Lake were several traditional houseboats. Nearby, a camel walking in a circular motion drew water from the ancient river. This was a sight commoner in the Middle East than on the subcontinent.

Before leaving Karachi, I spent a day in Hyderabad Sind. The Sind Museum was well worth a visit as they had excellent models of early villages and artifacts connected with Mohenjodaro. The place was brightened up with lots of local Hala tilework and memorable, rather faded, pictures of Tolpur rulers with huge beards and stove pipe hats! Shahi Bazaar was where I had purchased my Sindi Ajrak shawl. The bazaar is over one and a half miles long from Hyderabad fort to the market tower built by the British. The huge mud fort of Shaikh Makai surrounds the tomb of Saint Makai and being unlike any other fort I had seen, it reminded me of a huge mud cake. Nearby, Sind University, always a hot bed of student unrest, stood stranded on what looked like a desert island near Kotri Barrage several miles outside the city.

Northwards to Lahore, the train traversed date palms and paddy fields in the Kharpur area of Sind. Lahore, the capital of the Punjab was founded by Loh, son of Rama Chandra, the hero of the Hindu epic, the Ramayana. Formerly, I had stayed in Lahore with a wealthy traditional family of a woman who was secretary of the Pakistan Girl Guides Association. On this visit, I stayed at the YWCA near 'Charing Cross'. This was run by two Christian women called Miss Masih and Mrs Ghosh. Miss Masih had one ambition, to marry a European and migrate to Holland. Like many Christians, she was a fish out of water, living in a cloistered world of pre-Partition India.

My visit coincided with the Lahore Mela Chiraghan (Festival of Lights). This festival commemorates the life of a Punjabi Sufi poet and Saint Hazrat Madho Lal Hussain. In his tomb enclosure are two bodies but they are worshipped as one, the Muslim saint and his Hindu disciple. Madho Lal Hussain fought through his poetry against dogmatism and ritualism. Instead of the usual Persian or Arabic medium for poetry, he used his native Punjabi, thus reaching a wider audience. He was a Sufi and a member of the Qadariya brotherhood. He shaved off his hair and beard, and he and his Hindu disciple merged their personalities and are thus referred to as one person. The Hindu disciple did not convert to Islam probably because a true Sufi would not demand such an act. They were buried side by side.

For three days, mainly men and later women celebrated the mela. Temporary tents appeared and market stalls selling wooden toys, dazzling pots and mounds of stickly, sugary sweetmeats. A nearby fairground was packed with screaming kids and there was a mobile big wheel of rather a crude wooden construction but in good working order. Peep shows displayed headless bodies. A boy appeared with a performing bear standing on its hind legs. All the local villagers descended upon the cramped narrow streets by bullock carts and I appeared to be the only foreigner. Huge cooking pots stood near the tomb. The food would be distributed to all the pilgrims. Amongst the heaving throng, I noticed some foreigners. Three American girls were clinging onto each other for dear life. 'Are you alone? Oh, you are so brave!'

The best part of the mela was the dancing. There were strange looking sadhus who looked more like Hindus than Muslims with long, straggly Rastafarian-style matted locks. One man with a huge beard and wearing ten finger rings turned his head back and forth as if in a hashish-induced frenzy, waving money notes in a circular motion and then handing them over to some favoured people in the crowd. One section of the crowd was drawn to a man with a performing goat on stilts. The drummers thumping on their horizontal drums came while another musician banged two long metal strips. A third had castanets, which consisted of wooden boards with bells attached. Behind them were other players with flutes and rattles. All wore heavy anklets with bells attached. Nearer the tomb, a man danced in the body of a home-made horse. Permanent fires were burning and tea was served in handless cups while smoke smarted the eyes. Men moved rhythmically, and then women and one huge woman in a black burqa with coloured strips of cloth sewn on it joined in the dance. A comical bearded character was directing everybody. He wore a postman's red cap and a cloak. A picture of the Kaaba dangled down from his shoulder. He directed the dancers with a big stick while bells were ringing, which were stuck on a leather backing strapped to his legs. Everything smelt of sweat and smoke. Huge cauldrons of dal (split lentils) were ready for the celebrating masses.

Badshahi (Great King) mosque has a huge courtyard and towering domes, but after the beautiful exteriors of the Sindhi tombs and mosques, I felt disappointed. The Lahore Fort's lawns were being mowed by a lawn mower pulled by a buffalo. Inside the fort is the Moti Masjid (Pearl Mosque) constructed in white marble. The Shish Mahal (Palace of

Mirrors) has a glorious ceiling decorated with inlaid glass in the form of convex mirrors. The walls were constructed in white marble. I loved the little mosque of Wazir Khan, which is decorated with yellow and blue tile work. The internal frescoes were of bowls of fruit, a favourite motif in Islamic buildings on the subcontinent.

A gem of a place to visit in the old Mughal city was Faqir Khana, just inside Bhati Gate. This was a crumbling mansion belonging to the Faqir family. On arrival, the widow of the family brought me tea and sweetmeats. She then showed me around her inheritance full of dusty objects d'art. There were miniatures painted on ivory, hand-painted Qurans, ancient family photos, plastic flowers, Chinese chairs all cold and stately and endless expensive cups and saucers. One of her carpets was made in Emperor Akbar's factory in the sixteenth century. Carved wooden tables were everywhere covered in dust. We went up some steep back stairs to see some cloth-covered Qurans beside the remnants of frescoed wall paintings. A huge courtyard with a dark interior dominated the place below. Inside the upper rooms, many of the chairs were wooden with beaten copper covering and looked in better state than the aged sunken sofas. She had a few oval mortars for pounding Unani-Greek medicine.

The main Lahore museum was famous for its Buddhist Greco-Gandhara sculptures, the most famous being that of the living, starving Buddha, which looked rather gruesome with all its ribs and skull like face but it was an exquisite piece of bronze work.

Before leaving Lahore, I bumped into a relic of the Raj called Hussein. He was a gardening fanatic and he invited me for coffee at Faletti's Hotel, another relic of the British era. He told me how he used to dance in the presently deserted, sad-looking dining room, which once had a cabaret.

I travelled by train from Lahore to Montgomery (Sahiwal) to find my way to the other main remnant of the Indus Valley civilisation, Harappa. In the 1980's it was just a mass of mounds. A large granary remained and circular threshing platforms could be seen. By chance, when I was in the little museum, I was invited by Begum Zia Ul-Haq's mother's brother's son to his house. His family, like General Zia's were all members of the middle class Arain farming community, just the class of people who saw Zia as representing their interests. My friend's family had a thirty five acre farm growing pomegranates, bamboo and wheat. The average sized Punjabi farm (in Pakistan) then being about fifteen acres. At the end of the day, I was taken back by motorbike to the Harappa guest house.

The new capital of Pakistan, Islamabad, had some imaginative architecture amongst trees galore. The growing city was backed by the Shakapara Hills. At the time of my visit, the town had far more trees than buildings, which were all low level. Islamabad was really a city of government officials, hence it was a terrible place to get about without private transport. A jasmine and rose garden added to the uncity-like atmosphere and not so far away was the marvellous Heritage and Folk Life Centre, which was dedicated to the preservation and collection of folklore.

I took the minibus northwards to the Himalayan foothills and arrived at Murree hill station. On the first part of the journey, greenery predominated but on ascent, the awful results of deforestation could be witnessed. It became hard to tell the flat-roofed mud houses clinging to the terraced hillsides from the surrounding landscape.

The view from Murree's Cecil Hotel where I took lunch was spoilt because of the lack of trees. No bright fires gleamed from the dining room's empty fireplaces. Though it was quite cool, but the cost of firewood was prohibitive. An Egyptian Christian Coptic family sat at the next table and I got into conversation with them. They had been posted to dusty Multan.

While walking in Murree, I met a character called Meboob who was a servant at the Dutch Embassy's holiday home, which was perched over a commanding view of the hills. We actually met while peering at a dead dog being eaten by crows. Some mad dog had bitten all the chowkidar's (watchman) dogs. 'We miss you people,' he said. Meboob meant that he missed the British presence. He had served with the British army in China. On returning to the house, which was empty of embassy staff, he showed me his tiny room. The walls of the main rooms had photos of the children of past diplomats and one table was made out of a bullock cart wheel. Another wall was stacked with enough packets of tea for a year. I did not realise that the Dutch were such tea drinkers.

I then took another bus to Tarbela Dam but I had been offered incorrect information about the bus services by a useless tourist department officer.

He obviously was only accustomed to wealthier visitors with cars. The bus was a mobile scrap heap and appeared to be stuck together with rope. It stopped quite a distance from the dam but a kind Pakistani work site supervisor showed me as much as he could of the dam. The dam was eighty square miles wide and a lot of repair work was going on. Apparently, one engineer had committed suicide because dangers of flooding were caused by his faulty designs. On the return bus, my head ached because each time it slowed down, a light flashed on and off and irritating sirens went off! I finally arrived back at Rawalpindi near Islamabad late at night in the middle of Raja Chowk in the densely populated old city.

I spent another day in Islamabad. I was standing outside Gulf Oil and a very kind employee of that firm, Mr Rabnawaz offered me accommodation with his family as I had been staying at 'Pindi's' Y.W.C.A. His eldest son was very anti-Indian and he kept mocking Gandhi whom he knew little about. He also kept making fatuous remarks about the Hindu faith.

From Rawalpindi I spent a day in Taxila, which has the remains of an ancient Buddhist University. In its museum were sculptures of Atlantis, Hariti, Goddess of Fertility and a Buddha with hair piled high on his head. The Greek connection is linked to Alexander the Great's visit to North West India. Taxila later developed a huge quarry industry, which employed many stone cutters and carvers. Some were carving all sizes of bowls, grinders and mortars. Others were monotonously chipping away lumps of stone from giant chunks into manageable amounts for the carvers.

I decided to take one of the most beautiful plane flights in the world north to Gilgit, which is just west of Kashmir. The mountains were snow-capped and I took photos from the cockpit. The region of Gilgit and Hunza boards onto the Oxus region of the USSR and Chinese Sinkiang.

At Gilgit's Chenar Bagh, there is a memorial to Baba Khan who after independence, fought against the Hindu Dogras with help from the Gilgit forces. The sound of Scottish bagpipes came as I was standing in the small garden with its tomb. The British had handed over Gilgit and Hunza to Dogra rule. The area was a reluctant member of Pakistan.

The locals are small, very fair and many have blue eyes. I stayed at the best hotel in Gilgit, the Rakaposhi Inn, which faces the Karakoram Rakaposhi Mountain. The district was full of Afghan refugees whose tents could be seen dotted about. Pack donkeys, goats and bedraggled little cattle formed the bulk of the fauna apart from birds of prey. Little oases of lush green rice terraces were distributed along the stepped landscape and luckily some lovely mauve blossom was about to come out.

At nearby Kargah, there was a huge Buddha carved into the mountainside thirty feet above the ground on a rocky spur at the entrance to Kargah nullah. Deeply cut holes surrounded the figure but for what purpose I am not sure, perhaps they supported wooden way-side shrines, which may have surrounded the giant figure. From there, I visited a government trout farm. One English couple had been given a dead trout because Muslims cannot eat an animal that has died naturally and has not been ritually slaughtered.

Hunza, to the north of Gilgit, was formerly ruled by the Mir of Hunza. I was lucky to get to Hunza as the Karakoran Highway, after heavy rainfall, was forever having landslides. At one point, all the passengers had to change buses after crossing over a huge heap of rubble. The highway was built by the Frontier Works Department with the help of the Chinese. The Chinese contribution could be seen in the design of the bridges. Hundreds of workers died during its construction and scattered memorials could be found all along the road. A number of old British suspension bridges connected with stone tower-like structures were still noticeable. The occasional huge road blocks were also due to the results of explosives. At night time, one could hear many thunderous rumbles, which sounded rather eerie.

Walking to Sikandarabad village, I was offered a dried apricot drink and dried fruits. Hunza apricots are famous and exported overseas. In Huseinabad, a village near to Rakaposhi, all the family of one house had departed for the Jamaat Khana (an Ismaeli assembly hall) as nearly all Hunza folk are followers of the Agha Khan.

The local stone buildings and stone walls surrounding the tiny lanes were heavenly to walk by. The local school at Huseinabad had the name of the Agha Khan engraved on its wall. In one house, I sampled gin made of mulberries, which is euphemistically called 'Hunza water'. Of course it was illicit hooch in prohibition-stricken Pakistan, but it tasted all the better for that. They stored it in underground stone and wooden jars and it fermented in about twenty eight days. Potatoes, apples and the like were stored up to six months below ground.

On to Karimabad (named after Karim Agha Khan), the road upwards was steep and rough. High up above Karimabad is Baltit. The six hundred year old Baltit castle overlooks on its east the nine hundred year old Altit Castle, which appears to be perched on top of a vertical piece of rock. These two castle-forts are the former homes of the Mir. The later Mir (powerless and living much of the year in Islamabad) built a new palace where one could see woolly-haired local camels. Behind the palace is the old Mir's Mazar (tomb) within a little whitewashed walled graveyard.

Near Baltit fort a local man requested me to visit his family. He told me that his son had, 'gone to Pakistan'. 'But is this not Pakistan?' I asked. 'No, we Himalaya people would like to be separate'. I cannot deny that I felt some sympathy with that sentiment, as many of the elite of Pakistan seemed to be composed of migrants from India or Punjabis. Karachi seemed a million miles from up there.

Baltit fort is constructed of stone with wooden beams both inside and out. Within the fort, old faded photos of the Mir's family and the Agha Khan stood forgotten. A coat of mail lay crumpled into a heavy heap alongside a stone jar that once held wine. On the roof was a stone mosque. The approach to the fort hid under a wooden beamed bridge with a tiny mosque built upon its carved wooden door panels. A wooden alcove or mihrab (point facing Mecca) was in evidence. The old dilapidated mosque was partly supported with blackened upright beams.

Walking towards Altit, a local woman invited me to have tea with her. We sat in her kitchen and I was nearly suffocated by smoke from a central fire that went out by a hole in the roof.

Within Altit Castle, horizontal sticks stood against one wall and when sunlight streamed through the windows, the beams of light rested upon a given stick and a rough estimate of the time was shown. This fort offered magnificent views of the Karakoram Highway and an old camp belonging to the Chinese workers still in Pakistan. The highway went directly to the Chinese frontier. On the other side, flat-roofed stone and mud dwellings all clambered onto one another like groping seashells. One locked, wooden door on the roof was kept for alcohol and from another side, there was a steep drop from the rock face.

The countryside of Hunza is exquisite with its permanently snow-capped peaks and blue sky. Varied degrees of lush green fields stood within the stone terraces, added to the fact that the blossom was at its best.

I rented a tiny room at the Hunza Hotel, which was little more than a glorified tea shop. Two friends from the Rakaposhi Hotel turned up in the middle of the night with jerry cans filled with local red Hunza wine. They banged on my door and I joined them over fried chicken and bread. One of the men was local from Gilgit, and very fair skinned with cropped hair who was a professional mountaineer. He had spent many years teaching the subject in Germany and his German was still fluent. His native tongue was Shenar, which is spoken in Gilgit, whilst in Hunza, they speak Burusushki.

The following day, we went to Hindi village, famed for its red wine, by jeep. We were guests of the best wine maker who lived in his three hundred year old house, which one descended into by the roof. We ate delicious maize chapattis and potato. This was followed by gigantic wheat chapattis. The women of the district did not wear veils but there was an understanding amongst any visitors not to photograph them.

Amongst all the Ismaeli villages, there was one conventional Shi'ite Muslim village called Qaziabad, but no outsiders could enter this village, which was surrounded by the lushest scenery.

The area is famed for precious stones and the government had started a ruby project. The stones were cut in Peshawar. Sri Lankans had been used to get this work off the ground.

We returned to Gilgit in a jeep crammed with contraband wine stored in jerry cans and it was lucky there were no road blocks.

As soon as a plane came to Gilgit, the whole town descended upon the airport. It seemed to be the focus of social life, especially when the road was blocked. Everywhere jeeps and Suzukis (local group taxi-buses) converged.

At the Rakaposhi Inn, I had met an elderly British couple who had invited me to stay with them on my return to Lahore. They lived in Lahore Cantonment as he had a government post. One night we went to a party at a doctor's house. This doctor had worked in Iran and we saw slides of his hospital staff, many of whom had been killed by Khomeini's fanatics. It was at the party that I heard of what the expatriates called the 'bacon run'. When the Pakistani officials saw pig meat being brought in from India, they let the infidels pass through quickly, forgetting that alcohol could be lurking beneath.

Chapter Thirty Three

Farewell to India

Lahore to Amritsar and back in India. Up to the Himalayas again but this time to the gentle hill station of Moosoorie, still being surrounded by forests. I stayed at the YWCA, which was run by a fair-skinned woman and her ex-army husband, Colonel Mehta who had migrated from Lahore at Partition.

In Sisters Bazaar, I purchased homemade jam and wholewheat bread along with Cheddar cheese and made a pig of myself. I had arranged half board at the YWCA and during the evening meal, the Mehtas would sit with the visitors. They said that Christians were still underdogs in India but at Partition, Colonel Mehta preferred to serve the Indian rather than the Pakistani side.

I took a bumpy bus ride eastwards to Tehri Garwhal in Northern Uttar Pradesh. The valleys were deeply forested but as the bus entered Tehri, the forest covering had practically vanished. The bus stand at Tehri was extremely muddy after the rains. I was on my way to meet Gandhian leader Sunderlal Bahugana whom I had already met at Gandhi Nidhi in Delhi. Bahugana's wife and daughter looked after me as he was absent on a 'padayatra' across the Indian Himalayas in aid of tree protection. Deforestation is having a deleterious effect all over the world, here hill communities livelihoods were literally being swept away with top soil, and flooding had increased. This area is called Uttarkhand and the 'Chipko' movement (Chipko-Hug) for 'hugging the trees' aimed to stop big contractors moving in to chop down the trees. The wider aim of the movement was to prevent depopulation of the hills to the already overcrowded plains. Bahugana would always say that a tree was like ten sons as it gave air to breathe, fuel to cook, fruit to eat, clothes to wear, shade, wood, and so forth.

From Tehri, I eventually arrived at Rishikesh, which lay on the banks of the Ganges in the Himalayas foothills. Its name came from the ancient rishis or Hindu acetics. Throughout history, many such people came to live secluded lives in scattered caves.

The right bank of the river was heavily forested and it was from here that eager pilgrims climbed upwards to the snowy heights of Gangotri and Kidarnarth's sacred sites. Crossing the Ganges from bank to bank, the boat passengers dip their hands in the holy river and believe they are purified. 'It will wash all your sins away,' said all the optimists. They sprinkled it on all and sundry and consumed it gleefully.

I visited the famous Sivananda ashram named after Swami Sivananda. Their day began at four in the morning with Japa (the recital of sacred mantras) and meditation. The first monk I met who kept the office was not friendly and perhaps he thought I was a drop out looking for cheap digs. I hasten to add that I did look clean and tidy. The inmates observe a rigid routine as in most ashrams. I was put off by the number of sanctimonious-looking western disciples living there. It would not do for me, as I disliked to be tied to a timetable.

I ended up at a rather lowly ashram named Prakash Bharti Ashram. The baba, or founder, died of too much hashish. The buildings were set in a mango grove and a notice exclaimed, 'No hashish or alcohol allowed under the law'. Wishful thinking, as most of the ashramites smoked it. A dreary-looking French girl blew the conch in the Siva temple to announce the pot-smoking session. What a bogus load of wallies! Miserable faces all around me sat about the verandah outside the grotty little temple. They were a bad influence on Indian youth and nobody gained or received knowledge. An Indian boy with pretentions at being a hippie said to me, you are the only non freak'.

At dusk, down by the riverside at Triveni Ghat, the crowds descended. Beggars and pilgrims wrestled with each other for positions on the ghat. Pilgrims bought tiny leaf bowls of flowers and each had a little wick burning and sent it with blessing down the river. The tiny lights floated gently down the river, glistening and bobbing in the sunset.

I was disturbed to hear that my tea shop wallah, whose shop was planted near the ashram, was continually bothered by goondas (ruffians) who sat and smoked all day without paying for their tea. Nobody helped him.

My bus returned to New Delhi via Hardwar, locally called 'Door of the Gods', which was the main place to become free from temporal bondage. The great plains of the Ganges begin southwards from Hardwar. No alcohol, hashish or meat eating was allowed in this town. 'No opium, chang or hobnobbing,' exclaimed a large notice. Fat chance!

I met my mentor, Razi Sahib at Hoshiapur near the Himalayas. Prior to Partition, this had been a Muslim town. Razi Sahib was opening a clinic at an ashram run by local holy man Baba Faqir Chand. The hospital ashram also offered ayurvedic and homeopathic treatments. Outside, the streets were narrow and winding like a Muslim town of the Middle East. Baba was teaching meditation to a scheduled caste man when I first set eyes on him. I attended prayers the following morning and made my salaams to Baba who was sitting at the front of the hall.

Before leaving India, I made my final visit to the Verma family at Chandigarh. They showed me a marriage invitation, which had the following remarks on it. 'We implore the glee of your embellish accompaniment on the ceremonious exigency of the marriage of their loving son Ramesh in Holy Wedlock with Vidyotma'.

With sadness, I left India for England after a four year absence.